REAL WORLD
GLOBALIZATION

A READER IN ECONOMICS, BUSINESS, AND POLITICS FROM
DOLLARS&SENSE

EDITED BY RAVI BHANDARI, ALEJANDRO REUSS,

CHRIS STURR, AND THE *DOLLARS & SENSE* COLLECTIVE

REAL WORLD GLOBALIZATION, 12th edition

ISBN: 978-1-939402-01-1

Published by:
Economic Affairs Bureau, Inc. d/b/a *Dollars & Sense*
1 Milk Street, Boston, MA 02109
617-447-2177; dollars@dollarsandsense.org.
For order information, contact Economic Affairs Bureau or visit: www.dollarsandsense.org.

Real World Globalization is edited by the *Dollars & Sense* Collective, which also publishes *Dollars & Sense* magazine and the classroom books *Real World Macro, Real World Micro, Current Economic Issues, Real World Labor, Real World Latin America, Real World Banking and Finance, The Wealth Inequality Reader, The Environment in Crisis, Introduction to Political Economy, America Beyond Capitalism, Unlevel Playing Fields: Understanding Wage Inequality and Discrimination, Striking a Balance: Work, Family, Life,* and *Grassroots Journalism.*

The 2012 *Dollars & Sense* Collective:
Betsy Aron, Arpita Banerjee, Ben Collins, Leibiana Feliz, Shirley Kressel, Neal Meyer, John Miller, Larry Peterson, Linda Pinkow, Paul Piwko, Smriti Rao, Joe Ramsey, Alejandro Reuss, Dave Ryan, Dan Schneider, Bryan Snyder, Chris Sturr, and Jeanne Winner.

Editors of this volume: Ravi Bhandari, Alejandro Reuss, Chris Sturr

Cover design: Chris Sturr.
Cover photo: Special 45-foot car transport equipment at Zárate, Argentina, January 19, 2005. Credit: Claudio Elias (public domain, via wikipedia.org).

Production: Alejandro Reuss and Chris Sturr.
Printed in U.S.A.

CONTENTS

Chapter 1

CRITICAL PERSPECTIVES ON GLOBALIZATION

Article 1.1

THE GOSPEL OF FREE TRADE
The New Evangelists

BY ARTHUR MacEWAN
November 1991, updated July 2009

Free trade! With the zeal of Christian missionaries, for decades the U.S. government has been preaching, advocating, pushing, and coercing around the globe for "free trade."

As the economic crisis emerged in 2007 and 2008 and rapidly became a global crisis, it was apparent that something was very wrong with the way the world economy was organized. Not surprisingly, as unemployment rose sharply in the United States, there were calls for protecting jobs by limiting imports and for the government to "buy American" in its economic stimulus program. Similarly, in many other countries, as unemployment jumped upwards, pressure emerged for protection—and some actual steps were taken. Yet, free trade missionaries did not retreat; they continued to preach the same gospel.

The free-traders were probably correct in claiming that protectionist policies would do more harm than good as a means to stem the rising unemployment generated by the economic crisis. Significant acts of protectionism in one country would lead to retaliation—or at least copying—by other countries, reducing world trade. The resulting loss of jobs from reduced trade would most likely outweigh any gains from protection.

Yet the argument over international economic policies should not be confined simply to what should be done in a crisis. Nor should it simply deal with trade in goods and services. The free-traders have advocated their program as one for long-run economic growth and development, yet the evidence suggests that free trade is not a good economic development strategy. Furthermore, the free-traders preach the virtue of unrestricted global movement of finance as well as of goods and services. As it turns out, the free flow of finance has been a major factor in bringing about and spreading the economic crisis that began to appear in 2007—as well as earlier crises.

The Push

While the U.S. push for free trade goes back several decades, it has become more intense in recent years. In the 1990s, the U.S. government signed on to the North American Free Trade Agreement (NAFTA) and in 2005 established the Central American Free Trade Agreement (CAFTA). Both Republican and Democratic presidents, however, have pushed hard for a *global* free trade agenda. After the demise of the Soviet Union, U.S. advisers prescribed unfettered capitalism for Eastern and Central Europe, and ridiculed as unworkable any move toward a "third way." In low-income countries from Mexico to Malaysia, the prescription has been the same: open markets, deregulate business, don't restrict international investment, and let the free market flourish.

In the push for worldwide free trade, the World Trade Organization (WTO) has been the principal vehicle of change, establishing rules for commerce that assure markets are open and resources are available to those who can pay. And the International Monetary Fund (IMF) and World Bank, which provide loans to many governments, use their financial power to pressure countries around the world to accept the gospel and open their markets. In each of these international organizations, the United States—generally through the U.S. Treasury—plays a dominant role.

Of course, as with any gospel, the preachers often ignore their own sermons. While telling other countries to open their markets, the U.S. government continued, for instance, to limit imports of steel, cotton, sugar, textiles, and many other goods. But publicly at least, free-trade boosters insist that the path to true salvation—or economic expansion, which, in this day and age, seems to be the same thing—lies in opening our market to foreign goods. Get rid of trade barriers at home and abroad, allow business to go where it wants and do what it wants. We will all get rich.

Yet the history of the United States and other rich countries does not fit well with the free-trade gospel. Virtually all advanced capitalist countries found economic success through heavy government regulation of their international commerce, not in free trade. Likewise, a large role for government intervention has characterized those cases of rapid and sustained economic growth in recent decades—for example, Japan after World War II, South Korea in the 1970s through the 1990s, and China most recently.

Free trade does, however, have its uses. Highly developed nations can use free trade to extend their power and control of the world's wealth, and business can use it as a weapon against labor. Most important, free trade can limit efforts to redistribute income more equally, undermine social programs, and keep people from democratically controlling their economic lives.

A Day in the Park

At the beginning of the 19th century, Lowell, Massachusetts became the premier site of the U.S. textile industry. Today, thanks to the Lowell National Historical Park, you can tour the huge mills, ride through the canals that redirected the Merrimack River's power to those mills, and learn the story of the textile workers, from the Yankee "mill girls" of the 1820s through the various waves of immigrant laborers who poured into the city over the next century.

During a day in the park, visitors get a graphic picture of the importance of 19th-century industry to the economic growth and prosperity of the United States. Lowell and the other mill towns of the era were centers of growth. They not only created a demand for Southern cotton, they also created a demand for new machinery, maintenance of old machinery, parts, dyes, *skills*, construction materials, construction machinery, *more skills*, equipment to move the raw materials and products, parts maintenance for that equipment, *and still more skills*. The mill towns also created markets—concentrated groups of wage earners who needed to buy products to sustain themselves. As centers of economic activity, Lowell and similar mill towns contributed to U.S. economic growth far beyond the value of the textiles they produced.

The U.S. textile industry emerged decades after the industrial revolution had spawned Britain's powerful textile industry. Nonetheless, it survived and prospered. British linens inundated markets throughout the world in the early 19th century, as the British navy nurtured free trade and kept ports open for commerce. In the United States, however, hostilities leading up to the War of 1812 and then a substantial tariff made British textiles relatively expensive. These limitations on trade allowed the Lowell mills to prosper, acting as a catalyst for other industries and helping to create the skilled work force at the center of U.S. economic expansion.

Beyond textiles, however, tariffs did not play a great role in the United States during the early 19th century. Southern planters had considerable power, and while they were willing to make some compromises, they opposed protecting manufacturing in general because that protection forced up the prices of the goods they purchased with their cotton revenues. The Civil War wiped out the planters' power to oppose protectionism, and from the 1860s through World War I, U.S. industry prospered behind considerable tariff barriers.

Different Countries, Similar Experiences

The story of the importance of protectionism in bringing economic growth has been repeated, with local variations, in other advanced capitalist countries. During the late 19th century, Germany entered the major league of international economic powers with substantial protection and government support for its industries. Likewise, in 19th-century France and Italy, national consolidation behind protectionist barriers was a key to economic development.

Britain—which entered the industrial era first—is often touted as the prime example of successful development without tariff protection. Yet, Britain embraced free trade only after its industrial base was well established; as in the U.S., the early and important textile industry was erected on a foundation of protectionism. In addition, Britain built its industry through the British navy and the expansion of empire, hardly prime ingredients in any recipe for free trade.

Japan provides an especially important case of successful government protection and support for industrial development. In the post-World War II era, when the Japanese established the foundations for their economic "miracle," the government rejected free trade and extensive foreign investment and instead promoted its national firms.

In the 1950s, for example, the government protected the country's fledgling auto firms from foreign competition. At first, quotas limited imports to $500,000 (in current dollars) each year; in the 1960s, prohibitively high tariffs replaced the quotas. Furthermore, the Japanese allowed foreign investment only insofar as it contributed to developing domestic industry. The government encouraged Japanese companies to import foreign technology, but required them to produce 90% of parts domestically within five years.

The Japanese also protected their computer industry. In the early 1970s, as the industry was developing, companies and individuals could only purchase a foreign machine if a suitable Japanese model was not available. IBM was allowed to produce within the country, but only when it licensed basic patents to Japanese firms. And IBM computers produced in Japan were treated as foreign-made machines.

In the 20th century, no other country matched Japan's economic success, as it moved in a few decades from a relative low-income country, through the devastation of war, to emerge as one of the world's economic leaders. Yet one looks back in vain to find a role for free trade in this success. The Japanese government provided an effective framework, support, and protection for the country's capitalist development.

Likewise, in many countries that have been late-comers to economic development, capitalism has generated high rates of economic growth where government involvement, and not free trade, played the central role. South Korea is a striking case. "Korea is an example of a country that grew very fast and yet violated the canons of conventional economic wisdom," writes Alice Amsden in *Asia's Next Giant: South Korea and Late Industrialization,* widely acclaimed as perhaps the most important analysis of the South Korean economic success. "In Korea, instead of the market mechanism allocating resources and guiding private entrepreneurship, the government made most of the pivotal investment decisions. Instead of firms operating in a competitive market structure, they each operated with an extraordinary degree of market control, protected from foreign competition."

Free trade, however, has had its impact in South Korea. In the 1990s, South Korea and other East Asian governments came under pressure from the U.S. government and the IMF to open their markets, including their financial markets. When they did so, the results were a veritable disaster. The East Asian financial crisis that began in 1997 was a major setback for the whole region, a major disruption of economic growth. After extremely rapid economic growth for three decades, with output expanding at 7% to 10% a year, South Korea's economy plummeted by 6.3% between 1997 and 1998.

Mexico and Its NAFTA Experience

While free trade in goods and services has its problems, which can be very serious, it is the free movement of capital, the opening of financial markets that has sharp, sudden impacts, sometimes wrecking havoc on national economies. Thus, virtually as soon as Mexico, the United States and Canada formed NAFTA at the beginning of 1994, Mexico was hit with a severe financial crisis. As the economy turned downward at the beginning of that year, capital rapidly left the country, greatly reducing the value of the Mexican peso. With this diminished value of the peso, the cost of servicing international debts and the costs of imports skyrocketed—and the downturn worsened.

Still, during the 1990s, before and after the financial crisis, free-traders extolled short periods of moderate economic growth in Mexico —3% to 4% per year—as evidence of success. Yet, compared to earlier years, Mexico's growth under free trade has been poor. From 1940 to 1990 (including the no-growth decade of the 1980s), when Mexico's market was highly protected and the state actively regulated economic affairs, output grew at an average annual rate of 5%.

Most important, Mexico's experience discredits the notion that free-market policies will improve living conditions for the masses of people in low-income countries. The Mexican government paved the way for free trade policies by reducing or eliminating social welfare programs, and for many Mexican workers wages declined sharply during the free trade era. The number of households living in poverty rose dramatically, with some 75% of Mexico's population below the poverty line at the beginning of the 21st century.

China and Its Impact

Part of Mexico's problem and its economy's relatively weak performance from the 1990s onward has been the full-scale entrance of China into the international economy. While the Mexican authorities thought they saw great possibilities in NAFTA, with the full opening of the U.S. market to goods produced with low-wage Mexican labor, China (and other Asian countries) had even cheaper labor. As China also gained access to the U.S. market, Mexican expectations were dashed.

The Chinese economy has surely gained in terms of economic growth as it has engaged more and more with the world market, and the absolute levels of incomes of millions of people have risen a great deal. However, China's rapid economic growth has come with a high degree of income inequality. Before its era of rapid growth, China was viewed as a country with a relatively equal distribution of income. By the beginning of the new millennium, however, it was much more unequal than any of the other most populace Asian countries (India, Indonesia, Bangladesh, Pakistan), and more in line with the high-inequality countries of Latin America. Furthermore, with the inequality has come a great deal of social conflict. Tens of thousands of "incidents" of conflict involving violence are reported each year, and most recently there have been the major conflicts involving Tibetans and Ouigers.

In any case, the Chinese trade and growth success should not be confused with "free trade." Foundations for China's surge of economic growth were established through state-sponsored infra-structure development and the vast expansion of the country's educational system. Even today, while private business, including foreign business, appears to have been given free rein in China, the government still plays a controlling role—including a central role in affecting foreign economic relations.

A central aspect of the government's role in the county's foreign commerce has been in the realm of finance. As Chinese-produced goods have virtually flooded international markets, the government has controlled the uses of the earnings from these exports. Instead of simply allowing those earnings to be used by Chinese firms and citizens to buy imports, the government has to a large extent held those earnings as reserves. Using those reserves, China's central bank has been the largest purchaser of U.S. government bonds, in effect becoming a major financer of the U.S. government's budget deficit of recent years.

China's reserves have been one large element in creating a giant pool of financial assets in the world economy. This "pool" has also been built up as the doubling of oil prices following the U.S. invasion of Iraq put huge amounts of funds in the pockets of oil-exporting countries and firm and individuals connected to the oil industry. Yet slow growth of the U.S. economy and extremely low interest rates, resulting from the Federal Reserve Bank's efforts to encourage more growth, limited the returns that could be obtained on these funds. One of the consequences—through a complex set of connections—was the development of the U.S. housing bubble, as financial firms, searching for higher returns, pushed funds into more and more risky mortgage loans.

It was not simply free trade and the unrestricted flow of international finance that generated the housing bubble and subsequent crisis in the U.S. economy. However, the generally unstable global economy—both in terms of trade and finance—that has emerged in the free trade era was certainly a factor bringing about the crisis. Moreover, as is widely recognized, it was not only the U.S. economy and U.S. financial institutions that were affected. The free international flow of finance has meant that banking has become more and more a global industry. So as the U.S. banks got in trouble in 2007 and 2008, their maladies spread to many other parts of the world.

The Uses of Free Trade

While free trade is not the best economic growth or development policy and, especially through the free flow of finance, can precipitate financial crises, the largest and most powerful firms in many countries find it highly profitable. As Britain preached the loudest sermons for free trade in the early 19th century, when its own industry was already firmly established, so the United States—or at least many firms based in the United States—find it a profitable policy at the beginning of the 21st century. The Mexican experience provides an instructive illustration.

For U.S. firms, access to foreign markets is a high priority. Mexico may be relatively poor, but with a population of 105 million it provides a substantial market. Furthermore, Mexican labor is cheap relative to U.S. labor; and using modern production techniques, Mexican workers can be as productive as workers in the United States. For U.S. firms to obtain full access to the Mexican market, the United States has to open its borders to Mexican goods. Also, if U.S. firms are to take full advantage of cheap foreign labor and sell the goods produced abroad to U.S. consumers, the United States has to be open to imports.

On the other side of the border, wealthy Mexicans face a choice between advancing their interests through national development or advancing their interests through ties to U.S. firms and access to U.S. markets. For many years, they chose the former route. This led to some development of the Mexican economy but also—due to corruption and the massive power of the ruling party, the PRI—huge concentrations of wealth in the hands of a few small groups of firms and individuals. Eventually, these groups came into conflict with their own government over regulation and taxation. Having benefited from government largesse, they came to see their fortunes in greater freedom from government control and, particularly, in greater access to foreign markets and partnerships with large foreign companies. National development was a secondary concern when more involvement with international commerce would produce greater riches more quickly.

In addition, the old program of state-led development in Mexico ran into severe problems. These problems came to the surface in the 1980s with the international debt crisis. Owing huge amounts of money to foreign banks, the Mexican government was forced to respond to pressure from the IMF, the U.S. government, and large international banks which sought to deregulate Mexico's trade and investment. That pressure meshed with the pressure from Mexico's own richest elites, and the result was the move toward free trade and a greater opening of the Mexican economy to foreign investment.

Since the early 1990s, these changes for Mexico and the United States (as well as Canada) have been institutionalized in NAFTA. The U.S. government's agenda since then has been to spread free trade policies to all of the Americas through more regional agreements like CAFTA and ultimately through a Free Trade Area of the Americas. On a broader scale, the U.S. government works through the WTO, the IMF, and the World Bank to open markets and gain access to resources beyond the Western Hemisphere. In fact, while markets remain important everywhere, low-wage manufacturing is increasingly concentrated in Asia—especially China— instead of Mexico or Latin America.

The Chinese experience involves many of the same advantages for U.S. business as does the Mexican—a vast market, low wages, and an increasingly productive labor force. However, the Chinese government, although it has liberalized the economy a great deal compared to the pre-1985 era, has not abdicated its major role in the economy. For better (growth) and for worse (inequality and repression), the Chinese government has not embraced free trade.

Who Gains, Who Loses?

Of course, in the United States, Mexico, China and elsewhere, advocates of free trade claim that their policies are in everyone's interest. Free trade, they point out, will mean cheaper products for all. Consumers in the United States, who are mostly workers, will be richer because their wages will buy more. In Mexico and China, on the one hand, and in the United States, on the other hand, they argue that rising trade will create more jobs. If some workers lose their jobs because cheaper imported goods are available, export industries will produce new jobs.

In recent years this argument has taken on a new dimension with the larger entrance of India into the world economy and with the burgeoning there of jobs based in information technology—programming and call centers, for example. This "out-sourcing" of service jobs has received a great deal of attention and concern in the United States. Yet free-traders have defended this development as good for the U.S. economy as well as for the Indian economy.

Such arguments obscure many of the most important issues in the free trade debate. Stated, as they usually are, as universal truths, these arguments are just plain silly. No one, for example, touring the Lowell National Historical Park could seriously argue that people in the United States would have been better off had there been no tariff on textiles. Yes, in 1820, they could have purchased textile goods more cheaply, but in the long run the result would have been less industrial advancement and a less wealthy nation. One could make the same point with the Japanese auto and computer industries, or indeed with numerous other examples from the last two centuries of capitalist development.

In the modern era, even though the United States already has a relatively developed economy with highly skilled workers, a freely open international economy does not serve the interests of most U.S. workers, though it will benefit large firms. U.S. workers today are in competition with workers around the globe. Many different workers in many different places can produce the same goods and services. Thus, an international economy governed by the free trade agenda will tend to bring down wages for many U.S. workers. This phenomenon has certainly been one of the factors leading to the substantial rise of income inequality in the United States during recent decades.

The problem is not simply that of workers in a few industries—such as auto and steel, or call-centers and computer programming—where import competition is an obvious and immediate issue. A country's openness to the international economy affects the entire structure of earnings in that country. Free trade forces down the general level of wages across the board, even of those workers not directly affected by imports. The simple fact is that when companies can produce the same products in several different places, it is owners who gain because they can move their factories and funds around much more easily than workers can move themselves around. Capital is mobile; labor is much less mobile. Businesses, more than workers, gain from having a larger territory in which to roam.

Control Over Our Economic Lives

But the difficulties with free trade do not end with wages. In both low-income and high-income parts of the world, free trade is a weapon in the hands of business when it opposes any progressive social programs. Efforts to place environmental restrictions on firms are met with the threat of moving production abroad. Higher taxes to improve the schools? Business threatens to go elsewhere. Better health and safety regulations? The same response.

Some might argue that the losses from free trade for people in the United States will be balanced by gains for most people in poor countries—lower wages in the United States, but higher wages in Mexico and China. Free trade, then, would bring about international equality. Not likely. In fact, as pointed out above, free trade reforms in Mexico have helped force down wages and reduce social welfare programs, processes rationalized by efforts to make Mexican goods competitive on international markets. China, while not embracing free trade, has seen its full-scale entrance into global commerce accompanied by increasing inequality.

Gains for Mexican or Chinese workers, like those for U.S. workers, depend on their power in relation to business. Free trade or simply the imperative of international "competitiveness" are just as much weapons in the hands of firms operating in Mexico and China as they are for firms operating in the United States. The great mobility of capital is business's best trump card in dealing with labor and popular demands for social change—in the United States, Mexico, China and elsewhere.

None of this means that people should demand that their economies operate as fortresses, protected from all foreign economic incursions. There are great gains that can be obtained from international economic relations—when a nation manages those relations in the interests of the great majority of the people. Protectionism often simply supports narrow vested interests, corrupt officials, and wealthy industrialists. In rejecting free trade, we should move beyond traditional protectionism.

Yet, at this time, rejecting free trade is an essential first step. Free trade places the cards in the hands of business. More than ever, free trade would subject us to the "bottom line," or at least the bottom line as calculated by those who own and run large companies. ❏

Article 1.2

INEVITABLE, IRRESISTIBLE, AND IRREVERSIBLE?
Questioning the Conventional Wisdom on Globalization

BY ALEJANDRO REUSS
November 2012

Over the last three decades, the world's capitalist economies have become, by almost any measure, more "globalized." And over the same period, battles have erupted all over the world over the direction and pace of economic change. Time was that international institutions like the World Trade Organization (WTO), the World Bank, and the International Monetary Fund (IMF) could not hold international meetings without facing demonstrators by the thousands. Union members, indigenous people, environmentalists—you name it—showed up to protest the depredations of global corporations and the emerging new global order that enabled them. The battle was joined all over the world, from the protests against water privatization in Bolivia to the fight against new "intellectual property rights" over plant genomes in India; from the Zapatista uprising in Chiapas, Mexico, to the struggles over oil extraction and environmental ruination in Nigeria.

You would think that, in such a contentious environment, the main story told in newspapers and on television—the "first draft of history"—would have been about a raging battleground of conflicting interests and ideas. That was not, however, the main narrative to come from mainstream commentators. *New York Times* columnist and author Thomas Friedman, one of the United States' most prominent globalization advocates of that period, summed up the mainstream message perfectly in his 1999 bestseller *The Lexus and the Olive Tree*:

"I feel about globalization a lot like I feel about the dawn," one of the book's more famous passages began. "Generally speaking, I think it is a good thing the sun comes up every morning. It does more good than harm." The idea that globalization was, on balance, a good thing, however, was not the whole point, or even the main point, of Friedman's metaphor. His main thrust was that globalization was *inevitable, irresistible, and irreversible.* "[E]ven if I didn't much care for the dawn," Friedman continued, "there isn't much I could do about it. I didn't start globalization, I can't stop it—except at a huge cost to human development—and I'm not going to waste my time trying."

This kind of narrative—which Friedman penned before the 1999 WTO protests, but which he and other commentators continued after it and other major protests—stripped the politics and conflict out of the restructuring of the capitalist world economy. It recast these changes as just nature taking its course. Globalization advocates embraced this story with triumphalist glee, since it placed them on the winning side of history (and cast their opponents, at best, as fools who were "wasting their time" fighting the inevitable). Even globalization critics, though, often glumly accepted the logic that they were struggling against the tide of history—devoted though they might be to keeping it at bay as long as possible.

A decade or so later, how does this story look? Well, it has become harder to convince people around the world that "globalization" was for the best, and it would be "waste of time" to fight about it. Globalization advocates cast the crises that struck individual countries (Mexico, Argentina, Russia, etc.) as being rooted in the particular failings of those nations' policymakers. They even wrote off a crisis encompassing an entire major world region, East Asia, in the late 1990s as revealing the weaknesses of the region's insufficiently "free market" version of capitalism. Today's crisis, however, has engulfed virtually the entire capitalist world economy. The political tide had already turned—at least on a form of globalization that put giant corporations squarely in command—in much of Latin America, and may be turning today in Europe.

Inevitable, irresistible, and irreversible? Not so fast.

Inevitable? Is Globalization the Unavoidable Result of Technological Change?

Politicians, commentators, and members of the public often think of "globalization" as an inevitable and irreversible fact of life. This view is usually based on the assumption that technological change is the driving force behind global economic integration, and that technological change is like a powerful river that people can neither stop nor divert. (The idea that changes in technology drive all other kinds of changes in human societies is, in the social sciences, known as "technological determinism.")

Recent developments in transportation and communications certainly make some kinds of connections between people—even on opposite sides of the globe—much faster, cheaper, and easier. News from one place can travel almost instantaneously to almost anywhere else in the world. People can travel, in a matter of a few hours, over distances that less than a century ago would have taken days, even by the fastest and most exclusive forms of travel then available. Goods, too, can be more cheaply and easily transported, even over long distances.

The development of transportation and communications technology has certainly helped make global sourcing of production—one of the key features of the new global economy—as widespread as it has become. New transportation methods have brought down the costs of shipping goods over long distances. New communications technologies have made it possible to coordinate complex operations around the world.

The increasing global economic integration of recent years, however, has not resulted from technological change alone. It has also required dramatic changes in the economic policies of individual countries, the signing of new economic treaties between countries, and the creation of new international institutions—all issues over which people have fought bitterly. If these changes were of little importance to the current form of economic globalization (if globalization would have happened in much the same way without them), those who fought for them—governments, political parties, and many large corporations—probably would not have bothered. If, on the other hand, certain policies were required to create the new global economic order, different policies presumably could have created a different order.

No matter how low the cost of shipping goods from, say, Mexico to the United States, U.S.-based companies would not have been able to "offshore" production to Mexico (profitably) had there, say, been high tariffs on goods exported from Mexico to the United States. (Tariffs on goods exported from the United States to Mexico would have also impeded offshoring, since U.S. companies exported parts to their own operations in Mexico for assembly and re-export to the United States.) It is little wonder, then, that large U.S. companies campaigned so strongly for the passage of the North American Free Trade Agreement (NAFTA), bringing down tariffs and other barriers to trade between the two countries.

Restrictions on foreign investment in low-income countries would, likewise, have stood in the way. Governments in lower-income countries—often spurred by international financial institutions—helped promote offshoring by eliminating such restrictions, establishing assurances of equal treatment for foreign companies as for domestic ones, and offering incentives (such as tax breaks) for foreign investment. The rise of offshoring was not some inevitable consequence of technological change. It required changes in public policy. These policy outcomes, in turn, depended on the balance of political power between different social groups.

Irresistible? Does Globalization Spell Doom for Labor Movements Everywhere?

Some critics argue that the new structure of the global economy—especially the ability of large companies to locate operations virtually anywhere in the world—leads to what they call the "race to the bottom." All countries, they say, are dependent on business investment for economic growth, job creation, tax revenue, and so on. Since businesses can locate their operations anywhere, each country has to make itself an attractive place for multinational companies to invest. This means that governments are forced to cut taxes on business, offer subsidies, weaken labor and environmental protections, and adopt other "business friendly" policies to attract investment. Since other countries are doing the same thing, they end up leap-frogging each other "down" as they compete for investing—eventually settling at the lowest taxes, the least regulation, and so on.

Meanwhile, workers all over the world find themselves in a similar "race to the bottom." Workers in high-income (or even middle-income) countries, who have been used to relatively high wages and employment benefits, suddenly find that their employers no longer have to accede to their demands. If workers in one place will not accept lower pay, cuts to benefits, and worse working conditions, a company can just close its operations there and establish them elsewhere, generally where the wages are much lower. Employers can just abandon areas where unions have been traditionally strong, and set up in places where they are weak or, preferably, nonexistent. This has led some observers to conclude that globalization is turning unions into dinosaurs—if not quite extinct, then well on their way.

To a great extent, the "race to the bottom" story, about both governments and workers, is shared by globalization advocates and critics. The advocates may celebrate these effects, or at least argue that they are inevitable and so there is not point in trying to stop them. The critics, on the other hand, may argue that some aspects of globalization, in its current form, need to be reversed or changed in order to prevent what they see as these destructive effects.

In recent decades, union size and strength have declined not only in the United States, but in most other high-income countries as well. These trends make the view of unions as an endangered species at least superficially plausible. The reasons for union decline, however, are complex, and not due only to globalization.

The decline in employment in traditionally high-unionization industries, often attributed to "offshoring," has multiple causes. Changing patterns of demand—as incomes increase, people spend more on services compared to manufactured goods—have contributed to this decline. Mechanization and automation, too, have played a significant role in the loss of what had been highly unionized manufacturing jobs.

Changing employment patterns, meanwhile, are not the whole—or even the main—cause of union decline. The increasingly hostile atmosphere for existing unions and new union organizing, in the United States and in other countries, has brought down unionization rates in both traditional union strongholds (like manufacturing, mining, construction, transportation, and public utilities) and other industries. This is the main cause of the plummeting unionization rate in the United States. For over a quarter century, employers have been more aggressive and effective in both weakening existing unions and preventing workers from forming new ones. Governments, too, have often turned a blind eye to employer attacks (even illegal ones) on labor.

Global "outsourcing" or "offshoring" of production, certainly, has contributed to declining manufacturing employment in the United States, as in other high-income capitalist countries, in recent years. This can hardly, however, explain the entire history of U.S. union decline, since the U.S. unionization rate has been heading downhill since the mid 1950s, long before global sourcing became an important factor. U.S.-based companies, like those from other high-income capitalist economies, have long established overseas subsidiaries to produce goods for sale in the countries where they operated. (For example, a U.S. company might establish a factory in Mexico to avoid tariffs and sell goods more cheaply on the Mexican market.) That is a different beast, however, than today's "export platform" production—a company, headquartered in one country, establishing operations abroad in order to export the goods back to the home country or to the world market. We can date the explosion of this kind of global sourcing to the 1980s, when U.S. manufacturers started establishing *maquiladora* plants in the Mexican border zone, as well as in "free-trade zones" in other countries. Most of the effects of "offshoring" on U.S. employment have probably come in the last decade or two, with earlier declines due primarily to other causes.

New opportunities for global sourcing have also provided employers with a new trump card when workers try to organize unions: the threat to relocate, especially to low-wage countries. Labor researcher Kate Bronfenbrenner has found that, in more than half of all unionization campaigns, employers threatened to close down the plant, in whole or in part. Since the advent of the North American Free Trade Agreement (NAFTA), Bronfenbrenner reports, this has often taken the form of threatening to move production to Mexico. Actual plant closings in response to unionization, she notes, have also become more frequent since NAFTA went into effect.

To a greater or lesser extent, the effects of such threats are probably felt in all high-income countries. Unionization rates, however, have declined in some countries much more than in others. According to data compiled by economic historian Gerald Friedman, the unionization rate for the United States peaked earlier, peaked at a lower percentage, and has declined to a lower percentage today, compared to those of most other high-income countries. Today, fourteen high-income countries out of the 15 listed by Friedman have unionization rates higher than the United States' 14 percent. Ten have rates higher than the U.S. *peak* of about 26 percent (reached in 1956). Six have rates above 50 percent; three, above 80 percent.

Let's compare, in more detail, the trajectories of unionization in the United States and its neighbor to the north, Canada (shown in the graph below). Until the 1960s, the trends in the two countries were similar—declining in the 1920s, bottoming out in the early 1930s, growing dramatically through the rest of the 1930s, the 1940s, and into the 1950s. Since then, however, the two have diverged. The U.S. unionization rate has traced a long and nearly uninterrupted path of decline for the last half century. Meanwhile, the Canadian rate, which had gone into decline in the 1950s and 1960s, recovered between the 1970s and 1990s. It has declined again since then, but remains nearly three times the U.S. rate (almost 30%, compared to just over 10% for the United States). It would be difficult, even ignoring the Canadian data, to attribute U.S. union decline just to international factors, such as import competition (which became a major factor in the 1970s) or global sourcing. Looking at the comparison with Canada, however, drives the point home: "globalization" is simply not the irresistible tidal wave, wiping out unions across the globe, that many commentators claim.

There are a couple of possible explanations for the divergence of U.S. and Canadian unionization rates (or, more generally, the divergence of the unionization rates in any two capitalist economies in the era of globalization).

First, perhaps it is possible for a country to effectively insulate itself from the global economy. That is, it may use controls on international trade and investment to prevent its economy from becoming "globalized" or, more likely, to regulate the *ways* that it is integrated into the world capitalist economy. That is probably not, however, what is going on with Canada. It is a member of NAFTA; its economy is highly integrated with that of the United States, both in terms of trade and investment; its imports and exports, as a percentage of GDP, are actually much *larger* than those of the United States.

Second, even if a country's economy is highly integrated into the world capitalist economy, the political and legal environments for labor relations—as well as the history and culture of its labor movement—have tremendous effects on the ability of unions to survive in the age of globalization. A recent report from the Center for Economic and Policy Research (CEPR) attributes the much sharper decline of U.S. unions primarily to "employer opposition to unions—together with relatively weak labor law" in the United States compared to Canada, rather than "structural changes to the economy ... related to globalization or technological progress."

The report, in particular, focuses on two differences in labor law: In Canada, workers have the right to form a union once most of the workers in a bargaining unit have signed a union card (a system known as "card check unionization"). This prevents employers from fighting unionization—including by firing union supporters or threatening shut downs, as are common in the United States—during a long, drawn-out period before a union election. (U.S. unions have proposed a similar legislation at the national level, but employers have so far prevented such a bill from passing.) Also, Canadian law requires, in the event that a union and employer cannot arrive at a first collective bargaining agreement, for the two parties to enter arbitration. As the CEPR report put it, this "ensure[s] that workers who voted to unionize [are] able to negotiate a contract despite continued employer opposition." In the United States, in contrast, employers often stonewall in initial negotiations, and many new unions never actually get a union contract signed.

A third factor, not discussed in the CEPR report, is the difference in laws governing the right to strike between the United States and Canada. In the United States, it is legal for employers to fire striking workers and hire permanent replacements. Since the 1970s, when U.S. employers started routinely using permanent replacements, strikes have become much harder for workers to win and, as a result, much less frequent. This has deprived U.S. workers of their main form of bargaining power, the ability to withdraw their labor and shut down production, cutting off the source of the employer's profits. In contrast, most Canadian provinces ban employers from using permanent replacements.

Finally, the CEPR report does note the possibility that weaknesses of the U.S. labor movement itself—especially the "lack of focus on organizing new members"—accounts for at least part of the divergence. Indeed, the labor movements in most capitalist countries have faced changes in employment patterns, and the relative decline of traditional high-unionization industries. As economic historian Friedman notes, however, some have been able to make up for declining employment in their traditional strongholds by organizing workers in growing-employment sectors. The U.S. labor movement—mostly, to be sure, due to the hostile environment for new organizing—has not been able to do so. The Canadian labor movement also differs from U.S. labor in having created an explicitly labor-oriented political party, the New Democratic Party. (Most western European countries have strong labor, social democratic, or socialist parties with institutional and historical ties to unions.) In many countries, such parties have played an important role in gaining favorable labor legislation, and more generally blunting attacks on labor by employers and governments.

UNIONIZATION RATES, CANADA AND UNITED STATES, 1920-2009

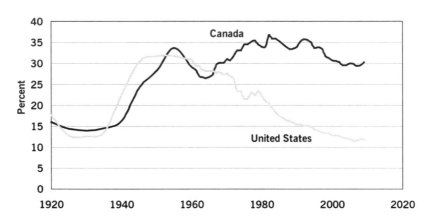

Source: Kris Warner, "Protecting Fundamental Labor Rights: Lessons from Canada for the United States," Center for Economic and Policy Research (CEPR), August 2012.

Global economic forces affecting all countries cannot, by themselves, explain the various patterns of union decline across different capitalist countries (or the patterns would be more similar). The differing political environments in different countries—such as the laws protecting workers' rights to form unions, to go on strike, and so on—likely explain most of the *differences* in the degree of union decline in different high-income countries.

Irreversible? Is Globalization Here to Stay, Whether We Like It or Not?

Even if one recognizes that global economic integration in its current form was not the inevitable process that some advocates make it out to be, one could still argue that there is no going back now. People may believe this regardless of their attitudes—favorable or critical—toward the new global economic order. But why would this be true? Laws that have been passed can, in principle, be repealed. Treaties that have been signed can be undone. Countries that have joined international organizations can withdraw from them.

The argument that "globalization" is here to stay, if we are to take it seriously, must depend on arguments about the interests and powers of different groups in society. For example, one might argue that elites in many countries benefit from the new global economic order, and that they are powerful enough to keep it in place, whether other people like it or not. Alternately, one might argue that "globalization" benefits a broad majority of people in most countries—and is here to stay because most people want to keep it.

Even these arguments, however, are only of much use in predicting the near future. Institutions that look unshakable can, under changed conditions, be swept away with surprising speed. In the last couple of centuries, many countries have abolished slavery. In many places, people have risen up and gained independence from global empires. They have overthrown dictatorships that, almost until the day of reckoning, appeared all-powerful. An earlier wave of economic "globalization," in the early twentieth century, crashed on the rocks of the Great Depression and the Second World War. That earlier surge of global economic integration—powered in part by the cutting-edge technologies of that time, like the steam ship and the telegraph—did not turn out to be irreversible.

Current events today have also resulted in some reversals of the current wave of "globalization," or at least changes in its forms. In the last two decades, governments across Latin America, the developing region that embraced "free trade" policies earliest and most fully, have turned sharply away from these policies. The so-called "pink tide" included governments led by self-described socialist or labor parties, as well as some other political currents, in Argentina, Bolivia, Brazil, Chile, Ecuador, and Venezuela. While differing from each other in many ways, most of these parties shared the view that globalization in its current form increases inequalities within countries, causes economic instability, and reinforces the domination of poorer countries by richer ones (and by large international corporations).

None of these countries has cut off all ties with the world economy—for example, by cutting off all imports and exports (a policy known as "autarky") or rejecting all international investment—but they have tried, in various ways, to use government policy to change their relationships with the world economy. For instance, some of the resource-rich countries (Venezuela is a major oil exporter; Bolivia, a major producer of natural gas) have instituted policies to capture more of the revenue from the sale of these resources, and to use these for domestic development projects. Some Latin American countries have withdrawn from international institutions associated with the World Bank and International Monetary Fund, and several have contributed to an alternative international lending institution—Banco del Sur, or "Bank of the South"—centered within the region (instead of in the United States or Europe).

In Europe, the current global economic crisis may also cause some forms of economic integration to unravel. Of the 27 countries in the European Union (EU)—which has eliminated most barriers to trade, investment, and migration between member countries—17 have adopted a common currency, the euro. The lower-income, or "peripheral" countries in this 17-member "eurozone" have been especially hard-hit by the current global crisis. Meanwhile, the higher-income countries—especially Germany, which has been able to keep its economy growing and unemployment low through increased exports—have balked at measures proposed to boost demand and employment in the EU as a whole. They have insisted that deeply indebted countries, like Greece, impose painful austerity measures (especially make deep cuts in public spending) to reduce their government deficits and external debts—even though these are likely to exacerbate the fall in incomes and the increase in unemployment.

The eurozone's peripheral countries find themselves in a bind of not having their own independent currencies. This means that they cannot unilaterally expand the money supply, preventing them from stimulating the economy by bringing down interest rates, from deliberately raising inflation to reduce the real burden of their debts, or, in the last resort, from printing more money to pay debts as they come due (instead of defaulting). Nor can they allow the value of their currency to fall in value against that of other countries, like Germany. This would increase the prices of imports from other countries, while making their exports less expensive, and therefore reduce their trade deficits. At this point, is seems possible, maybe even likely, that one or more countries will abandon the euro. If there is a domino effect—with one exit followed by another, and another—it is unclear whether the monetary union will survive at all.

Globalization and "Anti-Globalization" Movements

People may use terms like global economic integration, "economic globalization," or simply "globalization" to describe the simple fact that economies across the world are becoming more connected. They may also use these terms to refer to the *specific way* in which economies are becoming connected. It is important to understand the difference. Critics of "globalization" are not necessarily saying that they would prefer for economic activity to pull back behind national borders, for different countries to become economically self-sufficient, or for everyone to produce and consume locally.

An analogy from U.S. economic history may help explain the difference between opposing economic integration and opposing a particular form of economic integration: In the second half of the 1800s, railroads and the telegraph helped tie different regions of the United States (especially the Northeast and the Great Plains) together economically. Farmers in the plains states produced grains, livestock, and other agricultural goods for the growing cities of the East Coast. In return, the growing industries of the Northeast shipped manufactured goods to stores and individuals in the Midwest.

Farmers had little choice about how to get their products to eastern markets. They had to go to whatever railroad ran nearby, and had to pay virtually whatever rate the railroad demanded. Meanwhile, they depended on credit from eastern banks, which benefited from economic policies keeping interest rates high. Farmers saw a big part of their income lopped off by railroad fees and interest payments.

In the late 1800s, "populist" movements, which objected to the power of large banks and railroad companies, attracted growing support from farmers in the Midwest. The farmers probably did not object to being able to sell their goods in eastern markets, or to being able to buy goods manufactured in eastern factories. Rather, they objected to the aspects of the new national economic order that they saw as giving banks, railroads, and other large companies excessive power.

Many of the "anti-globalization" activists may have no objection to international economic relations, in and of themselves, but rather with the specific economic order that has come with "globalization." For this reason, some describe themselves not as "anti-globalization," but as critics of "globalization from above," "corporate globalization," or "globalization dominated by capital"—a form of global integration that favors the interests of large corporations over other values, like decent wages and conditions of work, or protection of the natural environment.

It is not clear what an alternative form of "globalization"—what some activists call "globalization from below"—would look like. Some may point to the development of international movements to resist the power of capital. As entire national economies became unified in the 19th and 20th centuries [< -we don't use super-script], workers in many countries created broad (mostly national, but to some extent, even international) unions and political movements to fight the growing power of giant corporations in the new economic order. Today, some activists imagine new international movements of workers (and others) whose interests have been bound together by the new global economic order.

Others suggest new, international systems of regulation and social welfare protection—the same kinds of protections that were once instituted at the national level, and that the new global mobility of capital has undermined. Some advocates of European unification dreamed of what they called "social Europe," with member countries having to adhere to high minimum standards of labor rights, environmental protection, and social-welfare provision. Instead of integration undermining these achievements—instead of a "race to the bottom" to attract international investment—they believed it could result in an "upwards harmonization." (That vision has not come to pass.)

Still others argue that no humane social order—at least not one that encompasses the majority of the world's people and protects the entire global environment—will be built on the foundation of a capitalist society. While today's anti-capitalist movements may recognize how workers, indigenous people, and the environment have been battered under the current system of global capitalism, that does not mean they aim for a future of self-contained national economies and distinct (if radically transformed) national states. Indeed, the historical call to arms of the revolutionary socialist movement—*Workers of all lands, unite!*—was nothing if not global. ❑

Sources: Thomas Friedman, *The Lexus and the Olive Tree* (New York: Farrar, Straus and Giroux, 1999); Kris Warner, *Protecting Fundamental Labor Rights: Lessons from Canada for the United States*, Center for Economic and Policy Research (CEPR), August 2012; World Bank, Data,

Imports of Goods and Services (% of GDP), Exports of Goods and Services (% of GDP) (data. worldbank.org); Kate Bronfenbrenner, "Final Report: The Effects of Plant Closing or Threat of Plant Closing on the Right of Workers to Organize," International Publications, Paper 1, 1996 (digitalcommons.ilr.cornell.edu/intl/1); Kate Bronfenbrenner, "We'll close! Plant closings, plant-closing threats, union organizing and NAFTA, *Multinational Monitor, 18*(3), pp. 8-14; Gerald Friedman, "Is Labor Dead?" *International Labor and Working Class History*, Vol. 75, Issue 1, Table One: The Decline of the Labor Movement; Peter Cramton, Morley Gunderson, and Joseph Tracy. "Impacts of Strike Replacement Bans in Canada," *Labor Law Journal* 50 (1999) (works. bepress.com/cramton/84); Gerald Friedman, "Greece and the Eurozone Crisis by the Numbers," *Dollars & Sense*, July/August 2012; Jayati Ghosh, "Europe and the Global Crisis," *Dollars & Sense*, November/December 2012; unionization rate series (in graph) calculated from data in W. Craig Riddell, "Unionization in Canada and the United States: A Tale of Two Countries" in David Card and Richard B. Freeman (eds.), Small Differences That Matter: Labor Markets and Income Maintenance in Canada and the United States, University of Chicago Press (1993) (for 1920-1955, nonagricultural workers only); ICTWSS Database, version 3.0. (uva-aias.net/208) (for 1960-2009, all workers).

Article 1.3

DEBUNKING THE "INDEX OF ECONOMIC FREEDOM"

Economic freedom for corporations has little to do with either political freedom or economic growth.

BY JOHN MILLER
March/April 2005

"HAIL ESTONIA!"

For the first time in the 11 years that the Heritage Foundation and *The Wall Street Journal* have been publishing the Index of Economic Freedom, the U.S. has dropped out of the top 10 freest economies in the world. ...

The 2005 Index, released today, ranks Hong Kong once again as the world's freest economy, followed by Singapore and Luxembourg. But it is Estonia at No. 4 that makes the point. This former Soviet satellite is a model reformer, setting the standard for how fast countries can move ahead in the realm of economic liberalization. ...

The U.S. ... scores well. But worrying developments like Sarbanes-Oxley in the category of regulation and aggressive use of antidumping law in trade policy have kept it from keeping pace with the best performers in economic freedom. Most alarming is the U.S.'s fiscal burden, which imposes high marginal tax rates for individuals and very high marginal corporate tax rates. ...

Policy makers who pay lip service to fighting poverty would do well to grasp the link between economic freedom and prosperity. This year the Index finds that the freest economies have a per-capita income of $29,219, more than twice that of the "mostly free" at $12,839, and more than four times that of the "mostly unfree." Put simply, misery has a cure and its name is economic freedom.

—*Wall Street Journal* op-ed by Mary Anastasia O'Grady,
January 4, 2005

I must be confused. I somehow thought that an Index of Economic Freedom would showcase countries that are reducing the democratic deficits of the global economy by giving people more control over their economic lives and the institutions that govern them. In the hands of the *Wall Street Journal* and the Heritage Foundation, Washington's foremost right-wing think tank, however, an economic freedom index merely measures corporate and entrepreneurial freedom from accountability. Upon examination, the index turns out to be a poor barometer of either freedom more broadly construed or of prosperity.

The index does not even pretend that its definition of economic freedom has anything to do with political freedom. Take the two city-states, Hong Kong and Singapore, which top the index's list of free countries. Both are only "partially free" according to *Freedom in the World*, an annual country-by-country assessment published by the nonpartisan think tank Freedom House, which the *Journal*'s editors themselves have called "the Michelin Guide to democracy's development." Hong Kong is still without direct elections for its legislature or its chief executive, and a proposed internal security law threatens press and academic freedom as well as political dissent. In Singapore, freedom of the press and the right to demonstrate are limited; films, TV, and other media are censored; preventive detention is legal; and you can do jail time for littering.

Moving further down the list of "free" countries, the rankings are no better correlated with any ordinary definition of "freedom," as economic journalist Robert Kuttner pointed out when the index was first published in 1997. For instance, Bahrain (#20), where the king holds an effective veto over parliament and freedom of expression is limited, ranks higher than Norway (#29), whose comprehensive social insurance and strong environmental regulation drag down its score. Likewise, Kuwait, an emirship no one would term free or democratic, is tied (at #54) with Costa Rica, long the most vigorous democracy in Latin America.

These results are not surprising, however, given the index's premise: the less a government intervenes in the economy, the higher its freedom ranking. Specifically, the index breaks "economic freedom" down into 10 components: trade policy; fiscal burden of government; level of government intervention; monetary policy; financial liberalization; banking and finance policies; labor market policies; enforcement of property rights; business, labor, and environmental regulations; and size of the black market. In other words, minimum-wage laws, environmental regulations, or requirements for transparency in corporate accounting make a country less free, whereas low business taxes, harsh debtor laws, and little or no regulation of occupational health and safety make a country more free.

Consider that the index docks the United States' ranking for passing Sarbanes-Oxley, a law that seeks to improve corporate accounting practices and to make CEOs responsible for their corporations' profit reports. The segment of the U.S. population whose economic freedom this law erodes is tiny, but it's obviously that segment—not workers and not even shareholders—whose freedom counts for the folks at the *Journal* and at Heritage.

The rather objective-looking list that results from assessing the ten components ranks 155 countries from freest (Hong Kong and Singapore) to most repressive (Burma and North Korea). The index then becomes a tool its authors can use to hammer home their message: economic freedom (as they define it) brings prosperity. As they point out, "the freest economies have a per-capita income more than twice that of the 'mostly free' and more than four times that of the 'mostly unfree.'"

Not so fast. For one thing, the index's creators used some oddball methods that compromise its linkage of prosperity to economic freedom.

For instance, according to the index, the fiscal burden of the Swedish and Danish welfare states is smaller than that of the United States, even though U.S. government spending is more than 20 percentage points lower relative to Gross Domestic Product (GDP, or the size of the economy). This bizarre result comes about because the index uses the change in government spending, not its actual level, to calculate fiscal burden.

To measure the tax side of a country's fiscal burden, the index uses the top rate of the personal and corporate income taxes—and that's equally misleading. Besides ignoring the burden of other taxes, these two figures don't get at *effective* tax rates, which also depend on what share of corporate profits and personal income is actually taxed. On paper, U.S. corporate tax rates are higher than those in Europe, as the *Journal* is quick to point out. But nearly half of U.S. corporate profits go untaxed. The average rate of taxation on U.S. corporate profits currently stands at 15%, far below the top corporate tax rate of 35%. And relative to GDP, U.S. corporate income taxes are no more than half those of other OECD countries.

The index's treatment of government intervention is flawed as well, for it fails to count industrial policy as a form of intervention. This is a serious mistake: it means that the index overestimates the degree to which some of the fastest growing economies of the last few decades, such as in Taiwan and South Korea, relied on the market and underestimates the positive role that government played in directing economic development in those countries by guiding investment and protecting infant industries.

The treatment of informal markets is downright strange. The index considers a large informal sector to indicate less economic freedom because government restrictions must have driven that economic activity underground. (Of course, you could take the opposite view: since the informal sector is for the most part unregulated, countries with larger informal sectors are, by the index's definition, more free!) But this way of looking at it biases the index. Developing countries tend to have large informal sectors while developed economies usually have small informal sectors. That means the index systematically lowers the economic freedom index of developing countries while boosting the scores of developed countries, thus artificially correlating income levels with economic freedom. Even right-wing economist Stefan Karlsson of the libertarian Ludwig Von Mises Institute has criticized the index on this point. Thanks in part to this bias, Estonia, Chile, and Bahrain are the only middle-income countries to make it into the top 20.

Whatever the biases in the index do to cement a tight relationship between economic freedom and income, they can't produce a tight correlation between economic freedom and *growth*. The fastest-growing countries are mostly unfree. Take China, India, and Vietnam, three of the fastest-growing countries in the world. They are way down in the rankings, at #112, #118, and #137 respectively. While all three countries have adopted market reforms in recent years that have improved their standing in the index, their trade policies and regulations remain "repressive." And there are plenty of relatively slow growers among the countries high up in the index, including Estonia (#4), the *Journal*'s poster child for economic freedom. How free or unfree a country is according to the index seems to have little to do with how quickly it grows.

An "Index of Economic Freedom" that tells us little about economic growth or political freedom is a slipshod measure that would seem to have no other purpose other than to sell the neoliberal policies that stand in the way of most people gaining control over their economic lives and obtaining genuine economic freedom in today's global economy. ❑

Sources: Mary Anastasia O'Grady, "Hail Estonia!" *Wall Street Journal*, January 4, 2005; *The 2005 Index of Economic Freedom*, Heritage Foundation, 2005; Johan Fernandez, "Malaysia climbs up economic freedom index," *The Star Online*, January 25, 2005; "Freedom & Growth: No Siamese twins," *The Economic Times*, May 27, 2002; Robert Kuttner, "A Weird Set of Values," *The American Prospect*, December 7, 1997; Stefan M. I. Karlsson, "The Failings of the Economic Freedom Index," Ludwig Von Mises Institute, January 21, 2005; "Freedom in the World 2005: Civic Power and Electoral Politics," Freedom House, 2005, freedomhouse.org.

Article 1.4

RICH AND POOR IN THE GLOBAL ECONOMY
An Interview with Bob Sutcliffe

BY ARTHUR MacEWAN
March/April 2005

Whether *economic inequality is rising or falling globally is a matter of intense debate, a key question in the larger dispute over how three decades of intensified economic globalization have affected the world's poor. Bob Sutcliffe is an economist at the University of the Basque Country in Bilbao, Spain, and the author of* 100 Ways of Seeing an Unequal World. *He has been analyzing both the statistical details and the broader political-economic import of the debate and shared some of his insights in a recent interview with Arthur MacEwan, an associate and founder of* Dollars & Sense.

DOLLARS & SENSE: If someone asked you whether global inequality has grown over the past 25 years, I assume you'd say, "It depends—on how inequality is defined, on what data is used, on how that data is analyzed." Is that fair?

BOB SUTCLIFFE: Yes, it's fair, but it's not enough. First, the most basic fact about world inequality is that it is monstrously large; that result is inescapable, whatever the method or definition. As to its direction of change in the last 25 years, to some extent there are different answers. But also there are different questions. Inequality is not a simple one-dimensional concept that can be reduced to a single number. Single overall measures of world inequality (where all incomes are taken into account) give a different result from measures of the relation of the extremes (the richest compared with the poorest). Over the last 25 years, you find that the bottom half of world income earners seems to have gained something in relation to the top half (so, in this sense, there is less inequality), but the bottom 10% have lost seriously in comparison with the top 10% (thus, more inequality), and the bottom 1% have lost enormously in relation to the top 1% (much more inequality). None of these measures is a single true measure of inequality; they are all part of a complex structure of inequalities, some of which can lessen as part of the same overall process in which others increase.

We do have to be clear about one data-related question that has caused huge confusion. To look at the distribution of income in the world, you have to reduce incomes of different countries to one standard. Traditionally it has been done by using exchange rates; this makes inequality appear to change when exchange rates change, which is misleading. But now we have data based on "purchasing power parity" (the comparative buying power, or real equivalence, of currencies). Using PPP values achieves for comparisons over space what inflation-adjusted index numbers have achieved for comparisons over time. Although many problems remain with PPP values, they are the only way to make coherent comparisons of incomes between countries. But they produce estimates that are astonishingly different from exchange rate-based calculations. For instance, U.S. income per head is 34 times Chinese income per head using exchange rates, but only 8 times as great using PPP values. (And, incidentally, on PPP estimates the total size of the U.S. economy is now only 1.7 times that of China, and is likely to be overtaken by it by 2011.) So when you make this apparently technical choice between two methods of converting one currency to another, you come up not only with different figures on income distribution but also with two totally different world economic, and thus political, perspectives.

D&S: So even if some consensus were reached on the choices of definition, data, and method, you're urging a complex, nuanced portrait of what is happening to global inequality, rather than a yes or no answer. Could you give a brief outline of what you think that portrait looks like?

BS: Most integral measures—integral meaning including the entire population rather than comparing the extremes—that use PPP figures suggest that overall income distribution at the global level during the last 25 years has shown a slight decline in inequality, though there is some dissent on this. In any event this conclusion is tremendously affected by China, a country with a fifth of world population which has been growing economically at an unprecedented rate. Second, there seems to me little room for debate over the fact that the relative difference between the very rich and the very poor has gotten worse. And the smaller the extreme proportions you compare, the greater the gap. So the immensely rich have done especially well in the last 25 years, while the extremely poor have done very badly. The top one-tenth of U.S. citizens now receive a total income equal to that of the poorest 2.2 billion people in the rest of the world.

There have also been clear trends within some countries. Some of the fastest growing countries have become considerably more unequal. China is an example, along with some other industrializing countries like Thailand. The most economically liberal of the developed countries have also become much more unequal—for instance, the United States, the United Kingdom, and Australia—and so have the post-communist countries. The most extreme figures for inequality are found in a group of poor countries including Namibia and Botswana in southern Africa and Paraguay and Panama in Latin America.

Finally, the overall index of world inequality (measured by the Gini coefficient, a measure of income distribution) is about the same as that for two infamously unequal countries, South Africa and Brazil. And in the last few years it has shown no signs of improvement whatsoever.

D&S: People use the terms "unimodal" and "bimodal" to describe the global distribution of income. Can you explain what these mean? Also, you have referred elsewhere to a possible trimodal distribution—what does that refer to?

BS: The mode of a distribution is its most common value. In many countries there is one level of income around which a large proportion of the population clusters; at higher or lower levels of income there are progressively fewer people, so the distribution curve rises to a peak and then falls off. That is a unimodal distribution. But in South Africa, for example, due to the continued existence of entrenched ethnic division and economic inequality, the curve of distribution has two peaks—a low one, the most common income received by black citizens, and another, higher one, the the most common received by whites. This is a bimodal distribution because there are two values that are relatively more common than those above or below them. Because of its origins you could call it the "Apartheid distribution." The world distribution is in many respects uncannily like that of South Africa. It could be becoming trimodal in the sense that the frequency distribution of income has three peaks—one including those in very poor countries which have not been growing economically (e.g., parts of Africa), one in those developing countries which really have been developing (e.g., in South and East Asia), and one in the high-income industrialized countries. It's a kind of "apartheid plus" form of distribution.

D&S: In 2002, you wrote that many institutions, like the United Nations and the World Bank, were not being exactly honest in this debate—for example, emphasizing results based on data or methods that they elsewhere acknowledged to be poor. Has this changed over the past few years? Has the quality of the debate over trends in global income inequality improved?

BS: The most egregious pieces of statistical opportunism have declined. But I think there is a strong tendency in general for institutions to seize on optimistic conclusions regarding distribution in order to placate critics of the present world order. This increasingly takes the form of putting too much weight on measures of welfare other than income, for instance, life expectancy, for which there has been more international convergence than in the case of income. But there has been very little discussion of the philosophical basis for using life expectancy instead of or combined with income to measure inequality. If poor people live longer but in income terms remain as relatively poor as ever, has the world become less unequal?

The problem of statistical opportunism is not confined to those who are defending the world economic order; it also exists on the left. So, on the question of inequality, there is a tendency to accept whatever numerical estimate shows greatest inequality on the false assumption that this confirms the wickedness of capitalism. But capitalist inequality is so great that the willful exaggeration of it is not needed as the basis of anti-capitalist propaganda. It is more important for the left to look at the best indicators of the changing state of capitalism, including indicators of inequality, in order to intervene more effectively.

Finally, the quality of the debate, regardless of the intentions of the participants, is still greatly restricted by the shortage of available statistics about inequalities. That has improved somewhat in recent years although there are many things about past and present inequalities which we shall probably never know.

D&S: Do you see any contexts in which it's more important to focus on absolute poverty levels and trends in those levels rather than on inequality?

BS: The short answer is no, I do not. Plans for minimum income guarantees or for reducing the number of people lacking basic necessities can be important. But poverty always has a relative as well as an absolute component. It is a major weakness of the Millenium Development Goals, for example, that they talk about halving the number of people in absolute extreme poverty without a single mention of inequality. [The Millenium Development Goals is a U.N. program aimed at eliminating extreme poverty and achieving certain other development goals worldwide by 2015. —*Eds.*] And there is now a very active campaign on the part of anti-egalitarian, pro-capitalist ideologues in favor of the complete separation of the two. That is wrong not only because inequality is what partly defines poverty but more importantly because inequality and poverty reduction are inseparable. To separate them is to say that redistribution should not form part of the solution to poverty. Everyone is prepared in some sense to regard poverty as undesirable. But egalitarians see riches as pathological too. The objective of reducing poverty is integrally linked to the objective of greater equality and social justice.

D&S: Can you explain the paradox that China's economic liberalization since the late 1970s has increased inequality within China and at the same time reduced global inequality? Some researchers and policymakers interpret China's experience over this period as teaching us that it may be necessary for poor countries to sacrifice some equality in order to fight poverty. Do you agree with this—if not, how would you respond?

BS: When you measure *global* inequality, you are not just totalling the levels of inequality in individual countries. In theory all individual countries could become more unequal and yet the world as a whole become more equal, or vice versa. In China, a very poor country in 1980, average incomes have risen much faster than the world average and this has reduced world inequality. But different sections of the population have done much better than others so that inequality within China has grown. If and when China becomes on average a richer country than it is now, further unequal growth there may contribute to increasing rather than decreasing world inequality.

China's growth has been very inegalitarian, but it has been very fast. And the proportion of the population in poverty seems to have been reduced. But it is possible to envisage a more egalitarian growth path which would have been slower in aggregate but which would have reduced the number of poor people at least as much if not more than China's actual record. So I do not think it is right to say that higher inequality is the cause of reduced poverty, though it may for a time be a feature of the rapid growth which in turn creates employment and reduces poverty.

This does not mean that all increases in inequality are necessarily pathological. The famous Kuznets curve sees inequality first rising and then falling during economic growth as an initially poor population moves by stages from low-income, low-productivity work into high-income, high-productivity work, until at the end of the process 100% of the population is in the second group. If you measure inequality during such a process, it does in fact rise and then fall again to its original level—in this example at the start everyone is equally poor, at the end everyone is equally richer. That might be called transitional inequality; many growth processes may include an element of it. In that case equality is not really being "sacrificed" to reduce poverty—poverty is reduced by a process which increases inequality and then eliminates it again. But at the same time inequality may be growing for many other reasons which are not, like the Kuznets effect, self-eliminating, but rather cumulative. When inequality grows, this malign variety tends to be more important than the self-eliminating variety. But many economists are far too ready to see growing inequality as the more benign, self-eliminating variety.

D&S: Where do you think the question of what is happening to global income inequality fits into the broader debate over neoliberalism and globalization?

BS: Many people say that since some measures of inequality started to improve in about 1980 and that is also when neoliberalism and globalization accelerated, it is those processes which have produced greater equality. There are many problems with this argument, among them the fact that at least on some measures global inequality has grown since 1980. In any case, measures which show global inequality falling in this period are, as we have seen, very strongly influenced by China. China's extraordinary growth has, of course, in part been expressed in and permitted by greater globalization (its internationalization has grown faster than its production), and it is also clear that liberalization of economic policy has played a role, though China hardly has a neoliberal economy. But to permit is not to cause. The real cause is surely to be found not so much in economic policy as in a profound social movement in which a new and highly dynamic capitalist class (combined with a supportive authoritarian state) has once again become an agent of massive capitalist accumulation, as seen before in Japan, the United States, and Western Europe. So, an important part of what we are observing in figures which show declining world inequality is not any growth of egalitarianism, but the dynamic ascent of Chinese and other Asian capitalisms. ❑

This interview also appears on the website of the Political Economy Research Institute at the University of Massachusetts-Amherst, along with Bob Sutcliffe's working paper "A More or Less Unequal World? World Income Distribution in the 20th Century." See <www.umass.edu/peri>.

Article 1.5

RISE OF THE GLOBAL CORPORATOCRACY
An Interview with John Perkins

BY RAVI BHANDARI
November 2012

> *Economic hit men (EHMs) are highly paid professionals who cheat countries around the globe out of trillions of dollars. They funnel money from the World Bank, the U.S. Agency for International Development (USAID), and other foreign "aid" organizations into the coffers of huge corporations and the pockets of a few wealthy families who control the planet's natural resources. Their tools include fraudulent financial reports, rigged elections, payoffs, extortion, sex, and murder. They play a game as old as empire, but one that has taken on new and terrifying dimensions during this time of globalization. I should know; I was an EHM. – John Perkins,* Confessions of an Economic Hit Man *(2004)*

Across several books, John Perkins exposes the lifestyles of the economic hit men. They inhabit a stateless global archipelago of privilege—a collection of private schools, tax havens and gated residential communities with little or no connection to the outside world. They are people to whom nations are as meaningless as they are to the global corporations and to the international aristocracy they serve.

The system of contemporary capitalist globalization operates for the exclusive benefit of a global plutocracy that has no national boundaries or loyalties. Oligarchy, a word that has been applied exclusively to the modern-day capitalist barons of Russia; is no less real in the triad of the United States, Japan, and Europe.

The operation of this global system and its current financial architecture is as far as it could possibly be from the fairytale version of "free market" liberal democracy glorified in standard economic textbooks and the mainstream media. That is the reality that John Perkins' *Confessions of an Economic Hit Man* has driven home for so many readers since it appeared in 2004. I spoke with him in September 2012.

—*Ravi Bhandari*

D&S: As a fellow EHM, pushing for the privatization of land in Nepal through the World Bank's market-led land reform of the 1990s, I feel that your work has helped to give me, like countless others around the world, a better understanding of the disastrous consequences of our actions on the vast majority of the people and the planet. Since you wrote the famous opening paragraph, quoted above, in *Confessions of an Economic Hit Man*, many people throughout the world have been shocked to learn about the operations of EHM and how globalization works in the real world. Were you surprised by the impact of the book?

JP: The public interest aroused by *Confessions* was not by any means a forgone conclusion. I spent a great deal of time working up the courage to try to publish it. By late 2003, the manuscript had been circulated to many publishers—and I had almost given up on ever seeing the book in print. Despite praising it as "riveting," "eloquently written," "an important exposé," and "a story that must be told," publisher after publisher—twenty-nine, in fact—rejected it. My literary agent and I concluded that it was just too anti-corporatocracy. [A word introduced to most readers in *Confessions*, , "corporatocracy" refers to the powerful group of people who run the world's biggest corporations, the most powerful governments, and history's first truly global empire. – *D&S*] The major publishing houses, we concluded, were too intimidated by, or perhaps too beholden to, the corporate elite.

Finally, Berrett-Koehler, a relatively small publishing house, took it on. Almost instantly it hit the bestseller lists. But despite all the success the book had, an important element was still missing. The major U.S. media refused to discuss *Confessions* or the fact that, because of it, terms such as "EHM" and "corporatocracy" were now appearing on college syllabi. It is interesting that a book entitled *Confessions of an Economic Hit Man* earned its author an international peace prize. I was recently awarded the Lennon Ono Grant for Peace—mainly because of that book but also recognizing my work on protecting the rainforests and indigenous peoples in Latin America. Fighting the global corporatocracy has led me most recently to Iceland and Ireland, where I have encouraged the voters to refuse to pay back the debt that the big banks claim they owe.

D&S: The degree of monopolization has reached an unprecendented level today. Oligarchy is established not just in Russia but throughout the rich capitalist countries. So is the industry of the EHM growing and adapting to meet the new needs of global capital?

JP: Absolutely, today there are many more types of EHMs and the role they play is more diverse. Moreover, the game is far more complex, its corruption more pervasive, and its operations more fundamental to world economy and politics. This makes the future of developing countries even more bleak today than the 1980s. In the *Secret History of the American Empire* (2007), I document how the veneer of responsibility remains a key factor in the dark side of globalization; subterfuges range from money laundering and tax evasion in luxurious office suites to activities that amount to economic war crimes. Real globalization is based on a system of deception, extortion, and rampant violence from IMF officers slashing education and health-care programs to mercenaries defending European oil interests in Nigeria to executives financing warlords in Congo to secure supplies of coltan ore.

One of the earliest robber barons noted in my book was J.P. Morgan. He set a course years ago that has been followed by many of today's billionaires—of mergers, acquisitions, and consolidations, deals that heap riches on those who mold them but wreak havoc on competitors, workers, and local economies. These transactions empower a few individuals with control of resources and markets; the CEOs who end up at the top of the conglomerates are in positions to exert excessive influence over government officials, the press, and buying trends. Because such deals are made on paper—in board rooms, law offices, and at investment banks—they seldom produce tangible goods or services or create new jobs. These paper transactions have played an ever increasing role in the U.S. economy in recent decades and are a major contributor to the failing of our economy.

D&S: Although the global financial crisis started in 2007 in the United States, now the international spotlight is on Europe and its debt crisis, and on Greece in particular. Many things you wrote about in *Hoodwinked*, your follow-up to *Confessions*, have come to pass as you predicted.

JP: Yes, Greece has clearly been struck by economic hit men. Set to default on its debts, the Athens government is leading the pack of the 17 eurozone states as the

---

The Global Corporatocracy and the Global Crisis

As Marx predicted over a century and a half ago, the degree of monopolization has grown continuously under capitalism. I has reached an unprecedented level today, giving global capitalism three distinguishing characteristics.

First, transnational corporations control the world economy as a whole, including the political and cultural spheres, even those sectors that are not directly monopolized. Second, corporations today are globalized due to neoliberal policies that, over the last 30 years, have pushed privatization, deregulation, and "liberalization" of international trade and investment at any cost. Third, the global oligopolies that dominate the world economy today are fully financialized. There is no longer a purely financial sector (banks, insurance companies, etc.) on the one hand, and a "productive" sector on the other.

The global corporatocracy—composed of a few giant industrial-financial oligopolies—makes a striking 75% of all profits in the Third World today. Giant corporations based in the world's richest countries—the "Triad" of the United States, Western Europe, and Japan—control the world's technology, natural resources, finance, communications and information, and weapons of mass destruction. These powers now substitute, for the ancient privilege of the exclusive industrialization of the West, in ensuring the worldwide dominion of this super-elite.

This global order is based on imperialism and continual war in the Third World. Predatory global capitalism (or what Marxian economists refer to as senile and obsolete capitalism) is incompatible with democracy, and helps explain the decline of democracy and increasing conflict and violence worldwide.

In the last few years, the world has witnessed the global corporatocracy successfully privatizing gains and socializing losses to the global public. It shifts, for example, eco-

first country where the common currency (the euro) is to be declared in "selective default" on its debt. In the process, this nation, where democracy was first defined more than 2000 years ago, is clearly demonstrating how predatory capitalism works to undo the freedoms of its citizens. The Greek people were not the ones who agreed to accept these debts and for the most part they did not benefit from them; yet they will be burdened for years to come because they were hoodwinked by the international banking community and their own corrupt leaders.

Bailouts serve the creditors; they enslave the debtors. Although protestors swarm the streets of Athens, objecting to the draconian measures being imposed by the EU and the IMF, the country's leaders are crumbling; they are accepting the bailouts. It has become evident that bailouts in our own U.S. crisis have only benefited the corporatocracy, with CEOs paying themselves truly outrageous bonuses. This method of borrowing against the well-being of the country's citizens merely serves to increase the power of the central banks, the IMF, and corporate CEOs.

In my books, I write about how world economics and politics today are controlled by a very few people—the corporatocracy. This is clearly demonstrated by

---

logical damage from the rich who generate it to the vast majority of our planet, the poorest in the Third World, who bear its greatest burden.

While many analysts today separate a supposedly artificial and negative financial capitalism from a supposedly good "real" sector where things are actually created and produced, they are actually two sides of the same coin. The same oligopolies own big manufacturing corporations and big financial institutions.

The relative stagnation of the global capitalist economy since the 1970s—the low rates of profit, investment, and growth that have prevailed in the United States, Europe, and Japan, despite the deep and widespread defeats of the working class— has left the oligopolies with excess cash relative to opportunities for profitable productive investment. It is this imbalance that, together with a Wild West environment of deregulation and derivatives, has fed the rampant financial bubbles of recent years. Speculation, which results in no productive investment or employment, has become the principal means to make profit.

It should not, therefore, be surprising that the 2008 financial collapse is producing not just a recession but a veritable global depression. Even before the financial meltdown, however, the crisis of global capitalism had already surfaced in the public consciousness in various way. This crisis manifests itself internationally as the energy crisis, food and agriculture crises, climate change and ecological degradation, increasing poverty in different world regions, and the fall of democracy worldwide.

All are, in fact, intimately connected, facets of the same underlying structural crisis of predatory global capitalism.

—*Ravi Bhandari*

the fact that whenever "debt restructuring" or "debt forgiveness" deals are struck they include privatizing parts of the economy that were previously considered public. Utilities, schools, pensions, even significant parts of the military are sold to multinational corporations. Those who demand smaller government are—knowingly or not—supporting a new brand of corporate imperialism.

These corporations are usurping the economic engines of growth that historically have been considered as belonging to the public domain. When I was an economic hit man during the 1970s, I was ordered to implement these policies in many "Third World" countries. It took me nearly a decade to see beyond the smoke and mirrors of the World Bank/business school models, but eventually I came to understand that this was nothing less than the Big Steal. Now it has struck Iceland, Ireland, and Greece; Spain, and Portugal are in the cross-hairs. The Big Steal is escalating in the U.S., with the current round of budget-cutting anti-government campaigns.

D&S: We are confronted daily with so many crises that are global in nature yet appear separate and unrelated Isn't the crisis now—including all its political, economic, environmental, and other aspects—a crisis of global capitalist system itself as opposed to merely a financial crisis or a sum of multiple systemic crises?

JP: What we have seen is that we are going through the throes of a failed global economy. I do not think that the depression or recession that we, and so many countries around the world are experiencing today, is temporary. It reflects a structural problem that we have around the world with the current form of capitalism. And I call this current form of capitalism predatory capitalism. I think it is a mutant viral form of capitalism that really took hold in the '70s and has been spreading ever since. As expressed by famous economist Milton Friedman, it is based on a single premise, a single goal, and that goal is to maximize profits, without taking into account social and environmental cost. In essence every U.S. president since Ronald Reagan has bought into this idea, and supported it, Democrat and Republican alike. The big businesses of the world, the multinationals, really have embraced this concept and they hire highly paid lobbyists and others to make sure that laws are written in a way that will support the goal of maximizing profits regardless of the social and environmental costs. They have been able to control politicians and the laws they implement, legally, and they achieve this through campaign financing. The people that run the corporations which I call the corporatocracy control the mainstream press. Specifically they own the media outlets or if they do not, they control its message through media advertising. Thus they have used their tremendous power to create a global economic system that is unstable, unjust, and rather insane. It is a wholly inefficient system in that it doesn't work for anyone except the very wealthy, in which case the system works beautifully. Even in times of recession, due to the power which they wield, all parties that make up this corporatocracy are able to be bailed out of their failed gambles.

D&S: Your work emphasizes how the First World continues to economically, politically, and militarily colonize the Third World—old wine in new bottles—through the games of EHMs in finance, debt, and so-called "development."

JP: Yes, the new form of imperialism is debt, and it is done through finance. The military is there as a back-up but the most used tool is imperialism through economics. The current control and scramble for natural resources throughout the "Third World" coupled with the corporatocracy once again calling for "radical structural reforms," more deregulation, and more financialization should not come as a surprise. Let me share with you a long-standing effort of mine to fight this imperialism by working with indigenous people to protect the rainforests.

In June, hundreds of indigenous demonstrators began dismantling the Belo Monte Dam in the heart of Brazil's rainforest to protest the destruction it will bring to lands they have loved and honored for centuries. The Brazilian government is determined to promote construction of this massive, $14 billion dam, which will be the world's third largest when it is completed in 2019. It is being developed by Norte Energia, a consortium of ten of the world's largest construction, engineering, and mining firms set up specifically for the project. Hydroelectric energy is anything but "clean" when measured in terms of the excruciating pain it causes individuals, social institutions, and local ecology. The indigenous people's occupation of the dam garnered international attention, connecting their situation to other events around the globe. Indigenous leaders from these groups have asked the Brazilian government to immediately withdraw the installation license for Belo Monte. They demand a halt to work until the government puts into place "effective programs and measures to address the impacts of the dam on local people." They point out that a promised monetary program to compensate for the negative impacts of the mega-dam has not yet been presented by local villages.

The indigenous peoples' occupation of the dam garnered international attention, interweaving their situation with other events across the globe—the Arab spring, democratic revolutions in Latin America, the Occupy Movement, and anti-austerity strikes in Spain and other European nations. Brazil's indigenous protestors have essentially joined protestors on every continent who are demanding that rights be restored to the people.

D&S: If global corporations are above the nation-state and have no global accountability or global institutions to regulate them, then how do countries not only in the Third World, but the periphery *within* Europe respond to these debt-dependency burdens?

JP: Iceland is a great case in point. I traveled around that country, met with the President and many top-ranking government officials and spoke at universities and other public forums. I urged the people not to pay the debts the international banking community said they owed. And they voted overwhelming not to in a national referendum. After refusing to pay the banks for the outrageous debt they didn't deserve, Iceland is now doing very well financially and economically speaking.

But now the banks including the IMF and the World Bank say that Ireland owes them. In May 2010, I was in Ireland lobbying against the referendum that would force the Irish people to pay back the enormous debt. After the vote, it appeared that Ireland, unlike Iceland, didn't listen to my advice. Today there is a large rumble in Ireland that the voting for the referendum was rigged and in fact the Irish people voted against the plan to repay the banks. And also and unfortunately in Ireland, there has been a history of the people voting down referendums like this one, and then having their politicians devise a similar referendum to vote on. Even though the people are making their voices heard, their politicians are only happy with a specific type of voice. What this shows, is that in Iceland where the population is around 300,000; democracy was able to work because essentially everyone knows everybody else, people can't get away with much. From a political standpoint, democracy is a very difficult thing to maintain, especially in countries with large and diverse populations, like the United States (e.g. Al Gore's loss that may have been due to election rigging—win the popular vote and lose the Electoral College).

The bigger issue today is that nations are not all that important. We have moved from religious organizations ruling the world to different types of governments (totalitarian, republican) to now multinational corporations that rule the world. Nowhere is this more evident than in the United States where no one is elected into a high-ranking position until they receive large support from these multinationals. Big corporations control the mainstream media as well. Big corporations' control is profound not only in Third World countries but here at home in the First World as well. In a sense, what they have been doing and continue to do in the Third World for decades they are now doing here: structural adjustment, predatory loans, and austerity which has now become business as usual in Europe and the United States.

D&S: From the countryside of Brazil to a rare success story in Iceland, people are beginning to respond to the unfolding and deepening global crisis with success, albeit limited. What lessons can be drawn from the Iceland experience, once the poster child of the 2008 financial crisis?

JP: In 2007 Iceland was considered the third richest country per capita by the World Bank. Suddenly the country collapses and goes into debt. Then it decides to go against this World Bank and not take their advice and is now back on top. It defied the logic of the World Bank, IMF, and business schools everywhere and now the country of Iceland is back on top. Now, for the first time people do not feel shame when they face debt, because they understand they incurred this debt under predatory capitalism.

As another example, we can use the case of big banks in the United States that in essence collapsed and went into debt. They refused to pay anything and were bailed out. Debt is the great enslaver of these times. But unlike actual metal chains around your ankles, you can slip out of debt by refusing to pay it. There are many success stories both on the individual and country level. All we have to do is come together (e.g. Nigeria, Spain, Ecuador, Greece) and say we are not going to pay our debts in this predatory capitalistic system in which we were forced to live. That is one reason why the Occupy movement is so important, because they preach this consciousness of not paying back debts under a corrupt system.

This is perhaps the most important revolution in human history. We are at a time that is comparable to or more important than the agricultural revolution or industrial revolution or technological revolution. This is a revolution in global consciousness, not merely a change that is necessary for the economic system. People everywhere, as well as nature, are facing the same crises. We are beginning to see how we relate to everything else and what an important role we humans play in protecting this planet. So it is about waking up. We are all waking up to the incredible potential that human beings have. ❏

Chapter 2

CORPORATE POWER AND THE GLOBAL ECONOMY

Article 2.1

U.S. BANKS AND THE DIRTY MONEY EMPIRE

BY JAMES PETRAS
September/October 2001

Washington and the mass media have portrayed the United States as being in the forefront of the struggle against narcotics trafficking, drug-money laundering, and political corruption. The image is of clean white hands fighting dirty money from the Third World (or the ex-Communist countries). The truth is exactly the opposite. U.S. banks have developed an elaborate set of policies for transferring illicit funds to the United States and "laundering" those funds by investing them in legitimate businesses or U.S. government bonds. The U.S. Congress has held numerous hearings, provided detailed exposés of the illicit practices of the banks, passed several anti-laundering laws, and called for stiffer enforcement by public regulators and private bankers. Yet the biggest banks continue their practices and the sums of dirty money grow exponentially. The $500 billion of criminal and dirty money flowing annually into and through the major U.S. banks far exceeds the net revenues of all the information technology companies in the United States. These yearly inflows surpass the net profits repatriated from abroad by the major U.S. oil producers, military industries, and airplane manufacturers combined. Neither the banks nor the government have the will or the interest to put an end to practices that provide such high profits and help maintain U.S. economic supremacy internationally.

Big U.S. Banks and Dirty Money Laundering

"Current estimates are that $500 billion to $1 trillion in illegal funds from organized crime, narcotics trafficking and other criminal misconduct are laundered through banks worldwide each year," according to Senator Carl Levin (D-Mich.), "with about half going through U.S. banks." The senator's statement, however, only covers proceeds from activities that are crimes under U.S. law. It does not include financial transfers by corrupt political leaders or tax evasion by overseas businesses, since in those cases any criminal activity takes place outside the United States. Raymond Baker, a leading U.S. expert on international finance and guest scholar in economic studies at the Brookings Institution, estimates the total "flow of corrupt money … into Western coffers" from Third World or ex-Communist economies at $20 to $40 billion a year. He puts the "flow stemming from mis-priced trade" (the difference between the price quoted, for tax purposes, of goods sold abroad, and their real price) at a minimum of $80 billion a year. "My lowest estimate is $100 billion per year by these two means … a trillion dollars in the decade, at least half to the United States," Baker concludes. "Including other elements of illegal flight capital would produce much higher figures."

The money laundering business, whether "criminal" or "corrupt," is carried out by the United States' most important banks. The bank officials involved in money laundering have backing from the highest levels of the banking institutions. These are not isolated offenses perpetrated by loose cannons. Take the case of Citibank's laundering of Raúl Salinas' $200 million account. The day after Salinas, the brother of Mexico's ex-President Carlos Salinas de Gortari, was arrested and his large-scale theft of government funds was exposed, his private bank manager at Citibank, Amy Elliott, said in a phone conversation with colleagues (the transcript of which was made available to Congressional investigators) that "this goes [on] in the very, very top of the corporation, this was known … on the very top. We are little pawns in this whole thing."

Citibank is the United States' biggest bank, with 180,000 employees worldwide, operating in 100 countries, with $700 billion in known assets. It operates what are known as "private banking" offices in 30 countries, with over $100 billion in client assets. Private banking is the sector of a bank which caters to extremely wealthy clients, with deposits of $1 million or more. The big banks charge customers for managing their assets and for providing the specialized services of the private banks. These services go beyond routine banking services like check clearing and deposits, to include investment guidance, estate planning, tax assistance, off-shore accounts, and complicated schemes designed to secure the confidentiality of financial transactions. Private banks sell secrecy to their clients, making them ideal for money laundering. They routinely use code names for accounts. Their "concentration accounts" disguise the movement of client funds by co-mingling them with bank funds, cutting off paper trails for billions of dollars in wire transfers. And they locate offshore private investment corporations in countries such as the Cayman

Islands and the Bahamas, which have strict banking secrecy laws. These laws allow offshore banks and corporations to hide a depositor's name, nationality, the amount of funds deposited, and when they were deposited. They do not require any declarations from bank officials about sources of funds.

Private investment corporations (PICs) are one particulary tricky way that big banks hold and hide a client's assets. The nominal officers, trustees, and shareholders of these shell corporations are themselves shell corporations controlled by the private bank. The PIC then becomes the official holder of the client's accounts, while the client's identity is buried in so-called "records of jurisdiction" in countries with strict secrecy laws. The big banks keep pre-packaged PICs on the shelf awaiting activation when a private bank client wants one. The system works like Russian matryoshka dolls, shells within shells within shells, which in the end can be impenetrable to the legal process.

Hearings held in 1999 by the Senate's Permanent Subcommittee on Investigations (under the Governmental Affairs Committee) revealed that in the Salinas case, private banking personnel at Citibank—which has a larger global private banking operation than any other U.S. bank— helped Salinas transfer $90 to $100 million out of Mexico while disguising the funds' sources and destination. The bank set up a dummy offshore corporation, provided Salinas with a secret codename, provided an alias for a third party intermediary who deposited the money in a Citibank account in Mexico, transferred the money in a concentration account to New York, and finally moved it to Switzerland and London.

Instead of an account with the name "Raúl Salinas" attached, investigators found a Cayman Islands account held by a PIC called "Trocca, Ltd.," according to Minority Counsel Robert L. Roach of the Permanent Committee on Investigations. Three Panama shell companies formed Trocca, Ltd.'s board of directors and three Cayman shell companies were its officers and shareholders. "Citibank controls all six of these shell companies and routinely uses them to function as directors and officers of PICs that it makes available to private clients," says Roach. Salinas was only referred to in Citibank documents as "Confidential Client No. 2" or "CC-2."

Historically, big-bank money laundering has been investigated, audited, criticized, and subjected to legislation. The banks have written their own compliance procedures. But the big banks ignore the laws and procedures, and the government ignores their non-compliance. The Permanent Subcommittee on Investigations discovered that Citibank provided "services," moving a total of at least $360 million, for four major political swindlers, all of whom lost their protection when the political winds shifted in their home countries: Raúl Salinas, between $80 and $100 million; Asif Ali Zardari (husband of former Prime Minister of Pakistan), over $40 million; El Hadj Omar Bongo (dictator of Gabon since 1967), over $130 million; Mohammed, Ibrahim, and Abba Sani Abacha (sons of former Nigerian dictator General Sani Abacha), over $110 million. In all cases Citibank violated all of its own procedures and government guidelines: there was no review of the client's background (known as the "client profile"), no determination of the source of the funds, and no inquiry into any violations of the laws of the country where the money originated. On the contrary, the bank facilitated the outflow in its prepackaged format: shell corporations were established, code names were provided, funds were moved through concentration accounts, and the funds were invested in legitimate businesses or in U.S. bonds. In none of these cases did the banks practice "due diligence," taking the steps required by law to ensure that they do not facilitate money laundering. Yet top banking officials have never been brought to court and tried. Even after the arrest of its clients, Citibank continued to provide them with its services, including moving funds to secret accounts.

Another route that the big banks use to launder dirty money is "correspondent banking." Correspondent banking is the provision of banking services by one bank to another. It enables overseas banks to conduct business and provide services for their customers in jurisdictions where the bank has no physical presence. A bank that is licensed in a foreign country and has no office in the United States can use correspondent banking to attract and retain wealthy criminal or corrupt clients interested in laundering money in the United States. Instead of exposing itself to U.S. controls and incurring the high costs of locating in the U.S., the bank will open a correspondent account with an existing U.S. bank. By establishing such a relationship, the foreign bank (called the "respondent") and its customers can receive many or all of the services offered by the U.S. bank (called the "correspondent"). Today, all the big U.S. banks have established multiple correspondent relationships throughout the world so they may engage in international financial transactions for themselves and their clients in places where they do not have a physical presence. The largest U.S. and European banks, located in financial centers like New York or London, serve as correspondents for thousands of other banks. Most of the offshore banks laundering billions for criminal clients have accounts in the United States. Through June 1999, the top five correspondent bank holding companies in the United States held correspondent account balances exceeding $17 billion; the total correspondent balances of the 75 largest U.S. correspondent banks was $34.9 billion. For billionaire criminals an important feature of correspondent relationships is that they provide access to international transfer systems. The biggest banks specializing in international fund transfers (called "money center banks") can process up to $1 trillion in wire transfers a day.

The Damage Done

Hundreds of billions of dollars have been transferred, through the private-banking and correspondent-banking systems, from Africa, Asia, Latin America, and Eastern Europe to the biggest banks in the United States and Europe. In all these regions, liberalization and privatization of the economy have opened up lucrative opportunities for corruption and the easy movement of booty overseas. Authoritarian governments and close ties to Washington, meanwhile, have ensured impunity for most of the guilty parties. Russia alone has seen over $200 billion illegally transferred out of the country in the course of the 1990s. The massive flows of capital out of these regions—really the pillaging of these countries' wealth through the international banking system—is a major factor in their economic instability and mass impoverishment. The resulting economic crises, in turn, have made these countries more vulnerable to the prescriptions of the International Monetary Fund and the World Bank, including liberalized banking and financial systems that lead to further capital flight.

Even by an incomplete accounting (including both "criminal" and "corrupt" funds, but not other illicit capital transfers, such as illegal shifts of real estate or securities titles, wire fraud, etc.), the dirty money coming from abroad into U.S. banks amounted to $3.5 to $6.0 trillion during the 1990s. While this is not the whole picture, it gives us a basis for estimating the significance of the "dirty money factor" in the U.S. economy. The United States currently runs an annual trade deficit of over $400 billion. The gap has to be financed with inflows of funds from abroad—at least a third of which is "dirty money." Without the dirty money the U.S. economy's external accounts would be unsustainable. No wonder the biggest banks in the United States and Europe are actively involved, and the governments of these countries turn a blind eye. That is today's capitalism— built around pillage, criminality, corruption, and complicity. ❏

Sources: "Private Banking and Money Laundering: A Case Study of Opportunities and Vulnerabilities," Permanent Subcommittee on Investigations of the Committee on Governmental Affairs, United States Senate, One Hundred Sixth Congress, November 9-10, 2000; "Report on Correspondent Banking: A Gateway to Money Laundering," Minority Staff of the U.S. Senate Permanent Subcommittee on Investigations, February 2001.

Article 2.2

SYNERGY IN SECURITY
The Rise of the National Security Complex

BY TOM BARRY
March/April 2010

In his January 17, 1961 farewell address, President Dwight D. Eisenhower cautioned: "In the councils of government, we must guard against the acquisition of unwarranted influence, whether sought or unsought, by the military-industrial complex."

Five decades later, this complex, which Eisenhower defined as the "conjunction of an immense military establishment and a large arms industry," is no longer new. And while Eisenhower's warning is still pertinent, the scale, scope, and substance of the complex have changed in alarming ways. It has morphed into a new type of public-private partnership—one that spans military, intelligence, and homeland-security contracting, and might be better called a "national security complex."

Not counting the supplemental authorizations for the wars in Iraq and Afghanistan, current levels of military spending are, adjusting for inflation, about 45% higher than the military budget when Eisenhower left office. Including the Iraq and Afghanistan war budgets, military spending stands about 30% higher, adjusted for inflation, than any of the post-WWII highpoints—Korea, Vietnam, and the Reagan build-up in the 1980s. Private military contracting, which constituted about half of the Pentagon's spending in the 1960s, currently absorbs about 70% of the Department of Defense (DoD) budget. No longer centered exclusively in the Pentagon, outsourcing to private contractors now extends to all aspects of government. But since 2001, the major surge in federal outsourcing has occurred in the "intelligence community" and in the new Department of Homeland Security (DHS).

Since Sept. 11, 2001, a vastly broadened government-industry complex has emerged—one that brings together all aspects of national security. Several interrelated trends are responsible for its formation and explosive growth: 1) the dramatic growth in government outsourcing since the early 1990s, and particularly since the beginning of the George W. Bush administration, 2) the post-Sept. 11 focus on homeland security, 3) the wars in Iraq and Afghanistan, 4) the Bush-era surge in intelligence budget and intelligence contracts, and 5) the cross-agency focus on information and communications technology.

The term "military-industrial complex" no longer adequately describes the multi-headed monster that has emerged in our times. The industrial (that is, big business) part of the military-industrial complex has become ever more deeply integrated into government—no longer simply providing arms but also increasingly offering their services on the fronts of war and deep inside the halls of government—commissioned to carry out the very missions of the DoD, DHS, and intelligence agencies. In the national security complex, it is ever more difficult to determine what is private sector and what is public sector—and whose interests are being served.

Different Departments, Same Companies

In 2008, the federal government handed out contracts to the private sector totaling $525.5 billion—up from $209 billion in 2000. That's about a quarter of the entire federal budget. The DoD alone accounts for about $390 billion, or nearly three-quarters of total federal contracts.

The living symbol of the new national security complex is Lockheed Martin, whose slogan is "We Never Forget Who We're Working For." That's the U.S. government—sales to which account for more than 80% of the company's revenues, with most of the balance coming from international weapons sales and other security contracts facilitated by Washington. In addition to its sales of military hardware, Lockheed is the government's top provider of IT services and systems integration (see Table 1).

Whether it is military operations, interrogations, intelligence gathering, or homeland security, the country's "national security" apparatus is largely in the same hands. Various components of the U.S. national-security state are divvied up among different federal bureaucracies. But increasingly, the main components are finding a common home within corporate America. Corporations such as Lockheed Martin, Boeing, L-3 Communications, and Northrop Grumman have the entire business—military, intelligence, and "homeland security"—covered.

Lockheed Martin, Northrop Grumman, and Boeing led the top ten military contractors in 2008 (see Table 2).

The 2003 creation of the Department of Homeland Security has helped spawn an explosion of new companies, and new divisions of existing companies, providing "homeland security" products and services. Before President Bush created DHS in

TABLE 1: TOP TEN GOVERNMENT CONTRACTORS, 2008	
Lockheed Martin	$34,785,141,737
Boeing	$23,784,593,887
Northrop Grumman	$18,177,546,625
BAE Systems	$16,137,793,437
General Dynamics	$15,992,669,588
Raytheon	$14,663,608,137
United Technologies	$8,927,106,729
L-3 Communications	$7,597,574,871
KBR	$5,995,025,351
SAIC	$5,945,115,101

Source: USAGovernmentSpending.gov

the wake of Sept. 11, the agencies that would be merged into the new department did very little outsourcing. From less than 1% of federal contracts (as a total dollar amount) in 2000, outsourcing by DHS has quadrupled as a portion of federal contracting from 2003 to 2009.

Although DHS contracts with scores of new companies, its top contractors are all leading military contractors that have established "homeland security" divisions and subsidiaries.

The top ten DHS contractors in 2008 were Lockheed Martin, Northrop Grumman, IBM, L-3 Communications, Unisys, SAIC, Boeing, Booz Allen Hamilton, General Electric, and Accenture, all leading military contractors. Other major military contractors among the top 25 DHS contractors include General Dynamics, Fluor, and Computer Sciences Corp (see Table 3).

There is no public list of corporations that contract for U.S. intelligence agencies. But based on company press releases and filings with the Securities and Exchange Commission, Tim Shorrock concludes in his new book *Spies for Hire* that the top five intelligence contractors are probably Lockheed Martin, Northrop Grumman, SAIC, General Dynamics, and L-3 Communications. Other major contractors include Booz Allen Hamilton, CACI International, DRS Technologies, and ManTech International, also leading military contractors.

Within the past eight years—since Sept. 11, 2001—the intelligence budget has soared, rising from an estimated $30 billion in 2000 to an estimated $66.5 billion today. Intelligence agencies have channeled most of the new funding to private contractors, both major companies like CACI and thousands of individual contractors. Private contracts now account for about 70% of the intelligence budget. Intelligence community sources told the *Washington Post* that private contractors constituted

TABLE 2: TOP TEN DoD CONTRACTORS, 2008	
Lockheed Martin	$29,363,894,334
Northrop Grumman	$23,436,442,251
Boeing	$21,838,400,709
BAE Systems	$16,227,370,773
Raytheon	$13,593,610,345
General Dynamics	$13,490,652,077
United Technologies	$8,283,275,612
L-3 Communications	$6,675,712,135
KBR	$5,997,147,425
Navistar Int'l	$4,761,740,206

Source: USAGovernmentSpending.gov

"a significant majority" of analysts working at the new National Counterterrorism Center, which provides the White House with terrorism intelligence.

The major military contractors are now moving their headquarters from their production centers, often in California and Texas, to the Washington Beltway in pursuit of more intelligence, military, and homeland security contracts. The gleaming Beltway office buildings of the security corporations are now the most visible symbol of this national security complex.

Boots on the Ground, Computers in Cubicles

Another feature of this evolving, ever-expanding complex is that all the U.S. government departments involved in national security—DoD, State Department, DHS, and intelligence—are outsourcing the boots-on-the-ground components of their missions through the use of private security and military provider firms. Companies such as ArmourGroup (which includes Wackhenhut), DynCorp, MPRI, and Xe (formerly Blackwater Worldwide) have injected the private sector directly into the public sector through their work as interrogators, military trainers, prison guards, intelligence agents, and war-fighters.

Five dozen of these security contractors have organized themselves into the International Peace Operations Association (IPOA). After Blackwater came under worldwide scrutiny for its massacre of unarmed Iraqis in central Baghdad on Sept. 17, 2007, the firm left IPOA, whose code of conduct for "peacekeeping" operations it

TABLE 3: TOP TEN HOMELAND SECURITY DEPARTMENT CONTRACTORS, 2008	
Boeing	$591,048,628
IBM	$486,219,723
Accenture Ltd	$392,700,978
General Dynamics	$391,294,040
Integrated Coast Guard Systems (Northrop Grumman/ Lockheed Martin joint venture)	$386,344,211
Unisys	$367,722,670
SAIC	$362,403,533
L-3 Communications	$329,431,785
Lockheed Martin	$294,412,822
Booz Allen Hamilton	$242,899,612

Source: USAGovernmentSpending.gov

had flagrantly ignored. Blackwater created a new association of private military contractors called Global Peace and Security Operations—conveniently without any potentially embarrassing code of conduct.

Private contractors are not only on the frontlines of war and clandestine operations, but have also penetrated the national security bureaucracy itself. Reacting to a March 2008 GAO report on conflicts of interest within the Pentagon, Frida Berrigan of the New America Foundation's Arms and Security Initiative observed that alarming numbers of "cubicle mercenaries" are now working within federal bureaucracies as administrators, contract managers, intelligence analysts, and cybersecurity chiefs. No longer does the "large arms industry" that Eisenhower warned about just peddle goods like weapons and missiles, it also sells itself through its services.

Common Dominators of the New Complex: Information and Security

Private contractors are also in control of the core of the complex's information and intelligence systems. Information and communications technology is the fastest-growing sector in government contracting. The DHS's expanding involvement in cybersecurity, information systems, and electronic identification programs, for example, is adding billions of dollars annually to the national security boom.

Lockheed Martin led the ranks of information technology (IT) contractors in 2008, followed by Boeing and Northrop Grumman. Although IT contracts are expanding rapidly, there are few new entrants to the list of top IT providers to the government. Among the top 100 IT contractors, there were just twelve new entrants, as traditional military giants dominated the list (see Table 4).

TABLE 4: TOP TEN FEDERAL IT AND SYSTEMS INTEGRATION CONTRACTORS, 2009	
Lockheed Martin	$14,983,515,367
Boeing	$10,838,231,984
Northrop Grumman	$9,947,316,207
General Dynamics	$ 6,066,178,545
Raytheon	$ 5,942,575,316
KBR	$5,467,721,429
SAIC	$4,811,194,880
L-3 Communications	$4,236,653,555
Computer Sciences	$3,435,767,906
Booz Allen Hamilton	$2,779,421,015

Source: Washington Technology, Eagle Eye Publishers Inc., and Houlihan Lokey

One of the largest sources of federal contracting at DHS has been the EAGLE (Enterprise Acquisition Gateway for Leading Edge Solutions) IT program, which awarded $8.2 billion in contracts in the past three years. Among the leading contractors are CACI, Booz Allen Hamilton, Lockheed Martin, SAIC, Northrop Grumman, General Dynamics, and BAE Systems—all major military contractors. Most of the EAGLE IT bonanza is in the form of "indefinite-delivery, indefinite quantity contracts" that provide generous operating room for IT firms to determine their own solutions to DHS' vast IT and cybersecurity requirements.

The major military corporations have quickly formed new branches to focus on these new opportunities outside of their traditional core contracts with the Pentagon. This year, for example, Northrop Grumman created a new Information Systems division to seek military, homeland security, and intelligence IT contracts. Recognizing the interest in the Obama administration in cyber-security and information war, corporations such as Booz Allen Hamilton and Hewlett-Packard, among others, have created new cybersecurity divisions or subsidiaries. Similarly, the new administration's focus on transnational disease has led military companies such as General Dynamics to acquire medical subsidiaries.

Revolving-Door Security Consultants

Another manifestation of the new national security complex is the rise of a new series of consulting agencies that act as an interface between government and their clients. That's an easy connection for such companies as the Chertoff Group, Ridge Global, and RiceHadley Group, since all their principals recently left government, where they had presided over the unprecedented wave of outsourcing.

Two of these national security agencies are headed by the DHS's first two secretaries, Michael Chertoff and Tom Ridge, while the newest group brings together Condoleezza Rice and Stephen Hadley, who only a year ago were serving as secretary of state and national security adviser, respectively.

When announcing his group's formation, Chertoff boasted, "Our principals have worked closely together for years, as leaders of the Department of Defense, the Department of Homeland Security, the Department of Justice, the National Security Agency and the CIA." Indeed, a leading member of this new group is former CIA director Michael Hayden (2005-2009), who also directed the National Security Agency (1999-2005). Others include former DHS deputy Paul Schneider (who was head of acquisitions for NSA and the U.S. Navy prior to his position at DHS); Admiral Jay Cohen (Ret.), who was DHS director of science and technology and previously the Navy's technology chief; and Charlie Allen, who was the intelligence chief at DHS and, according to Michael Chertoff, "pretty much head of everything you could be for the CIA."

The Chertoff Group has now hooked up with Blue Star Capital, a transatlantic investment company specializing in mergers and acquisitions in the security business. In its announcement of the new partnership, Blue Star emphasized their joint interest in "generating opportunities" across the national security spectrum—"in the homeland security, defense, and intelligence markets."

Chertoff himself applauded the value of the merger: "I believe there are many areas of opportunity within the Homeland Security, Intelligence and Defense sectors where the synergies between Blue Star and the Chertoff Group will provide real value."

Taking Back Security

The "unwarranted influence" that concerned Eisenhower during the Cold War now pervades national politics and is rarely questioned. Nor has there been any evaluation of the achievements of the increasingly privatized national security complex. In his 2010 State of the Union address, President Obama talked about the need for fiscal restraint, but exempted "national security" from the planned spending freeze. Despite manifold evidence of vast waste and scandalous profiteering in the security apparatus—to say nothing of "unnecessary wars"—the president didn't see fit to scale back the security agencies. By failing to do so, he has all but guaranteed that the outsourcing bonanza will continue. With "national security" off limits for budget cuts, Obama signaled that safeguarding the nation against the "unwarranted influence" and "rise of misplaced power" will not be priorities for this administration.

As major corporations such as Lockheed Martin and security consulting agencies such as the Chertoff Group extend their corporate tentacles into the intelligence, military, and homeland security terrains, the greater threat they pose. The corporate penetration of all the government's information-gathering, communications, intelligence, and data systems undermines democratic governance. The new corporate domination of data-mining, communications, and cybersecurity systems—with little or no government oversight —threatens individual liberty and privacy. This also creates a powerful vested interest in a large and growing "national security" apparatus—and one that is deeply integrated with the top echelons of the intelligence agencies, military, and other parts of this secretive state-within-the-state.

In the end, it's not the contractors that are the central problem with the national security complex—it's the outsourcers, that is, the elected politicians and the government administrators they appoint or confirm. The contractors are working to maximize profits, and are answerable mainly to company shareholders. The outsourcers, however, are ultimately answerable, at least in principle, to the public. What is at stake is who really controls public policy—a democratically accountable government, or an unaccountable fusion of governmental and corporate power. ❏

Sources: Center for Defense Information, "Military Budgets 1946-2009,"; Center for Arms Control and NonProliferation, "2008-2009 U.S. Defense Spending Highest Since WWII," Feb. 20, 2008; FedSpending, org, a project of OMB Watch; USASpending.gov; Tim Shorrock, *New Spies for Hire: The Secret World of Intelligence Outsourcing*, 2008; FY2009 Intelligence Budget, GlobalSecurity.org; F.J. Hillhouse, "Outsourcing Intelligence," *The Nation*, July 24, 2007; Walter Pincus, "Lawmakers Want More Data on Contracting Out Intelligence," *Washington Post*, May 7,

2006: David Horowitz, ed., *Corporations and the Cold War*, 1969; GAO, "Defense Contracting: Army Case Study Delineates Concerns with Use of Contractors as Contract Specialists," March 2008; Frida Berrigan, "Military Industrial Complex 2.0," TruthOut, Sept. 14, 2008; "2009 Top 100," Washington Technology; DHS, Enterprise Solutions Office, EAGLE contracts; *Global Homeland Security 2009-2019*, VisionGain, June 23, 2009; Chertoff Group web pages, chertoffgroup.com; Homeland Security & Defense Business Council web pages, homelandcouncil. org; Chalmers Johnson, "Military Industrial Complex: It's Much Later Than You Think," AntiWar. com, July 28, 2008; Allison Stanger, *One Nation Under Contract: The Outsourcing of American Power and the Future of Foreign Policy* (Yale University Press, 2009); Project on Government Oversight (POGO); Deborah Avant, *The Market for Force: The Consequences of Privatizing Security* (Cambridge University Press, 2005); Center for Public Integrity, "Making a Killing: The Business of War," 2002, "The Shadow Pentagon," 2004; Peter Singer, *Corporate Warriors* (Cornell University Press, 2003).

Article 2.3

THE OTHER COLOMBIA
The Economics and Politics of Depropriation

BY PATRICIA M. RODRIGUEZ
November/December 2010

It has rained for days, and the swampy ocean waters that surround this community of displaced fishermen in northern Colombia rise at their own whim, flooding people's houses and making life even harder than usual. Yet most of the families living in this tiny makeshift encampment in Boca de Aracataca in the Magdalena province of Colombia have gathered under a tarp to eloquently tell a group of activists from Witness for Peace, a Washington-based social justice organization, about their problems. "[The foreign companies] kicked us out of our land. We do not have water, electricity, food, nor any help from the government... we need to be respected, we need to be treated as people, and not as animals," says Alicia Camargo, who has been displaced three times already, once very violently, along with family and neighbors.

As it turns out, the source of the problems in this community—and others nearby—is the presence of multinational corporations. In this particular case, it involves a new port expansion project along the Caribbean coast near the otherwise-idyllic city of Santa Marta. The construction of this mega-port has been funded by foreign coal companies that have operated practically unrestrictedly in Colombia for nearly 15 years. When it is finished in 2013, the port will allow U.S.-based company Drummond and Swiss-based Glencore to ship an extra 30 to 60 million tons of coal per year to global markets, in addition to the nearly 69 million tons they already export. The Colombian government allegedly receives a royalty of 10% of this total export profit, but only a handful of people see this money. A large portion of the money is never transferred to the communities that are most impoverished and environmentally affected by corporate presence. Still, foreign direct investment is embraced wholeheartedly by Colombian elites who equate corporate ventures in the agricultural, mineral, and industrial sectors with growth and prosperity.

It is not uncommon to hear about how corporations bring investment to developing countries and even their "willingness" to address problem areas such as environmental contamination and child labor practices. It is sometimes said that corporations' business practices are completely socially responsible and that corporations give back to the communities in which they operate. The media give much less attention to stories about how corporations destroy local lives, directly and indirectly. Yet it happens, and in some cases it leaves a trail of unimaginable destruction and violence. In this Caribbean region of Colombia, to talk of displacement of communities by corporations does not do justice to the reality; rather, locals speak of depropriation, or the takeover of property and livelihoods with complete impunity.

In this corner of the world, multinational corporations in the coal industry like Drummond and Glencore, and in the banana sector, like Dole and Chiquita Brands (among others), are not just operating on the basis of government-granted licenses to exploit natural resources. Through alliances with authorities, legal and otherwise, these companies have crafted what amounts to an informal ownership of the region. They own a large part of the railroads, highways, ports, and mines, and they have little concern for how communities feel about their presence there.

But what is it about the nature of these enterprises and the context in which they operate that make for such dominance, and what facilitates their exploitation of workers and communities? How have local people resisted these infractions, and to what degree, considering the widespread corruption of their political representatives? To answer both these questions, it helps to understand more about the region. Whether due to its strategic location, its natural resources, or its distance from the centers of power in the capital city, Bogotá, this region is often referred to as "the other Colombia." It is an allusion both to its potential and to its stigma as something of a no man's land.

Free Reign in the "Other Colombia"

Multinational companies began to arrive in the Magdalena and Cesar provinces in large part because the location offers such natural advantages. Surrounded in the east by the Sierra Nevada mountains, several municipalities in Magdalena province have direct access to the rivers that originate in these slopes. This makes the land well suited for banana plantations and other kinds of large-scale agriculture, and therefore for elite and corporate interests. It comes as no surprise that one of the U.S.-based companies with most presence throughout Latin America, the United Fruit Company (UFCO), operated in Magdalena since the beginning of the 20th century. As with its operations elsewhere, UFCO labor practices in Colombia were exploitative and repressive. During a strike by UFCO banana workers on December 6, 1928, in which they asked for better treatment and working conditions, an indefinite number of workers were massacred by company and police security forces in Ciénaga. The Nobel Prize-winning Colombian writer Gabriel García Márquez wrote a fictional account of this massacre in One Hundred Years of Solitude. Though UFCO left the Magdalena region in 1950s and moved to other regions of Colombia, it continued subcontracting with local growers.

In the mid to late 1980s, Chiquita Brands (formerly UFCO) and Dole rediscovered the Zona Bananera, or the Caribbean Banana Zone, at a time when local landowners had already been paying a "security fee" to rebel guerrilla groups that operated from the largely uninhabited Sierra Nevada, like the National Liberation Army (ELN). Noticing the potential for exclusive control of land and/or lucrative contracts with local large-scale banana growers, Chiquita and Dole officials negotiated economic deals with the landowners and security deals with the guerrillas. Their aim was to guarantee the companies' unrestricted access to highways and railroads leading to the coastal ports. In just a few years, however, small private security gangs began brutal confrontations with guerrillas in the mountains and the cities. Aware of their stronger firepower, the companies began to pay these small groups for protection instead of the guerrillas. By the late 1990s, these gang-style private security groups multiplied and fought each other for control of the territory (and for the substantial payments from landowners and multinational companies). A handful of gang leaders emerged victorious, and soon formed more structured paramilitary organizations like the powerful United Self-Defense Forces of Colombia (AUC). AUC and other paramilitary groups are known to have solid ties to drug lords as well as to military and high-level state authorities.

One of the AUC leaders in the Caribbean region is Rodrigo Tovar, popularly known as Jorge 40. He was a former army official and comes from one of a handful of powerful traditional families in the region. In the mid 1990s, Jorge 40 began to work under the command of the Castaño family, who founded the AUC when the patriarch Jesús Castaño was kidnapped and assassinated in the mid 1990s by another guerrilla group, the Revolutionary Armed Forces of Colombia (FARC). To garner control, Jorge 40 was known to carry out "cleansings" of local communities in Magdalena and Cesar provinces, targeting anyone suspected of ties to ELN or FARC. In 2000, after a guerrilla attack on a group of business and mafia leaders in the town of Nueva Venezia, Jorge 40 ordered the massacre of 70 people from this community. According to witnesses, the armed paramilitaries then played soccer with victims' severed heads to show the community that they were in complete control. There are several others like Jorge 40 who have ties to the different landowning families and to different companies. In 2007, Chiquita Brands admitted in federal court that it paid nearly $2 million to paramilitary death squads over a period of seven years. On its end, Drummond is currently being sued in a United States court under the Alien Tort Claims Act for having contracted paramilitary forces to kill three union leaders. The violence in the region is widespread, and largely tied to corporate interest in acquiring lands and controlling the regions' vast resources. Between 1997 and 2007, 4,000 people died and at least 500 were disappeared. Moreover, during the height of the violence in between 2003 and 2006, 43,300 families from the region suffered forced displacement from their communities.

On their end, the companies suffered no major consequences from the bloodbath, other than occasionally having to rearrange their deals with different paramilitary leaders. As long as they kept scheduled payments, the companies enjoyed complete control over vast lands. By 2002 Chiquita and Dole decided to divvy up the 10,000 hectares of land in the Zona Bananera: the medium-to-large farms that grew bananas for Dole had their main houses painted red and white, and those that grew bananas for Chiquita were painted blue and white. They also happily shared the railroad. On the other hand, small farms that for one or another reason do not have contracts with these companies have hardly survived. Many peasants have agreed to sell their lands, only to lose most of their money to criminal and paramilitary gangs that extorted them shortly after the sale. Others, out of fear, have simply never returned after their violent displacement by paramilitary groups. In the near future, these corporations are likely to continue to buy lands in the region, especially with the impending passage of the free trade agreement (FTA) between the United States and Colombia. While former president Alvaro Uribe championed the push for the FTA deal with the United States, current president Juan Manuel Santos, a former defense minister and a millionaire who has solid ties to many traditional elite Colombian families, is likely to deepen the open-borders approach.

The free reign of foreign coal companies reflects a similar history. The mountainous terrain in neighboring Cesar province contains some of the biggest coal mines in Latin America. Drummond, Prodeco (a subsidiary of Glencore), and now Brazilian-owned Vale, have capitalized on this by buying part of the national railroad company Fenoco, so as to have unrestricted access to the approximately 300 miles of railroad line between the mines and the port of Ciénaga, near Santa Marta. The port installations now cover four kilometers (of a total twelve kilometers) of the coastal shores in Magdalena, but the mega-port currently under construction would extend them by another two kilometers. When the project got under way in 2008, several communities living in the swamps, or ciénaga, near the port were forcibly displaced by armed gunmen, and many ended in the encampment in Boca de Aracataca. The port expansion work has prevented the fishermen from being able to access close-by waters and they now have to fish in far away waters, if their boats are solid enough to make it there. The damage extends far beyond access. For years, the companies have been dumping millions of tons of coal onto communities where the railroad crosses, and into coastal waters. This is due to negligence, as residuals "accidentally" fall out when the coal is carried uncovered or dumped into the shipping containers. This has resulted in severe erosion and environmental contamination of local flora and fish. As if that did not suffice, Drummond was recently conceded the rights to Rio Toribio, including control over the station that supplies clean water to local communities. According to the fishermen, Drummond uses the water to wet down the coal so that it does not ignite in the containers on the way to global markets. This has generated the contamination of river water with coal dust, and has caused a variety of skin and respiratory diseases among the local population.

State Complicity

This depropriation and destruction occurs under the protective eye of the Colombian state. Though laws exist which delimit any alterations to the agro-ecological balance in much of the coastal area, the government blatantly disregards the laws. In December 2007 the national Ministry of Transportation declared that the entire municipality was a public interest zone for purposes of national development, paving the way for the expansion of the port. Though Drummond and Prodeco appear to have followed all the legal steps to begin the expansion project, the process has certainly faltered in many aspects. According to a report prepared by local community leaders, the companies and municipal authorities did not adequately consult local community groups about worrisome environmental and socio-economic effects. Though the royalties for mining concessions and banana profits by law should remain in the communities for social and infrastructural investment, a majority of this money is simply distributed privately to national and municipal authorities. As a community leader from Ciénaga states, "what we have here is a case of mafia triangulation, with companies, the central government, and local authorities keeping the municipal funds for themselves, and thereby diffusing any responsibility that they should have towards communities."

The foreign companies do as they please, with impunity. When unionized coal workers organize to demand respect for their labor rights, or to ask for appropriate paid sick time for work injuries, the companies fire them. Such is the case of Moisés Padilla, a former Drummond employee who belongs to the Sintraminergética (National Union of Industry and Energy Workers) union. He worked for 50 years as a welder (25 at Drummond), and is now incapacitated due to severe respiratory and heart conditions. The company has successfully resisted any outside intervention, despite legal efforts of the union. In a letter to Moisés Padilla, a company representative stated that it was not company policy to consent to third-party involvement, in this case a committee of independent and state officials that could evaluate his injury claims. Union workers have less and less job security, especially since the company has recently created its own union, Sintradrummond. Although the practice was previously prohibited, a recent judicial decision has opened a loophole for companies to begin organizing their own unions. Anibal Perez, another injured worker from Sintraminergética, affirms that "for us to belong to our union is considered by the state practically a crime…the state does not give us the tools and protections to make our voices heard, and the result is that we have communities full of widows, orphans, and sick workers." The union has had five of its leaders killed since 2001, and several others now live in exile after being threatened by paramilitaries.

The companies are also quick to hold on to the façade of being socially and environmentally responsible. One example: Drummond trains a certain number of people from the community to be mine workers, but rarely hires local trainees. Some think this is because it is cheaper for the company to hire migrants from other regions. Similarly, national companies like Augura (Association of Banana Workers of Colombia) organize some of their own workers in seemingly beneficial cooperatives. Though independent on paper, Augura does business strictly with Dole, and prices are arranged between top level managers from Augura and Dole. So even if cooperative workers would truly get a fair trade price for their bananas, the lack of liberty to make autonomous decisions within the company-run cooperatives is problematic at best.

Not that state intervention would do any good. For one thing, much of the state funding for social programs for local communities is channeled to the companies themselves, such as the Augura-run cooperatives. So while the state has funds that it invests in social programs, these are mostly captured by the companies.

Secondly, other state-funded social programs deliver subsidies as if community members were clients. The community at large, whether they belong to the category of low-income families, displaced families, or relatives and victims of violence, barely has access to a program that distributes about $40 every two months; most do not have enough of a connection with municipal authorities to receive even this small benefit. Thirdly, though the laws exist on paper to make the state more responsible and responsive, implementation is a problem. For instance, Colombia has had a Labor Statute since 1991, but the mechanisms for its implementation have not yet been discussed in Congress. Besides, corruption pervades the state. In 2009, a national scandal erupted over a government program aimed at helping struggling farmers, the Agro Ingreso Seguro (AIS) program. The funding (partly from the U.S. Agency for International Development) began in 2006 as part of an effort to ease concern over a potential negative impact of an impending FTA with the United States, but small farmers were not the ones benefiting; the bulk of AIS' $630 million per year was discovered to be going to rich landowners, narco-traffickers, and mobsters.

Organizing an Effective Resistance

Considering the pervasiveness of corporate interests, violence, and state complicity, what can the handful of community leaders, human rights defenders, and union workers do to organize effective resistance? The truth is that they cannot organize freely; their lives are threatened constantly. Despite the threats, is not so hard to understand why those who are still alive publicly denounce the companies, the Colombian government, and the United States for trampling on their dignity. "Our denunciations make us very public personas, and since we do not have money to pay for private security guards, speaking out publicly and internationally ironically gives us some sense of security," says Edgardo Alemán, a local human rights defender.

And so they do challenge, collectively when possible. One of the small victories of the sintramienergética union and other allied groups has been the Collective Labor Agreement signed between the union and Drummond, for the years 2010-2013. Even at quick glance, it is easy to find the voice of the workers, and their concern for community. Article 7 states that when a job opens at Drummond, the company will give preference to skilled members of the local community; upon the death of a worker, the company commits to hiring a family member of the victim. Union leaders concur that the agreement feels more like "our list of demands" than an actual commitment by Drummond representatives. Yet many insist that a more effective interaction between the communities and the companies is the only solution. "We need to guarantee a way to capture the resources, to have a social development policy that favors our communities. If we go through the politicians, we will get nothing," says local activist and economist, Luís Eduardo Rendón.

If the state's lack of responsiveness is any indication, negotiating with the companies might in fact be a viable approach. But the success of that strategy does not depend on the amount of pressure Colombian workers and community leaders exert. In this sense, the context (and place) in which they operate limits their impact. For their voice to mean anything in a system dominated by elite power in Bogotá and abroad, it will take the U.S. government and global citizens en masse to press the companies (American companies!) and the Colombian state to be honest, and to practice their activities legally, with true social responsibility. Perhaps then there can begin to be justice for these communities in the other Colombia. ❏

Sources: Luis E. Barranco, "Como el gobierno nacional convirtió una zona agroecológica en zona de interés público para fines portuarios," *EDUMAG*, Ciénaga, Colombia, 2010; Marcelo Bucheli, *Bananas and Business: The United Fruit Company in Colombia, 1899-2000* (New York University Press, 2005); Peter Chapman, *Bananas: How the United Fruit Company Shaped the World* (Canongate, 2007); Aviva Chomsky, Garry Leech, and Steve Striffler, *Bajo el manto del carbon: Pueblos y multinacionales en las minas de El Cerrejón* (Casa Editorial Pisando Callos, 2007).

Article 2.4

BANKRUPTCY AS CORPORATE MAKEOVER

ASARCO demonstrates how to evade environmental responsibility.

BY MARA KARDAS-NELSON, LIN NELSON, AND ANNE FISCHEL
May/June 2010

> "At around noon [every] July and August…our folks would bring us into the
> house, because the smoke, the pollution, the sulfur, would settle into our
> community for about two or three hours…when there was no breeze to take that
> away. When we would breathe that, we could not be outside because we were
> constantly coughing. So nobody can tell me that there was no ill effect on the
> majority of the folks that lived in Smeltertown."
>
> —Daniel Solis, resident of Smeltertown, a Mexican-American
> neighborhood in El Paso, Texas located next to an ASARCO smelter.

After five long years in court, the bankruptcy of the American Smelting and Refining Company, or ASARCO, has finally been determined.

Hailed as one of the earliest and largest multinational corporations and responsible for the employment of hundreds of thousands, ASARCO has a long history of polluting both the environment and the workplace. After racking up billions in environmental damages, the company filed for bankruptcy in 2005.

It has been billed as the largest environmental bankruptcy in United States history; 90 communities from 21 states will share a $1.79 billion settlement to cover the costs of environmental monitoring and cleanup and limited compensation to some of its workers. This figure, however, represents less than one percent of the funds originally identified as needed by claimants.

The ASARCO case emerged in the context of a diminished and disabled "Superfund," as the federal environmental program established to deal with hazardous waste sites is known. The fund was originally created by Congress to hold companies accountable for environmental damage and to ensure that communities are not left with large bills and no means to pay them. But years of corporate pressure on Capitol Hill has depleted Superfund, placing the financial burden of environmental cleanups on taxpayers, rather than on corporations.

This use of bankruptcies to avoid responsibility, coupled with a cash-strapped Superfund, offers a chilling glimpse into the world of corporate irresponsibility allowable under U.S. bankruptcy provisions and environmental policy. As the case closes, ASARCO is transforming from an aging corporation weighed down by shuttered factories and contaminated communities into a lean and profitable company. This is setting a precedent for how others can use legal loopholes to evade liability and undermine government protections.

Damaging Health and Environment, Yet Shaping Environmental Policy

ASARCO began operations in the late 1890s, mining, smelting, and refining essential ores (first lead, then copper) in order to provide base materials for industrial production. By the mid-20th century, the company had expanded to include holdings and operations in Latin America, Australia, Canada, Africa, and the Philippines. In 1914 company workers unionized through the Western Federation of Miners, which later became the Mine, Mill & Smelterworkers, eventually merging with the United Steelworkers in the 1960s. In its heyday, ASARCO operated in close to 90 U.S. communities in 22 states, employing thousands.

By the mid-1970s, employees and communities were growing concerned about environmental and public health risks resulting from company operations. Researchers, health departments, unions, and workers began tracking the impact of exposure to arsenic, lead, cadmium, and sulfur dioxide, all byproducts of the smelting process. In Tacoma, WA, site of one of ASARCO's largest smelting operations, dissident workers launched "The Smelterworker" newsletter, one of the first union-based occupational health efforts in the country. The Puget Sound Air Pollution Control Agency began to voice similar concerns when ASARCO's lobbying regarding federal laws and regulations successfully slowed development of a federal arsenic standard.

Health concerns also emerged in El Paso, Texas, site of a large ASARCO smelter that had polluted both sides of the U.S.-Mexico border. In 1970, following passage of the Clean Air Act, the City of El Paso sued ASARCO over its sulfur dioxide emissions. During the process of discovery, ASARCO submitted documentation of its emissions to the City for the first time. These reports showed that between 1969 and 1971, 1,012 metric tons of lead, 508 metric tons of zinc, eleven metric tons of cadmium, and one metric ton of arsenic had been released during operations.

By 1969 the city had a higher concentration of airborne lead than any other in the state. In the early 1970s a research team from the Centers for Disease Control (CDC), led by Dr. Philip Landrigan, confirmed a pattern of smelter-sourced lead threatening the children on the U.S. side.

Chronic arsenic exposure can lead to skin pigmentation, numbness, cardiovascular disease, diabetes, vascular disease, and a variety of cancers, including skin, kidney, bladder, lung, prostate and liver.

Lead exposure can result in damage to the kidneys, liver, brain, nerves, and other organs, and the development of osteoporosis, reproductive disorders, seizures, mental retardation, behavioral and learning disorders, lowered IQ, high blood pressure and elevated risk of heart disease.

The studies conducted by the CDC linked the high levels of lead in air, soil, and dust to the ASARCO smelter. They also linked the lead in soil and dust to elevated lead levels in children's blood. Landrigan's research team administered IQ tests and reaction time tests, and found significant differences in performance between lead-impacted children and those with lower blood levels. This pathbreaking research transformed scientific thinking about the impact of lead on children's development, and confirmed numerous dangers, even in children without obvious clinical symptoms.

At the time of research the threshold for lead in blood was 40 micrograms per deciliter. Today it is 10 micrograms per deciliter, and many health researchers and physicians want to see it set even lower. Yet some researchers had asserted that lead from smelters was not harmful to humans, and an El Paso pediatrician, in a study funded by an organization connected to the industry, claimed that levels of 40 to 80 micrograms were acceptable, as long as the children were properly nourished. As a result of the CDC studies, however, "it is now widely accepted in the scientific community that lead is toxic at extremely low levels," according to Landrigan.

Some of the affected children were treated with painful chelation therapy. Daniel Solis, a Smeltertown resident, recalls his siblings' reaction to the treatment:

> They would get hysterical because of how much the treatment would hurt, they would literally go underneath their cribs and they would hold on to the bottom of the bed. I would literally have to go underneath and drag them out…It was excruciating. My mom would cry to see…the pain that her kids would be going through. But we had no other choice, you know, my siblings were that infected with lead that they had to get that treatment.

In 1991, through its subsidiary Encycle, ASARCO received highly hazardous waste, sourced from a Department of Defense site at Rocky Mountain Arsenal in Colorado. Napalm, sarin nerve gas, cluster bombs, and white phosphorous had all been produced at this site, and private pesticide companies also rented space in the facility. At Encycle, hazardous waste labels were removed and materials were shipped to ASARCO facilities in El Paso and in East Helena, Mont. Neither facility was licensed to manage hazardous waste; it is possible that the waste was shipped to other sites as well. In El Paso, workers were not informed of the risks of such incineration and were not trained to deal with these hazardous materials. This lack of protection and withholding of information violates the federal right-to-know workplace law.

The Government Accountability Office (GAO) has verified that from 1991 to 1999, the El Paso and East Helena plants received and incinerated waste meant only for licensed hazardous waste facilities. This illegal disposal potentially exposed hundreds of workers and both communities. In 1998, the federal government fined ASARCO $50 million for these violations and problems at other ASARCO sites. The settlement did not include provisions for testing workers, soil, air, water, or community members for exposure to potential contaminants. The El Paso community was not informed about these illegal activities; the extent of knowledge in East Helena is unclear. The wrist-slap against the company—and the actions that provoked it—became public only through the investigative work of citizen activists in El Paso, leading to a *New York Times* exposé in 2006.

Although many communities endure severe health effects and environmental problems, ASARCO's ties to powerful politicians gave it substantial influence on public health policy. During the George W. Bush years, James Connaughton, one of ASARCO's key attorneys, served as head of the White House Council for Environmental Quality. A key ASARCO scientist was positioned for the federal Lead Advisory Board, while other prominent, independent scientists were pushed to the margins. ASARCO has also promoted the corporate "audit privilege," allowing companies to self-monitor hazards.

Superfund: Hope and Disappointment for Polluted Communities

ASARCO was hardly the only company polluting communities throughout the industrial boom of the 20th century. As research linked contamination to birth defects, higher cancer rates, and other serious illnesses, community advocates and municipal and state leaders took collective action. In 1980, in response to the discovery of hazardous waste at Love Canal, N.Y., Congress passed the Comprehensive Environmental Response, Compensation & Liability Act (CERCLA), better known as "Superfund." The Act made companies legally and financially responsible for environmental degradation that occurred as a result of their operations. Additionally, cleanup costs for "orphan sites" where specific companies could not be identified or held responsible would draw money from the Superfund, made of a series of corporate taxes, or "polluter-pays fees," and supported by government revenue. The legislation authorized the Environmental Protection Agency (EPA) to place heavily contaminated sites on the National Priorities List. If identified as a "Superfund site," a community qualified for enforced cleanup and funds. Since the inception of Superfund, the EPA has identified over 1,200 sites, including 20 ASARCO operations. One in four Americans lives within four miles of a Superfund site.

In 1995, under the watch of President Clinton and a Republican Congress, Superfund's polluter-pays fees expired, thus shifting most of the financial burden onto taxpayers. As of 2010, these fees have yet to be reinstated. By 2003, all corporate funds were exhausted and the Superfund now relies solely on taxpayer-funded government revenues. According to the U.S. Public Interest Research Group, in 1995 taxpayers paid only 18% ($300 million) of the Superfund, but by 2005, they contributed 100%—approximately $1.2 billion.

As a result of under-financing and lack of political will, the number of Superfund sites undergoing cleanup has diminished. While the EPA averaged 87 completed cleanups a year from 1997 to 2000, in 2008 only 30 sites were processed, representing a drop of over 50% in the pace of cleanups. Without polluter-pays fees and in light of the bankruptcy, the affected communities at ASARCO sites are left with few options to ensure comprehensive cleanup and reparations.

Penny Newman of the Center for Community Action & Environmental Justice calls the fund "impotent" without corporate contributions: "It's disingenuous to pretend a program exists without the funding." In spring 2009, the Obama administration directed $600 million in stimulus money to 50 Superfund sites—including the ASARCO site in Tacoma—that have shown significant progress in their cleanups. Obama and the EPA call this a "stopgap measure," setting the restoration of the polluter-pays tax as an important environmental health goal.

The Bankruptcy "Solution"

As environmental and community health concerns mounted, public pressure increased, and projected cleanup costs skyrocketed, ASARCO closed most of its operations. All of ASARCO's sites—operating, shuttered, or in remediation—were affected by the 2005 Chapter 11 bankruptcy filing. The company cited environmental liabilities as a primary explanation for the action.

The bankruptcy was not a last-minute act of desperation. On the contrary, the company had been rearranging itself for some time, shedding liabilities and cutting costs through sales and mergers. In 1999, ASARCO was "bought" by its major subsidiary, Grupo México, a Mexican-based company that is one of the largest metal producers in the world. This sale is significant because ASARCO's assets and records were shifted outside of the United States and therefore no longer under U.S. government jurisdiction; citizens requesting records and remediation from the company now had difficulty doing so. In 2002, ASARCO sold one of its most valuable mining complexes, Southern Peru Copper, to its new parent company, transferring even more valuable resources beyond national boundaries. Fearing a potential bankruptcy, the Department of Justice forced ASARCO to set up a $100 million trust to cover liabilities for impacted U.S. communities.

Chapter 11 of the U.S. Bankruptcy Code permits corporate reorganization and invokes "automatic stay," in which most litigation is put on hold until it can be resolved in court, with creditors ceasing collection attempts. This status allowed ASARCO to legally avoid paying for environmental damage at sites that required it for the duration of the bankruptcy. Additionally, pension payments and other monies owed to workers as negotiated by the United Steelworkers, which represents most employees, were threatened and delayed. As a result of the bankruptcy, the Steelworkers, a member of the bankruptcy creditors' committee, settled with a one-year extension of their collective bargaining agreement.

Complexities stemming from ASARCO's multinational status became more apparent during the 2005-2009 bankruptcy proceedings. During the case, Grupo México, by court ruling, was removed as the controlling agent of ASARCO. As such, Grupo México battled with another corporate suitor, India-based Sterilite/Vedanta Corporation, for control; Grupo México eventually prevailed. This competition prolonged proceedings, as the judge assessed competing purchase offers and changing promises to affected communities and workers.

Through bankruptcy negotiations, ASARCO significantly reduced its debts to damaged communities. The *Tacoma News Tribune* reported that more than a dozen states and the federal government originally collectively filed $6 billion in environmental claims involving 20 ASARCO sites. Other estimates placed cleanup and liability costs as high as $25.2 billion. This figure was subsequently reduced to $3.6 billion in early bankruptcy court proceedings, which was later sliced to the final settlement of $1.79 billion.

In the days following the announcement of the settlement, government spokespeople and community members expressed a mix of relief and disappointment. According to U.S. Associate Attorney General Tom Perrelli, "The effort to recover this money was a collaborative and coordinated response by the states and federal government. Our combined efforts have resulted in the largest recovery of funds to pay for past and future cleanup of hazardous materials in the nation's history. Today is a historic day for the environment and the people affected across the country."

But activists and affected communities insist the ruling did not go far enough. In addition to paying less than originally projected, ASARCO's parent company, Grupo México, faces fewer responsibilities than it did before the bankruptcy. While the company had previously been pegged with penalty payments for the transfer of Southern Peru Copper, the bankruptcy decision, which reinstated Grupo México control, nullified this.

The $1.79 billion settlement will also be unevenly split between affected communities. While Washington State celebrated the perseverance of their attorneys and coordinated work of departments, Texas, which had relatively little sustained support and attention by federal authorities, will not be as well served. The El Paso area has a modest $52 million to address complex and hazardous contamination.

ASARCO's Legacy and Communities' Call for Responsibility

Throughout the bankruptcy proceedings, U.S. Senator Maria Cantwell (D-WA) warned that ASARCO's use of bankruptcy will be imitated by other companies aiming to minimize their liability for environmental and health damages. The *Tacoma News Tribune* has reported that companies in eight of the ten regions under EPA jurisdiction have considered bankruptcy in order to elude responsibility. A 2007 study identified six companies connected to approximately 120 Superfund sites in 28 states filing for bankruptcy, with four of these companies successfully avoiding over half a billion dollars in cleanup costs. In 2009, eleven states involved in the ASARCO bankruptcy and the Justice Department reaffirmed the warning that more companies will follow suit.

Twice Cantwell has introduced bills to curtail companies' use of bankruptcies and other "legal" techniques to avoid responsibility; twice the bills have failed.

Texas State Senator Shapleigh has witnessed the city of El Paso's struggle with the high cost of environmental cleanup and jeopardized public health. Commenting on the bankruptcy and echoing Cantwell's concerns, he warns, "This is a strategy that will be used over and over again in the United States. The corporations will play out this environmental saga…this is the first one."

A Familiar Story

The story of ASARCO is a complicated one. It is a story of environmental degradation, of countless hidden occupational health hazards, of a corporation comfortably connected to federal and state administrations, and of a broken safety net that offers little compensation for communities impacted by a century of industrial operations.

Yet the story of ASARCO is not an unfamiliar one. The company's evasion of corporate responsibility in the face of weakened federal regulations demonstrates how companies can shift billions of dollars of environmental cleanup costs onto affected communities.

The special brew of corporate bankruptcies and an under-funded Superfund leaves us extremely vulnerable to industrial contamination. ASARCO's bankruptcy left thousands of exposed workers and family members, 21 states, two Indian tribal communities, and unions in limbo for years, and now with very limited reparation for life-altering health effects and degraded environments. Despite the company's responsibility for extensive environmental and health damage, the settlement holds them accountable for only a sliver of originally projected cleanup costs. A lack of political will from Congress to ensure corporate funding for Superfund and to pass legislation that tightens legal loopholes has left communities who believed they were protected by the 1980 CERCLA legislation strapped for cash and with few legal protections to enforce corporate responsibility.

Current and former ASARCO employees, affected communities, and allies are organizing to push for corporate accountability and government regulations. In El Paso, as a result of the bankruptcy, the Superfund dysfunction, and the special burden of illegal hazardous waste incineration, community advocates are working to shape a strategy for activating workplace right-to-know for former employees at high risk for illness. They are further insisting on transparency in the cleanup and corporate accountability for public health.

In February 2010, a group of over two dozen organizations and individuals, including current and former ASARCO employees and several Mexican government officials, wrote to the EPA with concerns that the cleanup plan for the El Paso site is "inadequate to protect the health of the [El Paso] community and does not address offsite-pollution in [New Mexico], Mexico and Texas." The current plan only addresses hazards in El Paso, but according to Mariana Chew of the Sierra Club, "Cuidad Juárez in Mexico and Sunland Park in [New Mexico] are the communities most affected by ASARCO's legal and illegal operations and yet are not taken in account." Chew and others are especially concerned about the health of children at an elementary school in Cuidad Juárez that sits just 400 feet downwind from the smelter.

The group demands larger payments from ASARCO, specifically for its illegal incineration of hazardous waste. In the interim, the group claims that federal monies from the Superfund should be used.

The 2010 National Latino Congress has also condemned ASARCO's contamination of the border region and the company's bankruptcy. The Congress, supported by hundreds of organizations and over 40 elected U.S. officials, demanded full disclosure of the illegal incineration of hazardous waste, and comprehensive testing and treatment for workers and community members who may have been exposed.

Meanwhile, in Hayden, Ariz., site of the company's only operating U.S. smelter, ASARCO officials have reassured residents that blowing dust from mine tailings is not a hazard. According to ASARCO vice president Thomas Aldrich, "Across the board these are very low in metals, about what you'd expect here, comparable to the background levels in soil."

Such statements offer little comfort for communities still struggling for information, protection, and accountability. ❏

This article is based on the project "No Borders: Communities Living and Working with Asarco" based at Evergreen and guided by Fischel and Nelson. The project examines the occupational and environmental health and social justice implications of ASARCO's operations with a focus on three communities: Ruston/Tacoma, Wash., Hayden, Ariz. and El Paso, Texas. A documentary film, "Borders of Resistance," to be released in the summer of 2010, documents the El Paso story of community and labor advocates pressing for accountability and health protections. Other films and writing are forthcoming.

Sources: Office of Texas Senator Eliot Shapleigh, "Asarco in El Paso," September 2008; Les Blumenthal, "Asarco Mess Reveals Superfund Failings," *Tacoma News Tribune*, March 21, 2006; Les Blumenthal, "Lawyers Dissect Asarco's cleanup obligation in the US," *Tacoma News Tribune*, May 20, 2006; Les Blumenthal, "Grupo México wins Asarco back in court ruling," *Tacoma News Tribune*, September 3, 2009; Joel Millman, "Asarco Bankruptcy Leaves Many Towns with Cleanup Mess," *Wall Street Journal*, May 24, 2006; Office of U.S. Senator Maria Cantwell, "Cantwell Introduces Legislation to Prevent Corporate Polluters from Evading Toxic Cleanup Responsibilities," June 15, 2006; Center for Health, Environment and Justice, "Superfund: In the Eye of the Storm," March 2009; Center for Health, Environment and Justice, "America's Safety Net in Crisis: 25th Anniversary of Superfund," 2005; *The Smelterworker* rank-and-file union newsletter, circa 1970-75, Tacoma Wash.; Marianne Sullivan, "Contested Science and Exposed Workers: ASARCO and the Occupational Standard for Inorganic Arsenic," *Public Health Chronicles*, July 2007; Ralph Blumenthal, "Copper Plant Illegally Burned Hazardous Waste, EPA Says," *New York Times*, October 11, 2006; Government Accountability Office, "Environmental Liabilities: EPA Should Do More to Ensure That Liable Parties Meet Their Cleanup Obligations," August 2005; Government Accountability Office, "Hazardous Waste: Information about How DOD and Federal and State Regulators Oversee the Off-site Disposal of Waste from DOD Installations," November 2007; Department of Justice, "Largest Environmental Bankruptcy in US History Will Result in Payment of $1.79 Billion Towards Environmental Cleanup and Restoration," December 10 2009;

Seattle and King County Department of Public Health, Arsenic Facts, 2010 (www.kingcounty. gov/healthservices/health/ehs/toxic/ArsenicFacts.aspx); The Center for Health, Environment & Justice, "Letter to the Environmental Protection Agency," February 16 2010; The Center for Health, Environment & Justice, "News Release," February 16 2010; The 2010 National Latino Congress, "Draft Amended ASARCO Resolution," 2010; Interview, Dr. Philip Landrigan, Mt Sinai Medical School, August 27 2009; Interview, Daniel Solis, El Paso, Tex, August 2007.

Chapter 3

TRADE, CURRENCY, AND DEBT

Article 3.1

COMPARATIVE ADVANTAGE

BY RAMAA VASUDEVAN
July/August 2007

> Dear Dr. Dollar:
>
> When economists argue that the outsourcing of jobs might be a plus for the U.S. economy, they often mention the idea of comparative advantage. So free trade would allow the United States to specialize in higher-end service-sector businesses, creating higher-paying jobs than the ones that would be outsourced. But is it really true that free trade leads to universal benefits?
> —*David Goodman, Boston, Mass.*

You're right: The purveyors of the free trade gospel do invoke the doctrine of comparative advantage to dismiss widespread concerns about the export of jobs. Attributed to 19th-century British political-economist David Ricardo, the doctrine says that a nation always stands to gain if it exports the goods it produces *relatively* more cheaply in exchange for goods that it can get *comparatively* more cheaply from abroad. Free trade would lead to each country specializing in the products it can produce at *relatively* lower costs. Such specialization allows both trading partners to gain from trade, the theory goes, even if in one of the countries production of *both* goods costs more in absolute terms.

For instance, suppose that in the United States the cost to produce one car equals the cost to produce 10 bags of cotton, while in the Philippines the cost to produce one car equals the cost to produce 100 bags of cotton. The Philippines would then have a comparative advantage in the production of cotton, producing one bag at a cost equal to the production cost of 1/100 of a car, versus 1/10 of a car in the United States; likewise, the United States would hold a comparative advantage in the production of cars. Whatever the prices of cars and cotton in the global market, the theory goes, the Philippines would be better off producing only cotton and importing all its cars from the United States, and the United States would be better off producing only cars and importing all of its cotton from the Philippines. If the international terms of trade—the relative price—is one car for 50 bags, then the United States will take in 50 bags of cotton for each car it exports, 40 more than the 10 bags it forgoes by putting its productive resources into making the car rather than growing cotton. The Philippines is also better off: it can import a car in exchange for the export of 50 bags of cotton, whereas it would have had to forgo the production of 100 bags of cotton in order to produce that car domestically. If the price of cars goes up in the global marketplace, the Philippines will lose out in relative terms—but will still be better off than if it tried to produce its own cars.

The real world, unfortunately, does not always conform to the assumptions underlying comparative-advantage theory. One assumption is that trade is balanced. But many countries are running persistent deficits, notably the United States, whose trade deficit is now at nearly 7% of its GDP. A second premise, that there is full employment within the trading nations, is also patently unrealistic. As global trade intensifies, jobs created in the export sector do not necessarily compensate for the jobs lost in the sectors wiped out by foreign competition.

The comparative advantage story faces more direct empirical challenges as well. Nearly 70% of U.S. trade is trade in similar goods, known as *intra-industry trade*: for example, exporting Fords and importing BMWs. And about one third of U.S. trade as of the late 1990s was trade between branches of a single corporation located in different countries (*intra-firm trade*). Comparative advantage cannot explain these patterns.

Comparative advantage is a static concept that identifies immediate gains from trade but is a poor guide to economic development, a process of structural change over time which is by definition dynamic. Thus the comparative advantage tale is particularly pernicious when preached to developing countries, consigning many to "specialize" in agricultural goods or be forced into a race to the bottom where cheap sweatshop labor is their sole source of competitiveness.

The irony, of course, is that none of the rich countries got that way by following the maxim that they now preach. These countries historically relied on tariff walls and other forms of protectionism to build their industrial base. And even now, they continue to protect sectors like agriculture with subsidies. The countries now touted as new models of the benefits of free trade—South Korea and the other "Asian tigers," for instance—actually flouted this economic wisdom, nurturing their technological capabilities in specific manufacturing sectors and taking advantage of their lower wage costs to *gradually* become effective competitors of the United States and Europe in manufacturing.

The fundamental point is this: contrary to the comparative-advantage claim that trade is universally beneficial, nations as a whole do not prosper from free trade. Free trade creates winners and losers, both within and between countries. In today's context it is the global corporate giants that are propelling and profiting from "free trade": not only outsourcing white-collar jobs, but creating global commodity

Article 3.2

FAIR TRADE AND FARM SUBSIDIES
How Big a Deal? Two Views

November/December 2003; updated, October 2009

In September of 2003, the global free-trade express was derailed—at least temporarily—when the World Trade Organization talks in Cancún, Mexico, collapsed. At the time, the inconsistency of the United States and other rich countries—pressing poor countries to adopt free trade while continuing to subsidize and protect selected domestic sectors, especially agriculture—received wide attention for the first time. Where does ending agricultural subsidies and trade barriers in the rich countries rank as a strategy for achieving global economic justice? Dollars & Sense *asked progressive researchers on different sides of this question to make their case.*

Make Trade Fair

BY GAWAIN KRIPKE

Trade can be a powerful engine for economic growth in developing countries and can help pull millions of people out of poverty. Trade also offers an avenue of growth that relies less than other development strategies on the fickle charity of wealthy countries or the self-interest of multinational corporations. However, current trade rules create enormous obstacles that prevent people in developing countries from realizing the benefits of trade. A growing number of advocacy organizations are now tackling this fundamental problem, hoping to open a route out of poverty for tens of millions of people who have few other prospects.

Why Trade? Poor countries have few options for improving the welfare of their people and generating economic growth. Large debt burdens limit the ability of governments in the developing world to make investments and provide education, clean water, and other critical services. Despite some recent progress on the crushing problem of debt, only about 15% of the global South's $300 billion in unpayable debt has been eliminated.

Poor countries have traditionally looked to foreign aid and private investment to drive economic development. Both of these are proving inadequate. To reach the goals of the United Nations' current Millenium Development campaign, including reducing hunger and providing universal primary education, wealthy countries would have to increase their foreign aid from a paltry 0.23% of GDP to 0.7%. Instead, foreign aid flows are stagnant and are losing value against inflation and population growth. In 2001, the United States spent just 0.11% of GDP on foreign aid.

Likewise, although global foreign direct investment soared to unprecedented levels in the late 1990s, most developing countries are not attractive to foreign investors. The bulk of foreign private investment in the developing world, more than 76%, goes to ten large countries including China, Brazil, and Mexico. For the majority of developing countries, particularly the poorest, foreign investment remains a modest contributor to economic growth, on a par with official foreign aid. Sub-Saharan Africa, with the highest concentration of the world's poor, attracted only $14 billion in 2001.

In this environment, trade offers an important potential source of economic growth for developing countries. Relatively modest gains in their share of global trade could yield large benefits for developing countries. Gaining an additional 1% share of the $8 trillion global export market, for example, would generate more revenue than all current foreign aid spending.

But today, poor countries are bit players in the global trade game. More than 40% of the world's population lives in low-income countries, but these countries generate only 3% of global exports. Despite exhortations from the United States and other wealthy countries to export, many of the poorest countries are actually losing share in export markets. Africa generated a mere 2.4% of world exports of goods in 2001, down from 3.1% in 1990.

Many factors contribute to the poorest countries' inability to gain a foothold in export trade, but the core problem is that the playing field is heavily tilted against them. This is particularly true in the farm sector. The majority of the global South population lives in rural areas and depends on agriculture for survival. Moreover, poverty is concentrated in the countryside: more than three-quarters of the world's poorest people, the 1.1 billion who live on less than one dollar a day, live in rural areas. This means that agriculture must be at the center of trade, development, and poverty-reduction strategies throughout the developing world.

Two examples demonstrate the unfair rules of the global trading system in agriculture: cotton and corn.

"It's Not White Gold Anymore". Cotton is an important crop in Central and West Africa. More than two million households depend directly on the crop for their livelihoods, with millions more indirectly involved. Despite serious social and environmental problems that have accompanied the expansion of cotton cultivation, cotton provides families with desperately needed cash for health care, education, and even food. The cotton crop can make a big difference in reducing poverty. For example, a 2002 World Bank study found a strong link between cotton prices and rural welfare in Benin, a poor West African country.

Cotton is important at a macroeconomic level as well; in 11 African countries, it accounts for more than one-quarter of export revenue. But since the mid-1990s, the cotton market has experienced chronic price depression. Though prices have rebounded in recent months, they remain below the long-term average of $0.72 a pound. Lower prices mean less export revenue for African countries and lower incomes for African cotton farmers.

But not for U.S. cotton farmers. Thanks to farm subsidies, U.S. cotton producers are insulated from the market and have produced bumper crops that depress prices worldwide. The global price of cotton is 20% lower than it would be without U.S. subsidies, according to an analysis by the International Cotton Advisory Committee. Oxfam estimates that in 2001, as a result of U.S. cotton subsidies, eight countries in Africa lost approximately $300 million—about one-quarter of the total amount the U.S. Agency for International Development will spend in Africa next year.

Dumping on Our Neighbor. Mexico has been growing corn (or maize) for 10,000 years. Today, nearly three million Mexican farmers grow corn, but they are facing a crisis due to sharply declining prices. Real prices for corn have fallen 70% since 1994. Poverty is widespread in corn-growing areas like Chiapas, Oaxaca, and Guerrero. Every year, large numbers of rural Mexicans leave the land and migrate to the cities or to the United States to try to earn a living.

The price drops are due to increased U.S. corn exports to Mexico, which have more than tripled since 1994. These exports result in large part from U.S. government policies that encourage overproduction. While Mexican farmers struggle to keep their farms and support their families, the United States pours up to $10 billion annually into subsidies for U.S. corn producers. By comparison, the entire Mexican government budget for agriculture is $1 billion. Between 2000 and 2002, a metric ton of American corn sold on export markets for $20 less than the average cost to produce it. The United States controls nearly 70% of the global corn market, so this dumping has a huge impact on prices and on small-scale corn farmers in Mexico.

To be fair, the Mexican government shares some of the responsibility for the crisis facing corn farmers. Although the North American Free Trade Agreement (NAFTA) opened trade between the United States and Mexico, the Mexican government voluntarily lowered tariffs on corn beyond what was required by NAFTA. As NAFTA is fully phased in, though, Mexico will lose the option of raising tariffs to safeguard poor farmers from a flood of subsidized corn.

What do Poor Countries Want? Cotton and corn illustrate the problems that current trade regimes pose for developing countries and particularly for the world's poorest people. African countries want to engage in global trade but are crowded out by subsidized cotton from the United States. The livelihood of Mexican corn farmers is undermined by dumped U.S. corn. In both of these cases, and many more, it's all perfectly legal. WTO and NAFTA rules provide near impunity to rich countries that subsidize agriculture, and increasingly restrict developing countries' ability to safeguard their farmers and promote development.

How much do subsidies and trade barriers in the rich countries really cost the developing world? One study estimates that developing countries lose $24 billion annually in agricultural income—not a trivial amount. In today's political climate, it's hard to see where else these countries are going to find $24 billion to promote their economic development.

The benefits of higher prices for farmers in the developing world have to be balanced against the potential cost to consumers, both North and South. However, it's important to remember that many Northern consumers actually pay more for food *because of* subsidies. In fact, they often pay twice: first in higher food costs, and then in taxes to pay for the subsidies. Consumers in poor countries will pay more for food if farm commodity prices rise, but the majority of people who work in agriculture will benefit. Since poverty is concentrated in rural areas, the gains to agricultural producers are particularly important.

However, some low-income countries are net food importers and could face difficulties if prices rise. Assuring affordable food is critical, but this goal can be achieved much more cheaply and efficiently than by spending $100 billion on farm subsidies in the rich countries. The World Bank says that low-income countries that depend on food imports faced a net agricultural trade deficit of $2.8 billion in 2000-2001. The savings realized from reducing agricultural subsidies could easily cover this shortfall.

Each country faces different challenges. Developing countries, in particular, need flexibility to develop appropriate solutions to address their economic, humanitarian, and development situations. Broad-stroke solutions inevitably fail to address specific circumstances. But the complexity of the issues must not be used as an excuse for inaction by policy-makers. Failure to act to lift trade barriers and agricultural subsidies will only mean growing inequity, continuing poverty, and endless injustice.

Sources: Xinshen Diao, Eugenio Diaz-Bonilla, and Sherman Robinson, "How Much Does It Hurt? The Impact of Agricultural Trade Policies on Developing Countries," International Food Policy Research Institute, Washington, D.C., 2003; "Global Development Finance: Striving for Stability in Development Finance," World Bank, 2003; Lyuba Zarksy and Kevin Gallagher, "Searching for the Holy Grail? Making FDI Work for Sustainable Development," Tufts Global Development and Environment Institute/WWF, March 2003; Oxfam's website on trade issues, www.maketradefair.com.

False Promises on Trade

BY DEAN BAKER AND MARK WEISBROT

Farmers throughout the Third World are suffering not from too much free trade, but from not enough. That's the impression you get from most media coverage of the recent World Trade Organization (WTO) meetings in Cancún. The *New York Times*, *Washington Post*, and other major news outlets devoted huge amounts of space to news pieces and editorials arguing that agricultural subsidies in rich countries are a major cause of poverty in the developing world. If only these subsidies were eliminated, and the doors to imports from developing countries opened, the argument goes, then the playing field would be level and genuinely free trade would work its magic on poverty in the Third World. The media decided that agricultural subsidies were the major theme of the trade talks even if evidence indicated that other issues—for example, patent and copyright protection, rules on investment, or developing countries' right to regulate imports—would have more impact on the well-being of people in those countries.

There is certainly some element of truth in the argument that agricultural subsidies and barriers to imports can hurt farmers in developing countries. There are unquestionably farmers in a number of developing countries who have been undersold and even put out of business by imports whose prices are artificially low thanks to subsidies the rich countries pay their farmers. It is also true that many of these subsidy programs are poorly targeted, benefiting primarily large farmers and often encouraging environmentally harmful farming practices.

However, the media have massively overstated the potential gains that poor countries might get from the elimination of farm subsidies and import barriers. The risk of this exaggeration is that it encourages policy-makers and concerned non-governmental organizations (NGOs) to focus their energies on an issue that is largely peripheral to economic development and to ignore much more important matters.

To put the issue in perspective: the World Bank, one of the most powerful advocates of removing most trade barriers, has estimated the gains from removing all the rich countries' remaining barriers to trade in manufactured and farm products *and* ending agricultural subsidies. The total estimated gain to low- and middle-income countries, when the changes are phased in by 2015, is an extra 0.6% of GDP. In other words, an African country with an annual income of $500 per person would see that figure rise to $503 as a result of removing these barriers and subsidies.

Simplistic Talk on Subsidies. The media often claim that the rich countries give $300 billion annually in agricultural subsidies to their farmers. In fact, this is not the amount of money paid by governments to farmers, which is actually less than $100 billion. The $300 billion figure is an estimate of the excess cost to consumers in rich nations that results from all market barriers in agriculture. Most of this cost is attributable to higher food prices that result from planting restrictions, import tariffs, and quotas.

The distinction is important, because not all of the $300 billion ends up in the pockets of farmers in rich nations. Some of it goes to exporters in developing nations, as when sugar producers in Brazil or Nicaragua are able to sell their sugar in the United States for an amount that is close to three times the world price. The higher price that U.S. consumers pay for this sugar is part of the $300 billion that many accounts mistakenly describe as subsidies to farmers in rich countries.

Another significant misrepresentation is the idea that cheap imports from the rich nations are always bad for developing countries. When subsides from rich countries lower the price of agricultural imports to developing countries, consumers in those countries benefit. This is one reason why a recent World Bank study found that the removal of *all* trade barriers and subsidies in the United States would have no net effect on growth in sub-Saharan Africa.

In addition, removing the rich countries' subsidies or barriers will not level the playing field—since there will still often be large differences in productivity—and thus will not save developing countries from the economic and social upheavals that such "free trade" agreements as the WTO have in store for them. These agreements envision a massive displacement of people employed in agriculture, as farmers in developing countries are pushed out by international competition. It took the United States 100 years, from 1870 to 1970, to reduce agricultural employment from 53% to under 5% of the labor force, and the transition nonetheless caused considerable social unrest. To compress such a process into a period of a few years or even a decade, by removing remaining agricultural trade barriers in poor countries, is a recipe for social explosion.

It is important to realize that in terms of the effect on developing countries, low agricultural prices due to subsidies for rich-country farmers have the exact same impact as low agricultural prices that stem from productivity gains. If the opponents of agricultural subsidies consider the former to be harmful to the developing countries, then they should be equally concerned about the impact of productivity gains in the agricultural sectors of rich countries.

Insofar as cheap food imports might have a negative impact on a developing country's economy, the problem can be easily remedied by an import tariff. In this situation, the developing world would gain the most if those countries that benefit from cheap imported food have access to it, while those that are better served by protecting their domestic agricultural sector are allowed to impose tariffs without fear of retaliation from rich nations. This would make much more sense, and cause much less harm, than simply removing all trade barriers and subsidies on both sides of the North-South economic divide. The concept of a "level playing field" is a false one. Mexican corn farmers, for example, are not going to be able to compete with U.S. agribusiness, subsidies or no subsidies, nor should they have to.

It is of course good that such institutions as the *New York Times* are pointing out the hypocrisy of governments in the United States, Europe, and Japan in insisting that developing countries remove trade barriers and subsidies while keeping some of their own. And the subsidy issue was exploited very skillfully by developing-country governments and NGOs at the recent Cancún talks. The end result—the collapse of the talks—was a great thing for the developing world. So were the ties that were forged among countries such as those in the group of 22, enabling them to stand up to the rich countries. But the WTO remedy of eliminating subsidies and trade barriers across the board will not save developing countries from most of the harm caused by current policies. Just the opposite: the removal of import restrictions in the developing world could wipe out tens of millions of farmers and cause enormous economic damage.

Avoiding the Key Issues. While reducing agricultural protection and subsidies just in the rich countries might in general be a good thing for developing countries, the gross exaggeration of its importance has real consequences, because it can divert attention from issues of far more pressing concern. One such issue is the role that the IMF continues to play as enforcer of a creditors' cartel in the developing world, threatening any country that defies its edicts with a cutoff of access to international credit. One of the most devastated recent victims of the IMF's measures has been Argentina, which saw its economy thrown into a depression after the failure of a decade of neoliberal economic policies. The IMF's harsh treatment of Argentina last year, while it was suffering from the worst depression in its history, is widely viewed in the developing world as a warning to other countries that might deviate from the IMF's recommendations. One result is that Brazil's new president, elected with an overwhelming mandate for change, must struggle to promote growth in the face of 22% interest rates demanded by the IMF's monetary experts.

Similarly, most of sub-Saharan Africa is suffering from an unpayable debt burden. While there has been some limited relief offered in recent years, the remaining debt service burden is still more than the debtor countries in that region spend on health care or education. The list of problems that the current world economic order imposes on developing countries is long: bans on the industrial policies that led to successful development in the West, the imposition of patents on drugs and copyrights on computer software and recorded material, inappropriate macroeconomic policies imposed by the IMF and the World Bank. All of these factors are likely to have far more severe consequences for the development prospects of poor countries than the agricultural policies of rich countries. ❑

Sources: Elena Ianchovichina, Aaditya Mattoo, and Marcelo Olareaga, "Unrestricted Market Access for Sub-Saharan Africa: How much is it worth and who pays," (World Bank, April 2001); Mark Weisbrot and Dean Baker, "The Relative Impact of Trade Liberalization on Developing Countries," (Center for Economic and Policy Research, June 2002).

Update: As of July 2008, the WTO negotiations have failed to reach an agreement, particularly on the issue of farm subsidies. Developing countries, especially India and China, demanded a deeper cut in the farm subsidies provided to U.S. and EU farmers and a much lower threshold for special safeguard mechanism for farmers in the developing countries. Meanwhile, developed countries, especially the United States, were not ready to budge from their position of reducing annual farm subsidies from $18 billion to $14.5 billion. The EU countries spend a total of $280 billion to support domestic farmers, while the official development assistance by the OECD countries to the developing world was $80 billion in 2004).

The IMF and the World Bank pushed the agenda of the structural adjustment program in more than 70 countries. The resulting decline in government spending has forced the farmers of the developing countries to deal with the mounting costs of cultivation. This, coupled with the vagaries of world farm-products prices (thanks to the Northern protectionism) has been driving the farmers in the South to much despair and hopelessness, and in the case of some 190,753 Indian farmers, suicide.

—*Arpita Banerjee*

Article 3.3

WHAT CAUSES EXCHANGE-RATE FLUCTUATIONS?

BY ARTHUR MacEWAN

March/April 2001, updated August 2009

Dear Dr. Dollar:

What are the primary forces that cause foreign exchange rates to fluctuate, and what are the remedies to these forces?

—*Mario Anthony, West Palm Beach, Fla.*

A foreign exchange rate is the price, in terms of one currency, that is paid for another currency. For example, at the end of December 2000, in terms of the U.S. dollar, the price of a British pound was $1.50, the price of a Japanese yen was 0.9 cents, and the price of a Canadian dollar was 67 cents. Like any other prices, currency prices fluctuate due to a variety of forces that we loosely categorize as "supply and demand." And as with other prices, the forces of "supply and demand" can have severe economic impacts and nasty human consequences.

Two factors, however, make exchange rates especially problematic. One is that they are subject to a high degree of speculation. This is seldom a significant problem for countries with stable economies—the "developed" countries. But for low-income countries, where instability is endemic, small changes in economic conditions can lead speculators to move billions of dollars in the time it takes to press a button, resulting in very large changes in the prices of currencies. This can quickly and greatly magnify small changes in economic conditions. In 1997 in East Asia, this sort of speculation greatly worsened the economic crisis that arose first in Thailand and then in several other countries. The speculators who drive such crises include bankers and the treasurers of multinational firms, as well as individuals and the operatives of investment companies that specialize in profiting off of the international movement of funds.

The second factor making exchange rates especially problematic is that they affect the prices of many other commodities. For a country that imports a great deal, a drop in the price of its currency relative to the currencies of the countries from which it imports means that a host of imported goods—everything from food to machinery—become more costly. When speculators moved funds out of East Asian countries in 1997, the price of foreign exchange (e.g., the price of the dollar in terms of local currencies) rose, imports became extremely expensive (in local currencies), and both living standards and investment fell dramatically. (Strong speculative movement of funds into a country can also create problems—driving up the price of the local currency, thereby hurting demand for the country's exports, and limiting economic growth.)

In the "normal" course of international trade, short-term exchange-rate fluctuations are seldom large. Consider, for example, trade between the United States and Canada. If people in the United States increasingly buy things from Canada—lumber, vacations in the Canadian Rockies, fish, minerals, auto parts—they will need Canadian dollars to do so. Thus these increased purchases of Canadian goods by people in the United States will mean an increased demand for Canadian dollars and a corresponding increased supply of U.S. dollars. If nothing else changes, the price of the Canadian dollar in terms of the U.S. dollar will tend to rise.

A great deal of the demand and supply of international currencies, however, is not for trade but for investment, often speculative investment. With the strong U.S. stock market in the late 1990s, investors in other countries bought a large amount of assets in the United States. To do so, they demanded U.S. dollars and supplied their own currencies. As a result, the price of the dollar in terms of the currencies of other countries rose substantially, by about 25% on average between the middle of 1995 and the end of 2000. One of the results has been to make imports to the U.S. relatively cheap, and this has been a factor holding down inflation in the United States. Also, as the cost of foreign currency dropped, the cost (in terms of dollars) of hiring foreign workers to supply goods also dropped. The result was more severe competition for many U.S. workers (including, for example, people employed in the production of auto parts, glass goods, textiles, and apparel) and, no surprise, their wages suffered.

There is little point in attempts by governments to constrain the "normal" fluctuations in foreign exchange rates that are associated with trade adjustments (as in the U.S.-Canada example above) or those associated with long-run investment movements (as in the case of the United States during the late 1990s). Although these fluctuations can create large problems—like their impact on U.S. wages—it would be very costly and very difficult, if not impossible, to eliminate them. There are other ways to deal with declining wages.

The experience of the East Asian countries in 1997 is another matter. Speculative investment drove huge exchange-rate changes and (along with other factors) severely disrupted these countries' economies. Between mid-1997 and early 1998, for example, the value of the Thai baht lost close to 60% of its value in terms of the U.S. dollar, and the Malaysian ringgit lost close to 50%. Governments can control such speculative swings by a variety of limits on the quick movement of capital into and out of countries. One mechanism would be a tax on short-term investments. Another would be direct limits on movements of funds. These sorts of controls are not easy to implement, but they have worked effectively in many cases—notably in Malaysia following the 1997 crisis.

It has become increasingly clear in recent years that effective development policies in low-income countries cannot be pursued in the absence of some sort of controls on the movement of funds in and out of those countries. Otherwise, any successful program—whatever its particular aims—can be disrupted and destroyed by the actions of international speculators.

Update, August 2009: The years leading into the economic crisis that appeared in 2007 and 2009 illustrate the way a variety of forces affect the value of the dollar relative to other currencies. Between 1995 and the end of the millennium, the value of the dollar relative to other currencies rose by almost 28%. Many factors were involved, but one important force was the demand by foreign interests for dollars to take part in the stock market boom of that period. After the dot-com stock market bubble of the late 1990s burst, however, the value of the dollar did not fall immediately. The value of the dollar was maintained (and even rose a bit through 2001) as the U.S. economy entered into the 2001 recession; with the recession, there was a fall off in demand for imports—which meant a reduction in the supply of dollars.

Then, however, the value of the dollar began to fall. By early 2008, it was back down to its 1995 level, more than 25% below the 2001 peak. Again, several factors account for the fall. In particular, the vary large trade deficit (imports greater than exports)—which more than doubled between 2001 and 2006—meant a growing supply of dollars relative to the demand for dollars. This was partly offset by the demand of foreign interests—for example, the central banks of China, Japan and other countries—for U.S. government bonds (which financed the growing federal budget deficit). But low interest rates in the United States kept the demand for U.S. assets from outweighing the huge supply of dollars generated by the trade deficit.

Ironically, from early 2008 through the beginning of 2009, as the U.S. economy plunged, the value of the dollar shot back up—rising by 14% between April 2008 and April 2009. The reason was simple: as the instability of world financial markets became increasingly apparent, there was a rush to security. That is, investors moved their money into U.S. government bonds, widely viewed as the most secure way to hold assets (in spite of the very low interest rates). This meant a strong demand for dollars.

These movements in the value of the dollar over the last two decades tell a story of instability in the world economy and in the economic relation of the United States to other countries. This instability in turn, can be extremely disruptive for a variety of industries—and for workers in those industries. ❑

Note: *In this discussion of recent experience, the value of the dollar is the "trade-weighted value of the dollar"—that is, the average value of the dollar relative to the values of the currencies of U.S. trading partners.*

Article 3.4

WHO WINS WHEN THE DOLLAR LOSES VALUE?

BY ARTHUR MacEWAN
July/August 2010

Dear Dr. Dollar:
When the dollar loses value in comparison with other currencies, which groups in the United States win and which lose? Do consumers benefit? Does the corporate elite profit? And how does a lower-valued dollar affect the trade deficit?
    —*Julia Willebrand, New York, NY*

When the dollar loses value in comparison with other currencies, imports to the United States tend to become more expensive. It takes more dollars to buy, for example, 100 yuan of Chinese goods because it takes more dollars to purchase that amount of yuan. So if you shop a lot at Target or Wal-Mart to buy the low-priced Chinese-made goods, you lose.

However, if you are producing goods for export—for example, U.S.-made semiconductors, software, aircraft, medical equipment, pharmaceutical preparations—then people in other countries will be able to buy your goods at lower prices in terms of their own currencies. In China, it will take less yuan to buy a dollar's worth of the goods you produce; in Europe, it will take less euros. So people in other countries will tend to buy more of the goods you produce. You win.

Higher-priced imports tend to push up prices generally, while lower-priced exports usually mean more jobs in the United States. At a time when inflation is not a threat but we are suffering from a lack of jobs, some loss in the value of the dollar would probably be a good thing.

In recent years, we in the United States have been spending a lot more on goods from abroad than people abroad have been spending on goods from the United States. That difference is the trade deficit. If the dollar falls in value, we can expect that the trade deficit will fall—meaning we would buy less from abroad and people abroad would buy more from us.

A trade deficit, however, has another side. When we import more than we export (each measured in dollars), people abroad are getting more dollars for what they sell to us than they are spending on things that they buy from us. They use these extra dollars to make financial investments (stocks and bonds) or real investments (factories and offices) in the United States. The Chinese government, in particular, has accumulated the dollars that we pay for Chinese goods and has used those dollars to buy U.S. assets. In early 2009, the Chinese central bank held $764 billion in U.S. Treasury bonds, financing a large part of the U.S. government's budget deficit.

If the dollar loses value against other currencies and if, as a result, the trade deficit declines, this means less foreign investment in the United States—i.e., fewer loans from abroad to finance the federal government's debt and also private debt. The result would tend to be an increase of interest rates in the United States. Higher interest rates could reduce real investment in the United States—which could counter the positive jobs impact of the expansion of exports.

But the big losers from rising interest rates could be the banks. They hold huge amounts of Treasury bonds. If interest rates were to rise, the value of those bonds would fall and the banks (and other creditors) could lose billions. For example, on ten-year Treasury bonds, with an increase from 3.5% (roughly the rate in mid-May) to 4.5%, the creditors' bonds would lose about 9% of their value. (That is, a $100 bond returning 3.5% would yield $141.06 in ten years. But at 4.5%, a $90.83 bond would yield $141.06 in ten years. So if interest rates jumped from 3.5% to 4.5%, that $100 bond would be worth only $90.83.)

It is not automatic that a fall in the value of the dollar relative to other currencies would lead to a rise in interest rates. The Federal Reserve could take action (buying more of the Treasury bonds itself) that would keep interest rates down. But this could create other problems—in particular, it could raise the likelihood of inflation.

Some things are pretty clear—a decline in the value of the dollar would lead to higher import prices and an increase in demand for exports. Other impacts depend on a variety of other actions that are difficult to predict—most important, the actions of monetary authorities in the United States and elsewhere.

Beyond the consequences of a loss in the value of the dollar, there are problems that arise from erratic fluctuations in the dollar's value. Over the last two years, the value of the dollar relative to the euro has swung widely, gaining or losing 15% to 20% in these swings. Such gyrations both mess things up and reflect the mess that already exists. ❑

Article 3.5

IS CHINA'S CURRENCY MANIPULATION HURTING THE U.S.?

BY ARTHUR MacEWAN
November/December 2010

Dear Dr. Dollar:

Is it true that China has been harming the U.S. economy by keeping its currency "undervalued"? Shouldn't the U.S. government do something about this situation?
—*Jenny Boyd, Edmond, W.Va.*

The Chinese government, operating through the Chinese central bank, does keep its currency unit—the yuan—cheap relative to the dollar. This means that goods imported *from* China cost less (in terms of dollars) than they would otherwise, while U.S. exports *to* China cost more (in terms of yuan). So we in the United States buy a lot of Chinese-made goods and the Chinese don't buy much from us. In the 2007 to 2009 period, the United States purchased $253 billion more in goods annually from China than it sold to China.

This looks bad for U.S workers. For example, when money gets spent in the United States, much of it is spent on Chinese-made goods, and fewer jobs are then created in the United States. So the Chinese government's currency policy is at least partly to blame for our employment woes. Reacting to this situation, many people are calling for the U.S. government to do something to get the Chinese government to change its policy.

But things are not so simple.

First of all, there is an additional reason for the low cost of Chinese goods—low Chinese wages. The Chinese government's policy of repressing labor probably accounts for the low cost of Chinese goods at least as much as does its currency policy. Moreover, there is a lot more going on in the global economy. Both currency problems and job losses involve much more than Chinese government actions—though China provides a convenient target for ire.

And the currency story itself is complex. In order to keep the value of its currency low relative to the dollar, the Chinese government increases the supply of yuan, uses these yuan to buy dollars, then uses the dollars to buy U.S. securities, largely government bonds but also private securities. In early 2009, China held $764 billion in U.S. Treasury securities, making it the largest foreign holder of U.S. government debt. By buying U.S. government bonds, the Chinese have been financing the federal deficit. More generally, by supplying funds to the United States, the Chinese government has been keeping interest rates low in this country.

If the Chinese were to act differently, allowing the value of their currency to rise relative to the dollar, both the cost of capital and the prices of the many goods imported from China would rise. The rising cost of capital would probably not be a serious problem, as the Federal Reserve could take counteraction to keep interest rates low. So, an increase in the value of the yuan would net the United States some jobs, but also raise some prices for U.S. consumers.

It is pretty clear that right now what the United States needs is jobs. Moreover, low-cost Chinese goods have contributed to the declining role of manufacturing in the United States, a phenomenon that both weakens important segments of organized labor and threatens to inhibit technological progress, which has often been centered in manufacturing or based in applications in manufacturing (e.g., robotics).

So why doesn't the U.S. government place more pressure on China to raise the value of the yuan? Part of the reason may lie in concern about losing Chinese financing of the U.S. federal deficit. For several years the two governments have been co-dependent: The U.S. government gets financing for its deficits, and the Chinese government gains by maintaining an undervalued currency. Not an easy relationship to change.

Probably more important, however, many large and politically powerful U.S.-based firms depend directly on the low-cost goods imported from China. Wal-mart and Target, as any shopper knows, are filled with Chinese-made goods. Then there are the less visible products from China, including a power device that goes into the Microsoft Xbox, computer keyboards for Dell, and many other goods for many other U.S. corporations. If the yuan's value rose and these firms had to pay more dollars to buy these items, they could probably not pass all the increase on to consumers and their profits would suffer.

Still, in spite of the interests of these firms, the U.S. government may take some action, either by pressing harder for China to let the value of the yuan rise relative to the dollar or by placing some restrictions on imports from China. But don't expect too big a change. ❏

Article 3.6

"PRESSURE FROM THE BOND MARKET"

BY ARTHUR MacEWAN
May/June 2010

> Dear Dr. Dollar:
>
> With the crisis in Greece and other countries, commentators have said that governments are "under pressure from the bond market" or that bond markets will "punish" governments. What does this mean?
> —*Nikolaos Papanikolaou, Queens, N.Y.*

It means that money is power.

The people and institutions that buy government bonds have the money. They are "the bond market." By telling governments the conditions under which they will make loans (i.e., buy the governments' bonds), they are able to greatly influence governments' policies.

But let's go back to some basics. When a government spends more than it takes in as taxes, it has to borrow the difference. It borrows by selling bonds, which are promises to pay. So the payments for the bonds are loans.

A government might sell a bond that is a promise to pay $103 a year from the date of sale. If bond buyers are confident that this promise will be kept and if the return they can get on other forms of investments is 3%, they will be willing to pay $100 for the bond. That is, they will be willing to loan the government $100 to be paid back in one year with 3% interest. This investment will then be providing the same return as their other investments.

But what if they are not confident that the promise will be kept? What if the investors ("the bond market") think that the government of Greece, for example, may not be able to make the payments as promised and will default on the bonds? Under these circumstances the investors will not pay $100 for the bonds that return $103 next year. They may be willing to pay only $97.

If the government then does meet its promise, the bond will provide a 6.2% rate of return. But if the "bond market's" fear of default turns out to be correct, then these bonds will have a much lower rate of return—or, in the extreme case, they will be a total loss. The "bond market" is demanding a higher rate of return to compensate for the risk. (The 3% - 6.2% difference was roughly the difference between the return on German and Greek bonds in March, when this column was written. By mid-April Greece was paying 9%.)

However, if the Greek government—or whatever government is seeking the loans—can sell these bonds for only $97, it will have to sell more bonds in order to raise the funds it needs. In a year, the payments (that 6.2%) will place a new, severe burden on the government's budget.

So the investors say, in effect, "If you fix your policies in ways that we think make default less likely, we will buy the bonds at a higher price—not $100, but maybe at $98 or $99." It is not the ultimate purchasers of the bonds who convey this message; it is the underwriters, the large investment banks—Goldman Sachs for example. As underwriters they handle the sale of the bonds for the Greek government (and take hefty fees for this service).

Even if the investment banks were giving good, objective advice, this would be bad enough. However, the nature of their advice—"the pressure from the bond market"—is conditioned by who they are and whom they represent.

Foremost, they push for actions that will reduce the government's budget deficit, even when sensible economic policy would call for a stimulus that would be provided by maintaining or expanding the deficit. Also, investment bankers will not tell governments to raise taxes on the rich or on foreign corporations in order to reduce the deficit. Instead, they tend to advocate cutting social programs and reducing the wages of public-sector workers.

It does not require great insight to see the class bias in these sorts of actions.

Yet the whole problem does not lie with the "pressure from the bond market." The Greek government and other governments have followed policies that make them vulnerable to this sort of pressure. Unwilling or unable to tax the rich, governments borrowed to pay for their operations in good times. Having run budget deficits in good times, these authorities are in a poor position to add more debt when it is most needed—in the current recession in particular. So now, when governments really need to borrow to run deficits, they—and, more important, their people—are at the mercy of the "bond markets."

Popular protests can push back, saving some social programs and forcing governments to place a greater burden on the wealthy. A real solution, however, requires long-term action to shift power, which would change government practices and reduce vulnerability to "the pressure from the bond market." ❑

Article 3.7

DISARMING THE DEBT TRAP

BY ELLEN FRANK
November/December 2000

This article was originally written in 2000, in the immediate wake of the "Jubilee 2000" campaign to cancel the external debts of the world's poorest countries. Author Ellen Frank argues that, admirable though the debt-cancellation campaign was, it would likely fail to keep low-income countries out of debt in the long run unless serious structural reforms were made to the international-payments system. More than ten years later, the international debt picture for developing countries is mixed. Over that period, the ratios of external debt to GDP and external debt payments (or "debt service") to exports are down for most of the world's low-income regions. In part, this is due to debt cancellation, and the fact that debt-cancellation campaigns forced international institutions like the World Bank and International Monetary Fund to accept broader and deeper debt reduction than they had initially planned. Today, however, storm clouds are again visible on the horizon, with debt burdens in some of the world's poorest countries again on the rise. Meanwhile, Frank's proposals have new and unexpected relevance for even high-income world regions, as several countries in Europe face deep debt crises as a result, in large measure, of not being able to repay debt in currencies they control. —Eds.

Sources: Nick Mead, "A Developing World of Debt," *The Guardian*, May 16, 2012 (guardian. co.uk); World Bank, Global Development Finance: External Debt of Developing Countries, 2012 (worldbank.org).

QUESTION: What if the IMF, World Bank and G-7 governments canceled the debts of the poorer countries right now, fully and with no strings attached?

ANSWER: Within five years, most would be up to their necks in debt again. While a Jubilee 2000 debt cancellation would provide short-term relief for heavily indebted countries, the bitter reality of the current global financing system is that poor countries are virtually doomed to be debtors.

When residents of Zambia or Zaire buy maize or medicine in America, they are required to pay in dollars. If they can't earn enough dollars through their own exports, they must borrow them—from the IMF, the World Bank, a Western government agency, or from a commercial lender. But foreign currency loans are problematic for poor countries. If CitiCorp loans funds to a U.S. business, it fully expects that the business will realize a stream of earnings from which the loan can be repaid. When the IMF or World Bank makes foreign currency loans to poor countries—to finance deficits or development projects—no such foreign currency revenue stream is generated and the debt becomes a burdensome obligation that can be met only by abandoning internal development goals in favor of export promotion.

Few poor countries can avoid the occasional trade deficit—of 93 low- and moderate-income countries, only 11 currently have trade surpluses—and most are heavily dependent on imports of food, oil, and manufactured goods. Even the most tightly managed economy is only an earthquake or crop failure away from a foreign currency debt. Once incurred, interest payments and other debt-servicing charges mount quickly. Because few countries can manage payment surpluses large enough to service the debt regularly, servicing charges are rolled over into new loans and the debt balloons. This is why, despite heroic efforts by many indebted less-developed countries (LDCs) to pump up exports and cut imports, the outstanding foreign currency debt of developing countries has more than tripled during the past two decades.

Many poorer nations, hoping to avoid borrowing, have attempted recently to attract foreign investor dollars with the bait of high interest rates or casino-style stock exchanges. But the global debt trap is not so easily eluded. An American financial firm that purchases shares on the Thai stock exchange with baht (the Thai currency) wants, eventually, to distribute gains to shareholders in dollars. Big banks and mutual funds are wary, therefore, of becoming ensnared in minor currencies and, to compensate against potential losses when local currencies are converted back into dollars, they demand sky-high interest rates on LDC bonds. Thailand, Brazil, Indonesia and many other countries recently discovered that speculative financial investors are quick to turn heel and flee, driving interest rates up and exchange rates down, and leaving debtor countries even deeper in the hole.

If plans to revamp the international "financial architecture" are to help anyone but the already rich, they must address these issues. Developing countries need many things from the rest of the world—manufactured goods, skilled advisors, technical know-how—but loans are not among them. A global payments system based on the borrowing and lending of foreign currencies is, for small and poor nations, a life sentence to debtor's prison.

There are alternatives. Rather than scrambling endlessly for the foreign currency they cannot print, do not control, and cannot earn in sufficient amounts through exporting, developing countries could be permitted to pay for foreign goods and services in their own currencies. Americans do this routinely, issuing dollars to cover a trade deficit that will exceed $300 billion this year. Europe, too, finances external deficits with issues of euro-denominated bonds and bank deposits. But private financial firms will generally not hold assets denominated in LDC currencies; when they do hold them, they frequently demand interest rates several times higher than those paid by rich countries. But the governments of the world could jointly agree to hold these minor currencies, even if private investors will not.

The world needs an international central bank, democratically structured and publicly controlled, that would allow countries to settle payment imbalances politically, without relying on loans of foreign currencies. The idea is not new. John Maynard Keynes had something similar in mind in the 1940s, when the International Monetary Fund was established. Cambridge economist Nicholas Kaldor toyed with the idea in the 1960s. Recently, Jane D'Arista of the Financial Markets Center and a number of other international financial specialists have revived this notion, calling for a global settlements bank that could act not as a lender of last resort to international banks (as the IMF does), but as a lender of first resort for payments imbalances between sovereign nations. Such a system would take the problems of debts, deficits, and development out of the marketplace and place them in the international political arena, where questions of fairness and equity could be squarely and openly addressed.

The idea is beguilingly simple, eminently practicable, and easy to implement. It would benefit poor and rich countries alike, since the advanced nations could export far more to developing countries if those countries were able to settle international payments on more advantageous terms. A global settlements bank, however, would dramatically shift the balance of power in the world economy and will be fiercely opposed by those who profit from the international debt trap. If developing countries were not so desperate for dollars, multinational corporations would find them less eager to sell their resources and citizens for a fistful of greenbacks. That nations rich in people and resources, like South Africa, can be deemed bankrupt and forced into debt peonage for lack of foreign exchange is not merely a shame. It is absurd, an unacceptable artifact of a global finance system that enriches the already rich. ❏

Article 3.8

W(H)ITHER THE DOLLAR?

The U.S. trade deficit, the global economic crisis, and the dollar's status as the world's reserve currency.

BY KATHERINE SCIACCHITANO

For more than half a century, the dollar was both a symbol and an instrument of U.S. economic and military power. At the height of the financial crisis in the fall of 2008, the dollar served as a safe haven for investors, and demand for U.S. Treasury bonds ("Treasuries") spiked. More recently, the United States has faced a vacillating dollar, calls to replace the greenback as the global reserve currency, and an international consensus that it should save more and spend less.

At first glance, circumstances seem to give reason for concern. The U.S. budget deficit is over 10% of GDP. China has begun a long-anticipated move away from Treasuries, threatening to make U.S. government borrowing more expensive. And the adoption of austerity measures in Greece—with a budget deficit barely 3% higher than the United States—hovers as a reminder that the bond market can enforce wage cuts and pension freezes on developed as well as developing countries.

These pressures on the dollar and for fiscal cut-backs and austerity come at an awkward time given the level of public outlays required to deal with the crisis and the need to attract international capital to pay for them. But the pressures also highlight the central role of the dollar in the crisis. Understanding that role is critical to grasping the link between the financial recklessness we've been told is to blame for the crisis and the deeper causes of the crisis in the real economy: that link is the outsize U.S. trade deficit.

Trade deficits are a form of debt. For mainstream economists, the cure for the U.S. deficit is thus increased "savings": spend less and the bottom line will improve. But the U.S. trade deficit didn't balloon because U.S. households or the government went on a spending spree. It ballooned because, from the 1980s on, successive U.S. administrations pursued a high-dollar policy that sacrificed U.S. manufacturing for finance, and that combined low-wage, export-led growth in the Global South with low-wage, debt-driven consumption at home. From the late nineties, U.S. dollars that went out to pay for imports increasingly came back not as demand for U.S. goods, but as demand for investments that fueled U.S. housing and stock market bubbles. Understanding the history of how the dollar helped create these imbalances, and how these imbalances in turn led to the housing bubble and sub-prime crash, sheds important light on how labor and the left should respond to pressures for austerity and "saving" as the solution to the crisis.

Gold, Deficits, and Austerity

A good place to start is with the charge that the Federal Reserve triggered the housing bubble by lowering interest rates after the dot-com bubble burst and plunged the country into recession in 2001.

In 2001, manufacturing was too weak to lead a recovery, and the Bush administration was ideologically opposed to fiscal stimulus other than tax cuts for the wealthy. So the real question isn't why the Fed lowered rates; it's why it was able to. In 2000, the U.S. trade deficit stood at 3.7% of GDP. Any other country with this size deficit would have had to tighten its belt and jump-start exports, not embark on stimulating domestic demand that could deepen the deficit even more.

The Fed's ability to lower interest rates despite the U.S. trade deficit stemmed from the dollar's role as the world's currency, which was established during the Bretton Woods negotiations for a new international monetary system at the end of World War II.

A key purpose of an international monetary system—Bretton Woods or any other—is to keep international trade and debt in balance. Trade has to be mutual. One country can't do all the selling while other does all the buying; both must be able to buy and sell. If one or more countries develop trade deficits that persist, they won't be able to continue to import without borrowing and going into debt. At the same time, some other country or countries will have corresponding trade surpluses. The result is a global trade imbalance. To get back "in balance," the deficit country has to import less, export more, or both. The surplus country has to do the reverse.

In practice, economic pressure is stronger on deficit countries to adjust their trade balances by importing less, since it's deficit countries that could run out of money to pay for imports. Importing less can be accomplished with import quotas (which block imports over a set level) or tariffs (which decrease demand for imports by imposing a tax on them). It can also be accomplished with "austerity"—squeezing demand by lowering wages.

Under the gold standard, this squeezing took place automatically. Gold was shipped out of a country to pay for a trade deficit. Since money had to be backed by gold, having less gold meant less money in domestic circulation. So prices and wages fell. Falling wages in turn lowered demand for imports and boosted exports. The deficit was corrected, but at the cost of recession, austerity, and hardship for workers. In other words, the gold standard was deflationary.

Bretton Woods

The gold standard lasted until the Great Depression, and in fact helped to cause it. Beyond the high levels of unemployment, one of the most vivid lessons from the global catastrophe that ensued was the collapse of world trade, as country after country tried to deal with falling exports by limiting imports. After World War II, the industrialized countries wanted an international monetary system that could correct trade imbalances without imposing austerity and risking another depression. This was particularly important given the post-war levels of global debt and deficits, which could have suppressed demand and blocked trade again. Countries pursued these aims at the Bretton Woods negotiations in 1944, in Bretton Woods, New Hampshire.

John Maynard Keynes headed the British delegation. Keynes was already famous for his advocacy of government spending to bolster demand and maintain employment during recessions and depressions. England also owed large war debts to the United States and had suffered from high unemployment for over two decades. Keynes therefore had a keen interest in creating a system that prevented the build-up of global debt and avoided placing the full pressure of correcting trade imbalances on debtor countries.

His proposed solution was an international clearing union—a system of accounts kept in a fictitious unit called the "bancor." Accounts would be tallied each year to see which countries were in deficit and which were in surplus. Countries with trade deficits would have to work to import less and export more. In the meantime, they would have the unconditional right—for a period—to an "overdraft" of bancors, the size of the overdraft to be based on the size of previous surpluses. These overdrafts would both support continued imports of necessities and guarantee uninterrupted global trade. At the same time, countries running trade surpluses would be expected to get back in balance too by importing more, and would be fined if their surpluses persisted.

Keynes was also adamant that capital controls be part of the new system. Capital controls are restrictions on the movement of capital across borders. Keynes wanted countries to be able to resort to macroeconomic tools such as deficit spending, lowering interest rates, and expanding money supplies to bolster employment and wages when needed. He worried that without capital controls, capital flight—investors taking their money and running—could veto economic policies and force countries to raise interest rates, cut spending, and lower wages instead, putting downward pressure on global demand as the gold standard had.

Keynes's system wouldn't have solved the problems of capitalism—in his terms, the problem of insufficient demand, and in Marx's terms the problems of overproduction and under-consumption. But by creating incentives for surplus countries to import more, it would have supported global demand and job growth and made the kind of trade imbalances that exist today—including the U.S. trade deficit—much less likely. It would also have taken the pressure off deficit countries to adopt austerity measures. And it would have prevented surplus countries from using the power of debt to dictate economic policy to deficit countries.

At the end of World War II, the United States was, however, the largest surplus country in the world, and it intended to remain so for the foreseeable future. The New Deal had lowered unemployment during the Depression. But political opposition to deficit spending had prevented full recovery until arms production for the war restored manufacturing. Many feared that without continued large U.S. trade surpluses and expanded export markets, unemployment would return to Depression-era levels.

The United States therefore blocked Keynes' proposal. Capital controls were permitted for the time being, largely because of the danger that capital would flee war-torn Europe. But penalties for surplus countries were abandoned; pressures remained primarily on deficit countries to correct. Instead of an international clearing union with automatic rights to overdrafts, the International Monetary Fund (IMF) was established to make short-term loans to deficit countries. And instead of the neutral bancor, the dollar— backed by the U.S. pledge to redeem dollars with gold at $35 an ounce —would be the world currency.

Limits of the System

The system worked for just over twenty-five years, not because trade was balanced, but because the United States was able and willing to recycle its huge trade surpluses. U.S. military spending stayed high because of the U.S. cold-war role as "global cop." And massive aid was given to Europe to rebuild. Dollars went out as foreign aid and military spending (both closely coordinated). They came back as demand for U.S. goods.

At the same time, memory of the Depression created a kind of Keynesian consensus in the advanced industrial democracies to use fiscal and monetary policy to maintain full employment. Labor movements, strengthened by both the war and the post-war boom, pushed wage settlements and welfare spending higher. Global demand was high.

Two problems doomed the system. First, the IMF retained the power to impose conditions on debtor countries, and the United States retained the power to control the IMF.

Second, the United States stood outside the rules of the game: The larger the world economy grew, the more dollars would be needed in circulation; U.S. trade deficits would eventually have to provide them. Other countries would have to correct their trade deficits by tightening their belts to import less, exporting more by devaluing their currencies to push down prices, or relying on savings from trade surpluses denominated in dollars (known as "reserves") to pay for their excess of imports over exports. But precisely because countries needed dollar reserves to pay for international transactions and to provide cushions against periods of deficits, other countries would need to hold the U.S. dollars they earned by investing them in U.S. assets. This meant that U.S. dollars that went out for imports would come back and be reinvested in the United States. Once there, these dollars could be used to finance continued spending on imports—and a larger U.S. trade deficit. At that point, sustaining world trade would depend not on recycling U.S. surpluses, but on recycling U.S. deficits. The ultimate result would be large, destabilizing global capital flows.

The Crisis of the 'Seventies

The turning point came in the early 'seventies. Europe and Japan had rebuilt from the war and were now export powers in their own right. The U.S. trade surplus was turning into a deficit. And the global rate of profit in manufacturing was falling. The United States had also embarked on its "War on Poverty" just as it increased spending on its real war in Vietnam, and this "guns and butter" strategy—an attempt to quell domestic opposition from the civil right and anti-war movements while maintaining global military dominance—led to high inflation.

The result was global economic crisis: the purchasing power of the dollar fell, just as more and more dollars were flowing out of the United States and being held by foreigners.

What had kept the United States from overspending up to this point was its Bretton Woods commitment to exchange dollars for gold at the rate of $35 an ounce. Now countries and investors that didn't want to stand by and watch as the purchasing power of their dollar holdings fell—as well as countries that objected to the Vietnam War—held the United States to its pledge.

There wasn't enough gold in Ft. Knox. The United States would have to retrench its global military role, reign in domestic spending, or change the rules of the game. It changed the rules of the game. In August 1971, Nixon closed the gold window; the United States would no longer redeem dollars for gold. Countries and individuals would have to hold dollars, or dump them and find another currency that was more certain to hold its value. There was none.

The result was that the dollar remained the global reserve currency. But the world moved from a system where the United States could spend only if could back its spending by gold, to a system where its spending was limited only by the quantity of dollars the rest of the world was willing to hold. The value of the dollar would fluctuate with the level of global demand for U.S. products and investment. The value of other currencies would fluctuate with the dollar.

Trading Manufacturing for Finance

The result of this newfound freedom to spend was a decade of global inflation and crises of the dollar. As inflation grew, each dollar purchased less. As each dollar purchased less, the global demand to hold dollars dropped—and with it the dollar's exchange rate. As the exchange rate fell, imports became even more expensive, and inflation ratcheted up again. The cycle intensified when OPEC—which priced its oil in dollars—raised its prices to compensate for the falling dollar.

Owners of finance capital were unhappy because inflation was eroding the value of dollar assets. Owners of manufacturing capital were unhappy because the global rate of profit in manufacturing was dropping. And both U.S. politicians and elites were unhappy because the falling dollar was eroding U.S. military power by making it more expensive.

The response of the Reagan administration was to unleash neoliberalism on both the national and global levels—the so-called Reagan revolution. On the domestic front, inflation was quelled, and the labor movement was put in its place, with high interest rates and the worst recession since the Depression. Corporate profits were boosted directly through deregulation, privatization, and tax cuts, and indirectly by attacks on unions, unemployment insurance, and social spending.

When it was over, profits were up, inflation and wages were down, and the dollar had changed direction. High interest rates attracted a stream of investment capital into the United States, pushing up demand for the currency, and with it the exchange rate. The inflows paid for the growing trade and budget deficits—Reagan had cut domestic spending, but increased military spending. And they provided abundant capital for finance and overseas investment. But the high dollar also made U.S. exports more expensive for the rest of the world. The United States had effectively traded manufacturing for finance and debt.

Simultaneously, debt was used as a hammer to impose neoliberalism on the Third World. As the price of oil rose in the seventies, OPEC countries deposited their growing trade surpluses—so-called petro-dollars—in U.S. banks, which in turn loaned them to poor countries to pay for the soaring price of oil. Initially set at very low interest rates, loan payments skyrocketed when the United States jacked up its rates to deal with inflation. Third World countries began defaulting, starting with Mexico in 1981. In response, and in exchange for more loans, the U.S.-controlled IMF imposed austerity programs, also known as "structural adjustment programs."

The programs were similar to the policies in the United States, but much more severe, and they operated in reverse. Instead of pushing up exchange rates to attract finance capital as the United States had done, Third World countries were told to devalue their currencies to attract foreign direct investment and export their way out of debt. Capital controls were dismantled to enable transnational corporations to enter and exit at will. Governments were forced to slash spending on social programs and infrastructure to push down wages and demand for imports. Services were privatized to create opportunities for private capital, and finance was deregulated.

Policies dovetailed perfectly. As the high dollar hollowed out U.S. manufacturing, countries in the Global South were turned into low-wage export platforms. As U.S. wages stagnated or fell, imports became cheaper, masking the pain. Meanwhile, the high dollar lowered the cost of overseas production. Interest payments on third world debt—which continued to grow—swelled the already large capital flows into the United States and provided even more funds for overseas investment.

The view from the heights of finance looked promising. But Latin America was entering what became known as "the lost decade." And the United State was shifting from exporting goods to exporting demand, and from recycling its trade surplus to recycling its deficit. The world was becoming dependent on the United States as the "consumer of last resort." The United States was becoming dependent on finance and debt.

Consolidating Neoliberalism

The growth of finance in the eighties magnified its political clout in the nineties. With the bond market threatening to charge higher rates for government debt, Clinton abandoned campaign pledges to invest in U.S. infrastructure, education, and industry. Instead, he balanced the budget; he adopted his own high-dollar policy, based on the theory that global competition would keep imports cheap, inflation low, and the living standard high—regardless of sluggish wage growth; and he continued deregulation of the finance industry—repealing Glass-Steagall and refusing to regulate derivatives. By the end of Clinton's second term, the U.S. trade deficit had hit a record 3.7% of GDP; household debt had soared to nearly 69% of GDP and financial profits had risen to 30% of GDP, almost twice as high as they had been at any time up to the mid 1980s.

Internationally, Clinton consolidated IMF-style structural adjustment policies under the rubric of "the Washington Consensus," initiated a new era of trade agreements modeled on the North American Free Trade Agreement, and led the charge to consolidate the elimination of capital controls.

The elimination of capital controls deepened global economic instability in several ways.

First, eliminating restrictions on capital mobility made it easier for capital to go in search of the lowest wages. This expanded the globalization of production, intensifying downward pressure on wages and global demand.

Second, removing capital controls increased the political power of capital by enabling it to "vote with its feet." This accelerated the deregulation of global finance and—as Keynes predicted—limited countries' abilities to run full-employment policies. Regulation of business was punished, as was deficit spending, regardless of its purpose. Low inflation and deregulation of labor markets—weakening unions and making wages more "flexible"—were rewarded.

Finally, capital mobility fed asset bubbles and increased financial speculation and exchange rate volatility. As speculative capital rushed into countries, exchange rates rose; as it fled, they fell. Speculators began betting more and more on currencies themselves, further magnifying rate swings. Rising exchange rates made exports uncompetitive, hurting employment and wages. Falling exchange rates increased the competitiveness of exports, but made imports and foreign borrowing more expensive, except for the United States, which borrows in its own currency. Countries could try to prevent capital flight by raising interest rates, but only at the cost of dampening growth and lost of jobs. Lacking capital controls, there was little countries could do to prevent excessive inflows and bubbles.

Prelude to a Crash

This increased capital mobility, deregulation, and speculation weakened the real economy, further depressed global demand, and greatly magnified economic instability.

From the eighties onward, international financial crises broke out approximately every five years, in countries ranging from Mexico to the former Soviet Union.

By far the largest crisis prior to the sub-prime meltdown took place in East Asia in the mid-nineties. Speculative capital began flowing into East Asia in the mid nineties. In 1997, the bubble burst. By the summer of 1998, stock markets around the world were crashing from the ripple effects. The IMF stepped in with $40 billion in loans, bailing out investors but imposing harsh conditions on workers and governments. Millions were left unemployed as Asia plunged into depression.

When the dust settled, Asian countries said "never again." Their solution was to build up large dollar reserves—savings cushions—so they would never have to turn to the IMF for another loan. To build up reserves, countries had to run large trade surpluses. This meant selling even more to the United States, the only market in the world able and willing to run ever-larger trade deficits to absorb their exports.

In addition to further weakening U.S. manufacturing, the Asia crisis set the stage for the sub-prime crisis in several ways.

First, as capital initially fled Asia, it sought out the United States as a "safe haven," igniting the U.S. stock market and nascent housing bubbles.

Second, the longer-term recycling of burgeoning Asian surpluses ensured an abundant and ongoing source of capital to finance not only the mounting trade deficit, but also the billowing U.S. consumer debt more generally.

Third, preventing their exchange rates from rising with their trade surpluses and making their exports uncompetitive required Asian central banks to print money, swelling global capital flows even more.

Between 1998 and 2007, when the U.S. housing bubble burst, many policy makers and mainstream economists came to believe this inflow of dollars and debt would never stop. It simply seemed too mutually beneficial to end. By financing the U.S. trade deficit, Asian countries guaranteed U.S. consumers would continue to purchase their goods. The United States in turn got cheap imports, cheap money for consumer finance, and inflated stock and real estate markets that appeared to be self-financing and to compensate for stagnating wages. At the same time, foreign holders of dollars bought increasing quantities of U.S. Treasuries, saving the U.S. government from having to raise interest rates to attract purchasers, and giving the United States cheap financing for its budget deficit as well.

It was this ability to keep interest rates low—in particular, the Fed's ability to lower rates after the stock market bubble collapsed in 2000—that set off the last and most destructive stage of the housing bubble. Lower interest rates simultaneously increased the demand for housing (since lower interest rates made mortgages cheaper) and decreased the returns to foreign holders of U.S. Treasuries. These lower returns forced investors to look for other "safe" investments with higher yields. Investors believed they found what they needed in U.S. mortgage securities.

As Wall Street realized what a lucrative international market they had, the big banks purposefully set out to increase the number of mortgages that could be repackaged and sold to investors by lowering lending standards. They also entered into complicated systems of private bets, known as credit default swaps, to insure against the risk of defaults. These credit default swaps created a chain of debt that exponentially magnified risk. When the bubble finally burst, only massive stimulus spending and infusions of capital by the industrialized countries into their banking systems kept the world from falling into another depression.

Deficit Politics

The political establishment—right and center—is now licking its chops, attacking fiscal deficits as if ending them were a solution to the crisis. The underlying theory harks back to the deflationary operation of the gold standard and the conditions imposed by the IMF: Government spending causes trade deficits and inflation by increasing demand. Cutting spending will cut deficits by diminishing demand.

Like Clinton before him, Obama is now caving in to the bond market, fearful that international lenders will raise interest rates on U.S. borrowing. He has created a bi-partisan debt commission to focus on long-term fiscal balance—read: cutting Social Security and Medicare—and revived "PAYGO," which requires either cuts or increases in revenue to pay for all new outlays, even as unemployment hovers just under 10%.

By acquiescing, the U.S. public is implicitly blaming itself for the crisis and offering to pay for it twice: first with the millions of jobs lost to the recession, and again by weakening the safety net. But the recent growth of the U.S. budget deficit principally reflects the cost of cleaning up the crisis and of the wars in Iraq and Afghanistan. Assumptions of future deficits are rooted in projected health-care costs in the absence of meaningful reform. And the U.S. trade deficit is driven mainly by the continued high dollar.

The economic crisis won't be resolved by increasing personal savings or enforcing fiscal discipline, because its origins aren't greedy consumers or profligate governments. The real origins of the crisis are the neoliberal response to the crisis of the 1970s—the shift from manufacturing to finance in the United States, and the transformation of the Global South into a low-wage export platform for transnational capital to bolster sagging profit rate. The U.S. trade and budget deficits may symbolize this transformation. But the systemic problem is a global economic model that separates consumption from production and that has balanced world demand—not just the U.S. economy—on debt and speculation.

Forging an alternative will be the work of generations. As for the present, premature tightening of fiscal policy as countries try to "exit" from the crisis will simply drain global demand and endanger recovery. Demonizing government spending will erode the social wage and undermine democratic debate about the public investment needed for a transition to an environmentally sustainable global economy.

In the United States, where labor market and financial deregulation have garnered the most attention in popular critiques of neoliberalism, painting a bulls-eye on government spending also obscures the role of the dollar and U.S. policy in the crisis. For several decades after World War II, U.S. workers benefited materially as the special status of the dollar helped expand export markets for U.S. goods. But as other labor movements throughout the world know from bitter experience, it's the dollar as the world's currency, together with U.S. control of the IMF, that ultimately provided leverage for the United States to create the low-wage export model of growth and financial deregulation that has so unbalanced the global economy and hurt "first" and "third" world workers alike.

Looking Ahead

At the end of World War II, John Maynard Keynes proposed an international monetary system with the bancor at its core; the system would have helped balance trade and avoid the debt and deflation in inherent in the gold standard that preceded the Great Depression. Instead, Bretton Woods was negotiated, with the dollar as the world's currency. What's left of that system has now come full circle and created the very problems it was intended to avoid: large trade imbalances and deflationary economic conditions.

For the past two and a half decades, the dollar enabled the United States to run increasing trade deficits while systematically draining capital from some of the poorest countries in the world. This money could have been used for development in the Global South, to replace aging infrastructure in the United States, or to prepare for and prevent climate change. Instead, it paid for U.S. military interventions, outsourcing, tax cuts for the wealthy, and massive stock market and housing bubbles.

This mismanagement of the dollar hasn't served the long-term interests of workers the United States any more than it has those in of the developing world. In domestic terms, it has been particularly damaging over the last three decades to U.S. manufacturing, and state budgets and workers are being hit hard by the crisis. Yet even manufacturing workers in the United States cling to the high dollar as if it were a life raft. Many public sector workers advocate cutting back on government spending. And most people in the United States would blame bankers' compensation packages for the sub-prime mess before pointing to the dismantling of capital controls.

After suffering through the worst unemployment since the Depression and paying for the bailout of finance, U.S. unions and the left are right to be angry. On the global scale, there is increased space for activism. Since the summer of 2007, at least 17 countries have imposed or tightened capital controls. Greek workers have been in the streets protesting pension cuts and pay freezes for months now. And a global campaign has been launched for a financial transactions tax that would slow down speculation and provide needed revenue for governments. Together, global labor and the left are actively rethinking and advocating reform of the global financial system, the neoliberal trade agreements, and the role and governance of the International Monetary Fund. And there is increasing discussion of a replacement for the dollar that won't breed deficits, suck capital out of the developing world, impose austerity on deficit countries—or blow bubbles.

All these reforms are critical. All will require more grassroots education. None will come without a struggle. ❑

Sources: C. Fred Bergsten, "The Dollar and the Deficits: How Washington Can Prevent the Next Crisis," Peterson Institute for International Economics, *Foreign Affairs*, Volume 88 No. 6, November 2009; Dean Baker, "The Budget, the Deficit, and the Dollar," Center for Economic Policy and Research, www.cepr.net; Martin Wolf, "Give us fiscal austerity, but not quite yet," *Financial Times* blogs, November 24, 2009; Tom Palley, "Domestic Demand-led Growth: A New Paradigm for Development," paper presented at the Alterantives to Neoliberalism Conference sponsored by the New Rules for Global Finance Coalition, May 21-24, 2002, www. economicswebinstitute.org; Sarah Anderson, "Policy Handcuffs in the Financial Crisis: How U.S. Government And Trade Policy Limit Government Power To Control Capital Flows, " Institute for Policy Studies, February 2009; Susan George, "The World Trade Organisation We Could Have Had," *Le Monde Diplomatique*, January 2007.

Chapter 4

INTERNATIONAL INSTITUTIONS AND TRADE AGREEMENTS

Article 4.1

THE INTERNATIONAL MONETARY FUND (IMF) AND WORLD BANK

From "The ABCs of the Global Economy"

BY THE *DOLLARS & SENSE* COLLECTIVE
March/April 2000, last revised November 2012

The basic structure of the postwar international capitalist economy was created in 1944, at an international conference in Bretton Woods, New Hampshire. While the Bretton Woods conference included representatives of the U.S. and British governments, the Americans dominated the outcome.

The British delegation (including the legendary economist John Maynard Keynes) argued for an international currency for world trade and debt settlements. The Americans insisted on the U.S. dollar being the de facto world currency (with the dollar's value fixed in terms of gold and the values of other currencies fixed in proportion to the dollar). The British wanted countries that ran trade surpluses and those that ran trade deficits (and became indebted to the "surplus" countries) to share the costs of "adjustment" (bringing the world economy back into balance). The U.S. insisted on a system in which the "deficit" countries would have to do the adjusting, and a central aim would be making sure that the debtors would pay back their creditors at any cost.

Among the institutions coming out of Bretton Woods were the World Bank and the International Monetary Fund (IMF). For this reason, they are sometimes known as the "Bretton Woods twins." Both institutions engage in international lending. The IMF primarily acts as a "lender of last resort" to countries (usually, but not always, lower-income countries) that have become heavily indebted and cannot get loans elsewhere. The World Bank, meanwhile, focuses primarily on longer-term "development" lending.

At both the World Bank and the IMF, the number of votes a country receives is closely proportional to how much capital it contributes to the institution, so the voting power of rich countries like the United States is disproportionate to their numbers. Eleven rich countries, for example, account for more than 50% of the voting power in the IMF Board of Governors. At both institutions, five powerful countries—the United States, the United Kingdom, France, Germany, and Japan—get to appoint their own representatives to the institution's executive board, with 19 other directors elected by the rest of the 180-odd member countries. The president of the World Bank is elected by the Board of Executive Directors, and traditionally nominated by the U.S. representative. The managing director of the IMF is traditionally a European.

The IMF and the World Bank wield power vastly greater than the share of international lending they account for because private lenders follow their lead in deciding which countries are credit-worthy. The institutions have taken advantage of this leverage—and of debt crises in Latin America, Africa, Asia, and even Europe—to push a "free-market" (or "neoliberal") model of economic development.

The IMF

The IMF was a key part, from the very start of the "debtor pays" system the U.S. government had insisted on at Bretton Woods. When a country fell heavily into debt, and could no longer get enough credit from private sources, the IMF would step in as the "lender of last resort." This made it possible for the debtor to continue to pay its creditors in the short run. The typical IMF adjustment program, however, demanded painful "austerity" or "shock therapy"—elimination of price controls on basic goods (such as food and fuel), cuts in government spending, services, and employment, and "devaluation" of the country's currency. All three of these austerity measures hit workers and poor people the hardest, the first two for fairly obvious reasons. The impact of currency devaluation, however, requires a little more explanation.

Devaluation meant that the currency would buy fewer dollars—and fewer of every other currency "pegged" to the dollar. This made imports to the country more expensive. (Suppose that a country's peso had been pegged at a one-to-one ratio to the dollar. An imported good that cost $10 would cost 10 pesos. If the currency was devalued to a two-to-one ratio to the dollar, an imported good that cost $10 would now cost 20 pesos.) Devaluation also caused domestic prices to rise, since domestic producers faced less import competition. Meanwhile, it made the country's exports less expensive to people in other countries. The idea was that the country would

corrected page proofs.
conomic Affairs Bureau, Inc.CHAPTER 4: INTERNATIONAL INSTITUTIONS AND TRADE AGREEMENTS | 103
not reproduce or distribute.

export more, earn more dollars in return, and—this is the key—be able to pay back its debts to U.S. and European banks. In other words, the people of the country (especially workers and the poor) would consume less of what they produced, and send more of it abroad to "service" the country's debt.

For many years, these kinds of measures were the core of IMF "adjustment" plans. Starting in the 1970s, however, the IMF broadened its standard program to include deeper "structural" changes to debtor countries' economies. "Structural adjustment programs" (SAPs) included not only the austerity measures described above, but also the elimination of trade barriers and controls on international investment, the privatization of public enterprises, and the "deregulation" of labor markets (including elimination of minimum wage laws, hours laws, occupational safety and health regulations, and protections for unions). These were the basic ingredients for overturning "regulated" (or "interventionist") forms of capitalism in many lower-income countries, and replacing it with "free-market" (or "neoliberal") capitalism.

Structural adjustment also prepared the ground for the system of globalized production—making it easier for multinational companies to locate operations in affected countries (thanks to the removal of restrictions on foreign investment), employ a relatively cheap and controllable workforce (thanks to the removal of labor regulations), and export the goods back to their home countries or elsewhere in the world (thanks to the elimination of trade barriers). Structural adjustment programs became the lance-point of "free-market" reform, especially in Latin America during the 1980s debt crisis, but also in other low-income regions.

The World Bank

In its early years, just after World War II, the World Bank mostly loaned money to Western European governments to help rebuild their war-ravaged economies. This was an important factor in the postwar reconstruction of the world capitalist economy. European reconstruction bolstered demand for exported goods from the United States, and ultimately promoted the reemergence of Western Europe as a global manufacturing powerhouse.

During the long period (1968-1981) that former U.S. Defense Secretary Robert S. McNamara headed the World Bank, however, the bank turned toward "development" loans to lower-income countries. McNamara brought the same philosophy to development that he had used as a chief architect of the U.S. war against Vietnam: big is good and bigger is better. Since then, the World Bank has favored large, expensive projects regardless of their appropriateness to local conditions, and with little attention to environmental and social impacts. The Bank has been especially notorious, for example, for supporting large dam projects that have flooded wide areas, deprived others of water, and uprooted the people living in affected regions. The Bank's support for large, capital-intensive "development" projects has also been a disguised way of channeling benefits to large global companies. Many of these projects require inputs—like high-tech machinery—that are not produced in the countries where the projects take place. Instead, they have to be imported, mostly from high-income countries. Such projects may also create long-run dependencies, since the spare parts and technical expertise for proper maintenance may only be available from the companies that produced these inputs in the first place.

While the Bank's main focus is long-term "development" lending, it has also engaged in "structural adjustment" lending. The Bank's structural adjustment policies, much like those from the IMF, have imposed heavy burdens on workers and poor people. In the 1980s and 1990s, during its "structural adjustment era," the Bank went so far as to advocate that governments charge fees even for public primary education. (Predictably, in countries that adopted such policies, many poor families could not afford the fees and school enrollment declined.) The Bank has since publicly called for the abolition of school fees. Critics argue, however, that the shift is at least partly rhetorical. Katarina Tomasevski, founder of the organization Right to Education, argues that the Bank presents itself as opposing fees, but does not oppose hidden charges, as for textbooks, school uniforms, and other costs of attending school.

The World Bank has also made development loans conditional on the adoption of "free-market" policies, like privatization of public services. Most notoriously, the Bank has pushed for the privatization of water delivery. Where privatization of water or other public services has not been possible, the Bank has urged governments to adopt "cost-recovery" strategies—including raising fees on users. Both privatization and cost-recovery strategies have undermined poor people's access to water and other essentials.

Recent developments

Since the 1990s, opposition to World Bank and IMF policies have shaken the two institutions' power—especially in Latin America, the world region to which "neoliberalism" came first and where it went furthest. This is part of a broader backlash against neoliberal policies, which opponents (especially on the Latin American left) blame for persistent poverty and rising inequality in the region. The last decade or so has seen a so-called "pink wave" in Latin America, with "center-left" parties coming to power in Argentina, Bolivia, Brazil, Chile, Ecuador, and Venezuela. (The center-left has since lost the presidency in Chile.) Different governments have adopted different policies in power, some staying close to the neoliberal path, others veering sharply away from it. Venezuela has, along with several other countries, withdrawn from the World Bank-affiliated International Centre for the Settlement of Investment Disputes (ICSID). Several South American governments, including Argentina, Brazil, and Venezuela, have also jointly formed a new regional lending institution, the Bank of the South, which aims to act as an alternative lender (for both long-term development and short-term "liquidity crises") to the IMF and World Bank.

On the other hand, the IMF has emerged, surprisingly, as a powerful influence in Western Europe. For many years, acute debt crises seemed to be confined to lower income economies, and most observers did not dream that they could happen in Europe or other high-income regions. (For this reason, the IMF was widely criticized as a hammer that high-income countries used on low-income countries.) During the current economic crisis, however, several Western European countries have fallen deeply into debt. The IMF has stepped in as part of "bailout" programs for Greece, Iceland, and Ireland. True to its origins, it has also pushed for austerity—especially cuts in public spending—in highly indebted countries. Many economists—especially proponents of "Keynesian" views—have argued that weakness in total demand is the main cause of the current economic crisis in Europe and the rest of the world. Under these conditions, they argue, cuts in government spending will only reduce total demand further, and likely cause the crisis to drag on. ❑

Sources: International Monetary Fund, "IMF Members' Quotas and Voting Power, and IMF Board of Governors" (www.imf.org); International Monetary Fund, "IMF Executive Directors and Voting Power" (www.imf.org); World Bank, "Executive Directors and Alternates" (www.worldbank.org); World Bank, "Cost Recovery for Water Supply and Sanitation and Irrigation and Drainage Projects (www.worldbank.org); Zoe Godolphin, "The World Bank as a New Global Education Ministry?" Bretton Woods Project, January 21, 2011 (www.brettonwoodsproject.org); Katerina Tomasevski, "Both Arsonist and Fire Fighter: The World Bank on School Fees," Bretton Woods Project, January 23, 2006 (www.brettonwoodsproject.org); Katerina Tomasevski, "Six Reasons Why the World Bank Should Be Debarred From Education ," Bretton Woods Project, September 2, 2006 (www.brettonwoodsproject.org).

Article 4.2

THE WORLD TRADE ORGANIZATION (WTO)
From "The ABCs of the Global Economy"

BY THE *DOLLARS & SENSE* COLLECTIVE
March/April 2000, last revised November 2012

If you know one thing about the World Trade Organization (WTO), it is probably that the organization's ministerial meetings have been the target of massive "anti-globalization" protests. The most famous was the "Battle in Seattle." Over 50,000 people went to Seattle in 1999 to say no to the WTO's corporate agenda, success-fully shutting down the first day of the ministerial meeting. African, Caribbean, and other least-developed country representatives, in addition, walked out of the meeting. But what is the WTO? Where did it come from? And what does it do?

Where did it come from?

Starting in the 1950s, government officials from around the world began to meet irregularly to hammer out the rules of a global trading system. Known as the General Agreements on Trade and Tariffs (GATT), these negotiations covered, in excruciating detail, such matters as what level of taxation Japan could impose on foreign rice, how many American automobiles Brazil could allow into its market, and how large a subsidy France could give its vineyards. Every clause was carefully crafted, with constant input from business representatives who hoped to profit from expanded international trade.

The GATT process however, was slow, cumbersome and difficult to monitor. As corporations expanded more rapidly into global markets they pushed governments to create a more powerful and permanent international body that could speed up trade negotiations as well as oversee and enforce provisions of the GATT. The result was the World Trade Organization, formed out of the ashes of GATT in 1995.

Following the shocking demonstrations in Seattle, the WTO held its 2001 ministerial meeting in Doha, Qatar, safe from protest. The WTO initiated a new round of trade talks that it promised would address thee need s of developing coun-tries. The Doha Development round, however, continued the WTO's pro-corporate agenda. Two years later "the Group of 20 developing countries" at the Cancún min-isterial refused to lower their trade barriers until the United States and EU cleaned up their unfair global agricultural systems. By the summer of 2006, five years after it began, the Doha round had collapsed and the WTO suspended trade negotiations.

What does it do?

The WTO functions as a sort of international court for adjudicating trade dis-putes. Each of its 153 member countries has one representative, who participates in negotiations over trade rules. The heart of the WTO, however, is not its delegates, but its dispute resolution system. With the establishment of the WTO, corporations now have a place to complain to when they want trade barriers—or domestic regulations that limit their freedom to buy and sell—overturned.

Though corporations have no standing in the WTO—the organization is, officially, open only to its member countries—the numerous advisory bodies that provide technical expertise to delegates are overflowing with corporate representation. The delegates themselves are drawn from trade ministries and confer regularly with the corporate lobbyists and advisors who swarm the streets and offices of Geneva, where the organization is headquartered. As a result, the WTO has become, as an anonymous delegate told the *Financial Times*, "a place where governments can collude against their citizens."

Lori Wallach and Michelle Sforza, in their book *The WTO: Five Years of Reasons to Resist Corporate Globalization*, point out that large corporations are essentially "renting" governments to bring cases before the WTO, and in this way, to win in the WTO battles they have lost in the political arena at home. Large shrimping corporations, for example, got India to dispute the U.S. ban on shrimp catches that were not sea-turtle safe. Once such a case is raised, the resolution process violates most democratic notions of due process and openness. Cases are heard before a tribunal of "trade experts," generally lawyers, who, under WTO rules, are required to make their ruling with a presumption in favor of free trade. The WTO puts the burden squarely on governments to justify any restriction of what it considers the natural order of things. There are no amicus briefs (statements of legal opinion filed with a court by outside parties), no observers, and no public records of the deliberations.

The WTO's rule is not restricted to such matters as tariff barriers. When the organization was formed, environmental and labor groups warned that the WTO would soon be rendering decisions on essential matters of public policy. This has proven absolutely correct. The organization ruled against Europe for banning hormone-treated beef and against Japan for prohibiting pesticide-laden apples. Also WTO rules prohibit selective purchasing laws, even those targeted at human rights abuses. In 1998 the WTO court lodged a complaint against the Massachusetts state law that banned government purchases from Burma in an attempt to punish its brutal dictatorship. Had the WTO's rules been in place at the time at the time of the anti-Apartheid divestment movement, laws barring trade with or investment in South Africa would have violated them as well.

Why should you care?

At stake is a fundamental issue of popular sovereignty—the rights of the people to regulate economic life, whether at the level of the city, state, or nation. The U.S. does not allow businesses operating within its borders to produce goods with child labor, for example, so why should we allow those same businesses—Disney, Gap, or Walmart—to produce their goods with child labor in Haiti and sell the goods here? ❏

Article 4.3

NAFTA AND CAFTA

From "The ABCS of Free-Trade Agreements and Other Regional Economic Blocs"

BY THE *DOLLARS & SENSE* COLLECTIVE

January/February 2001, last revised November 2012

In the early 1990s, as the North American Free Trade Agreement (NAFTA) was under consideration in the Canada, Mexico, and the United States, supporters of the pact argued that both business owners and workers in all three countries would gain from the removal of trade and investment barriers. For example, the argument went, U.S. firms that produce more efficiently than their Mexican counterparts would enjoy larger markets, gain more profits, generate more jobs, and pay higher wages. The winners would include information technology firms, biotech firms, larger retailers, and other U.S. corporations that had an advantage because of skilled U.S. labor or because of experience in organization and marketing. On the other hand, Mexican firms that could produce at low cost because of low Mexican wages will be able to expand into the U.S. market. The main examples were assembly plants or *maquiladoras*.

Critics of the agreement, meanwhile, focused on problems resulting from extreme differences among the member countries in living standards, wages, unionization, environmental laws, and social legislation. The options that NAFTA would create for business firms, the critics argued, would put them at a great advantage in their dealings with workers and communities.

As it turned out, NAFTA was approved by the governments of all three countries, and went into effect on January 1, 1994. The agreement eliminated most barriers to trade and investment among the United States, Canada and Mexico. For some categories of goods—certain agricultural goods, for example—NAFTA promised to phase out restrictions on trade over a few years, but most goods and services were to be freely bought and sold across the three countries' borders from the start. Likewise, virtually all investments—financial investments as well as investments in fixed assets such as factories, mines, or farms (foreign direct investment)—were freed from cross-border restrictions.

The agreement, however, made no changes in the restrictions on the movement of labor. Mexican—and, for that matter, Canadian—workers who wish to come to the United States must enter under the limited immigration quotas, or illegally. Thus NAFTA gave new options and direct benefits to those who obtain their income from selling goods and making investments, but the agreement included no parallel provision for those who make their incomes by working.

For example, U.S. unions were weakened because firms could more easily shut down domestic operations and substitute operations in Mexico. With the government suppressing independent unions in Mexico, organization of workers in all

corrected page proofs.
Economic Affairs Bureau, Inc. CHAPTER 4: INTERNATIONAL INSTITUTIONS AND TRADE AGREEMENTS | 109
not reproduce or distribute.

three countries was undermined. (Actually, the formal Mexican labor laws are probably as good or better than those in the United States but they are usually not enforced.) While NAFTA may mean more jobs and better pay for computer software engineers in the United States, manufacturing workers in the United States, for example, have seen their wages stagnate or fall. Similarly, the greater freedom of international movement that NAFTA affords to firms has given them greater bargaining power over communities when it comes to environmental regulations. One highly visible result has been severe pollution problems in Mexican *maquiladora* zones along the U.S. border.

An additional and important aspect of NAFTA is that it creates legal mechanisms for firms based in one country to contest legislation in the other countries when it might interfere with their "right" to carry out their business. Thus, U.S. firms operating in Mexico have challenged stricter environmental regulations won by the Mexican environmental movement. In Canada, the government rescinded a public-health law restricting trade in toxic PCBs as the result of a challenge by a U.S. firm; Canada also paid $10 million to the complaining firm, in compensation for "losses" it suffered under the law. These examples illustrate the way in which NAFTA, by giving priority to the "rights" of business, has undermined the ability of governments to regulate the operation of their economies in an independent, democratic manner.

Finally, one of NAFTA's greatest gifts to business was the removal of restrictions on the movement of financial capital. The immediate result for Mexico was the severe financial debacle of 1994. Investment funds moved rapidly into Mexico during the early 1990s, and especially after NAFTA went into effect. Without regulation, these investments were able to abandon Mexico just as rapidly when the speculative "bubble" burst, leading to severe drops in production and employment.

CAFTA: Extending the Free Trade Agenda

After the implementation of NAFTA, it looked like the Americas were on a fast track to a hemisphere-wide free-trade zone. In 1994, then-President Bill Clinton proposed to have the world's largest trading block in place by 2005. Instead, the Free Trade Area of the Americas (FTAA) stalled in its tracks when, in 1997, Congress denied Clinton "fast-track" negotiating authority. President George W. Bush revived the fast-track push in 2001 and succeeded in getting fast-track legislation through both the House of Representatives and the U.S. Senate in 2002. Nonetheless, the entire decade of the 2000s came and went without the FTAA.

The NAFTA model, however, has been extended into Central America and the Caribbean through the Central American Free Trade Agreement (CAFTA). CAFTA is now in effect for trade between the United States and Costa Rica, El Salvador, Guatemala, Honduras, Nicaragua, and the Dominican Republic. Economic size alone assures that U.S. interests dominate the agreement. The combined economic output of the countries in Central America is smaller than the total income of just two U.S.-based agribusiness companies that will benefit from the accord: Cargill and Archer Daniels Midland.

CAFTA, modeled after NAFTA, shares all of its shortcomings and will do as much to hamper sustainable development and no more to further human rights and labor abuses in Central America than NAFTA did in Mexico. A report from the "Stop CAFTA Coalition" documented the problems evident just one year into the agreement. First, CAFTA did not appear to be creating the promised regional textile complex to offset competition from China. Central American garment exports continued to lose market share to their Asian competitors. In addition, CAFTA contributed to making difficult conditions in the Central American countryside yet worse. U.S. imports of fresh beef, poultry, and dairy products increased dramatically, displacing local producers, and food prices rose. Finally, CAFTA did nothing to improve human rights or extend labor rights in Central America.

And CAFTA poses yet another danger. Rules buried in the technical language of the agreement's investment chapter would make it more difficult for the Central American and Caribbean nations to escape their heavy debt burdens or recover from a debt crisis. ❑

Article 4.4

THE EUROPEAN UNION (EU) AND THE EUROZONE

From "The ABCS of Free-Trade Agreements and Other Regional Economic Blocs"

BY THE *DOLLARS & SENSE* COLLECTIVE
January/February 2001, last revised November 2012

The European Union (EU) forms the world's largest single market—larger than the United States or even the three NAFTA countries together. From its beginnings in 1951 as the six-member European Coal and Steel Community, the association has grown both geographically (now including 27 countries) and especially in its degree of unity. All national border controls on goods, capital, and people were abolished between member countries in 1993. And seventeen of the EU's members now share a common currency (the euro), collectively forming the "eurozone."

The EU and the "Social Charter": Promises Unkept

At first glance, open trade within the EU seemed to pose less of a threat for wages and labor standards than NAFTA or the WTO. Even the poorer member countries, such as Spain, Portugal, and Greece, were fairly wealthy and had strong unions and decent labor protections. Moreover, most EU countries, including top economic powers like France, Germany, Italy, and the United Kingdom, had strong parties (whether "socialist," social democratic, or labor) with roots in the working-class movement. This relationship had grown increasingly distant over time; still, from the perspective of labor, the EU represented a kind of best-case scenario for freeing trade. The results are, nonetheless, cautionary.

The main thrust of the EU, like other trade organizations, has been trade and investment. Labor standards were never fully integrated into the core agenda of the EU. In 1989, 11 of the then-12 EU countries signed the "Charter of the Fundamental Social Rights of Workers," more widely known as the "Social Charter." (Only the United Kingdom refused to sign.) Though the "Social Charter" did not have any binding mechanism—it is described in public communications as "a political instrument containing 'moral obligations'"—many hoped it would provide the basis for "upward harmonization," that is, pressure on European countries with weaker labor protections to lift their standards to match those of member nations with stronger regulations. The years since the adoption of the "Social Charter" have seen countless meetings, official studies, and exhortations but few appreciable results.

Since trade openness was never directly linked to social and labor standards and the "Social Charter" never mandated concrete actions from corporations, European business leaders have kept "Social Europe" from gaining any momentum simply by ignoring it. Although European anti-discrimination rules have forced countries like Britain to adopt the same retirement age for men and women, and regional funds are dispersed each year to bring up the general living standards of the poorest nations, the social dimension of the EU has never been more than an appendage for buying off opposition. As a result, business moved production, investment, and employment in Europe toward countries with lower standards, such as Ireland and Portugal.

The EU also exemplifies how regional trading blocs indirectly break down trade regulations with countries outside the bloc. Many Europeans may have hoped that the EU would insulate Europe from competition with countries that lacked social, labor, and environmental standards. While the EU has a common external tariff, each member can maintain its own non-tariff trade barriers. EU rules requiring openness between member countries, however, made it easy to circumvent any EU country's national trade restrictions. Up until 1993, member states used to be able to block indirect imports through health and safety codes or border controls, but with the harmonization of these rules across the EU, governments can no longer do so. Since then, companies have simply imported non-EU goods into the EU countries with the most lax trade rules, and then freely transported the goods into the countries with higher standards. (NAFTA similarly makes it possible to circumvent U.S. barriers against the importation of steel from China by sending it indirectly through Mexico.)

EU members that wished to uphold trade barriers against countries with inadequate social, labor, and environmental protections ended up becoming less important trading hubs in the world economy. This has led EU countries to unilaterally abolish restrictions and trade monitoring against non-EU nations. The logic of trade openness seems to be against labor and the environment even when the governments of a trading bloc individually wish to be more protective.

The Eurozone: Caught in a Bind

The process of European economic integration, which began with the formation of the six-country European Coal and Steel Community in 1951, culminated with the establishment of a common currency (the euro) between 1999 and 2002. The creation of the euro seemed to cap the rise of Europe, over many years, from the devastation of the Second World War. Step by step, Western Europe had rebuilt vibrant economies. The largest "core" economy, Germany, had become a global manufacturing power. Even some countries with historically lower incomes, like Ireland, Italy, and Spain, had converged toward the affluence of the core countries. The euro promised to be a major new world currency, ultimately with hundreds of millions of users in one of the world's richest and seemingly most stable regions. Some commentators viewed the euro as a potential rival to the dollar as a key currency in world trade, and as a "reserve" currency (in which individuals, companies, and national banks would hold financial wealth).

Of the 27 European Union (EU) member countries, only 17 have adopted the euro as their currency (joined the "eurozone"). One of the most important EU economies, the United Kingdom, for example, has retained its own national currency (the pound). The countries that did adopt the euro, on the other hand, retired their national currencies. There is no German deutschmark, French franc, or Italian lira anymore. These currencies, and the former national currencies of other eurozone countries, stopped circulating in 2001 or 2002, depending on the country. Bank balances held in these currencies were converted to euros. People holding old bills and coins were also able to exchange them for euros.

The adoption of the euro meant a major change in the control over monetary policy for the eurozone countries. Countries that have their own national currencies generally have a central bank (or "monetary authority") responsible for policies affecting the country's overall money supply and interest rates. In the United States, for example, the Federal Reserve (or "the Fed") is the monetary authority. To "tighten" the money supply, the Fed sells government bonds to "the public" (really, to private banks). It receives money in return, and so reduces the amount of money held by the public. The Fed may do this at the peak of a business cycle boom, in order to combat or head off inflation. Monetary tightening tends to raise interest rates, pulling back on demand for goods and services. Reduced overall demand, in turn, tends to reduce upward pressure on prices. To "loosen" the money supply, on the other hand, the Fed buys government bonds back from the banks. This puts more money into the banks' hands, which tends to reduce interest rates and stimulate spending. The Fed may do this during a business-cycle downturn or full-blown recession, in order to raise output and employment. As these examples suggest, monetary policy can be an important lever through which governments influence overall demand, output, and employment. Adopting the euro meant giving up control over monetary policy, a step many EU countries, like the UK, were not willing to make.

For eurozone countries, monetary policy is made not by a national central bank, but by the European Central Bank (ECB). ECB policy is made by 23-member "governing council," including the six members of the bank's executive board and the directors of each of the 17 member countries' central banks. The six executive-board members, meanwhile, come from various eurozone countries. (The members in late 2011 are from France, Portugal, Italy, Spain, Germany, and Belgium.) While all countries that have adopted the euro are represented on the governing council, Germany has a much greater influence on European monetary policy than other countries. Germany's is the largest economy in the eurozone. Among other eurozone countries, only France's economy is anywhere near its size. (Italy's economy is less than two-thirds the size of Germany's, in terms of total output; Spain's, less than half; the Netherlands', less than one-fourth.) German policymakers, meanwhile, have historically made very low inflation rates their main priority (to the point of being "inflation-phobic"). In part, this harkens back to a scarring period of "hyperinflation" during the 1920s; in part, to the importance of Germany as a financial center. Even during the current crisis, as economist

Paul Krugman puts it, "what we're seeing is an ECB catering to German desires for low inflation, very much at the expense of making the problems of peripheral economies much less tractable."

For countries, like Germany, that have not been hit so hard by the current crisis, the "tight money" policy is less damaging than for the harder-hit countries. With Germany's unemployment rate at 6.5% and the inflation rate at only 2.5%, as of late 2011, an insistence on a tight money policy does reflect an excessive concern with maintaining very low inflation and insufficient concern with stimulating demand and reducing unemployment. If this policy torpedoes the economies of other European countries, meanwhile, it may drag the whole of Europe—including the more stable "core" economies—back into recession.

For the harder-hit countries, the results are disastrous. These countries are mired in a deep economic crisis, in heavy debt, and unable to adopt a traditional "expansionary" monetary policy on their own (since the eurozone monetary policy is set by the ECB). For them, a looser monetary policy could stimulate demand, production, and employment, even without causing much of an increase in inflation. When an economy is producing near its full capacity, increased demand is likely to put upward pressure on prices. (More money "chasing" the same amount of goods can lead to higher inflation.) In Europe today, however, there are vast unused resources—including millions of unemployed workers—so more demand could stimulate the production of more goods, and need not result in rising inflation.

Somewhat higher inflation, moreover, could actually help stimulate the harder-hit European economies. Moderate inflation can stimulate demand, since it gives people an incentive to spend now rather than wait and spend later. It also reduces the real burdens of debt. Countries like Greece, Ireland, Italy, Portugal, and Spain are drowning in debt, both public and private. These debts are generally specified in nominal terms—as a particular number of euros. As the price level increases, however, it reduces the real value of a nominal amount of money. Debts can be paid back in euros that are worth less than when the debt was incurred. As real debt burdens decrease, people feel less anxious about their finances, and may begin to spend more freely. Inflation also redistributes income from creditors, who tend to be wealthier and to save more of their incomes, to debtors, who tend to be less wealth and spend most of theirs. This, too, helps boost demand.

The current crisis has led many commentators to speculate that some heavily indebted countries may decide to abandon the euro. This need not mean that they would repudiate (refuse to pay) their public debt altogether. They could, instead, convert their euro debts to their new national currencies. This would give them more freedom to pursue a higher-inflation policy, which would reduce the real debt burden. (Indeed, independent countries that owe their debt in their own currency need not ever default. A country that controls its own money supply can "print" more money to repay creditors—with the main limit being how the money supply can be expanded without resulting in unacceptably high inflation. Adopting the euro, however, deprived countries in the eurozone of this power.) The current crisis, some economists argue, shows how the euro project was misguided from the start. Paul Krugman, for example, argues that the common currency was mainly driven by a political (not economic) aim—the peaceful unification of a region that had been torn apart by two world wars. It did not make much sense economically, given the real possibility for divergent needs of different national economies. Today, it seems a real possibility that the eurozone, at least, will come apart again. ❑

Sources: Paul Krugman, "European Inflation Targets," *New York Times* blog, January 18, 2011 (krugman.blogs.nytimes.com); European Central Bank, Decision-making, Governing Council (www.ecb.int/); European Central Bank, Decision-making, Executive Board (www.ecb.int/); Federal Statistical Office (Statistisches Bundesamt Deutschland), Federal Republic of Germany, Short-term indicators, Unemployment, Consumer Price Index (www.destatis.de); Paul Krugman, "Can Europe Be Saved?" *New York Times*, January 12, 2011 (nytimes.com).

Article 4.5

WOUNDED TIGER
Ireland submits to the IMF.

BY DAN READ
July/August 2011

Guinness is, apparently, now good for public relations. President Barack Obama, in his recent visit to Ireland, seemed to develop a fondness for the drink, or at least put on a brave face when he posed for the cameras with a pint in his hand. Less than twenty-four hours later, though, he had departed the country, after promising to do "everything that we can to be helpful" on Ireland's economic woes that have led to not just one, but potentially two bailouts by the International Monetary Fund (IMF).

The initial three-year Extended Fund Facility granted by the IMF in December 2010 amounted to a loan of over 22.5 billion euros (roughly $32 billion). Coupled with loans from the European Union and state intervention from Dublin, the grand total comes to around $121 billion. The extraordinary price tag came with conditions: Ireland has had to make structural adjustments to its economy that align with IMF goals.

On the surface there is a lot of financial jargon involving "debt restructuring" that will ostensibly render the Irish economy "solvent" once again. The practical implications of these vague and somewhat strange phrases are spelled out in a National Recovery Plan enacted by the government and endorsed by the IMF.

The plan aims to cut government spending by over $21 billion within three years, with $8.5 billion being taken out of the public sector in 2011 alone.

Government pay and staffing levels are thus being downscaled, with the state payroll having already been slashed in 2010 to the tune of over $2 billion. Wages for "new entrants" have also been hit with a blanket 10% reduction, with recruitment to the state sector limited to 3,300 new personnel each year. In conjunction with measures to fire existing staff, the government hopes to have a leaner, less well-paid public sector, with fewer than 294,000 employees by 2014. Taking public-sector employment figures for late 2008, this entails a decline of 75,100 employees.

Downgrading for Growth

In their online press releases, the IMF has lauded the plan for laying the foundations for recovery while still paying "due regard to a social safety net." The safety net is looking a little worn, however. Some measures proposed by the plan involved the withdrawal of $144 million from state pension funds, as well as raising the retirement age to 66 in 2014, to 67 in 2021, and to 68 in 2028. Furthermore, for 2011 alone $1.1 billion is to be taken from Social Protection (welfare), which will see a total cut of $4.3 billion by 2014.

The plan paves new ground for political institutions worldwide in that it openly admits the measures "will negatively affect the living standards of citizens," but claims that this is necessary to "to return [the Irish] economy to a sustainable medium-term economic growth path."

The state sector employs workers from a diverse set of industries, ranging from hospital nurses to postmen to police officers. Policies threatening these workers' jobs have prompted renewed militancy on the part of trade unions and leftist political organizations.

"We have had several huge workers demonstrations in the past couple of years," Macdara Doyle, a spokesman for the Irish Congress of Trade Unions (ICTU), told *Dollars & Sense.* "These were some of the largest in Europe—I mean, if you factor in the overall size of the population of Ireland, one hundred thousand or so people on the streets of Dublin is like several million in London and Paris."

The ICTU has not been slow to note a mounting pressure on working families. Speaking to a meeting of trade unionists in April, the congress's economic advisor, Paul Sweeney, took note of a deteriorating economic situation made worse by a global rise in food and oil prices.

Coupled with a recent rise in interest rates for Ireland's existing consumer debts, Sweeney cited "extra hardship for people all over the country" due to people "being squeezed on too many fronts. There is a limit to the burden of austerity that any society, or household, can tolerate."

Yet the Dail, the principal house of Ireland's parliament, seemed more than willing to engage in economic austerity measures even before the IMF received its not-so-warm welcome last December. The national budget for 2010 detailed "savings" on expenditure to the tune of $4.3 billion. Of this sizeable sum, $1.1 billion was taken from "Social and Family Affairs"—in part welfare measures such as benefit payments to the unemployed—alongside $576 million from child care and health services.

"We have actually had four austerity budgets in this country," says Doyle of the ICTU, "December's bailout was actually triggered by the European Central Bank [ECB] in response to a broken and busted banking system that has brought down the whole country. We were in debt to the ECB to the tune of around 130 billion euros [$187 billion], and the government just kept going to them for aid until the ECB just said 'No, we can't do this anymore, this debt needs to be restructured.'"

IMF spokesmen are in agreement with Doyle on this point. In a document released shortly after the December bailout, the IMF emphasized the flaws of "an oversized banking system" that had become "overly dependent on financing from the European Central Bank."

The paradox here is that the ECB is still intimately involved in the recovery process and remains an important participant in the Extended Fund Facility. What has changed, however, is that the IMF intervention seems to have mollified the ECB into acting as creditors to what they might otherwise have viewed as a lost cause.

Fewer Resources

The case of Ireland's banks is similar to the British or American experience—except that the Irish government does not have the capital reserves to implement extensive banking bailouts. Figures compiled by the World Bank during the height of the recession in 2009 show Irish GDP sitting at just over $227 billion. The corresponding figure for the UK showed British GDP leagues ahead at over $2.1 trillion.

The Wrong Medicine: Why Fiscal Austerity Is a Bad Idea for a Slumping Economy

As protesters take to the streets in Europe to oppose government spending cuts, proponents of austerity in the United States and Europe claim that immediate moves to reduce government deficits are the way to renewed economic growth. Accepting a little pain now, they argue, will reduce the pain in the long run.

Those familiar with Keynesian economic theory will find the austerity-to-growth claims surprising. Fiscal austerity, or a "contractionary fiscal policy," means either spending cuts or tax increases, or a combination of the two. Reductions in government spending reduce total demand directly. Government spending on real goods and services is just as much a part of total demand as private consumption or investment spending. Spending cuts can also reduce demand indirectly, as those who would have received income as a result of government spending cut back on their spending as well. Tax increases reduce demand by reducing the disposable incomes of private individuals, who then spend less. Either way, lower demand for goods and services can translate into less output and employment.

How, then, is fiscal contraction supposed to lead to growth? Austerity proponents argue that balancing government budgets and reducing public debt will boost private-sector "confidence." As public debt increases, the argument goes, people may become wary about spending, since they will be on the hook (through taxes) to pay down that debt in the future. Individuals and firms will spend more freely now if they do not have future taxes hanging over their heads.

The pro-austerity faction has relied heavily on a few recent studies, especially one by Harvard economists Alberto Alesina and Silvia Ardagna claiming to have identified 26 cases in which fiscal contraction led to renewed growth. This conclusion, however, has not stood up to careful scrutiny. Economists Arjun Jayadev and Mike Konczal, after studying the cases that Alesina and Ardagna describe, find that "in virtually none did the country a) reduce the deficit when the economy was in a slump and b) increase growth rates while reducing the debt-to-GDP ratio."

In 20 of the 26 cases, Jayadev and Konczal argue, the government did not carry out a fiscal contraction during the low (or "slump") phase of a business cycle. (Budgets are much easier to balance, and debt easier to pay down, during the "boom" phase of a business cycle. With output and incomes high, total tax revenue is bound to be high as well,

corrected page proofs.
conomic Affairs Bureau, Inc.**CHAPTER 4: INTERNATIONAL INSTITUTIONS AND TRADE AGREEMENTS | 119**
not reproduce or distribute.

Unsurprisingly, the United States won first with a GDP of well over $14 trillion. If the response to the crisis has been somewhat similar in these countries, the facts on the ground show that the Irish economy, despite its reputation as a "Celtic Tiger" in the 1990s, is simply unable to cope with the aftershocks of recession.

What prompted the crisis is, again, a somewhat familiar story: Ireland's former prosperity has been attributed to a housing bubble that lifted the country from depression in the late 1980s into the lofty heights of financial stardom less than ten

---

while expenditures on things like unemployment insurance are bound to be low.) Out of the six remaining cases, they find, the rate of economic growth actually declined in five. Looking at a broader sample of countries engaging in austerity, Jayadev and Konczal find that, in most cases, deficit cutting during a slump results in lower growth. Even in most of the cases where the growth rate did increase, the ratio of debt to gross domestic product actually increased as well. This suggests that, even if fiscal austerity had some effect in reducing the growth of total debt, it also resulted in such weak overall economic growth that the debt burden (relative to GDP) continued to rise.

Austerity can actually undermine a country's ability to reduce its government deficit and debt, and increase the interest rates a government is forced to pay on its debt. A government's ability to borrow depends on the size and stability of the economy that it has the power to tax. By cutting demand, a government may prolong a slump. The longer the slump goes on, the longer tax revenues will remain below normal, and the longer the government will have above-normal expenditures on items like unemployment insurance. If investors conclude that the slump is bound to go on for a long time, and that the government will therefore be a bad credit risk for the foreseeable future, they will demand a higher interest rate (to compensate them for that risk). This, too, will tend to increase the government's debt burden.

Austerity advocates present themselves as tough-minded and pragmatic—not flinching from the painful sacrifices necessary for a better future. The facts might suggest, instead, that fiscal austerity during a slump amounts to cutting off one's nose to spite one's face. Except that, as the protests raging in Europe show, it is other people's noses that the pro-austerity faction aims to lop off.

—*Alejandro Reuss*

Sources: Arjun Jayadev and Mike Konczal, "The Boom Not the Slump: Not the Right Time for Austerity," The Roosevelt Institute, August 23, 2010; Alberto Alesina and Silvia Ardagna, "Large Changes in Fiscal Policy: Taxes Versus Spending," NBER Working Paper No. 15438, 2009; Andrew G. Biggs, Kevin A. Hassett, and Matthew Jensen, "A Guide for Deficit Reduction in the United States Based on Historical Consolidations That Worked," American Enterprise Institute, December 2010; International Monetary Fund, "Will It Hurt? Macroeconomic Effects of Fiscal Consolidation," World Economic Outlook, Chapter 3, October 2010; Paul Krugman, "Does Fiscal Austerity Reassure Markets?" June 13, 2010 (krugman.blogs.nytimes.com).

years later. This claim is further substantiated by a 6.5% annual GDP growth rate between 1991 and 2007. *The Economist* had this to say in May 1997: "just yesterday, it seems, Ireland was one of Europe's poorest countries. Today it is about as prosperous as the European average and getting richer all the time."

Yet *The Economist* in its optimism overlooked some important facts. At the time of the article, house prices were already soaring dramatically; between 1992 and 2006 they rose by around 300%. In a story that is no doubt familiar, Irish banks were all too willing to lend at low interest rates while believing it safe to imitate the behavior of their American and British counterparts. But the property boom—and with it the banks' reckless lending and low interest rates—was not to last, and despite its former prosperity, Dublin is not the financial hub that London or New York can claim to be.

If the Dail cannot match Westminster in financial prosperity, however, it can match it in how it handles recession, and that's by passing the burden onto ordinary people. The Value Added Tax (VAT) has been hiked in both countries, despite the fact that, in Ireland in particular, a burden on the spending of the individual consumer is also an extra weight on small businesses, which are typically more dependent on the internal market than larger franchises with potential holdings overseas. "Obviously, it depends on what kind of small business we are talking about," said Sean Murphy, deputy chief executive for Chambers Ireland, Ireland's largest business advocacy organization, "but on the domestic side we are seeing a lowering of consumer confidence which is going to be affecting them. Outside of that, we can see that Irish exports are growing, but when dealing with the internal market and VAT rises and so on, things are not going so well."

A Second Bailout?

So far, talk of a second bailout in 2013 has been confined to supposition that the government will be forced to default on existing debts despite the implementation of the recovery plan. An additional bailout has therefore been raised as a possibility for boosting revenue, although the economic "adjustments" involved may differ in severity from those contained in the National Recovery Plan.

The possible additional bailout comes recommended by former IMF deputy director Donal Donovan. Donovan claimed last March that the country would need assistance until at least 2015, with further "debt restructuring" on the agenda should the economy prove "insolvent."

The Irish people themselves appear to disagree. The United Left Alliance (ULA), an umbrella organization of leftist groups founded last November, has already started to make waves on the political scene after winning five seats in the Dail in March.

"The only people who are in denial about a second bailout actually happening are the main political parties," Michael O'Brien, a member of the ULA's national interim steering committee, told *Dollars & Sense*. "It could be said that the reason why the original terms brought in last December were so harsh is that the IMF knew there would be a default, but not an immediate one, it's just that in the three-year period the first bailout is in effect foreign investors will be able to get more of a hold over the Irish banking sector before a second bailout becomes necessary."

"Both the left and the right don't seem to want to talk about this, but unless we reject these harsh terms we will certainly default, and that's when a second bailout becomes likely. Even if we reduce ourselves to serfdom there will be a default."

O'Brien is also a believer in Irish economist Richard Douthwait's theory that duplicity is integral to the IMF's strategy. If the IMF apparently believes a default will occur, then why have they bothered with a bailout in the first place? Douthwait believes, as does O'Brien, that the secret lies in the interests of foreign depositors in Irish banks. Writing in the magazine *Construct Ireland*, Douthwait poses the question: "If a default is inevitable, why is Ireland being paid, via the bailout money, not to default now? The answer is clear. A default now would mean that the foreign banks and other institutions which have lent to Ireland would suffer massive losses and might need to be rescued by the governments of the countries in which they are based. Big firms with deposits in Irish banks in excess of the 100,000 euros [$145,000] state guarantee would suffer big losses too. Indeed, if the two major banks collapsed, the government could find itself unable to honour its deposit guarantees at all."

Donovan, Douthwait, and O'Brien seem set on the belief that a second bailout will therefore be necessary, although they clearly have differing opinions as to why. Douthwait and O'Brien believe the priority of the IMF and ECB is to safeguard foreign deposits, or permit them to withdraw in time in order to avert further losses while adopting a wait-and-see approach to the Irish recovery. The IMF's Donovan, however, is slightly more optimistic. The British newspaper The Guardian quotes Donovan as being amenable to the notion of writing off some of Ireland's debt, provided that the nation continues to follow the measures prescribed by the National Recovery Plan. Once this is done, he argues, the ECB may be more willing to let Ireland off the hook, at least to a degree.

PIIGS

But talk of partial relief at some point in the future does little for those already facing unemployment and falling living standards. Moreover, economists at the IMF and elsewhere seem to have developed a contemptuous attitude towards Ireland and other countries still reeling from the economic crisis—an attitude that hardly endears them to the populations they claim to be helping.

Over the years, economists have referred to the weaker economies of Europe, such as Italy, as being "sick" or otherwise suffering some kind of ailment. The acronym "PIIGS" (as in Portugal, Ireland, Italy, Greece, and Spain) is now in use by economists and pundits to describe the economically troubled parts of the continent.

Being referred to as a pig is hardly likely to prompt a positive reaction, yet hardship and the contempt of powerful foreigners is not something that is new to Ireland. In the past, the Irish have often dealt with economic woes by moving abroad; almost a million Irish headed to the United States during the Potato Famine of the late 1840s. Although the Irish are now in different straits, their tried-and-tested method of seeking greener pastures abroad has resurfaced.

The ICTU has estimated that perhaps a thousand citizens leave the country each week, although according to Doyle "some of them are immigrants anyway." According to the Economic and Social Research Institute, a Dublin-based research organization, 60,000 people left the country in the twelve months leading up to April 2010 alone. Over the course of 2010 and 2011 this trend has only continued.

"The problem," said Doyle, "is that we are losing a lot of people who are very qualified and very skilled; the kind of people you need to help an economy recover."

Economic Freedom

The Irish socialist James Connelly once said that half-measures on the road to independence would ensure "England will still rule" through "the whole array of commercial institutions she has planted in this country and watered with the tears of our mothers and the blood of our martyrs."

Prophetic words, yet Connelly could not have envisaged the future scale of the problem. What Ireland now faces is not so much a single foreign aggressor but multiple economic ties to a globe-spanning organization imposing privation through financial means.

With the National Recovery Plan viewed more as a National Austerity Plan by large segments of the population, unemployment at over 13%, and discontent on the rise, the days of Irish prosperity appear to be over. The demand for a politically and economically free Ireland, as put forth by the likes of Connelly before his execution by the British in 1916, still remains valid. ❑

Sources: Irish Congress of Trade Unions (www.ictu.ie); International Monetary Fund (imf.org); "National Recovery Plan 2010-2014," An Roinn Airgeadais Department of Finance (www.budget. gov.ie); United Left Alliance (unitedleftalliance.org); Chambers Ireland (www.chambers.ie); Dáil Éireann (www.oireachtas.ie); Central Statistics Office Ireland (www.cso.ie); Economic and Social Research Institute (www.esri.ie); Richard Douthwait, "Ireland's inevitable default," Construct Ireland, May 9, 2011 (www.constructireland.ie); Lisa O'Carroll, "Ireland will need another bailout, says former IMF director," The Guardian, April 7, 2011 (www.guardian.co.uk); "Ireland Shines," The Economist, May 15, 1997 (economist.com).

Article 4.6

STRUCTURAL ADJUSTMENT, HERE AND THERE

BY ARTHUR MacEWAN
November/December 2012

Dear Dr. Dollar:
What are the similarities and differences between structural adjustment
in the rest of the world/Third World and structural adjustment in the
United States?   —*Vicki Legion, San Francisco, Calif.*

The similarities are pretty clear. The differences? Not so great.
The term "structural adjustment" came into vogue in the 1980s with the debt
crises in many low- and middle-income countries, especially in Latin America. The situation presented two related problems. On the one hand, many countries, devoting large
amounts of their resources to paying their debts to globally operating banks, saw their
economies spin downward. On the other hand, the banks, most of them based in the
United States and western Europe, were on the verge of not getting paid. Horrors!

So in stepped the World Bank and the International Monetary Fund (IMF).
They told the governments of the debtor counties, in effect: "We'll loan you money
to help meet your debts on the condition that you *adjust the structure* of your economies in ways that we say will get you on a path to economic recovery. Oh, and by
the way, the banks must get paid."

Structural adjustment, then, was the particular set of policies that the World
Bank and IMF claimed would solve the debtor countries' problems. In a nutshell,
these policies required governments to:

- Cut their spending to reduce the budget deficit.
- Restrict the growth of the money supply, curtailing inflation but also
  bringing higher unemployment.
- Reduce restrictions on foreign investment and imports, providing freer
  access to multinational firms.
- Sell off government enterprises—i.e., privatize.
- "Rationalize" labor markets—i.e., get rid of protections for workers.
- Cut regulations on business—e.g., environmental regulation.

The slogan supporting all of this was: Reduce the role of the government! In
reality, these policies do not so much reduce the role of the government as they shift
the government towards supporting business and the well-being of the elites at the
expense of lower-income groups.

Familiar? Of course. In the United States, the term "structural adjustment"
isn't used, but this is the same set of policies that elite groups here have pushed over

the past several decades—and are pushing today as the solution to the country's economic malaise.

Cut the deficit, that's first on the list. And the U.S. government has long taken the lead in establishing agreements that open up the economy to unfettered global trade and investment. The privatization of U.S. education, health care, prisons, and even many aspects of the military has been well underway for years. Hold the line on the minimum wage, and, for god's sake, get rid of the Environmental Protection Agency.

It's not quite that simple of course. In the current U.S. situation, the Federal Reserve has not fully followed the structural adjustment script. (It has taken steps to bring down unemployment that "inflation hawks" opposed.) And for some of the other policies, the process has not been smooth. There is resistance here and there—for example, the Chicago teachers' strike may slow the process of privatizing education in that city, some gains have been made on the minimum wage, and popular concerns about the environment have held back the destruction of environmental regulations. But the drumbeat for structural adjustment in the United States, for leaving things to the market, has not stopped.

In many other countries, structural adjustment has moved more rapidly, partly because of pressure from the Bank and IMF. But don't believe that they imposed these policies without support from elite groups within those countries. The elites were the beneficiaries of many structural adjustment policies. For example, with the privatization of government enterprises, they were able to take control of government assets at fire-sale prices. And "rationalizing" the labor market pushed down wages and shifted the distribution of income and power in favor of business owners. All the while, they could point their fingers at the IMF and the Bank, and say, "They made us do it."

U.S. elites have not had such a convenient scapegoat, and they have not been able to move ahead so rapidly—though the severe crisis of recent years and the slow recovery present a fine opportunity for more structural adjustment at home.

In resisting structural adjustment, people in the United States can learn from what happened during earlier rounds of structural adjustment elsewhere. Destruction of the environment in the Philippines. Devastation of the livelihoods of small farmers in Mexico. Rising inequality in many countries. And, by and large, sluggish economic growth in most structurally adjusted countries.

There have been many popular responses and some popular victories. In Bolivia in 2000, for example, a popular movement reversed the privatization of the water supply, which had been put in the hands of a multinational resource firm. In Ecuador, an indigenous peoples' movement emerged, opposing the depredation of the environment by oil companies and the government's imposition of austerity in 1999 and 2000 (at the behest of the IMF). In Mexico, structural adjustment (along with long-standing grievances) inspired the 1994 Zapatista uprising. Indeed, in many countries of Latin America, the debacles generated by structural adjustment in the 1980s have led to the election of progressive governments.

Good lessons for resistance right here at home. ❑

Article 4.7

OBAMA'S DOUBLE GAME ON OUTSOURCING

BY ROGER BYBEE
September/October 2012

A wickedly barbed Barack Obama TV ad features Mitt Romney croaking "America the Beautiful" while the camera pans over scenes of Bain Capital sending jobs to Mexico and China and Romney's use of tropical tax havens.

The ad, designed to define Mitt Romney as a job destroyer in the eyes of working-class voters in industrial states, has reportedly been effective. With 86% of Americans convinced that the offshoring of jobs contributes significantly to the nation's economic problems, the 2012 election's outcome may very well hinge on the perception of Obama as the defender of the public interest versus Romney the "vulture capitalist" and offshorer.

But is Obama's record much better? Obama has aggressively promoted a set of ew "free-trade" agreements that foster the shift of production from the United States to low-wage offshore sites—often in authoritarian nations denying basic labor rights. At the same time, these agreements directly and severely constrain democratically elected governments under an emerging doctrine of global corporate supremacy privileging maximum investor profits over protections for workers, consumers, and the environment. Instead of challenging the corporate prerogative to relocate family- and community-sustaining U.S. jobs to low-wage dictatorships, Obama has resorted to high-profile but hollow gestures.

About-Face on Trade Agreements

Since Obama took office, he has expressed ardent support for "free trade" agreements that provide the ground rules under which companies like Bain can generate such massive profits. Obama's backing for these agreements, modeled on the investor rights-centered North American Free Trade Agreement (NAFTA), directly contradicts his hard-hitting message in the 2008 presidential campaign. "Decades of trade deals like NAFTA and China have been signed with plenty of protections for corporations and their profits," he declared before GM workers in Janesville, Wisconsin, "but none for our environment or our workers who've seen factories shut their doors and millions of jobs disappear."

Despite his campaign rhetoric, Obama has championed George W. Bush-negotiated "free-trade" deals with labor-rights pariah Colombia, tax-haven Panama, and South Korea. Trade economist Robert Scott of the Economic Policy Institute (EPI) estimated that the South Korea deal alone will cost 159,000 U.S. workers their jobs. Union leaders also worry that the agreement will serve as a "funnel" for component parts produced under near-slavery conditions in North Korea and

China under a South Korean label, says Matt McKinnon, political director for the International Association fo Machinists and Aerospace Workers (IAMAW).

Meanwhile, the Obama administration is hammering out the biggest, farthest-reaching, and most secretive "free trade" deal ever, the Trans-Pacific Partnership (TPP). The TPP would include numerous nations on the Pacific Rim, including Australia, Brunei, Canada, Chile, Malaysia, Mexico, New Zealand, Peru, Singapore and Vietnam. U.S. Trade representatives have negotiated its terms under such an unusual level of secrecy, with only 600 corporate executives apprised of the content, that even pro-"free trade" members of Congress have complained about being excluded from the talks.

An analysis of leaked TPP documents led Public Citizen's Global Trade Watch to conclude in June that the deal would "extend the incentives for U.S. firms to offshore investment and jobs to lower-wage countries." The TPP would also create expanded powers for corporations to challenge—before secretive dispute resolution tribunals—protective regulations on finance, the environment, workplace safety, and other vital measures enacted by democratically elected governments.

Phantom "Insourcing"

Obama is promoting the notion of tax incentives for firms to "insource"—i.e., bring jobs back to the United States. Since last fall, he has been busy declaring that U.S.-based manufacturers are suddenly returning to America's shores. Obama has suggested that rising labor costs in China are a central factor in these decisions by U.S. firms.

The purported insourcing trend would be reinforced by substantial tax credits equalling 20% of the costs of relocating jobs back to America. There are fundamental problems with this model, under which "good firms" would be rewarded with taxpayer money, "bad" firms engaged in offshoring would be punished with the loss of tax credits, and U.S. workers would, presumably, benefit from a greater supply of family-supporting jobs.

For one thing, there is almost no evidence of a meaningful trend toward insourcing. EPI's Robert Scott told Dollars & Sense, "I have seen no evidence of this [insourcing] in our trade performance. The U.S. trade deficit [in goods] has risen much faster than the GDP the past three years," reaching $738.4 billion in goods for 2011. (The total deficit including services was $599.9 billion.)

Labor costs are rising in China, but not sharply enough to drive away U.S. companies, both EPI's Scott and University of Wisconsin labor economist Frank Emspak told Dollars & Sense. Chinese labor costs—starting from a base as low as 30 cents an hour—are climbing in the range of 5% to 30% per year, hardly enough to make a significant difference to the U.S. firms that have invested so heavily in China. For example, Milwaukee-based Johnson Controls has continued to expand rapidly in China, and now has no fewer than 60 plants there. General Electric recently shifted the headquarters of its medical equipment division from Wisconsin to Beijing.

Moreover, U.S.-based firms like Apple have developed intricate and effective supply chains in China. As global justice advocate Walden Bello has pointed out, "Chinese suppliers, with subsidies from the state, have established an unbeatable supply chain of contiguous factories, radically bringing down transport cost, enabling rapid assembly of an iPod or phone, and thus satisfying customers in a highly competitive market in record time."

In any case, since so many U.S.-based firms can legally avoid paying corporate income taxes, it is hard to imagine how sufficient incentives can be constructed, at least through tax credits alone, to influence their conduct. David Cay Johnston, tax expert and writer for Reuters, sees little hope that Obama's tax plans will yield more jobs in the United States, though they will likely produce a further windfall of tax benefits for the corporations. Scott of EPI agrees. "The corporations will use their ability to set up subsidiaries overseas, manipulate their prices and profits, and shift revenues," predicted Scott.

Labor's Response

AFL-CIO President Richard Trumka, frustrated with Democrats selling out labor, fumed last year that he'd had "a snootful of this shit." While he seems to be aware of the emptiness of Obama's pledges against the offshoring of jobs, Trumka is holding off on public criticism of the administration on volatile trade issues as we draw closer to the November election. Asked about the TPP, Trumka told Mike Elk of In These Times, "This president has been better on trade than the last several presidents. He has enforced the trade laws better than I think anybody else and done a good job at that. Do we disagree on some things? Absolutely we do.... We will continue to work with them."

But others in and around the labor movement view the current moment as our last chance to pressure Obama to step back from promoting the TPP and instead start taking effective action against offshoring. That is the stance adopted by the 5,000-member Association of Western Paper and Pulp Workers (AWPPW), which recently held a demonstration of several hundred outside an Obama fundraiser in Portland, Ore.

For many in labor, it's now-or-never. "Where is the sense of urgency that the TPP must be stopped?" demands Chris Townsend, political director of the United Electrical, Radio, and Machine Workers (UE). "It's an absurd moment when people in the Administration are saying that 'free trade' and the TPP will do anything but create more destruction."

John R. MacArthur, who detailed the Clinton administration's machinations for NAFTA in his 2001 book The Selling of Free Trade, sees close parallels between the manipulative strategies of Obama and Clinton on trade. While adopting a populist tone of concern about the fate of workers and the U.S. manufacturing base, they both remained committed to the "free trade" policies enriching their large donors. MacArthur points to the contributions pouring into Obama's campaign "from hedge-fund partners and law firms structuring deals based on 'free trade'."

While Obama has drawn criticism from Democrats close to Wall Street—Newark Mayor Cory Booker, former Pennsylvania Gov. Ed Rendell, and Massachusetts Gov. Deval Patrick—over his attacks on Bain Capital and the private equity industry as a whole, MacArthur regards this conflict as a mere "pantomime" to confer illusory populist credentials on Obama. "It helps to keep people ignorant," argues MacArthur, "about the push for free trade going on behind the scenes."

Not all of labor has been diverted by the pantomime. The critical "action behind the scenes" has riveted the attention of some unions like the UE and the APPW, whose leadership sees passivity on the TPP and offshoring as ultimately suicidal for workers. "These trade agreements have been the number one job killer for our members," the APPW's vice president, Greg Pallesen, told Dollars & Sense. "Our members have made it clear they are sick and tired of the trade agreements. If we don't take this moment to act and put pressure on the president, when will he listen?" ❑

Sources: Roger Bybee, "Offshoring and Obama," Z Magazine, July 2011; John Nichols, "Obama Talks Tough(er) on Trade to Win Wisconsin," TheNation.com blog, February 13, 2008; Public Citizen, "Controversial Trade Pact Text Leaked, Shows U.S. Trade Officials Have Agreed to Terms That Undermine Obama Domestic Agenda," citizen.org, June 13, 2012; John Nichols, "AFL's Trumka on Pols Selling Out Workers: 'I've Had a Snootful of This S**t!'," TheNation.com blog, June 11, 2011; Lynn Sweet, "Ten Giant U.S. Companies Avoiding Income Taxes," Chicago Sun-Times, March 27, 2011; John R. MacArthur, The Selling of Free Trade: NAFTA, Washington, and the Subversion of Democracy (Hill and Wang, 2000).

Chapter 5

LABOR IN THE INTERNATIONAL ECONOMY

Article 5.1

INTERNATIONAL LABOR STANDARDS

BY ARTHUR MacEWAN
September/October 2008

Dear Dr. Dollar:

U.S. activists have pushed to get foreign trade agreements to include higher labor standards. But then you hear that developing countries don't want that because cheaper labor without a lot of rules and regulations is what's helping them to bring industries in and build their economies. Is there a way to reconcile these views? Or are the activists just blind to the real needs of the countries they supposedly want to help?

—*Philip Bereaud, Swampscott, Mass.*

In 1971, General Emilio Medici, the then-military dictator of Brazil, commented on economic conditions in his country with the infamous line: "The economy is doing fine, but the people aren't."

Like General Medici, the government officials of many low-income countries today see the well-being of their economies in terms of overall output and the profits of firms—those profits that keep bringing in new investment, new industries that "build their economies." It is these officials who typically get to speak for their countries. When someone says that these countries "want" this or that—or "don't want" this or that—it is usually because the countries' officials have expressed this position.

Do we know what the people in these countries want? The people who work in the new, rapidly growing industries, in the mines and fields, and in the small shops and market stalls of low-income countries? Certainly they want better conditions—more to eat, better housing, security for their children, improved health and safety. The officials claim that to obtain these better conditions, they must "build their economies." But just because "the economy is doing fine" does not mean that the people are doing fine.

In fact, in many low-income countries, economic expansion comes along with severe inequality. The people who do the work are not getting a reasonable share of the rising national income (and are sometimes worse off even in absolute terms). Brazil in the early 1970s was a prime example and, in spite of major political change, remains a highly unequal country. Today, in both India and China, as in several other countries, economic growth is coming with increasingly severe inequality.

Workers in these countries struggle to improve their positions. They form—or try to form—independent unions. They demand higher wages and better working conditions. They struggle for political rights. It seems obvious that we should support those struggles, just as we support parallel struggles of workers in our own country. The first principle in supporting workers' struggles, here or anywhere else, is supporting their right to struggle—the right, in particular, to form independent unions without fear of reprisal. Indeed, in the ongoing controversy over the U.S.-Colombia Free Trade Agreement, the assassination of trade union leaders has rightly been a major issue.

Just how we offer our support—in particular, how we incorporate that support into trade agreements—is a complicated question. Pressure from abroad can help, but applying it is a complex process. A ban on goods produced with child labor, for example, could harm the most impoverished families that depend on children's earnings, or could force some children into worse forms of work (e.g., prostitution). On the other hand, using trade agreements to pressure governments to allow unhindered union organizing efforts by workers seems perfectly legitimate. When workers are denied the right to organize, their work is just one step up from slavery. Trade agreements can also be used to support a set of basic health and safety rights for workers. (Indeed, it might be useful if a few countries refused to enter into trade agreements with the United States until we improve workers' basic organizing rights and health and safety conditions in our own country!)

There is no doubt that the pressures that come through trade sanctions (restricting or banning commerce with another country) or simply from denying free access to the U.S. market can do immediate harm to workers and the general populace of low-income countries. Any struggle for change can generate short-run costs, but the long-run gains—even the hope of those gains—can make those costs acceptable. Consider, for example, the Apartheid-era trade sanctions against South Africa. To the extent that those sanctions were effective, some South African workers were deprived of employment. Nonetheless, the sanctions were widely supported by mass organizations in South Africa. Or note that when workers in this country strike or advocate a boycott of their company in an effort to obtain better conditions, they both lose income and run the risk that their employer will close up shop.

Efforts by people in this country to use trade agreements to raise labor standards in other countries should, whenever possible, take their lead from workers in those countries. It is up to them to decide what costs are acceptable. There are times, however, when popular forces are denied even basic rights to struggle. The best thing we can do, then, is to push for those rights—particularly the right to organize independent unions—that help create the opportunity for workers in poor countries to choose what to fight for. ❑

Article 5.2

CAMPUS STRUGGLES AGAINST SWEATSHOPS CONTINUE

Indonesian workers and U.S. students fight back against Adidas.

BY SARAH BLASKEY AND PHIL GASPER

September/October 2012

Abandoning his financially ailing factory in the Tangerang region of Indonesia, owner Jin Woo Kim fled the country for his home, South Korea, in January 2011 without leaving money to pay his workers. The factory, PT Kizone, stayed open for several months and then closed in financial ruin in April, leaving 2,700 workers with no jobs and owed $3.4 million of legally mandated severance pay.

In countries like Indonesia, with no unemployment insurance, severance pay is what keeps workers and their families from literal starvation. "The important thing is to be able to have rice. Maybe we add some chili pepper, some salt, if we can," explained an ex-Kizone worker, Marlina, in a report released by the Worker Rights Consortium (WRC), a U.S.-based labor-rights monitoring group, in May 2012. Marlina, widowed mother of two, worked at PT Kizone for eleven years before the factory closed. She needs the severance payment in order to pay her son's high school registration fee and monthly tuition, and to make important repairs to her house.

When the owner fled, the responsibility for severance payments to PT Kizone workers fell on the companies that sourced from the factory—Adidas, Nike, and the Dallas Cowboys. Within a year, both Nike and the Dallas Cowboys made severance payments that they claim are proportional to the size of their orders from the factory, around $1.5 million total. But Adidas has refused to pay any of the $1.8 million still owed to workers.

Workers in PT Kizone factory mainly produced athletic clothing sold to hundreds of universities throughout the United States. All collegiate licensees like Adidas and Nike sign contracts with the universities that buy their apparel. At least 180 universities around the nation are affiliated with the WRC and have licensing contracts mandating that brands pay "all applicable back wages found due to workers who manufactured the licensed articles." If wages or severance pay are not paid to workers that produce university goods, then the school has the right to terminate the contract.

Using the language in these contracts, activists on these campuses coordinate nationwide divestment campaigns to pressure brands like Adidas to uphold previously unenforceable labor codes of conduct.

Unpaid back wages and benefits are a major problem in the garment industry. Apparel brands rarely own factories. Rather, they contract with independent manufacturers all over the world to produce their wares. When a factory closes for any reason, a brand can simply take its business somewhere else and wash its hands of any responsibilities to the fired workers.

Brands like Nike and Russell have lost millions of dollars when, pressed by United Students Against Sweatshops (USAS), universities haver terminated their contracts. According to the USAS website, campus activism has forced Nike to pay severance and Russell to rehire over 1,000 workers it had laid off, in order to avoid losing more collegiate contracts. Now many college activists have their sights set on Adidas.

At the University of Wisconsin (UW) in Madison, the USAS-affiliated Student Labor Action Coalition (SLAC) and sympathetic faculty are in the middle of a more than year-long campaign to pressure the school to terminate its contract with Adidas in solidarity with the PT Kizone workers.

The chair of UW's Labor Licensing Policy Committee (LLPC) says that Adidas is in violation of the code of conduct for the school's licensees. Even the university's senior counsel, Brian Vaughn, stated publicly at a June LLPC meeting that Adidas is "in breach of the contract based on its failure to adhere to the standards of the labor code." But despite the fact that Vaughn claimed at the time that the University's "two overriding goals are to get money back in the hands of the workers and to maintain the integrity of the labor code," the administration has dragged its feet in responding to Adidas.

Instead of putting the company on notice for potential contract termination and giving it a deadline to meet its obligations as recommended by the LLPC, UW entered into months of fruitless negotiations with Adidas in spring of 2012. In July, when these negotiations had led nowhere, UW's interim chancellor David Ward asked a state court to decide whether or not Adidas had violated the contract (despite the senior counsel's earlier public admission that it had). This process will delay a decision for many more months--perhaps years if there are appeals.

Since the Adidas campaign's inception in the fall of 2011, SLAC members have actively opposed the school's cautious approach, calling both the mediation process and the current court action a "stalling tactic" by the UW administration and Adidas to avoid responsibility to the PT Kizone workers. In response, student organizers planned everything from frequent letter deliveries to campus administrators, to petition drives, teach-ins, and even a banner drop from the administration building that over 300 people attended, all in hopes of pressuring the chancellor (who ultimately has the final say in the matter) to cut the contract with Adidas.

While the administration claims that it is moving slowly to avoid being sued by Adidas, it is also getting considerable pressure from its powerful athletics director, Barry Alvarez, to continue its contract with Adidas. As part of the deal, UW's sports programs receive royalties and sports gear worth about $2.5 million every year.

"Just look at the money—what we lose and what it would cost us," Alvarez told the *Wisconsin State Journal*, even though other major brands would certainly jump at the opportunity to replace Adidas. "We have four building projects going on. It could hurt recruiting. There's a trickle-down effect that would be devastating to our whole athletic program."

But Tina Treviño-Murphy, a student activist with SLAC, rejects this logic. "A strong athletics department shouldn't have to be built on a foundation of stolen labor," she told Dollars & Sense. "Our department and our students deserve better.".

Adidas is now facing pressure from both campus activists in the United States and the workers in Indonesia--including sit-ins by the latter at the German and British embassies in Jakarta. (Adidas' world headquarters are in Germany, and the company sponsored the recent London Olympics.) This led to a meeting between their union and an Adidas representative, who refused to admit responsibility but instead offered food vouchers to some of the workers. The offer amounted to a tiny fraction of the owed severance and was rejected as insulting by former Kizone workers.

In the face of intransigence from university administrations and multinational companies prepared to shift production quickly from one location to another to stay one step ahead of labor-rights monitors, campus activism to fight sweatshops can seem like a labor of Sisyphus. After more than a decade of organizing, a recent fundraising appeal from USAS noted that "today sweatshop conditions are worse than ever."

Brands threaten to pull out of particular factories if labor costs rise, encouraging a work environment characterized by "forced overtime, physical and sexual harassment, and extreme anti-union intimidation, even death threats," says Natalie Yoon, a USAS member who recently participated in a delegation to factories in Honduras and El Salvador.

According to Snehal Shingavi, a professor at the University of Texas, Austin who was a USAS activist at Berkeley for many years, finding ways to build links with the struggles of the affected workers is key. "What I think would help the campaign the most is if there were actually more sustained and engaged connections between students here and workers who are in factories who are facing these conditions," Shingavi told Dollars & Sense. Ultimately, he said, only workers' self-activity can "make the kind of changes that I think we all want, which is an end to exploitative working conditions."

But in the meantime, even small victories are important. Anti-sweatshop activists around the country received a boost in September, when Cornell University President David Skorton announced that his school was ending its licensing contract with Adidas effective October 1, because of the company's failure to pay severance to PT Kizone workers. The announcement followed a sustained campaign by the Sweatfree Cornell Coalition, leading up to a "study in" at the president's office. While the contract itself was small, USAS described the decision as the "first domino," which may lead other campuses to follow suit. Shortly afterwards, Oberlin College in Ohio told Adidas that it would not renew its current four-year contract with the company if the workers in Indonesia are not paid severance.

Perhaps just as significant are the lessons that some activists are drawing from these campaigns. "The people who have a lot of power are going to want to keep that power and the only way to make people give some of that up is if we make them," Treviño-Murphy said. "So it's really pressure from below, grassroots organizing, that makes the difference. We see that every day in SLAC and I think it teaches us to be not just better students but better citizens who will stand up to fight injustice every time." ❑

Sources: Worker Rights Consortium, "Status Update Re: PT Kizone (Indonesia)," May 15, 2012 (workersrights.org); Andy Baggot, "Alvarez Anxiously Awaits Adidas Decision," Wisconsin State Journal, July 13, 2012 (host.madison.com); United Students Against Sweatshops (usas.org), PT Kizone update, June 15, 2012 (cleanclothes.org/urgent-actions/kizoneupdate).

Article 5.3

NIKE TO THE RESCUE?

Africa needs better jobs, not sweatshops.

BY JOHN MILLER
September/October 2006

"In Praise of the Maligned Sweatshop"
WINDHOEK, Namibia—Africa desperately needs Western help in the form of schools, clinics and sweatshops.

On a street here in the capital of Namibia, in the southwestern corner of Africa, I spoke to a group of young men who were trying to get hired as day laborers on construction sites.

"I come here every day," said Naftal Shaanika, a 20-year-old. "I actually find work only about once a week."

Mr. Shaanika and the other young men noted that the construction jobs were dangerous and arduous, and that they would vastly prefer steady jobs in, yes, sweatshops. Sure, sweatshop work is tedious, grueling and sometimes dangerous. But over all, sewing clothes is considerably less dangerous or arduous—or sweaty—than most alternatives in poor countries.

Well-meaning American university students regularly campaign against sweatshops. But instead, anyone who cares about fighting poverty should campaign in favor of sweatshops, demanding that companies set up factories in Africa.

The problem is that it's still costly to manufacture in Africa. The headaches across much of the continent include red tape, corruption, political instability, unreliable electricity and ports, and an inexperienced labor force that leads to low productivity and quality. The anti-sweatshop movement isn't a prime obstacle, but it's one more reason not to manufacture in Africa.

Imagine that a Nike vice president proposed manufacturing cheap T-shirts in Ethiopia. The boss would reply: "You're crazy! We'd be boycotted on every campus in the country."

Some of those who campaign against sweatshops respond to my arguments by noting that they aren't against factories in Africa, but only demand a "living wage" in them. After all, if labor costs amount to only $1 per shirt, then doubling wages would barely make a difference in the final cost.

One problem … is that it already isn't profitable to pay respectable salaries, and so any pressure to raise them becomes one more reason to avoid Africa altogether.

One of the best U.S. initiatives in Africa has been the African Growth and Opportunity Act, which allows duty-free imports from Africa—and thus has stimulated manufacturing there.

—Op-ed by Nicholas Kristof, *New York Times*, June 6, 2006

Nicholas Kristof has been beating the pro-sweatshop drum for quite a while. Shortly after the East Asian financial crisis of the late 1990s, Kristof, the Pulitzer Prize-winning journalist and now columnist for the *New York Times*, reported the story of an Indonesian recycler who, picking through the metal scraps of a garbage dump, dreamed that her son would grow up to be a sweatshop worker. Then, in 2000, Kristof and his wife, *Times* reporter Sheryl WuDunn, published "Two Cheers for Sweatshops" in the *Times Magazine*. In 2002, Kristof's column advised G-8 leaders to "start an international campaign to promote imports from sweatshops, perhaps with bold labels depicting an unrecognizable flag and the words 'Proudly Made in a Third World Sweatshop.'"

Now Kristof laments that too few poor, young African men have the opportunity to enter the satanic mill of sweatshop employment. Like his earlier efforts, Kristof's latest pro-sweatshop ditty synthesizes plenty of half-truths. Let's take a closer look and see why there is still no reason to give it up for sweatshops.

A Better Alternative?

It is hardly surprising that young men on the streets of Namibia's capital might find sweatshop jobs more appealing than irregular work as day laborers on construction sites.

The alternative jobs available to sweatshop workers are often worse and, as Kristof loves to point out, usually involve more sweating than those in world export factories. Most poor people in the developing world eke out their livelihoods from subsistence agriculture or by plying petty trades. Others on the edge of urban centers work as street-hawkers or hold other jobs in the informal sector. As economist Arthur MacEwan wrote a few years back in *Dollars & Sense*, in a poor country like Indonesia, where women working in manufacturing earn five times as much as those in agriculture, sweatshops have no trouble finding workers.

But let's be clear about a few things. First, export factory jobs, especially in labor-intensive industries, often are just "a ticket to slightly less impoverishment," as even economist and sweatshop defender Jagdish Bhagwati allows.

Beyond that, these jobs seldom go to those without work or to the poorest of the poor. One study by sociologist Kurt Ver Beek showed that 60% of first-time Honduran *maquila* workers were previously employed. Typically they were not destitute, and they were better educated than most Hondurans.

Sweatshops don't just fail to rescue people from poverty. Setting up export factories where workers have few job alternatives has actually been a recipe for serious worker abuse. In *Beyond Sweatshops*, a book arguing for the benefits of direct foreign investment in the developing world, Brookings Institution economist Theodore Moran recounts the disastrous decision of the Philippine government to build the Bataan Export Processing Zone in an isolated mountainous area to lure foreign investors with the prospect of cheap labor. With few alternatives, Filipinos took jobs in the garment factories that sprung up in the zone. The manufacturers typically paid less than the minimum wage and forced employees to work overtime in factories filled with dust and fumes. Fed up, the workers eventually mounted a series of crippling strikes. Many factories shut down and occupancy rates in the zone plummeted, as did the value of exports, which declined by more than half between 1980 and 1986.

Kristof's argument is no excuse for sweatshop abuse: that conditions are worse elsewhere does nothing to alleviate the suffering of workers in export factories. They are often denied the right to organize, subjected to unsafe working conditions and to verbal, physical, and sexual abuse, forced to work overtime, coerced into pregnancy tests and even abortions, and paid less than a living wage. It remains useful and important to combat these conditions even if alternative jobs are worse yet.

The fact that young men in Namibia find sweatshop jobs appealing testifies to how harsh conditions are for workers in Africa, not the desirability of export factory employment.

Oddly, Kristof's desire to introduce new sweatshops to sub-Saharan Africa finds no support in the African Growth and Opportunity Act (AGOA) that he praises. The Act grants sub-Saharan apparel manufacturers preferential access to U.S. markets. But shortly after its passage, U.S. Trade Representative Robert Zoellick assured the press that the AGOA would not create sweatshops in Africa because it requires protective standards for workers consistent with those set by the International Labor Organization.

Antisweatshop Activism and Jobs

Kristof is convinced that the antisweatshop movement hurts the very workers it intends to help. His position has a certain seductive logic to it. As anyone who has suffered through introductory economics will tell you, holding everything else the same, a labor standard that forces multinational corporations and their subcontractors to boost wages should result in their hiring fewer workers.

But in practice does it? The only evidence Kristof produces is an imaginary conversation in which a boss incredulously refuses a Nike vice president's proposal to open a factory in Ethiopia paying wages of 25 cents a hour: "You're crazy! We'd be boycotted on every campus in the country."

While Kristof has an active imagination, there are some things wrong with this conversation.

First off, the antisweatshop movement seldom initiates boycotts. An organizer with United Students Against Sweatshops (USAS) responded on Kristof's blog: "We never call for apparel boycotts unless we are explicitly asked to by workers at a particular factory. This is, of course, exceedingly rare, because, as you so persuasively argued, people generally want to be employed." The National Labor Committee, the largest antisweatshop organization in the United States, takes the same position.

Moreover, when economists Ann Harrison and Jason Scorse conducted a systematic study of the effects of the antisweatshop movement on factory employment, they found no negative employment effect. Harrison and Scorse looked at Indonesia, where Nike was one of the targets of an energetic campaign calling for better wages and working conditions among the country's subcontractors. Their statistical analysis found that the antisweatshop campaign was responsible for 20% of the increase in the real wages of unskilled workers in factories exporting textiles, footwear, and apparel from 1991 to 1996. Harrison and Scorse also found that "antisweatshop activism did not have significant adverse effects on employment" in these sectors.

Campaigns for higher wages are unlikely to destroy jobs because, for multinationals and their subcontractors, wages make up a small portion of their overall costs. Even Kristof accepts this point, well documented by economists opposed to sweatshop labor. In Mexico's apparel industry, for instance, economists Robert Pollin, James Heintz, and Justine Burns from the Political Economy Research Institute found that doubling the pay of nonsupervisory workers would add just $1.80 to the production cost of a $100 men's sports jacket. A recent survey by the National Bureau of Economic Research found that U.S. consumers would be willing to pay $115 for the same jacket if they knew that it had not been made under sweatshop conditions.

Globalization in Sub-Saharan Africa

Kristof is right that Africa, especially sub-Saharan Africa, has lost out in the globalization process. Sub-Saharan Africa suffers from slower growth, less direct foreign investment, lower education levels, and higher poverty rates than most every other part of the world. A stunning 37 of the region's 47 countries are classified as "low-income" by the World Bank, each with a gross national income less than $825 per person. Many countries in the region bear the burdens of high external debt and a crippling HIV crisis that Kristof has made heroic efforts to bring to the world's attention.

But have multinational corporations avoided investing in sub-Saharan Africa because labor costs are too high? While labor costs in South Africa and Mauritius are high, those in the other countries of the region are modest by international standards, and quite low in some cases. Take Lesotho, the largest exporter of apparel from sub-Saharan Africa to the United States. In the country's factories that subcontract with Wal-Mart, the predominantly female workforce earns an average of just $54 a month. That's below the United Nations poverty line of $2 per day, and it includes regular forced overtime. In Madagascar, the region's third largest exporter of clothes to the United States, wages in the apparel industry are just 33 cents per hour, lower than those in China and among the lowest in the world. And at Ramatex Textile, the large Malaysian-owned textile factory in Namibia, workers only earn about $100 per month according to the Labour Resource and Research Institute in Windhoek. Most workers share their limited incomes with extended families and children, and they walk long distances to work because they can't afford better transportation.

On the other hand, recent experience shows that sub-Saharan countries with decent labor standards *can* develop strong manufacturing export sectors. In the late 1990s, Francis Teal of Oxford's Centre for the Study of African Economies compared Mauritius's successful export industries with Ghana's unsuccessful ones. Teal found that workers in Mauritius earned ten times as much as those in Ghana—$384 a month in Mauritius as opposed to $36 in Ghana. Mauritius's textile and garment industry remained competitive because its workforce was better educated and far more productive than Ghana's. Despite paying poverty wages, the Ghanaian factories floundered.

Kristof knows full well the real reason garment factories in the region are shutting down: the expiration of the Multifiber Agreement last January [2008]. The agreement, which set national export quotas for clothing and textiles, protected the garment industries in smaller countries around the world from direct competition with China. Now China and, to a lesser degree, India, are increasingly displacing other garment producers. In this new context, lower wages alone are unlikely to sustain the sub-Saharan garment industry. Industry sources report that sub-Saharan Africa suffers from several other drawbacks as an apparel producer, including relatively high utility and transportation costs and long shipping times to the United States. The region also has lower productivity and less skilled labor than Asia, and it has fewer sources of cotton yarn and higher-priced fabrics than China and India.

If Kristof is hell-bent on expanding the sub-Saharan apparel industry, he would do better to call for sub-Saharan economies to gain unrestricted access to the Quad markets—the United States, Canada, Japan, and Europe. Economists Stephen N. Karingi, Romain Perez, and Hakim Ben Hammouda estimate that the welfare gains associated with unrestricted market access could amount to $1.2 billion in sub-Saharan Africa, favoring primarily unskilled workers.

But why insist on apparel production in the first place? Namibia has sources of wealth besides a cheap labor pool for Nike's sewing machines. The *Economist* reports that Namibia is a world-class producer of two mineral products: diamonds (the country ranks seventh by value) and uranium (it ranks fifth by volume). The mining industry is the heart of Namibia's export economy and accounts for about 20% of the country's GDP. But turning the mining sector into a vehicle for national economic development would mean confronting the foreign corporations that control the diamond industry, such as the South African De Beers Corporation. That is a tougher assignment than scapegoating antisweatshop activists.

More and Better African Jobs

So why have multinational corporations avoided investing in sub-Saharan Africa? The answer, according to international trade economist Dani Rodrik, is "entirely due to the slow growth" of the sub-Saharan economies. Rodrik estimates that the region participates in international trade as much as can be expected given its economies' income levels, country size, and geography.

Rodrik's analysis suggests that the best thing to do for poor workers in Africa would be to lift the debt burdens on their governments and support their efforts to build functional economies. That means investing in human resources and physical infrastructure, and implementing credible macroeconomic policies that put job creation first. But these investments, as Rodrik points out, take time.

In the meantime, international policies establishing a floor for wages and safe-guards for workers across the globe would do more for the young men on Windhoek's street corners than subjecting them to sweatshop abuse, because grinding poverty leaves people willing to enter into any number of desperate exchanges. And if Namibia is closing its garment factories because Chinese imports are cheaper, isn't that an argument for trying to improve labor standards in China, not lower them in sub-Saharan Africa? Abusive labor practices are rife in China's export factories, as the National Labor Committee and *BusinessWeek* have documented. Workers put in 13- to 16-hour days, seven days a week. They enjoy little to no health and safety enforcement, and their take-home pay falls below the minimum wage after the fines and deductions their employers sometimes withhold.

Spreading these abuses in sub-Saharan Africa will not empower workers there. Instead it will take advantage of the fact that they are among the most marginalized workers in the world. Debt relief, international labor standards, and public investments in education and infrastructure are surely better ways to fight African poverty than Kristof's sweatshop proposal. ❑

Sources: Arthur MacEwan, "Ask Dr. Dollar," *Dollars & Sense*, Sept–Oct 1998; John Miller, "Why Economists Are Wrong About Sweatshops and the Antisweatshop Movement," *Challenge*, Jan–Feb 2003; R. Pollin, J. Burns, and J. Heintz, "Global Apparel Production and Sweatshop Labor: Can Raising Retail Prices Finance Living Wages?" Political Economy Research Institute, Working Paper 19, DATE; N. Kristof, "In Praise of the Maligned Sweatshop,"*New York Times*, June 6, 2006; N. Kristof, "Let Them Sweat," *NYT* , June 25, 2002; N. Kristof, "Two Cheers for Sweatshops," *NYT* , Sept 24, 2000; N. Kristof, "Asia'[s Crisis Upsets Rising Effort to Confront Blight of Sweatshops," *NYT*, June 15, 1998; A. Harrison and J. Scorse, "Improving the Conditions of Workers? Minimum Wage Legislation and Anti-Sweatshop Activism," *Calif. Management Review*, Oct 2005; Herbert Jauch, "Africa's Clothing and Textile Industry: The Case of Ramatex in Namibia," in *The Future of the Textile and Clothing Industry in Sub-Saharan Africa*, ed. H. Jauch and R. Traub-Merz (Friedrich-Ebert-Stiftung, 2006); Kurt Alan Ver Beek, "Maquiladoras: Exploitation or Emancipation? An Overview of the Situation of Maquiladora Workers in Honduras," *World Development*, 29(9), 2001; Theodore Moran, *Beyond Sweatshops: Foreign Direct Investment and Globalization in Developing Countries* (Brookings Institution Press, 2002); "Comparative Assessment of the Competitiveness of the Textile and Apparel Sector in Selected Countries," in *Textiles and Apparel: Assessment of the Competitiveness of Certain Foreign Suppliers to the United States Market*, Vol. 1, U.S. International Trade Commission, Jan 2004; S. N. Karingi, R. Perez, and H. Ben Hammouda, "Could Extended Preferences Reward Sub-Saharan Africa's Participation in the Doha Round Negotiations?," *World Economy*, 2006; Francis Teal, "Why Can Mauritius Export Manufactures and Ghana Can Not?," *The World Economy*, 22 (7), 1999; Dani Rodrik, "Trade Policy and Economic Performance in Sub-Saharan Africa," Paper prepared for the Swedish Ministry for Foreign Affairs, Nov 1997.

Article 5.4

OUTSIZED OFFSHORE OUTSOURCING

The scope of offshore outsourcing gives some economists and the business press the heebie-jeebies.

BY JOHN MILLER
September/October 2007

At a press conference introducing the 2004 *Economic Report of the President*, N. Gregory Mankiw, then head of President Bush's Council of Economic Advisors, assured the press that "Outsourcing is probably a plus for the economy in the long run [and] just a new way of doing international trade."

Mankiw's comments were nothing other than mainstream economics, as even Democratic Party-linked economists confirmed. For instance Janet Yellen, President Clinton's chief economist, told the *Wall Street Journal*, "In the long run, outsourcing is another form of trade that benefits the U.S. economy by giving us cheaper ways to do things." Nonetheless, Mankiw's assurances were met with derision from those uninitiated in the economics profession's free-market ideology. Sen. John Edwards (D-N.C.) asked, "What planet do they live on?" Even Republican House Speaker Dennis Hastert (Ill.) said that Mankiw's theory "fails a basic test of real economics."

Mankiw now jokes that "if the American Economic Association were to give an award for the Most Politically Inept Paraphrasing of Adam Smith, I would be a leading candidate." But he quickly adds, "the recent furor about outsourcing, and my injudiciously worded comments about the benefits of international trade, should not eclipse the basic lessons that economists have understood for more than two centuries."

In fact Adam Smith never said any such thing about international trade. In response to the way Mankiw and other economists distort Smith's writings, economist Michael Meeropol took a close look at what Smith actually said; he found that Smith used his invisible hand argument to favor domestic investment over far-flung, hard-to-supervise foreign investments. Here are Smith's words in his 1776 masterpiece, *The Wealth of Nations*:

> By preferring the support of domestic to that of foreign industry, he [the investor] intends only his own security; and by directing that industry in such a manner as its produce may be of the greatest value, he intends only his own gain, and he is in this, as in many other cases, led by an invisible hand to promote an end, which was no part of his intention.

Outsized offshore outsourcing, the shipping of jobs overseas to take advantage of low wages, has forced some mainstream economists and some elements of the business press to have second thoughts about "free trade." Many are convinced that the painful transition costs that hit before outsourcing produces any ultimate benefits may be the biggest political issue in economics for a generation. And some recognize, as Smith did, that there is no guarantee unfettered international trade will leave the participants better off even in the long run.

Keynes's Revenge

Writing during the Great Depression of the 1930s, John Maynard Keynes, the pre-eminent economist of the twentieth century, prescribed government spending as a means of compensating for the instability of private investment. The notion of a mixed private/government economy, Keynes's prosthesis for the invisible hand of the market, guided U.S. economic policy from the 1940s through the 1970s.

It is only fitting that Paul Samuelson, the first Nobel Laureate in economics, and whose textbook introduced U.S. readers to Keynes, would be among the first mainstream economist to question whether unfettered international trade, in the context of massive outsourcing, would necessarily leave a developed economy such as that of the United States better off—even in the long run. In an influential 2004 article, Samuelson characterized the common economics wisdom about outsourcing and international trade this way:

> Yes, good jobs may be lost here in the short run. But ...the gains of the winners
> from free trade, properly measured, work out to exceed the losses of the losers. ...
> Never forget to tally the real gains of consumers alongside admitted possible
> losses of some producers. ... The gains of the American winners are big enough
> to more than compensate the losers.

Samuelson took on this view, arguing that this common wisdom is "dead wrong about [the] *necessary* surplus of winning over losing" [emphasis in the original]. In a rather technical paper, he demonstrated that free trade globalization can sometimes give rise to a situation in which "a productivity gain in one country can benefit that

---

Offshored? Outsourced? Confused?

The terms "offshoring" and "outsourcing" are often used interchangeably, but they refer to distinct processes:

Outsourcing—When a company hires another company to carry out a business function that it no longer wants to carry on in-house. The company that is hired may be in the same city or across the globe; it may be a historically independent firm or a spinoff of the first company created specifically to outsource a particular function.

Offshoring or *Offshore Outsourcing*—When a company shifts a portion of its business operation abroad. An offshore operation may be carried out by the same company or, more typically, outsourced to a different one.

country alone, while permanently hurting the other country by reducing the gains from trade that are possible between the two countries."

Many in the economics profession do admit that it is hard to gauge whether intensified offshoring of U.S. jobs in the context of free-trade globalization will give more in winnings to the winners than it takes in losses from the losers. "Nobody has a clue about what the numbers are," as Robert C. Feenstra, a prominent trade economist, told *BusinessWeek* at the time.

The empirical issues that will determine whether offshore outsourcing ultimately delivers, on balance, more benefits than costs, and to whom those benefits and costs will accrue, are myriad. First, how wide a swath of white-collar workers will see their wages reduced by competition from the cheap, highly skilled workers who are now becoming available around the world? Second, by how much will their wages drop? Third, will the U.S. workers thrown into the global labor pool end up losing more in lower wages than they gain in lower consumer prices? In that case, the benefits of increased trade would go overwhelmingly to employers. But even employers might lose out depending on the answer to a fourth question: Will cheap labor from abroad allow foreign employers to out-compete U.S. employers, driving down the prices of their products and lowering U.S. export earnings? In that case, not only workers, but the corporations that employ them as well, could end up worse off.

Bigger Than A Box

Another mainstream Keynesian economist, Alan Blinder, former Clinton economic advisor and vice-chair of the Federal Reserve Board, doubts that outsourcing will be "immiserating" in the long run and still calls himself "a free-trader down to his toes." But Blinder is convinced that the transition costs will be large, lengthy, and painful before the United States experiences a net gain from outsourcing. Here is why.

First, rapid improvements in information and communications technology have rendered obsolete the traditional notion that manufactured goods, which can generally be boxed and shipped, are tradable, while services, which cannot be boxed, are not. And the workers who perform the services that computers and satellites have now rendered tradable will increasingly be found offshore, especially when they are skilled and will work for lower wages.

Second, another 1.5 billion or so workers—many in China, India, and the former Soviet bloc—are now part of the world economy. While most are low-skilled

---

Attributes of Jobs Outsourced

- No Face-to-Face Customer Servicing Requirement
- High Information Content
- Work Process is Telecommutable and Internet Enabled
- High Wage Differential with Similar Occupation in Destination Country
- Low Setup Barriers
- Low Social Networking Requirement

workers, some are not; and as Blinder says, a small percentage of 1.5 billion is none-theless "a lot of willing and able people available to do the jobs that technology will move offshore." And as China and India educate more workers, offshoring of high-skill work will accelerate.

Third, the transition will be particularly painful in the United States because the U.S. unemployment insurance program is stingy, at least by first-world stan-dards, and because U.S. workers who lose their jobs often lose their health insurance and pension rights as well.

How large will the transition cost be? "Thirty million to 40 million U.S. jobs are potentially offshorable," according to Blinder's latest estimates. "These include scientists, mathematicians and editors on the high end and telephone operators, clerks and typists on the low end."

Blinder arrived at these figures by creating an index that identifies how easy or hard it will be for a job to be physically or electronically "offshored." He then used the index to assess the Bureau of Labor Statistics' 817 U.S. occupational categories. Not surprisingly, Blinder classifies almost all of the 14.3 million U.S. manufactur-ing jobs as offshorable. But he also classifies more than twice that many U.S. service sector jobs as offshorable, including most computer industry jobs as well as many others, for instance, the 12,470 U.S. economists and the 23,790 U.S. multimedia artists and animators. In total, Blinder's analysis suggests that 22% to 29% of the jobs held by U.S. workers in 2004 will be potentially offshorable within a decade or two, with nearly 8.2 million jobs in 59 occupations "highly offshorable." Table 1 provides a list of the broad occupational categories with 300,000 or more workers that Blinder considers potentially offshorable.

Mankiw dismissed Blinder's estimates of the number of jobs at risk to offshor-ing as "out of the mainstream." Indeed, Blinder's estimates are considerably larger than earlier ones. But these earlier studies either aim to measure the number of U.S. jobs that will be outsourced (as opposed to the number at risk of being outsourced), look at a shorter period of time, or have shortcomings that suggest they underes-timate the number of U.S. jobs threatened by outsourcing. (See sidebar, "Studying the Studies," pp. 148-9.)

Global Arbitrage

Low wages are the reason U.S. corporations outsource labor. Table 2 shows just how large the international wage differentials were for computer programmers in 2002. Programmers in the United States make wages nearly *ten times* those of their coun-terparts in India and the Philippines, for example.

Today, more and more white-collar workers in the United States are finding themselves in direct competition with the low-cost, well-trained, highly educated workers in Bangalore, Shanghai, and Eastern and Central Europe. These workers often use the same capital and technology and are no less productive than the U.S. workers they replace. They just get paid less.

TABLE 1: MAJOR OCCUPATIONS RANKED BY OFFSHORABILITY

Occupation	Category	Index Number	Number of Workers
Computer programmers	I	100	389,090
Telemarketers	I	95	400,860
Computer systems analysts	I	93	492,120
Billing and posting clerks and machine operators	I	90	513,020
Bookkeeping, accounting, and auditing clerks	I	84	1,815,340
Computer support specialists	I and II	92/68	499,860
Computer software engineers: Applications	II	74	455,980
Computer software engineers: Systems software	II	74	320,720
Accountants	II	72	591,311
Welders, cutters, solderers, and brazers	II	70	358,050
Helpers—production workers	II	70	528,610
First-line supervisors/managers of production and operating workers	II	68	679,930
Packaging and filling machine operators and tenders	II	68	396,270
Team assemblers	II	65	1,242,370
Bill and account collectors	II	65	431,280
Machinists	II	61	368,380
Inspectors, testers, sorters, samplers, and weighers	II	60	506,160
General and operations managers	III	55	1,663,810
Stock clerks and order fillers	III	34	1,625,430
Shipping, receiving, and traffic clerks	III	29	759,910
Sales managers	III	26	317,970
Business operations specialists, all other	IV	25	916,290

Source: Alan Blinder, "How Many U.S. Jobs Might Be Offshorable?" *CEPS Working Paper* #142, March 2007, figures from Bureau of Labor Statistics and author's judgments.

This global labor arbitrage, as Morgan Stanley's chief economist Stephen Roach calls it, has narrowed international wage disparities in manufacturing, and now in services too, by unrelentingly pushing U.S. wages down toward international norms. ("Arbitrage" refers to transactions that yield a profit by taking advantage of a price differential for the same asset in different locations. Here, of course, the "asset" is wage labor of a certain skill level.) A sign of that pressure: about 70% of laid-off workers in the United States earn less three years later than they did at the time of the layoff; on average, those reemployed earn 10% less than they did before.

And it's not only laid-off workers who are hurt. A study conducted by Harvard labor economists Lawrence F. Katz, Richard B. Freeman, and George J. Borjas finds that every other worker with skills similar to those who were displaced also loses out. Every 1% drop in employment due to imports or factories gone abroad shaves 0.5% off the wages of the remaining workers in that occupation, they conclude.

Global labor arbitrage also goes a long way toward explaining the poor quality and low pay of the jobs the U.S. economy has created this decade, according to Roach. By dampening wage increases for an ever wider swath of the U.S. workforce, he argues, outsourcing has helped to drive a wedge between productivity gains and wage gains and to widen inequality in the United States. In the first four years of this decade, nonfarm productivity in the United States has recorded a cumulative increase of 13.3%—more than double the 5.9% rise in real compensation per hour over the same period. ("Compensation" includes wages, which have been stagnant for the average worker, plus employer spending on fringe benefits such as health insurance, which has risen even as, in many instances, the actual benefits have been cut back.) Roach reports that the disconnect between pay and productivity growth during the current

TABLE 2: AVERAGE SALARIES OF PROGRAMMERS

Country	Salary Range
Poland and Hungary	$4,800 to $8,000
India	$5,880 to $11,000
Philippines	$6,564
Malaysia	$7,200
Russian Federation	$5,000 to $7,500
China	$8,952
Canada	$28,174
Ireland	$23,000 to $34,000
Israel	$15,000 to $38,000
USA	$60,000 to $80,000

Source: CIO magazine, November 2002, from Merrill Lynch Smart Access Survey.

economic expansion has been much greater in services than in manufacturing, as that sector weathers the powerful forces of global labor arbitrage for the first time.

Doubts in the Business Press?!

Even in the business press, doubts that offshore outsourcing willy-nilly leads to economic improvement have become more acute. Earlier this summer, a *BusinessWeek* cover story, "The Real Cost of Offshoring," reported that government statistics have underestimated the damage to the U.S. economy from offshore outsourcing. The

---

Studying the Studies

When economist Alan Blinder raised alarm bells in 2006 about the potentially large-scale offshoring of U.S. jobs, his results were inevitably compared to earlier research on offshore outsourcing. Three studies have been especially influential. The 2002 study (revised in 2004) by Forrester Research, a private, for-profit market research firm, which estimated that 3.3 million U.S. service sector jobs would move offshore by 2015, caused perhaps the biggest media stir. It was picked up by BusinessWeek and the Wall Street Journal, and hyped by Lou Dobbs, the CNN business-news anchor and outspoken critic of offshoring.

Forrester researcher John McCarthy developed his estimate by poring over newspaper clippings and Labor Department statistics on 505 white-collar occupations and then making an educated guess about how many jobs would be shipped offshore by 2015.

The Forrester study projects actual offshoring, not the number of jobs at risk of offshoring, so its estimate is rightfully lower than Blinder's. But the ample possibilities for technological change between now and 2015 convince Blinder that the Forrester estimate is nonetheless too low.

A 2003 study by University of California economists Ashok Bardhan and Cynthia Kroll estimated that about 11% of all U.S. jobs in 2001 were vulnerable to offshoring. Bradhan and Kroll applied the "outsourceability attributes" listed in "Attributes of Jobs Outsourced" to occupations where at least some outsourcing either has already taken place or is being planned.

Blinder considers the Bardhan and Kroll estimate for 2001 to be comparable to his estimate that 20% to 30% of the employed labor force will be at risk of offshore outsourcing within the next ten to twenty years, especially considering that Bardhan and Kroll do not allow for outsourcing to spread beyond the occupations it is currently affecting. This is like "looking only slightly beyond the currently-visible tip of the iceberg," according to Blinder.

The McKinsey Global Institute (MGI), a research group known for its unabashedly favorable view of globalization, has done its best to put a positive spin on offshore

problem is that since offshoring took off, *import* growth, adjusted for inflation, has been faster than the official numbers show. That means improvements in living standards, as well as corporate profits, depend more on cheap imports, and less on improving domestic productivity, than analysts thought.

Growing angst about outsourcing's costs has also prompted the business press to report favorably on remedies for the dislocation brought on by offshoring that deviate substantially from the non-interventionist, free-market playbook. Even the most unfazed pro-globalization types want to beef up trade adjustment assistance for displaced workers and strengthen the U.S. educational system. But both proposals are inadequate.

---

outsourcing. Its 2003 study, which relied on the Forrester offshoring estimates, concluded that offshoring is already benefiting the U.S. economy. For instance, MGI calculates that for every dollar spent on a business process outsourced to India, the U.S. economy gains at least $1.12. The largest chunk—58 cents—goes back to the original employer in the form of cost savings, almost exclusively in the form of lower wages. In addition, 30% of Indian offshoring is actually performed by U.S. companies, so the wage savings translate into higher earnings for those companies. The study also argues that offshore outsourcing frees up U.S. workers to do other tasks.

A second MGI study, in 2005, surveyed dozens of companies in eight sectors, from pharmaceutical companies to insurers. The study predicted that multinational companies in the entire developed world will have located only 4.1 million service jobs in low-wage countries by 2008—a figure equal to only 1% of the total number of service jobs in developed countries.

But the MGI outsourcing studies have serious limitations. For instance, Blinder points out that MGI's analysis looks at a very short time frame, and that the potential for outsourcing in English-speaking countries such as the United States is higher than elsewhere, a fact lost in the MGI studies' global averages.

In their 2005 book Outsourcing America, published by the American Management Association, public policy professors Ron Hira and Anil Hira argue that MGI's 2003 report "should be viewed as a self-interested lobbying document that presents an unrealistically optimistic estimate of the impact of offshore outsourcing." For instance, most of the data for the report came from case studies conducted by MGI that are unavailable to the public and unsupported by any model. Moreover, the MGI analysis assumes that the U.S. economy will follow its long-term trend and create 3.5 million jobs a year, enough to quickly reemploy U.S. workers displaced by offshoring. But current U.S. job creation falls far short of that trend. A recent White House fact sheet brags that the U.S. economy has created 8.3 million jobs since August 2003. Still, that is less than 2.1 million jobs a year, and only 1.8 million jobs over the last 12 months.

MGI's Farrell is right about one thing. "If the economy were stronger," she says, "there wouldn't be such a negative feeling" about work getting offshored. But merely assuming high job growth doesn't make it so.

More education, the usual U.S. prescription for any economic problem, is off the mark here. Cheaper labor is available abroad up and down the job-skill ladder, so even the most rigorous education is no inoculation against the threat of offshore outsourcing. As Blinder emphasizes, it is the need for face-to-face contact that stops jobs from being shipped overseas, not the level of education necessary to perform them. Twenty years from now, home health aide positions will no doubt be plentiful in the United States; jobs for highly trained IT professionals may be scarce.

Trade adjustment assistance has until now been narrowly targeted at workers hurt by imports. Most new proposals would replace traditional trade adjustment assistance and unemployment insurance with a program for displaced workers that offers wage insurance to ease the pain of taking a lower-paying job and provides for portable health insurance and retraining. The pro-globalization research group McKinsey Global Institute (MGI), for example, claims that for as little as 4% to 5% of the amount they've saved in lower wages, companies could cover the wage losses of all laid-off workers once they are reemployed, paying them 70% of the wage differential between their old and new jobs (in addition to health care subsidies) for up to two years.

While MGI confidently concludes that this proposal will "go a long way toward relieving the current anxieties," other globalization advocates are not so sure. They recognize that economic anxiety is pervasive and that millions of white-collar workers now fear losing their jobs. Moreover, even if fears of actual job loss are overblown, wage insurance schemes do little to compensate for the downward pressure offshoring is putting on the wages of workers who have not been laid off.

Other mainstream economists and business writers go even further, calling for not only wage insurance but also taxes on the winners from globalization. And globalization has produced big winners: on Wall Street, in the corporate boardroom, and among those workers in high demand in the global economy.

Economist Matthew Slaughter, who recently left President Bush's Council of Economic Advisers, told the *Wall Street Journal*, "Expanding the political support for open borders [for trade] requres making a radical change in fiscal policy." He proposes eliminating the Social Security-Medicare payroll tax on the bottom half of workers—roughly, those earning less than $33,000 a year—and making up the lost revenue by raising the payroll tax on higher earners.

The goal of these economists is to thwart a crippling political backlash against trade. As they see it, "using the tax code to slice the apple more evenly is far more palatable than trying to hold back globalization with policies that risk shrinking the economic apple."

Some even call for extending global labor arbitrage to CEOs. In a June 2006 *New York Times* op-ed, equity analyst Lawrence Orlowski and New York University assistant research director Florian Lengyel argued that offshoring the jobs of U.S. chief executives would reduce costs and release value to shareholders by bringing the compensation of U.S. CEOs (on average 170 times greater than the compensation of average U.S. workers in 2004) in line with CEO compensation in Britain (22 times greater) and in Japan (11 times greater).

Yet others focus on the stunning lack of labor mobility that distinguishes the current era of globalization from earlier ones. Labor markets are becoming increasingly free and flexible under globalization, but labor enjoys no similar freedom of movement. In a completely free market, the foreign workers would come here to do the work that is currently being outsourced. Why aren't more of those workers coming to the United States? Traditional economists Gary Becker and Richard Posner argue the answer is clear: an excessively restrictive immigration policy.

Onshore and Offshore Solidarity

Offshoring is one of the last steps in capitalism's conversion of the "physician, the lawyer, the priest, the poet, the man of science, into its paid wage laborers," as Marx and Engels put it in the *Communist Manifesto* 160 years ago. It has already done much to increase economic insecurity in the workaday world and has become, Blinder suggests, the number one economic issue of our generation.

Offshoring has also underlined the interdependence of workers across the globe. To the extent that corporations now organize their business operations on a global scale, shifting work around the world in search of low wages, labor organizing must also be global in scope if it is to have any hope of building workers' negotiating strength.

Yet today's global labor arbitrage pits workers from different countries against each other as competitors, not allies. Writing about how to improve labor standards, economists Ajit Singh and Ann Zammit of the South Centre, an Indian non-governmental organization, ask the question, "On what could workers of the world unite" today? Their answer is that faster economic growth could indeed be a positive-sum game from which both the global North and the global South could gain. A pick-up in the long-term rate of growth of the world economy would generate higher employment, increasing wages and otherwise improving labor standards in both regions. It should also make offshoring less profitable and less painful.

The concerns of workers across the globe would also be served by curtailing the ability of multinational corporations to move their investment anywhere, which weakens the bargaining power of labor both in advanced countries and in the global South. Workers globally would also benefit if their own ability to move between countries was enhanced. The combination of a new set of rules to limit international capital movements and to expand labor mobility across borders, together with measures to ratchet up economic growth and thus increase worldwide demand for labor, would alter the current process of globalization and harness it to the needs of working people worldwide. ❏

Sources: Alan S. Blinder, "Fear of Offshoring," CEPS Working Paper #119, Dec. 2005; Alan S. Blinder, "How Many U.S. Jobs Might Be Offshorable?" CEPS Working Paper #142, March 2007; N. Gregory Mankiw and P. Swagel, "The Politics and Economics of Offshore Outsourcing," Am. Enterprise Inst. Working Paper #122, 12/7/05; "Offshoring: Is It a Win-Win Game?" McKinsey Global Institute, August 2003; Diane Farrell et al., "The Emerging Global Labor Market, Part 1: The Demand for Talent in Services," McKinsey Global Institute, June 2005; Ashok Bardhan and Cynthia Kroll, "The New Wave of Outsourcing," Research Report #113, Fisher Center for Real Estate and Urban Economics, Univ. of Calif., Berkeley, Fall 2003; Paul A. Samuelson, "Where Ricardo and Mill Rebut and Confirm Arguments of Mainstream Economists Supporting Globalization," *J Econ Perspectives* 18:3, Summer 2004; Alan S. Blinder, "Free Trade's Great, but Offshoring Rattles Me," *Wash. Post,* 5/6/07; Michael Mandel, "The Real Cost of Offshoring," *BusinessWeek,* 6/18/07; Aaron Bernstein, "Shaking Up Trade Theory," *BusinessWeek,* 12/6/04; David Wessel, "The Case for Taxing Globalization's Big Winners," *WSJ,* 6/14/07; Bob Davis, "Some Democratic Economists Echo Mankiw on Outsourcing," *WSJ;* N. Gregory Mankiw, "Outsourcing Redux," gregmankiw.blogspot.com/2006/05/outsourcing-redux; David Wessel and Bob Davis, "Pain From Free Trade Spurs Second Thoughts," *WSJ,* 3/30/07; Ajit Singh and Ann Zammit, "On What Could Workers of the World Unite? Economic Growth and a New Global Economic Order," from *The Global Labour Standards Controversy: Critical Issues For Developing Countries,* South Centre, 2000; Michael Meeropol, "Distorting Adam Smith on Trade," *Challenge,* July/Aug 2004.

Article 5.5

ARE LOW WAGES AND JOB LOSS INEVITABLE?

BY ARTHUR MacEWAN
May/June 2011

Dear Dr. Dollar:

The main narrative that I hear in mainstream press is that U.S. workers are being undercut and eventually displaced by global competition. I think this narrative has a tone of inevitability, that low wages and job loss are driven by huge impersonal forces that we can't do much about. Is this right?

—*Vicki Legion, San Francisco, Calif.*

Yes, that is the main narrative. But, no, it's not right.

Globalization, in the sense of increasing international commerce over long distances, has been going on since human beings made their way out of Africa and spread themselves far and wide. Trade between China and the Mediterranean seems to have been taking place at least 3,000 years ago. (We know this through chemical analysis of silk found in the hair of an Egyptian mummy interred around 1000 BCE; the silk was identified as almost certainly from China.) The long history of long-distance commerce does cast an aura of inevitability over globalization.

But the spread of international commerce has not taken shape outside of human control. Globalization takes many forms; its history has variously involved colonial control, spheres of influence, and forms of regulated trade.

The current era of globalization was quite consciously planned by the U.S. government and U.S. business during and after World War II. They saw the United States replacing the British Empire as the dominant power among capitalist countries. But in place of 19th century-style colonial control, they looked to a "free trade" regime to give U.S. firms access to resources and markets around the world. While U.S. business and the U.S. government did not achieve the "free trade" goal immediately, this has been what they have promoted over the last 65 years.

This U.S.—sponsored form of globalization has given great advantage to U.S. business. And it has put many U.S. workers in direct competition with more poorly paid workers elsewhere in the world, who are often denied the right to organize and have little choice but to work long hours in often unsafe conditions. U.S. business can make its profits off these workers elsewhere—often by sub-contracting to local firms. But there is nothing inevitable about this set-up.

Furthermore, there are ways to counter these developments. Just as the current global economic arrangements were created by political decisions, they can be altered by political decisions. Two examples:

- The development of better social programs in the United States would put workers here in a stronger bargaining position, regardless of global competition. With universal health care (a "single-payer" system), for instance, U.S. workers would be in a better position to leave a bad job or turn down a bad offer.

- Rebuilding the labor movement is essential for placing U.S. workers in a stronger bargaining position in relation to their employers. Equally important, stronger unions would give workers more leverage in the political arena, where many decisions about the nature of global commerce are made.

No, we may not be able to create the same labor movement of decades past. However, lest one think that the decline of the labor movement has been itself inevitable in the face of globalization, consider some of the political decisions that have undermined labor's strength:

- The National Labor Relations Board has not done its job. In the '50s, '60s, and early 1970s, fewer than one in ten union elections were marred by illegal firings of union organizers. By the early 1980s, over 30% of union elections involved illegal firings. While the figure declined to 16% by the late 1990s, it was back up to 25% in the early 2000s.

- Or consider the minimum wage. Even with the recent increase of the federal minimum wage to $7.25 per hour, adjusted for inflation it is still below what it was in the 1960s and 1970s.

These are crucial political decisions that have affected organized labor, wage rates, and jobs. But they were not inevitable developments.

It would be folly to think that the changes in the global economy have not affected economic conditions in the United States, including the position of organized labor. But it would also be folly to assume that conditions in the United States are inevitably determined by the global economy. Political action matters.

(Caveat: Advocating a "different shape" for globalization is not a call for protectionism. It is possible to engage in world commerce and protect the interest of U.S. workers without resorting to traditional protectionism. But that is a topic for another day.) ❑

Article 5.6

ON STRIKE IN CHINA
A Chinese New Deal in the Making?

BY CHRIS TILLY AND MARIE KENNEDY
September/October 2010

> "[There will] never be a strike [at the Hyundai plant in Beijing]. Strikes in China would jeopardize the company's reputation."
> —*Zhang Zhixiong, deputy chairman of the union at that plant, 2003*

> "About 1,000 workers at Hyundai's auto parts factory [in Beijing] staged a two-day strike and demanded wage increases. The action only ended when bosses offered an initial 15% pay rise followed by another 10% in July."
> —*China Daily/Asia News Network, June 4, 2010*

Workers in China are on the move. The media initially fixed on the downward trajectory of desperate workers jumping from the roofs of Foxconn, the enormous electronics manufacturer that assembles the iPhone and numerous other familiar gadgets, but soon shifted to the upward arc of strike activity concentrated in the supply chains of Honda and Toyota.

But the auto-sector strikes in China's industrialized Southeast, as well as in the northeastern city of Tianjin, are just the tip of the iceberg. June strikes also pulled out thousands of workers at Brother sewing machine factories and a Carlsberg brewery in the central part of the country; machinery, LCD, and rubber parts plants in the east-central Shanghai area; a shoe manufacturer further inland in Jiujiang; and apparel and electronics workers outside the auto sector in the Southeast and Tianjin. "There are fifteen factories launching strikes now," Qiao Jian of the Chinese Institute of Industrial Relations (CIIR) told us in mid-June. Since that time, still more strikes have been reported, and many others are likely going unreported by Chinese media, which despite their growing independence remain sensitive to government pressure. None of the strikes had approval by the All China Federation of Trade Unions (ACFTU), the only labor movement authorized by Chinese law.

This explosion of wildcat walkouts prompts several questions. Why did it happen? What do the strikes mean for China's low-wage, low-cost manufacturing model? Equally important, what do they imply for China's party- and state-dominated labor relations? China's labor relations scholars—an outspoken bunch—are animatedly discussing that last question in public and in private.

What Happened and Why

The spark for the recent strike wave was the May 17th walkout of hundreds of workers from a Honda transmission plant in Nanhai, near Guangzhou in the Southeast. According to research by Wang Kan of CIIR, the strike was an accident: two employees embroiled in a dispute with Honda consulted a lawyer who advised them to threaten a strike as a bluff and even drew up a set of demands for them. They apparently were as shocked as anyone when workers spontaneously walked out. Accident or not, the workers demanded a 67% raise. Two weeks later, they agreed to return to work with a 42% wage increase. By that time, copycat strikes had erupted at other Honda suppliers in the Southeast and at Hyundai; workers at Toyota suppliers soon followed suit, as did employees from other sectors and regions. Most of these actions won wage settlements in the twenty-percent range.

Why did this strike wave happen now? The first thing to understand is that strikes in China did not begin in 2010. As Berkeley doctoral student Eli Friedman points out, "the number of strikes and officially mediated labor disputes in China [has] been increasing rapidly for at least fifteen years." So-called "mass incidents," of which experts estimate about a third to be strikes, numbered 87,000 in 2005, and were unofficially pegged at 120,000 in 2008. Mediated labor disputes, many of which only involve an individual, have grown even faster, rising in round figures from 19,000 in 1994 to 135,000 in 2000, 350,000 in 2007, and 700,000 in 2008. The huge increase in 2008 is due at least in part to new laws on labor contracts and labor mediation passed that year that bolster workers' ability to bring complaints.

Still, "the Honda strike marks a turning point," in the words of law professor Liu Cheng of Shanghai Normal University. "Previous strikes were mainly about enforcing labor law. This is the first successful strike about collective bargaining." Anita Chan, a labor researcher at the University of Technology in Sydney, agrees, saying the current strikers "are negotiating for their interests and not for their rights—it's a very different set of stakes." The Nanhai Honda action was also a breakthrough in that for the first time strikers demanded the right to elect their own union representatives—a demand to which the provincial union federation has agreed, though the election has not yet taken place. Many subsequent strikes reiterated this demand, although they have focused more on economic issues. Even the economic demands extend beyond wages: at Honda Lock, strikers demanded noise reduction measures to improve the work environment.

The long-term growth in strike activity owes much to demographic changes. Predominantly women, China's industrial workers hail overwhelmingly from the ranks of rural migrants, 140 million of whom live and work in the cities but lack long-term permission to stay there or receive social benefits there. When Deng Xiaoping's market liberalization first spurred rapid industrial growth in the 1980s, migrants were willing to "eat bitterness," enduring hardships and low wages to send remittances home to families who were worse off than they. This stoic attitude and decades of policies aimed at growth at almost any cost are reflected in the decline of labor's share of total national income from 57% in 1983 to 37% in 2005. Unpaid or underpaid overtime and only one or two days off a month—violations of Chinese law—became common in China's manufacturing sector.

But the new generation of migrants, reared in a time of relative prosperity and comparing themselves to their peers in the cities, expect more. "Our demands are higher because we have higher material and spiritual needs," a young Honda striker who identified himself only as Chen told Agence France-Presse. "Our strike demands are based on our need to maintain our living standards." With urban housing costs soaring, this has become a pressing issue. "I dream of one day buying a car or apartment," said Zhang, a 22-year-old man working at the same plant, "but with the salary I'm making now, I will never succeed."

Another long-run factor is the government's new willingness to tolerate strikes as long as they stay within bounds, in contrast to the harsh repression meted out in the 1980s and early 1990s.

Still the "Workshop of the World"?

The current wave of strikes owes its energy, too, to the lopsided policies China's government adopted in response to the global economic crunch. "With the global financial crisis, the income gap and social disparities worsened," commented Qiao of the CIIR. Panicking at the fall-off in demand for Chinese exports, authorities froze the minimum wage in 2009 even as the cost of living continued its upward march. They also put hundreds of billions of dollars into loans to help exporters and allowed employers to defer their tax payments and social insurance contributions.

Perhaps most important for workers' quality of life, provincial and local governments relaxed their enforcement of labor regulations—at a time when examples of hard-pressed businesses closing down and cheating workers out of months of back pay were becoming increasingly common. In Foshan, a government official declared in 2009 that employers violating the Labor Contract Law protecting basic worker rights would "not be fined, and will not have their operating licenses revoked." A year later, Honda workers in the city walked off the job.

But the business-friendly, worker-unfriendly government response to the crisis does not explain why autoworkers went out. "I don't know why the Honda workers went on strike, because their salaries and conditions are better than ours," Chen Jian, a 24-year-old worker at Yontai Plastics, not far from the Nanhai Honda plant, said to the Guardian newspaper. "We are not satisfied, but we will not go on strike. Some workers tried that last year and they were all fired. That is normal."

Despite Chen's puzzlement, his comments touch on the reason autoworkers led the way: power rooted in the specifics of the auto production process. Autoworkers wield a degree of skill that makes them more difficult to replace. Assembly line technology within the plant, and a division of labor that often locates fabrication of a particular part in a single plant, make it possible for a small number of strategically located workers to shut down the whole production process, a fact exploited by autoworkers around the world going back to the Flint sit-down strike in 1937. And Japanese-initiated just-in-time techniques have cut down inventories, speeding up the impact of strikes. Friedman reports that by the fourth day of the Nanhai strike, work at all four Honda assembly plants in China had ground to a halt due to lack of transmissions.

Pundits have speculated on whether the Chinese workforce's new demands will upend China's export machine. Andy Xie, a Hong Kong-based economist and business analyst formerly with Morgan Stanley, remarks, "To put it bluntly, the key competence of a successful [manufacturer] in China is to squeeze labor to the maximum extent possible." But in fact, Chinese manufacturing wages had already begun rising significantly in the years before the crisis—in part because of earlier strikes and protests. Some companies had already begun relocating work to Vietnam or Bangladesh. Most observers, including Xie, expect incremental adjustment by businesses, not a stampede. Limited worker demands could even play into the Chinese government's goal of increasing productivity and shifting into higher value-added manufacturing, as well as expanding the buying power of Chinese consumers. But as James Pomfret and Kelvin Soh of Reuters write, China's Communist Party "has faced a policy tightrope. It must also ensure that strikes don't proliferate and scare investors or ignite broader confrontation that erodes Party rule."

"Taking the Same Boat Together to Protect Growth"

Where was the All China Federation of Trade Unions as the working class rose up? Friedman points out that though ACFTU leaders were concerned about defending worker interests in the crisis, they were equally concerned with defending employers' interests. The result was what the ACFTU called "mutually agreed upon actions," which combined promises to desist from job actions with what Friedman describes as "weakly worded requests for employers." "Taking the same boat together to protect growth," a joint March 2009 release by government, unions, and the employer association in Guangdong, was typical, imploring businesses to "work hard" to avoid layoffs and wage cuts—an appeal that seems to have had little real impact on employers.

This ACFTU stance grows directly out of the federation's longstanding focus on "harmonious enterprises," which is rooted in the unions' historic role in state enterprises. "Each trade union is under the control of the local Party branch," Lin Yanling of the CIIR told us. "So, Party, company, and union leadership are often the same." Indeed, the ACFTU typically invites companies to name their union officials; as a result, middle managers often hold those posts. Along the same lines, Shanghai Normal's Liu Cheng stated, "These company unions don't work. They have nothing to do but entertainment. In the summer, they buy watermelon for the workers to celebrate the festivals." Lin Yanling concluded, "Now is the time to change trade unions in China!"

Recommendations for change circulating within China vary widely. "Some local trade union leaders say to reform the trade union, you must sever the relation between the trade union and the local Party branch," said Lin. "If the local union would only listen to upper trade union officials, the problem could be solved." Local state and Party representatives are particularly closely tied to the local businesses, whereas the national officialdom has more often advocated for workers' interests, for example through the new 2008 labor laws. He Zengke, executive director of the Center for Comparative Politics and Economics, expressed support for shifting control to the national level: "Local government has historically supported business, but the [Party Secretary] Hu government is now asking them to pursue a balanced policy—also pro-people, pro-poor."

But Lin is skeptical of this limited fix, arguing that "if you want the unions to change, you need the workers to elect the trade union chairperson." Liu Cheng agrees, but also advocates for unions to have the right to litigate on behalf of workers. Liu argues it is premature to push for the right to strike, whereas Zheng Qiao of CIIR holds that this is a good opportunity to define that right. Qiao Jian of CIIR advocates democratizing unions within a revitalized tripartite (union federation/employer association/government) system, but his colleague Lin insists, "That system will not function," because the unions don't yet have enough independence within the triad to adequately represent workers. The disagreements are passionate, if good-humored, since these scholars see the future of their country at stake.

Western observers, and some Hong Kong-based worker-rights groups, have gone farther to call for the right for workers to form their own independent unions—what the International Labor Organization calls "freedom of association." But labor relations experts within mainland China, and the strikers themselves, have so far steered clear of such radical proposals. Liu Cheng commented, "Without reform of the unions, I think freedom of association would result in disorder, and destroy the process of evolution. I don't like revolution—with most revolutions, there is no real progress, just a change of emperors." However, he did express the view that as the Chinese labor movement matures, it will reach a point when freedom of association will be possible and desirable.

"If People Are Oppressed, They Must Rebel"

But will the unions change—and will the Party and state let them? The question is complicated by the conflicting currents within the union federation itself and within China's official ideology. The same Party that promotes "harmonious enterprises" also enshrines Mao Zedong's dictum, "It's right to rebel." So perhaps it's not surprising that Li, a young striker at Honda's exhaust plant, told Agence France-Presse, "Safeguarding your own rights is always legitimate … . If people are oppressed they must rebel. This is only natural."

ACFTU responses to date, reported by Friedman and labor activist and blogger Paul Garver, reflect this mixed consciousness. At the Nanhai Honda strike that inaugurated the current wave, the local ACFTU leadership sent a group of 100 people with union hats and armbands to persuade the strikers to stand down. Whether by design or not, the conversation degenerated into a physical confrontation in which some strikers were injured, none severely. On the other hand, provincial-level union leaders then agreed to the strikers' demands to elect their own representatives. The top two Guangdong ACFTU officials, Deng Weilong and Kong Xianghong, subsequently spoke out in favor of the right to strike and pledged to replace current management-appointed officials with worker-elected ones.

When workers at the Denso (Nansha) car-parts factory in Guangzhou (also in Guangdong province) later went on strike, the local union response was different from that in Nanhai. The municipal union federation publicly supported the strikers, refusing to mediate between labor and management. There have even been signs of life from unions in other sectors: about a month after the Nanhai strike, the municipal union federation in Shenyang, in the far northeast of the country, hammered out the nation's first collective bargaining contract with KFC (whose fast-food restaurants blanket China), including a wage increase of nearly 30%.

On the government side, authorities in many provinces have responded to the strike wave with a wave of minimum-wage hikes. Premier Wen Jiabao declared in a June address to migrant workers, "Your work is a glorious thing, and it should be respected by society," and in August told the Japanese government that its companies operating in China should raise wages. Acknowledging that "a wide range of social conflicts have occurred recently," Zhou Yongkang, another top Party official, stated, "Improving people's livelihoods should be the starting and end point of all our work." In August, BusinessWeek reported that Guangdong's state legislature was discussing a law formalizing collective bargaining, empowering workers to elect local representatives, and even recognizing the right to strike—particularly noteworthy since Guangdong is China's industrial heartland. Still, pro-worker rhetoric is nothing new, the Guangdong provincial union federation is more progressive and powerful than most, and right around the time of Wen's June speech the Chinese government shut down a website calling for ACFTU democratization.

Amidst these cross-currents, China's labor relations scholars, aware that their own role is "marginal," as one of them put it, remain cautiously optimistic. "I think the situation will lead to union reform," said the CIIR's Zheng Qiao. When asked how activists in the United States can support the Chinese workers, her colleague Lin suggested, "Ask the big American brands to give a larger percentage back to the workers at their suppliers!" At Shanghai Normal, Liu Cheng reasoned through the prospects for change. "If the ACFTU does not do more, there will be more and more independent strikes, and in the end some kind of independent union. So the ACFTU will be scared, and the party will be angry with the ACFTU."

"So," Liu Cheng concluded, "the strike wave is a very good thing." ❏

Sources : Eli Friedman, "Getting through hard times together? Worker insurgency and Chinese unions' response to the economic crisis," paper presented at the International Sociological Association annual conference, Gothenburg, Sweden, July 2010; LabourStart page on China labor news, www.labourstart.org; James Pomfret and Kelvin Soh, "Special Report: China's new migrant workers pushing the line," Reuters, July 5, 2010; "The right to strike may be coming to China," Bloomberg Businessweek, August 5, 2010; ITUC/GUF Hong Kong Liaison Office, "A political economic analysis of the strike in Honda and the auto parts industry in China," July 2010.

Chapter 6

MIGRATION

Article 6.1

THE NEW POLITICAL ECONOMY OF IMMIGRATION

Since Sept. 11, 2001, immigrants have become America's most wanted.

BY TOM BARRY
January/February 2009

The terrorist attacks of Sept. 11 drastically altered the traditional political economy of immigration.

The millions of undocumented immigrants—those who crossed the border illegally or overstayed their visas—who were living and working in the United States were no longer simply regarded as a shadow population or as surplus cheap labor. In the public and policy debate, immigrants were increasingly defined as threats to the nation's security. Categorizing immigrants as national security threats gave the government's flailing immigration law-enforcement and border-control operations a new unifying logic that has propelled the immigrant crackdown forward.

Responsibility for immigration law-enforcement and border control passed from the Justice Department to the new Department of Homeland Security (DHS). In Congress Democrats and Republicans alike readily supported a vast expansion of the country's immigration control apparatus—doubling the number of Border Patrol agents and authorizing a tripling of immigrant prison beds.

Today, after the shift in the immigration debate, the $15 billion-plus DHS budget for immigration affairs has fueled an immigrant-crackdown economy that has greatly boosted the already-bloated prison industry. Even now, with the economy imploding, immigrants are currently behind one of the country's most profitable industries: they are the nation's fastest growing sector of the U.S. prison population.

Across the country new prisons are hurriedly being constructed to house the hundreds of thousands of immigrants caught each year. State and local governments are vying with each other to attract new immigrant prisons as the foundation of their rural "economic development" plans.

While DHS is driving immigrants from their jobs and homes, U.S. firms in the business of providing prison beds are raking in record profits from the immigrant crackdown. Although only one piece of the broader story of immigration, it's all a part of the new political economy of immigration.

Dangerous People

In the new national security context, undocumented immigrants are not just outlaws: They are "dangerous people" who threaten the homeland.

The two DHS agencies involved in immigration enforcement—Immigration and Customs En-forcement (ICE) and Customs and Border Enforcement (CBP)—have seen their funds increased disproportionately over the last several years,

---

Detention Profiteers

There may be a new boom in immigrant detention, but captive immigrants as good business is a concept that dates back two decades. Immigrants were the industry's first prisoners.

It all began in 1983 when a klatch of wealthy Tennessee Republicans decided private prisons were just what the country needed to solve the problems of prison riots, overcrowding, and increasing costs. They formed the Corrections Corporation of America (CCA), with the mission to "provide in partnership with government meaningful public service," and succeeded in persuading the Reagan administration to help launch prison privatization by having the Immigration and Naturalization Service (ICE's legacy agency) issue CCA a contract to keep immigrants locked up in Houston.

Wackenhut Corrections (recently renamed GEO Group), a private security services firm, branched into the private prison industry when it entered a contract in 1987 to operate an INS immigrant detention center in Colorado.

Using their experience in immigrant detention, CCA and Wackenhut soon began successfully soliciting states and counties to enter into private prison pacts, while winning dozens of new contracts with the federal government. However, the initial enthusiasm of governments at all levels faded with increasing abuse scandals at CCA and Wackenhut prisons, leading some states to cancel contracts and pull prisoners out.

But immigrant detention once again saved the day for CCA, Wackenhut, and other teetering private prison firms. The 1996 immigration law that broadened the guidelines for deporting undocumented and legal immigrants started to kick in, resulting in a rising federal demand for more immigrant detention beds that the private prison industry was happy to supply.

doubling in size while total DHS funding has increased by just a third. The funding for these two agencies is set to rise 19.1% in 2009 while the overall DHS budget will increase by only 6.8%. Hunting down immigrants has become a top DHS priority. As, DHS says its mission is "to prevent terrorist attacks against the nation and to protect our nation from dangerous people."

Immigrants caught up in DHS dragnets, worksite enforcement raids, and border patrols were the "metrics of success" that DHS Secretary Michael Chertoff pointed to in his July 18, 2008 congressional testimony. He used the dramatically increased number of immigrant apprehensions and "removals" as metrics to show that DHS is succeeding in its goal to "secure the homeland and protect the American people."

While the increased numbers of immigrants being arrested, imprisoned, and deported certainly demonstrate that DHS is busy, they don't demonstrate that DHS is stopping terrorism. Never in its congressional testimonies or media releases does DHS present evidence that show how the number of immigrants captured improves national security.

A 2007 study by the Transnational Records Access Clearinghouse (TRAC) at Syracuse University found that there has been no increase in terrorism or national security charges against immigrants since 2001. In fact, despite the increased enforcement operations by Homeland Security, more immigrants were charged annually in immigration courts with national security or terrorism-related offenses in a three-year period in the mid-1990s (1994–96) than in a comparable period (2004– 06) since Sept. 11. According to the TRAC study, "A decade later, national security charges were brought against 114 individuals, down about a third. Meanwhile for the same period, terrorism charges are down more than three-fourths, to just 12."

Enforcing the "Rule of Law"

Rather than addressing immigration as the complex socioeconomic issue that it is, Homeland Security has reduced immigration policy to a system of crime and punishment. Applying the simplistic law-and-order logic propagated by restrictionists, DHS regards undocumented immigrants not as workers, community members, and parents but as criminals.

Following the lead of the anti-immigration institutes and right-wing think tanks, Chertoff came to Homeland Security with a new interpretation of the department's immigration law enforcement and border control operations: Commitment to a strict enforcement regime to protect the country against foreign terrorists, and to reassert the "rule of law."

In the aftermath of Sept. 11, the restrictionist camp found that their messaging about the "illegality" and "criminality" of undocumented immigrants took on a new resonance. They proceeded to upscale their "what don't you understand about illegal?" message, to a more conceptual framing of undocumented immigration. Undocumented immigrants now represented a threat to the "rule of law" inside a nation that had just come under foreign attack by foreign outlaws.

Their new language about immigration policy started popping up everywhere, from the pronouncements of immigrant-rights groups to the Democratic Party platform.

Instead of promising an "earned path to citizenship," as it has in the past, the party stated that undocumented immigrants will be required to "get right with the law."

Looking ahead, Janet Napolitano, President Obama's nominee to replace Chertoff, while no anti-immigration hardliner, still seems poised to adopt the same law-and-order logic. As a lawyer, former federal prosecutor, and a governor who has insisted on more border control and stood behind a tough employer-sanctions law, Napolitano can be expected to follow the lead of Chertoff and the Democratic Party in insisting that current immigration laws be strictly enforced "to reassert the rule of law."

Immigrants Mean Business

Political imperatives—protecting the homeland and enforcing the "rule of law"—have over the past eight years countervailed against the economic forces that have historically led in setting immigration policy. Although the immigrant labor market persists, the increased risks for both employer and worker, along with the recessionary economy, appear to be exercising downward pressure on both supply and demand.

But even in the flagging economy, the immigrant crackdown has invigorated other market forces. Eager to cash in on immigrant detention, private prison firms and local governments are rushing to supply Homeland Security and the Justice Department with the prisons needed to house the hundreds of thousands of immigrants captured by ICE and Border Patrol agents.

In the prison industry, bed is a euphemism for a place behind bars. Even President Bush talked the prison-bed language when discussing immigration policy. When visiting the Rio Grande Valley in south Texas in 2006 to promote the immigrant crackdown, the president said: "Beds are our number one priority."

The number of beds for detained immigrants in DHS centers has increased by more than a third since 2002. There are now 32,000 beds available for the revolving population of immigrants on the path to deportation, and another 1,000 are scheduled to come on line in 2009. This doesn't include beds for immigrants in Homeland Security custody that are provided by county, state, and the federal Bureau of Prisons.

At the insistence of such immigration restrictionists as Rep. Tom Tancredo (R-Colo.), the Intelligence Reform and Terrorism Prevention Act of 2004 contained an authorization for an additional 40,000 beds to accommodate immigrants under U.S. government custody.

At the onset of the immigration crackdown two years ago, ICE dubbed its promise to find a detention center or prison bed for all arrested immigrants "Operation Reservation Guaranteed." The Justice Department has a similar initiative to ensure that the U.S. Marshals Service has beds available for detainees—about 180,000 a year, of whom more than 30% are held on immigration charges.

Most of the prison beds contracted by ICE and DOJ's Office of Federal Detention Trustee are with local governments; ICE has more than 300 intergovernmental agreements with county and city governments to hold immigrants, while

DOJ has some 1200 such agreements. In many cases, particularly with contracts for hundreds of prison beds, the local government then subcontracts with a private prison company to operate the facility.

Prison beds translate into per diem payments from the federal government that are well above the hotel room rates in the remote rural communities where most of these immigrant prisons are located. With these per diems running from $70 to $95 for each immigrant imprisoned, local governments and private firms are hurrying to expand existing facilities or to create new ones.

Depending on Immigrants

The uptick in immigrant detention that saved the industry in 2000 (see sidebar) turned into a mighty upswing in demand for immigrant prison beds after Sept. 11 and the ensuing immigrant crackdown. The Corrections Corporation of America (CCA) has reported record profits for the last few years, largely on the strength of increasing demand from its ICE and USMS "customers."

Forty percent of total CCA revenue comes from three federal contractors: Bureau of Prisons, U.S. Marshals Service, and ICE. In its 2007 Security and Exchange Commission filing, CCA stated: "We are dependent on government appropriations." CCA Chairman William Andrews warned investors that the company's high returns could be threatened by a change in the policy environment: "The demand for our facilities and services could be adversely affected by the relaxation of enforcement efforts...or through the decriminalization of certain activities that are currently proscribed by our criminal laws."

But to understand just how well the prison business is faring and how immigrants are key to prison profits, you can listen in on the prison firms' quarterly conference call with major Wall Street investment firms of November 2008.

Corrections Corporation of America boasted that it enjoyed a $33.6 million increase in the third quarter over last year, while earnings rose 15% during the same period. Formerly known as Wackenhut, GEO Group, the nation's second largest prison company, saw its earnings jump 29% over 2007. Cornell Companies, another private prison firm that imprisons immigrants, reported a 9% increase in net revenues in the third quarter.

Private prison companies aren't worried that the Democratic Party sweep will mean fewer beds. GEO Group's chairman George Zoley on Nov. 3 assured investors: "These federal initiatives to target, detain and deport criminal aliens throughout the country will continue to drive the need for immigration detention beds over the next several years and these initiatives have been fully funded by Congress on a bipartisan basis."

Addressing investor fears that recent decreases in undocumented immigration inflows might dampen company returns, CCA CEO and board chairman John Ferguson said, "So even though we have seen the border crossings and apprehensions decline in the last couple of years, we are really talking about dealing with a population well north of 12 million illegal immigrants residing in the United States."

The CCA chief assured investors that the company's dependence on detained immigrants is not a factor of policy but rather of law enforcement. "The Federal Bureau of Prisons, U.S. Marshals Service, Immigration and Custom Enforcement are carrying out statutory obligations for their responsibility....We should continue to see their utilization of the private sector to meet their statutory obligations and requirements."

The prison executives even intimate that the economic crisis will fatten their business. When asked by an investment company representative about a possible downturn in detained immigrants, James Hyman, president of Cornell Companies, said, "We do not believe we will see a decline in the need for detention beds particularly in an economy with rising unemployment among American workers."

Immigrant Prisons as Economic Development

Hundreds of local governments are also attempting to take advantage of this rising demand for immigrant prison beds by opening their jails to immigrants under ICE and DOJ custody and by building new jails to meet the anticipated increased demand.

Financial considerations weigh heavily for cash-strapped county commissions and sheriff departments. As Sheriff Roger Mulch told Jefferson County (Illinois) commissioners in late February 2008, "ICE, during the last three months, has been hot to do business with us." Each locality negotiates independently with ICE and USMS to set the per diem rates, and as the demand from the feds for local jail beds increases, county sheriff departments are negotiating ever-higher rates.

Along the U.S.-Mexico border, particularly in Texas, prisons are a booming industry. Near the bor-der town of Del Rio, the county's Val Verde Correctional Facility, which is owned and run by GEO Group, had only 180 beds eight years ago. Today, after undergoing its second 600-bed expansion, the maximum-security jail can fit 1,425 prisoners.

In Texas' Willacy County, the county government opened the country's largest immigrant detention center in 2006, and is currently pursuing a federal contract to host one of three new family detention centers for immigrants. County Commissioner Ernie Chapa, explaining how the county government financially depends on jailing immigrants, said: "We would love to have 2,500 [illegal immigrants] but we know that's not going to be . . . If we get 2,200 to 2,300, we'd be very happy."

Joining in the celebration of the opening of the new jail for immigrants, Willacy County Judge Simone Salinas said, "We are proud to have been able to bring on these new detention beds in record time, which will result in improved border security not only for county residents but also our nation."

"You talk about economic development, this is it," Salinas told a reporter, noting the county's initial cut is $2.25 a day per occupied bed.

A year later, a new agreement with ICE for another thousand beds was greeted enthusiastically by some officials in what is one of the poorest counties in the nation. The new county judge Eliseo Barnhart said the expansion of the immigrant detention center run by CCA will "bring jobs that are needed in Willacy County and it means income, which we desperately need."

"It's almost like a futures market. You have private prison companies gambling on expansion of the immigrant detention system, and basically prison speculators who are convincing communities to do this," Bob Libal, director of Grassroots Leadership in Austin and an organizer with South Texans Opposing Private Prisons, told the *Denver Post*. "It's a sick market, but a market nonetheless," Libal said.

New Political Economy of Immigration

What started off as a war against terrorism has devolved into a war against immigrants. The current "enforcement-only" approach to immigration policy has created a morass of new problems, including a host of human rights and financial issues associated with the annual detention and removal of immigrants. The immigrant crackdown has given rise to an unregulated complex of jails, detention centers, and prisons that create profit from the immigrant crackdown.

At the outset of a new administration and new era, the political economy of immigration is decidedly anti-immigrant. Political and economic factors have combined to create a harsh environment for undocumented immigrants, present and future. Immigration reform may not be a top priority, but the Obama administration and new Congress would do well to begin to address the challenge of reshaping the political economy of immigration.

First steps could include a more careful articulation of the intersection of immigration, rule of law, and national security. Napolitano should explain that the real threat to the rule of law is not having an immigration policy that provides a legal pathway to integration for the 11 million immigrants already within the U.S.

What's more, she would do well to disarticulate the links established by the Bush administration between immigrants and terrorists. At the same time, closer links must be made between immigration policy and economic policy, guarding against labor exploitation while considering domestic economic need.

Instead of a policy based on a calm assessment of the costs and benefits of immigrant labor to the U.S. economy, current immigration policy has been hijacked by the politics of fear, resentment, scapegoating, and nativism. The "enforcement only" immigration policy has fostered a national immigrant prison complex that feeds on ever-increasing numbers of arrested immigrants. As County Commissioner Ernie Chapa said, "Any time the numbers are high, it's good for the county because it brings more income." ❏

Sources: "Immigration Enforcement: The Rhetoric, The Reality," TRAC Immigration, 2007; "Corrections Corp. of America Q3 2008 Earnings Call Transcript," Seeking Alpha, November 2008; "The GEO Group, Inc. Q3 2008 (Qtr End 9/28/08) Earnings Call Transcript," Seeking Alpha, November 2008; "Cornell Companies Inc. Q3 2008 Earnings Call Transcript," Seeking Alpha, November 2008; "Mulch: Jail May Soon House Immigrants", Register News February 2008; "Willacy County Goes $50 Million More In Debt to Expand MTC's Tent City," Texas Prison Bid'ness Blog, August 2007; "Federal detention center in Willacy to expand," The Monitor, July 2007; "Inmate count continues to climb at detention center," Brownsville Herald, April 2008.

Article 6.2

"THEY WORK HERE, THEY LIVE HERE, THEY STAY HERE!"

French immigrants strike for the right to work—and win.

BY MARIE KENNEDY AND CHRIS TILLY

July/August 2007

France has an estimated half-million undocumented immigrants, including many from France's former colonies in Africa. The *sans-papiers* (literally, "without papers"), as the French call them, lead a shadowy existence, much like their U.S. counterparts. And as U.S. immigrants did in 2006 with rousing mass demonstrations, the French undocumented have recently taken a dramatic step out of the shadows. But the *sans-papiers* did it in a particularly French way: hundreds of them occupied their workplaces.

Snowballing Strikes

The snowflake that led to this snowball of sit-in strikes was a November immigration law, sponsored by the arch-conservative government of President Nicolas Sarkozy, that cracked down on family reunification and ramped up expulsions of unauthorized immigrants. The law also added a pro-business provision permitting migration, and even "regularization" of undocumented workers, in occupations facing labor shortages. The French government followed up with a January notice to businesses in labor-starved sectors, opening the door for employers to apply to local authorities for work permits for workers with false papers whom they had "in good faith" hired. However, for low-level jobs, this provision was limited to migrants from new European Union member countries. Africans could only qualify if they were working in highly skilled occupations such as science or engineering—but not surprisingly, most Africans in France are concentrated in low-wage service sector jobs.

At that point, African *sans-papiers* took matters into their own hands. On February 13, Fodie Konté of Mali and eight co-workers at the Grande Armée restaurant in Paris occupied their workplace to demand papers. All nine were members of the Confédération Générale du Travail (CGT), France's largest union federation, and the CGT backed them up. In less than a week, Parisian officials agreed to regularize seven of the nine, with Konté the first to get his papers.

The CGT and *Droits Devant!!* (Rights Ahead!!), an immigrant rights advocacy group, saw an opportunity and gave the snowball a push. They escorted Konté and his co-workers to meetings and rallies with other undocumented CGT workers, where they declared, "We've started it, it's up to you to follow." Small groups began to do just that. Then on April 15, fifteen new workplaces in Paris and the surrounding region sprouted red CGT flags as several hundred "irregular" workers held sit-ins. At France's Labor Day parade on May 1, a contingent of several thousand undocumented, most from West African countries such as Mali, Senegal, and Ivory Coast, were the stars.

But local governments were slow to move on their demands, so with only 70 workers regularized one month into the sit-ins, another 200 *sans-papiers* upped the ante on May 20 by taking over twenty more job sites. Still others have joined the strike since. As of early July, 400 former strikers have received papers (typically one-year permits), and the CGT estimates that 600 are still sitting tight at 41 workplaces.

Restaurants, with their visible locations on main boulevards, are the highest profile strike sites. But strikers are also camping out at businesses in construction, cleaning, security, personal services, and landscaping. Though the movement reportedly includes North Africans, Eastern Europeans, and even Filipinos, its public presence has consisted almost entirely of sub-Saharan Africans, a stunning indication of the degree of racial segregation in immigrant jobs. Strikers are overwhelmingly men, though the female employees of a contract cleaning business, Ma Net, made a splash when they joined the strike on May 26, and groups representing domestics and other women workers began to demonstrate around the same time.

"To Go Around Freely..."

The *sans-papiers* came to France by different means. Some overstayed student or tourist visas. Others paid as much as 7,500 euros ($12,000) to a trafficker to travel to the North African coast, clandestinely cross by boat to Spain, and then find their way to France. Strike leader Konté arrived in Paris, his target, two long years after leaving Mali. A set of false papers for 200 euros, and he was ready to look for work.

But opportunities for the undocumented are, for the most part, limited to jobs with the worst pay and working conditions. The French minimum wage is 8.71 euros an hour (almost $13), but strikers tell of working for 3 euros or even less. "With papers, I would get 1,000 euros a month," Issac, a Malian cleaner for the Quick restaurant chain who has been in France eleven years, told *Dollars & Sense*. "Without papers, I get 300." Even so, he and many others send half their pay home to families who depend on them. Through paycheck withholding, the *sans-papiers* pay taxes and contribute to the French health care and retirement funds. But "if I get sick, I don't have any right to reimbursement," said Camara, a dishwasher from Mali. He told *L'Humanité*, the French Communist Party newspaper, how much he wished "to go around freely." "In the evening I don't go out," he said. "When I leave home in the morning, I don't even know if I will get home that night. I avoid some subway stations" that are closely monitored by the police.

When asked how he would reply to the claim that the undocumented are taking jobs from French workers, Issac replied simply, "We are French workers—just without any rights. Yes, we're citizens, because France owned all of black Africa!"

Business Allies

The surprise allies in this guerrilla struggle for the right to work are many of the employers. When workers seized the Samsic contract cleaning agency in the Paris suburb of Massy, owner Mehdi Daïri first called the police. When they told him there was nothing they could do, he pragmatically decided to apply for permits for his 300-plus employees. "It's in everybody's best interest," he told *Le Monde*, the French daily newspaper. "Their action is legitimate. They've been here for years, working, contributing to the social security system, paying taxes, and we're satisfied with their work." He even has his office staff make coffee for the strikers every morning.

Though some businesses have taken a harder line against the strikers, the major business associations have called for massive regularization of their workforces. According to *L'Humanité*, André Dauguin, president of the hotel operators association, is demanding that 50,000 to 100,000 undocumented workers be given papers. Didier Chenet, president of another association of restaurant and hotel enterprises, declared that with 20,000 jobs going unfilled in these sectors, the *sans-papiers* "are not taking jobs away from other workers."

For the CGT, busy with defensive battles against labor "reforms" such as cutbacks in public employees' pensions, the strike wave represents a step in a new direction. The core of the CGT remains white, native-born French workers. As recently as the 1980s, the Communist Party, to which the CGT was then closely linked, took some controversial anti-immigrant stands. Raymond Chauveau, the general secretary of the CGT's Massy local, acknowledged to *Le Monde* that some union members still have trouble understanding why the organization has taken up this issue. But he added, "Today, these people are recognized for what they are: workers. They are developing class consciousness. Our role as a union is to show that these people are not outside the world of work." While some immigrant rights groups are critical of the CGT for suddenly stepping into the leadership of a fight other groups had been pursuing for years, it is hard to deny the importance of the labor organization's clout.

Half Empty or Half Full?

With only 400 of 1,400 applications for work permits granted four months into the struggle, the CGT is publicly voicing its impatience at the national government's insistence that local authorities make each decision on a case-by-case basis rather than offering broader guidelines. But Chauveau said he is proud that they have compelled the government to accept regularization of Africans in low-end jobs, broadening the opening beyond the intent of the 2007 law. And on its website, the CGT boasted that the *sans-papiers* "have compelled the government to take its first steps back, when that had seemed impossible since the [May 2007] election of Nicolas Sarkozy." Perhaps even more important for the long term is that class consciousness Chauveau mentioned. This is "a struggle that has changed my life," stated Mamadou Dembia Thiam of Senegal, a security guard who won his work authorization in June. "Before the struggle, I was really very timid. I've changed!" Changes like that seem likely to bring a new burst of energy to the struggling French labor movement. ❑

Resources: Confédération Générale du Travail, www.cgt.fr; Droits Devant!!, www.droitsdevant.org.

Article 6.3

MADE IN ARGENTINA
Bolivian Migrant Workers Fight Neoliberal Fashion

BY MARIE TRIGONA
January/February 2007

Dubbed "the Paris of the South," Buenos Aires is known for its European architecture, tango clubs, and *haute couture*. But few people are aware that Argentina's top fashion brands employ tens of thousands of undocumented Bolivian workers in slave-labor conditions. In residential neighborhoods across Buenos Aires, top clothing companies have turned small warehouses or gutted buildings into clandestine sweatshops. Locked in, workers are forced to live and work in cramped quarters with little ventilation and, often, limited access to water and gas. The *Unión de Trabajadores Costureros* (Union of Seamstress Workers—UTC), an assembly of undocumented textile workers, has reported more than 8,000 cases of labor abuses inside the city's nearly 400 clandestine shops in the past year. Around 100,000 undocumented immigrants work in these unsafe plants with an average wage—if they are paid at all—of $100 per month.

According to Olga Cruz, a 29-year-old textile worker, slave-labor conditions in textile factories are systematic. "During a normal workday in a shop you work from 7 a.m. until midnight or 1 a.m. Many times they don't pay the women and they owe them two or three years' pay. For not having our legal documents or not knowing what our rights are in Argentina, we've had to remain silent. You don't have rights to rent a room or to work legally."

Another Bolivian textile worker, Naomi Hernández, traveled to Argentina three years ago in hopes of a well-paying job. "I ended up working in a clandestine sweatshop without knowing the conditions I would have to endure. For two years I worked and slept in a three-square-meter room along with my two children and three sewing machines my boss provided. They would bring us two meals a day. For breakfast a cup of tea with a piece of bread and lunch consisting of a portion of rice, a potato, and an egg. We had to share our two meals with our children because according to my boss, my children didn't have the right to food rations because they aren't workers and don't yield production." She reported the subhuman conditions in her workplace and was subsequently fired.

Diseases like tuberculosis and lung complications are common due to the sub-human working conditions and constant exposure to dust and fibers. Many workers suffer from back injuries and tendonitis from sitting at a sewing machine 12 to 16 hours a day. And there are other hazards. A blaze that killed six people last year brought to light abusive working conditions inside a network of clandestine textile plants in Buenos Aires. The two women and four children who were killed had been locked inside the factory.

The situation of these workers shows that exploitation of migrant labor is not just a first-world/third-world phenomenon. The system of exploitative subcontracting of migrant workers that has arisen in U.S. cities as a result of neoliberal globalization also occurs in the countries of the global south—as does organized resistance to such exploitation.

Survival for Bolivian Workers

Buenos Aires is the number one destination for migrants from Bolivia, Paraguay, and Peru, whose numbers have grown in the past decade because of the declining economic conditions in those countries. More than one million Bolivians have migrated to Argentina since 1999; approximately one-third are undocumented.

Even when Argentina's economy took a nosedive in the 1990s, Bolivians were still driven to migrate there given their homeland's far more bleak economic conditions. Over two-thirds of Bolivians live in poverty, and nearly half subsist on less than a dollar a day. For decades, migration of rural workers (44% of the population) to urban areas kept many families afloat. Now, facing limited employment opportunities and low salaries in Bolivia's cities, many workers have opted to migrate to Argentina or Brazil.

Buenos Aires' clandestine network of sweatshops emerged in the late 1990s, following the influx of inexpensive Asian textile imports. Most of the textile factory owners are Argentine, Korean, or Bolivian. The workers manufacture garments for high-end brands like Lacár, Kosiuko, Adidas, and Montage in what has become a $700 million a year industry.

In many cases workers are lured by radio or newspaper ads in Bolivia promising transportation to Buenos Aires and decent wages plus room and board once they arrive. Truck drivers working for the trafficking rings transport workers in the back of trucks to cross into Argentina illegally.

For undocumented immigrants in Argentina, survival itself is a vicious cycle. The undocumented are especially susceptible to threats of losing their jobs. Workers can't afford to rent a room; even if they could, many residential hotel managers are unwilling to rent rooms to immigrants, especially when they have children.

Finding legal work is almost impossible without a national identity card. For years, Bolivian citizens had reported that Alvaro Gonzalez Quint, the head of Bolivia's consulate in Buenos Aires, would charge immigrants up to $100—equivalent to a textile worker's average monthly pay—to complete paperwork necessary for their documentation. The Argentine League for Human Rights has also brought charges against Gonzalez Quint in federal court, alleging he is tied to the network of smugglers who profit from bringing immigrants into Argentina to work in the sweatshops.

A New Chapter in Argentina's Labor Struggles

Argentina has a notable tradition of labor organizing among immigrants. Since the 19th century, working-class immigrants have fought for basic rights, including

Sundays off, eight-hour workdays, and a minimum wage. The eight-hour workday became law in 1933, but employers have not always complied. Beginning with the 1976-1983 military dictatorship, and continuing through the neoliberal 1990s, many labor laws have been altered to allow flexible labor standards. University of Buenos Aires economist Eduardo Lucita, a member of UDI (Economists from the Left), says that although the law for an eight-hour workday stands, the average work-day in Argentina is 10 to 12 hours. "Only half of workers have formal labor con-tracts; the rest are laboring as subcontracted workers in the unregulated, informal sector. For such workers there are no regulations for production rates and lengths of a workday—much less criteria for salaries." The average salary for Argentines is only around $200 a month, in contrast to the minimum of $600 required to meet the basic needs of a family of four.

Today, the extreme abuses in the new sweatshops have prompted a new genera-tion of immigrant workers to organize.

"We have had to remain silent and accept abuse. I'm tired of taking the blows. We are starting to fight, *compañeros*; thank you for attending the assembly." These are the words of Ana Salazar at an assembly of textile workers that met in Buenos Aires on a Sunday evening last April. The UTC formed out of a neighborhood assembly in the working class neighborhood of Parque Avalleneda. Initially, the assembly was a weekly social event for families on Sundays, the only day textile workers can leave the shop. Families began to gather at the assembly location, situ-ated at the corner of a park. Later, because Argentina's traditional unions refuse to accept undocumented affiliates, the workers expanded their informal assembly into a full-fledged union.

Since the factory fire that killed six on March 30, 2006, the UTC has stepped up actions against the brand-name clothing companies that subcontract with clan-destine sweatshops. The group has held a number of *escraches*, or exposure protests, outside fashion makers' offices in Buenos Aires to push the city government to hold inspections inside the companies' textile workshops. Workers from the UTC also presented legal complaints against the top jean manufacturer Kosiuko.

At a recent surprise protest, young women held placards: "I kill myself for your jeans," signed, "a Bolivian textile worker." During the protest, outside Kosiuko's offices in the exclusive Barrio Norte neighborhood, UTC presented an in-depth research report into the brand's labor violations. "The Kosiuko company is conceal-ing slave shops," said Gustavo Vera, member of the La Alemeda popular assembly. "They disclosed false addresses to inspectors and they have other workshops which they are not reporting to the city government." The UTC released a detailed list of the locations of alleged sweatshops. Most of the addresses that the Kosiuko com-pany had provided turned out to be private residences or stores.

To further spotlight large brand names that exploit susceptible undocumented workers, the UTC held a unique fashion show in front of the Buenos Aires city legisla-ture last September. "Welcome to the neoliberal fashion show—Spring Season 2006," announced the host, as spectators cheered—or jeered—the top brands that use slave labor. Models from a local theatre group paraded down a red carpet in brands like Kosiuko, Montagne, Porte Said, and Lacar, while the host shouted out the addresses of the brands' sweatshops and details of subhuman conditions inside shops.

"I repressed all of my rage about my working conditions and violations of my rights. Inside a clandestine workshop you don't have any rights. You don't have dignity," said Naomi Hernández, pedaling away at a sewing machine during the "fashion show."

After the show, Hernández stood up in front of the spectators and choked down tears while giving testimony of her experience as a slave laborer in a sweatshop: "I found out what it is to fight as a human being." She says her life has changed since joining the UTC.

Inspection-Free Garment Shops

To date, the union's campaign has had some successes. In April of 2006, the Buenos Aires city government initiated inspections of sweatshops employing Bolivians and Paraguayans; inspectors shut down at least 100. (Perhaps not surprisingly, Bolivian consul Gonzalez Quint has protested the city government's moves to regulate sweatshops, arguing that the measures discriminate against Bolivian employers who run some of the largest textile shops.) But since then, inspections have been suspended and many clothes manufacturers have simply moved their sweatshops to the suburban industrial belt or to new locations in the city. The UTC has reported that other manufacturers force workers to labor during the night to avoid daytime inspections.

Nestor Escudero, an Argentine who participates in the UTC, says that police, inspectors, and the courts are also responsible for the documented slave-labor conditions inside textile factories. "They bring in illegal immigrants to brutally exploit them. The textile worker is paid 75 cents for a garment that is later sold for $50. This profit is enough to pay bribes and keep this system going."

Since 2003, thousands of reports of slave-labor conditions have piled up in the courts without any resolution. In many cases when workers have presented reports to police of poor treatment, including threats, physical abuse, and forced labor, the police say they can't act because the victims do not have national identity cards.

Seeing their complaints go unheeded is sometimes the least of it. Escudero has confirmed that over a dozen textile workers have received death threats for reporting to media outlets on slave-labor conditions inside the textile plants. Shortly after the UTC went public last spring with hundreds of reports of abuses, over a dozen of the union's representatives were threatened. And in a particularly shocking episode, two men kidnapped the 9-year-old son of José Orellano and Monica Frías, textile workers who had reported slave-labor conditions in their shop. The attackers held the boy at knifepoint and told him to "tell your parents that they should stop messing around with the reports against the sweatshops." The UTC filed criminal charges of abandonment and abuse of power against Argentina's Interior Minister Aníbal Fernández in November for not providing the couple with witness protection.

The Road Ahead

Although the Buenos Aires city government has yet to make much headway in regulating the city's sweatshops, the UTC continues to press for an end to sweatshop slavery, along with mass legalization of immigrants and housing for immigrants living in poverty. Organizing efforts have not been in vain. In an important victory, the city government has opened a number of offices to process immigration documents free of charge for Bolivian and Paraguayan citizens, circumventing the Bolivian Consulate.

The UTC has also proposed that clandestine textile shops be shut down and handed over to the workers to manage them as co-ops and, ultimately, build a cooperative network that can bypass the middlemen and the entire piece-work system. Already, the Alameda assembly has joined with the UTC to form the Alameda Workers' Cooperative as an alternative to sweatshops. Nearly 30 former sweatshop workers work at the cooperative in the same space where the weekly assemblies are held.

Olga Cruz now works with the cooperative sewing garments. She says that although it's a struggle, she now has dignity that she didn't have when she worked in one of the piece-work shops. "We are working as a cooperative, we all make the same wage. In the clandestine shops you are paid per garment: they give you the fabric and you have to hand over the garment fully manufactured. Here we have a line system, which is more advanced and everyone works the same amount."

Fired for reporting on abusive conditions at her sweatshop, Naomi Hernández has also found work at the cooperative. "We are freeing ourselves, that's what I feel. Before I wasn't a free person and didn't have any rights," said Hernández to a crowd of spectators in front of the city legislature. She sent a special message and invitation: "Now we are fighting together with the Alameda cooperative and the UTC. I invite all workers who know their rights are being violated to join the movement against slave labor." ❑

Resources: To contact UTC activists at La Alameda assembly in Parque Avellaneda, email: asambleaparqueavellaneda@hotmail.com. To see videos of recent UTC actions, go to: www. revolutionvideo.org/agoratv/secciones/luchas_obreras/costureros_utc.html; www.revolutionvideo. org/agoratv/secciones/luchas_obreras/escrache_costureros.html.

Article 6.4

THE RIGHT TO STAY HOME

Transnational communities are creating new ways of looking at citizenship and residence that correspond to the realities of migration.

BY DAVID BACON
September/October 2008

For almost half a century, migration has been the main fact of social life in hundreds of indigenous towns spread through the hills of Oaxaca, one of Mexico's poorest states. That's made migrants' rights, and the conditions they face, central concerns for communities like Santiago de Juxtlahuaca. Today the right to travel to seek work is a matter of survival. But this June in Juxtlahuaca, in the heart of Oaxaca's Mixteca region, dozens of farmers left their fields, and weavers their looms, to talk about another right—the right to stay home.

In the town's community center two hundred Mixtec, Zapotec, and Triqui farmers, and a handful of their relatives working in the United States, made impassioned speeches asserting this right at the triannual assembly of the Indigenous Front of Binational Organizations (FIOB). Hot debates ended in numerous votes. The voices of mothers and fathers arguing over the future of their children echoed from the cinderblock walls of the cavernous hall. In Spanish, Mixteco, and Triqui, people repeated one phrase over and over: *el derecho de no migrar*—the right to *not* migrate. Asserting this right challenges not just inequality and exploitation facing migrants, but the very reasons why people have to migrate to begin with. Indigenous communities are pointing to the need for social change.

About 500,000 indigenous people from Oaxaca live in the United States, including 300,000 in California alone, according to Rufino Dominguez, one of FIOB's founders. These men and women come from communities whose economies are totally dependent on migration. The ability to send a son or daughter across the border to the north, to work and send back money, makes the difference between eating chicken or eating salt and tortillas. Migration means not having to manhandle a wooden plough behind an ox, cutting furrows in dry soil for a corn crop that can't be sold for what it cost to plant it. It means that dollars arrive in the mail when kids need shoes to go to school, or when a grandparent needs a doctor.

Seventy-five percent of Oaxaca's 3.4 million residents live in extreme poverty, according to EDUCA, an education and development organization. For more than two decades, under pressure from international lenders, the Mexican government has cut spending intended to raise rural incomes. Prices have risen dramatically since price controls and subsidies were eliminated for necessities like gasoline, electricity, bus fares, tortillas, and milk.

Raquel Cruz Manzano, principal of the Formal Primary School in San Pablo Macuiltianguis, a town in the indigenous Zapotec region, says only 900,000

Oaxacans receive organized health care, and the illiteracy rate is 21.8%. "The educational level in Oaxaca is 5.8 years," Cruz notes, "against a national average of 7.3 years. The average monthly wage for non-governmental employees is less than 2,000 pesos [about $200] per family," the lowest in the nation. "Around 75,000 children have to work in order to survive or to help their families," says Jaime Medina, a reporter for Oaxaca's daily *Noticias*, "A typical teacher earns about 2200 pesos every two weeks [about $220]. From that they have to purchase chalk, pencils and other school supplies for the children." Towns like Juxtlahuaca don't even

CITIZENSHIP, POLITICAL RIGHTS, AND LABOR RIGHTS

Citizenship is a complex issue in a world in which transnational migrant communities span borders and exist in more than one place simultaneously. Residents of transnational communities don't see themselves simply as victims of an unfair system, but as actors capable of reproducing culture, of providing economic support to families in their towns of origin, and of seeking social justice in the countries to which they've migrated. A sensible immigration policy would recognize and support migrant communities. It would reinforce indigenous culture and language, rather than treating them as a threat. At the same time, it would seek to integrate immigrants into the broader community around them and give them a voice in it, rather than promoting social exclusion, isolation, and segregation. It would protect the rights of immigrants as part of protecting the rights of all working people.

Transnational communities in Mexico are creating new ways of looking at citizenship and residence that correspond more closely to the reality of migration. In 2005 Jesús Martínez, a professor at California State University in Fresno, was elected by residents of the state of Michoacán in Mexico to their state legislature. His mandate was to represent the interests of the state's citizens living in the United States. "In Michoacán, we're trying to carry out reforms that can do justice to the role migrants play in our lives," Martínez said. In 2006 Pepe Jacques Medina, director of the Comité Pro Uno in Los Angeles' San Fernando Valley, was elected to the Federal Chamber of Deputies on the ticket of the left-leaning Party of the Democratic Revolution (PRD) with the same charge. Transnational migrants insist that they have important political and social rights, both in their communities of origin and in their communities abroad.

The two parties that control the Mexican national congress, the Institutional Revolutionary Party (PRI) and the National Action Party (PAN), have taken steps to provide political rights for migrants. But while Mexico's congress voted over a decade ago to enfranchise Mexicans in the United States, it only set up a system to implement that decision in April 2005. They imposed so many obstacles that in the 2006 presidential elections only 40,000 were able to vote, out of a potential electorate of millions.

While it is difficult for Mexicans in the United States to vote in Mexico, they are barred from voting in the United States altogether. But U.S. electoral politics can't remain forever immune from expectations of representation, and they shouldn't. After all, the slogan of the Boston Tea Party was "No taxation without representation"; those who make economic contributions have political rights. That principle requires recognition of the legitimate social status of everyone living in the United States. Legalization isn't just important to migrants—it is a basic step in the preservation and extension of democratic rights for all people. With and without

have waste water treatment. Rural communities rely on the same rivers for drinking water that are also used to carry away sewage.

"There are no jobs here, and NAFTA [the North American Free Trade Agreement] made the price of corn so low that it's not economically possible to plant a crop anymore," Dominguez asserts. "We come to the U.S. to work because we can't get a price for our product at home. There is no alternative." Without large-scale political change, most communities won't have the resources for productive projects and economic development that could provide a decent living.

visas, 34 million migrants living in the United States cannot vote to choose the political representatives who decide basic questions about wages and conditions at work, the education of their children, their health care or lack of it, and even whether they can walk the streets without fear of arrest and deportation.

Migrants' disenfranchisement affects U.S. citizens, especially working people. If all the farm workers and their families in California's San Joaquin Valley were able to vote, a wave of living wage ordinances would undoubtedly sweep the state. California's legislature would pass a single-payer health plan to ensure that every resident receives free and adequate health care. If it failed to pass, San Joaquin Valley legislators, currently among the most conservative, would be swept from office.

When those who most need social change and economic justice are excluded from the electorate, the range of possible reform is restricted, not only on issues of immigration, but on most economic issues that affect working people. Immigration policy, including political and social rights for immigrants, are integral parts of a broad agenda for change that includes better wages and housing, a national healthcare system, a national jobs program, and the right to organize without fear of being fired. Without expanding the electorate, it will be politically difficult to achieve any of it. By the same token, it's not possible to win major changes in immigration policy apart from a struggle for these other goals.

Anti-immigrant hysteria has always preached that the interests of immigrants and the native born are in conflict, that one group can only gain at the expense of the other. In fact, the opposite is true. To raise wages generally, the low price of immigrant labor has to rise, which means that immigrant workers have to be able to organize effectively. Given half a chance, they will fight for better jobs, wages, schools, and health care, just like anyone else. When they gain political power, the working class communities around them benefit too. Since it's easier for immigrants to organize if they have permanent legal status, a real legalization program would benefit a broad range of working people, far beyond immigrants themselves. On the other hand, when the government and employers use employer sanctions, enforcement, and raids to stop the push for better conditions, organizing is much more difficult, and unions and workers in general suffer the consequences.

The social exclusion and second-class status imposed by guestworker programs only increases migrants' vulnerability. De-linking immigration status and employment is a necessary step to achieving equal rights for migrant workers, who will never have significant power if they have to leave the country when they lose their jobs. Healthy immigrant communities need employed workers, but they also need students, old and young people, caregivers, artists, the disabled, and those who don't have traditional jobs.

Because of its indigenous membership, FIOB campaigns for the rights of migrants in the United States who come from those communities. It calls for immigration amnesty and legalization for undocumented migrants. FIOB has also condemned the proposals for guestworker programs. Migrants need the right to work, but "these workers don't have labor rights or benefits," Dominguez charges. "It's like slavery."

At the same time, "we need development that makes migration a choice rather than a necessity—the right to not migrate," explains Gaspar Rivera Salgado, a professor at UCLA. "Both rights are part of the same solution. We have to change the debate from one in which immigration is presented as a problem to a debate over rights. The real problem is exploitation." But the right to stay home, to not migrate, has to mean more than the right to be poor, the right to go hungry and be homeless. Choosing whether to stay home or leave only has meaning if each choice can provide a meaningful future.

In Juxtlahuaca, Rivera Salgado was elected as FIOB's new binational coordinator. His father and mother still live on a ranch half an hour up a dirt road from the main highway, in the tiny town of Santa Cruz Rancho Viejo. There his father Sidronio planted three hundred avocado trees a few years ago, in the hope that someday their fruit would take the place of the corn and beans that were once his staple crops. He's fortunate—his relatives have water, and a pipe from their spring has kept most of his trees, and those hopes, alive. Fernando, Gaspar's brother, has started growing mushrooms in a FIOB-sponsored project, and even put up a greenhouse for tomatoes. Those projects, they hope, will produce enough money that Fernando won't have to go back to Seattle, where he worked for seven years.

This family perhaps has come close to achieving the *derecho de no migrar*. For the millions of farmers throughout the indigenous countryside, not migrating means doing something like what Gaspar's family has done. But finding the necessary resources, even for a small number of families and communities, presents FIOB with its biggest challenge.

Rivera Salgado says, "we will find the answer to migration in our communities of origin. To make the right to not migrate concrete, we need to organize the forces in our communities, and combine them with the resources and experiences we've accumulated in 16 years of cross-border organizing." Over the years FIOB has organized women weavers in Juxtlahuaca, helping them sell their textiles and garments through its chapters in California. It set up a union for rural taxis, both to help farming families get from Juxtlahuaca to the tiny towns in the surrounding hills, and to provide jobs for drivers. Artisan co-ops make traditional products, helped by a cooperative loan fund.

The government does have some money for loans to start similar projects, but it usually goes to officials who often just pocket it, supporters of the ruling PRI, which has ruled Oaxaca since it was formed in the 1940s. "Part of our political culture is the use of *regalos*, or government favors, to buy votes," Rivera Salgado explains. "People want *regalos*, and think an organization is strong because of what it can give. It's critical that our members see organization as the answer to problems, not a gift from the government or a political party. FIOB members need political education."

But for the 16 years of its existence, FIOB has been a crucial part of the political opposition to Oaxaca's PRI government. Juan Romualdo Gutierrez Cortéz, a school teacher in Tecomaxtlahuaca, was FIOB's Oaxaca coordinator until he stepped down at the Juxtlahuaca assembly. He is also a leader of Oaxaca's teachers union, Section 22 of the National Education Workers Union, and of the Popular Association of the People of Oaxaca (APPO).

A June 2006 strike by Section 22 sparked a months-long uprising, led by APPO, which sought to remove the state's governor, Ulises Ruíz, and make a basic change in development and economic policy. The uprising was crushed by Federal armed intervention, and dozens of activists were arrested. According to Leoncio Vásquez, an FIOB activist in Fresno, "the lack of human rights itself is a factor contributing to migration from Oaxaca and Mexico, since it closes off our ability to call for any change." This spring teachers again occupied the central plaza, or *zócalo*, of the state capital, protesting the same conditions that sparked the uprising two years ago.

In the late 1990s Gutierrez was elected to the Oaxaca Chamber of Deputies, in an alliance between FIOB and Mexico's left-wing Democratic Revolutionary Party (PRD). Following his term in office, he was imprisoned by Ruíz' predecessor, José Murat, until a binational campaign won his release. His crime, and that of many others filling Oaxaca's jails, was insisting on a new path of economic development that would raise rural living standards and make migration just an option, rather than an indispensable means of survival.

Despite the fact that APPO wasn't successful in getting rid of Ruíz and the PRI, Rivera Salgado believes that "in Mexico we're very close to getting power in our communities on a local and state level." FIOB delegates agreed that the organization would continue its alliance with the PRD. "We know the PRD is caught up in an internal crisis, and there's no real alternative vision on the left," Rivera Salgado says. "But there are no other choices if we want to participate in electoral politics. Migration is part of globalization," he emphasizes, "an aspect of state policies that expel people. Creating an alternative to that requires political power. There's no way to avoid that." ❑

Article 6.5

THE RISE OF MIGRANT WORKER MILITANCY

IMMANUEL NESS
September/October 2006

Testifying before the Senate immigration hearings in early July, Mayor Michael Bloomberg affirmed that undocumented immigrants have become indispensable to the economy of New York City: "Although they broke the law by illegally crossing our borders or overstaying their visas, and our businesses broke the law by employing them, our city's economy would be a shell of itself had they not, and it would collapse if they were deported. The same holds true for the nation." Bloomberg's comment outraged right-wing pundits, but how much more outraged would they be if they knew that immigrant workers, beyond being economically indispensable, are beginning to transform the U.S. labor movement with a bold new militancy?

After years of working in obscurity in the unregulated economy, migrant workers in New York City catapulted themselves to the forefront of labor activism beginning in late 1999 through three separate organizing drives among low-wage workers. Immigrants initiated all three drives: Mexican immigrants organized and struck for improved wages and working conditions at greengroceries; Francophone African delivery workers struck for unpaid wages and respect from labor contractors for leading supermarket chains; and South Asians organized for improved conditions and a union in the for-hire car service industry. (In New York, "car services" are taxis that cannot be hailed on the street, only arranged by phone.) These organizing efforts have persisted, and are part of a growing militancy among migrant workers in New York City and across the United States.

Why would seemingly invisible workers rise up to contest power in their workplaces? Why are vulnerable migrant workers currently more likely to organize than are U.S.-born workers? To answer these questions, we have to look at immigrants' distinct position in the political economy of a globalized New York City and at their specific economic and social niches, ones in which exploitation and isolation nurture class consciousness and militancy.

Labor Migration and Industrial Restructuring

New immigrant workers in the United States, many here illegally, stand at the crossroads of two overwhelming trends. On one hand, industrial restructuring and capital mobility have eroded traditional industries and remade the U.S. political economy in the last 30 years in ways that have led many companies to create millions of low-wage jobs and to seek vulnerable workers to fill them. On the other hand, at the behest of international financial institutions like the International Monetary Fund, and to meet the requirements of free-trade agreements such as NAFTA, governments throughout the global South have adopted neoliberal policies that have restructured their economies, resulting in the displacement of urban workers and rural farmers alike. Many have no choice but to migrate north.

A century ago the United States likewise experienced a large influx of immigrants, many of whom worked in factories for their entire lives. There they formed social networks across ethnic lines and developed a class consciousness that spurred the organizing of unions; they made up the generation of workers whose efforts began with the fight for the eight-hour day around the turn of the last century and culminated in the great organizing victories of the 1930s and 1940s across the entire spectrum of mining and manufacturing industries.

Today's immigrants face an entirely different political-economic landscape. Unlike most of their European counterparts a century ago, immigration restrictions mean that many newcomers to the United States are now here illegally. Workers from Latin America frequently migrate illegally without proper documentation; those from Africa, Asia, and Europe commonly arrive with business, worker, student, or tourist visas, then overstay them.

The urban areas where many immigrants arrive have undergone a 30-year decline in manufacturing jobs. The growing pool of service jobs which have come in their stead tend to be dispersed in small firms throughout the city. The proliferation of geographically dispersed subcontractors who compete on the basis of low wages encourages a process of informalization—a term referring to a redistribution of work from regulated sectors of the economy to new unregulated sectors of the underground or informal economy. As a result, wages and working conditions have fallen, often below government-established norms.

Although informal work is typically associated with the developing world—or Global South—observers are increasingly recognizing the link between the regulated and unregulated sectors in advanced industrial regions. More and more the regulated sector depends on unregulated economic activity through subcontracting and outsourcing of work to firms employing low-wage immigrant labor. Major corporations employ or subcontract to businesses employing migrant workers in what were once established sectors of the economy with decent wages and working conditions.

Informalization requires government regulatory agencies to look the other way. For decades federal and state regulatory bodies have ignored violations of laws governing wages, hours, and workplace safety, leading to illegally low wages and declining workplace health and safety practices. The process of informalization is furthered by the reduction or elimination of protections such as disability insurance, Social Security, health care coverage, unemployment insurance, and workers compensation.

By the 1990s, substandard jobs employing almost exclusively migrant workers had become crucial to key sectors of the national economy. Today, immigrants have gained a major presence as bricklayers, demolition workers, and hazardous waste workers on construction and building rehab sites; as cooks, dishwashers, and busboys in restaurants; and as taxi drivers, domestic workers, and delivery people.

Employers frequently treat these workers as self-employed. They typically have no union protection and little or no job security. With government enforcement shrinking, they lack the protection of minimum-wage laws and they have been excluded from Social Security and unemployment insurance.

These workers are increasingly victimized by employers who force them to accept 19th-century working conditions and sub-minimum wages. Today, New York City, Los Angeles, Miami, Houston, and Boston form a nexus of international labor migration, with constantly churning labor markets. As long as there is a demand for cheap labor, immigrants will continue to enter the United States in large numbers. Like water, capital always flows to the lowest level, a state of symmetry where wages are cheapest.

In turn, the availability of a reserve army of immigrant labor provides an enormous incentive for larger corporations to create and use subcontracting firms. Without this workforce, employers in the regulated economy would have more incentive to invest in labor-saving technology, increase the capital-labor ratio, and seek accommodation with unions.

New unauthorized immigrants residing and working in the United States are ideal workers in the new informalized sectors: Their undocumented legal status makes them more tractable since they constantly fear deportation. Undocumented immigrants are less likely to know about, or demand adherence to, established labor standards, and even low U.S. wages represent an improvement over earnings in their home countries.

Forging Migrant Labor Solidarity

The perception that new immigrants undermine U.S.-born workers by undercutting prevailing wage and work standards cannot be entirely dismissed. The entry of a large number of immigrants into the underground economy unquestionably reduces the labor market leverage of U.S.-born workers. But the story is more complicated. In spite of their vulnerability, migrant workers have demonstrated a willingness and a capacity to organize for improvements in their wages and working conditions; they arguably are responding to tough conditions on the job with greater militancy than U.S.-born workers.

New York City has been the site of a number of instances of immigrant worker organizing. In 1998, Mexicans working in greengroceries embarked on a citywide organizing campaign to improve their conditions of work. Most of the 20,000 greengrocery workers were paid below $3.00 an hour, working on average 72 hours a week. Some did not make enough to pay their living expenses, no less send remittances back home to Mexico. Following a relentless and coordinated four-year organizing campaign among the workers, employers agreed to raise wages above the minimum and improve working conditions. Moreover, the campaign led state Attorney General Eliot Spitzer to establish a Greengrocer Code of Conduct and to strengthen enforcement of labor regulations.

In another display of immigrant worker militancy, beginning in 1999 Francophone African supermarket delivery workers in New York City fought for and won equality with other workers in the same stores. The workers were responsible for bagging groceries and delivering them to affluent customers in Manhattan and throughout the city. As contractors, the delivery workers were paid no wage, instead relying on the goodwill of customers in affluent neighborhoods to pay tips for each delivery.

The workers were employed in supermarkets and drug stores where some others had a union. Without union support themselves, delivery workers staged a significant strike and insurrection that made consumers aware of their appalling conditions of work. In late October, workers went on strike and marched from supermarket to supermarket, demanding living wages and dignity on the job. At the start of their campaign, wages averaged less than $70 a week. In the months following the strike the workers all won recognition from the stores through the United Food and Commercial Workers that had earlier neglected to include them in negotiations with management. The National Employee Law Project, a national worker advocacy organization, filed landmark lawsuits against the supermarkets and delivery companies and won backwage settlements as the courts deemed them to be workers—not independent contractors in business for themselves.

Immigrant workers have organized countless other campaigns, in New York and across the country. How do new immigrants, with weak ties to organized labor and the state, manage to assert their interests? The explanation lies in the character of immigrant work and social life; the constraints immigrant workers face paradoxically encourage them to draw on shared experiences to create solidarity at work and in their communities.

The typical migrant worker can expect to work twelve-hour days, seven days a week. When arriving home, immigrant workers frequently share the same apartments, buildings, and neighborhoods. These employment ghettos typify immigrant communities across the nation. Workers cook for one another, share stories about their oppressively long and hard days, commiserate about their ill treatment at work, and then go to sleep only to start anew the next day.

Migrant women, surrounded by a world of exploitation, typically suffer even more abuse their male counterparts, suffering from low wages, long hours, and dangerous conditions. Patterns of gender stratification found in the general labor market are even more apparent among migrant women workers. Most jobs in the nonunion economy, such as construction and driving, are stereotypically considered "men's work." Women predominate in the garment industry, as domestic and child care workers, in laundries, hotels, restaurants, and ever more in sex work. A striking example of migrant women's perilous work environment is the massive recruitment of migrant women to clean up the hazardous materials in the rubble left by the collapse of the World Trade Center without proper safety training.

Isolated in their jobs and communities, immigrant workers have few social ties to unions, community groups, and public officials, and few resources to call upon to assist them in transforming their workplaces. Because new immigrants have few social networks outside the workplace, the ties they develop on the job are especially solid and meaningful—and are nurtured every day. The workers' very isolation and status as outsiders, and their concentration into industrial niches by employers who hire on the basis of ethnicity, tend to strengthen old social ties, build new ones, and deepen class solidarity.

Immigrant social networks contribute to workplace militancy. Conversely, activism at work can stimulate new social networks that can expand workers' power. It is through relationships developed on the job and in the community that shared social identities and mutual resentment of the boss evolves into class consciousness and class solidarity: migrant workers begin to form informal organizations, meet with coworkers to respond to poor working conditions, and take action on the shop floor in defiance of employer abuse.

Typically, few workplace hierarchies exist among immigrants, since few reach supervisory positions. As a result, immigrant workers suffer poor treatment equally at the hands of employers. A gathering sense of collective exploitation usually transforms individualistic activities into shared ones. In rare cases where there are immigrant foremen and crew leaders, they may recognize this solidarity and side with the workers rather than with management. One former manager employed for a fast-food sandwich chain in New York City said: "We are hired only to divide the workers but I was really trying to help the workers get better pay and shorter hours."

Migrant workers bring social identities from their home countries, and those identities are shaped through socialization and work in this country. In cities and towns across the United States, segmentation of migrant workers from specific countries reinforces ethnic, national, and religious identities and helps to form other identities that may stimulate solidarity. Before arriving in the United States, Mexican immigrant workers often see themselves as peasants but not initially as "people of color," while Francophone Africans see themselves as Malian or Senegalese ethnics but not necessarily "black." Life and work in New York can encourage them to adopt new identifications, including a new class consciousness that can spur organizing and militancy.

Once triggered, organizing can go from workplace to workplace like wildfire. When workers realize that they can fight and prevail, this creates a sense of invincibility that stimulates militant action that would otherwise be avoided at all costs. This demonstration effect is vitally important, as was the case in the strikes among garment workers and coal miners in the history of the U.S. labor movement.

"Solidarity Forever" vs. "Take This Job and Shove It"

The militancy of many migrant workers contrasts sharply with the passivity of many U.S.-born workers facing the same low wages and poor working conditions. Why do most workers at chain stores and restaurants like Wal-Mart and McDonalds—most of whom were born in the United States—appear so complacent, while new immigrants are often so militant?

Migrants are not inherently more militant or less passive. Instead, the real workplace conditions of migrant workers seem to produce greater militancy on the job. First, collective social isolation engenders strong ties among migrants in low-wage jobs where organizing is frequently the only way to improve conditions. Because migrants work in jobs that are more amenable to organizing, they are highly represented among newly unionized workers. Strong social ties in the workplace drive migrants to form their own embryonic organizations at work and in their communities that are ripe for union representation. Organizing among migrant workers gains the attention of labor unions, which then see a chance to recruit new members and may provide resources to help immigrant workers mobilize at work and join the union.

Employers also play a major role. Firms employing U.S. workers tend to be larger and are often much harder to organize than the small businesses where immigrants work. In 2003, the Merriam-Webster dictionary added the new word McJob, defined as "a low-paying job that requires little skill and provides little opportunity for advancement." The widely accepted coinage reflects the relentless 30-year economic restructuring creating low-end jobs in the retail sector.

Organizing against Home Depot, McDonalds, Taco Bell, or Wal-Mart is completely different from organizing against smaller employers. Wal-Mart uses many of the same tactics against workers that immigrants contend with: failure to pay overtime, stealing time (intentionally paying workers for fewer hours than actually worked), no health care, part-time work, high turnover, and gender division of labor. The difference is that Wal-Mart has far more resources to oppose unionization than do the smaller employers who are frequently subcontractors to larger firms. But Wal-Mart's opposition to labor unions is so forceful that workers choose to leave rather than stay and fight it out. Relentless labor turnover mitigates against the formation of working class consciousness and militancy.

The expanding non-immigrant low-end service sector tends to produce unskilled part-time jobs that do not train workers in skills that keep them in the same sector of the labor market. Because jobs at the low end of the economy require little training, workers frequently move from one industry to the next. One day a U.S.-born worker may work as a sales clerk for Target, the next day as a waiter at Olive Garden. Because they are not stuck in identity-defined niches, U.S. workers change their world by quitting and finding a job elsewhere, giving them less reason to organize and unionize.

The fact that U.S.-born workers have an exit strategy and migrant workers do not is a significant and important difference. Immigrant workers are more prone to take action to change their working conditions because they have far fewer options than U.S.-born workers. Workers employed by companies like Wal-Mart are unable to change their conditions, since they have little power and will be summarily fired for any form of dissent. If workers violate the terms of Wal-Mart's or McDonalds' employee manual by, say, arriving late, and then are summarily fired, no one is likely to fend for them, as is usually the case among many migrant workers. While migrant workers engage in direct action against their employers to obtain higher wages and respect on the job, U.S. workers do not develop the same dense connections in labor market niches that forge solidarity. Employers firing new immigrants may risk demonstrations, picket lines, or even strikes.

Immigrant workers are pushed into low-wage labor market niches as day laborers, food handlers, delivery workers, and nannies; these niches are difficult if not impossible to escape. Yet immigrant workers relegated to dead-end jobs in the lowest echelons of the labor market in food, delivery, and car service work show a greater eagerness to fight it out to improve their wages and conditions than do U.S. workers who can move on to another dead-end job.

The Role of Unions

Today's labor movement is in serious trouble; membership is spiraling downward as employers demand union-free workplaces. Unionized manufacturing and service workers are losing their jobs to low-wage operations abroad. Unions and, more importantly, the U.S. working class, are in dire straits and must find a means to triumph over the neoliberal dogma that dominates the capitalist system.

As organizing campaigns in New York City show, migrant workers are indispensable to the revitalization of the labor movement. As employers turn to migrant labor to fill low-wage jobs, unions must encourage and support organizing drives that emerge from the oppressive conditions of work. As the 1930s workers' movement demonstrates, if conditions improve for immigrants, all workers will prosper. To gain traction, unions must recognize that capital is pitting migrant workers against native-born laborers to lower wages and improve profitability. Although unions have had some success organizing immigrants, most are circling the wagons, disinterested in building a more inclusive mass labor movement. The first step is for unions to go beyond rhetoric and form a broad and inclusive coalition embracing migrant workers. ❑

Chapter 7

ECONOMIC DEVELOPMENT

Article 7.1

WORLD HISTORY AND ECONOMIC DEVELOPMENT
Lessons from New Comparisons of Europe and East Asia

BY RAVI BHANDARI AND **KENNETH POMERANZ**
August 2009

Development prescriptions that assume that the rest of the world can (or should) mimic a stylized North Atlantic path to the modern world dominated the 1950s to 1970s, with limited success. The neo-liberal prescriptions of the last 30 years were no better at creating long-term dynamism, and often imposed horrific social costs.

Most of the success stories of post-1945 development are clustered in East Asia: Taiwan, South Korea, Hong Kong, Singapore, and (with more caveats), coastal China. Among other things, almost the entire *net* reduction in global poverty numbers during the last 30 years has occurred in China, which largely ignored the "Washington Consensus" on development strategy. This geographic clumping has encouraged discussion of an "East Asian development path." Sometimes this is said to derive from 20th century corporatist institutions, sometimes from supposedly timeless "Asian values" of discipline and respect for education; but none of these are sufficiently "East Asian" to explain very much.

A new comparative history of economic development yields different lessons. It highlights differences in political-economic relations between cores and peripheries and differential access to fossil fuels in explaining why the most dynamic regions in the West out-distanced their East Asian counterparts in the 19th century, casting particular doubt on arguments that focus on allegedly more perfect markets in the West. A second theme is the role of labor-intensive industries, often based in the countryside and employing people from households still connected to agriculture (creating relatively low rates of both urbanization and proletarianization). This period of catch-up growth unfolds with less growth of landlessness and less inequality than in most of the industrializing West. However, in China (by far the biggest East Asian country) we also see problems related to trade-dependence, resource shortages, and environmental degradation. These problems have made the indefinite extension of this path highly unlikely, and have engendered familiar strategies—socially and environmentally disquieting—for China's interior.

Comparative-Historical Theories of Development

Recent scholarship suggests a rough comparability in living standards between advanced areas in 18th century China and those in Europe. This allows us to use China to raise questions about Europe, and its 19th century breakthrough to sustained per capita growth. If the divergence in economic performance was quite late, it makes untenable any simple contrast between Western growth and non-Western stagnation. It also means that any explanation resting on cultural or institutional differences (which preceded the divergence by centuries) face a new burden of proof. We must either explain why some difference that was not particularly advantageous earlier became so later, or find offsetting disadvantages that fell away at a particular point, rather than looking only for "advantages" within Europe.

By contrast, most social science in both the Marxist and Weberian traditions was born from contemplation of a West that (briefly) held the world's only industrial societies, and took Western Europe as the standard of "real" historical change; other places were examples of failed, absent, or deviant development. The "new world history," or "California School," of which the work discussed here forms a part, does not deny that this approach yielded many insights, but suggests that reciprocal comparisons may be more valuable today: comparisons in which we also ask, "Why wasn't England the Yangzi Delta or the Kinai—wealthy agro-commercial areas with lots of handicrafts that did not initiate large-scale energy-intensive manufacturing?" Such comparisons are useful for separating the necessary and the contingent in North Atlantic growth; many structures happened to be in place as the West industrialized, and were adapted to serve that process—e.g. financial markets originally designed mostly to finance war were also useful for financing new technologies like railways that required lots of patient capital—but it does not follow that they were necessary to the process. Reciprocal comparisons allow us to take more seriously the possibilities that other societies had advantages as well as disadvantages, and to see the possibilities for transformative change that draws upon, rather than simply overcoming, indigenous institutions and expectations.

Others have taken these elements and combined them in other ways. André Gunder Frank, for instance, shared the emphasis here on the relative prosperity of early modern East Asia—indeed, he went much further, suggesting that Europe did not become more prosperous until the middle of the 19th century—and also used it to raise doubts about whether Western institutions were more conducive to growth. He also questioned the significance of any differences in local institutions, favoring an exclusive significance on the dynamics of a world system. Others, such as R. Bin Wong and Jack Goldstone, have differed from the analysis here in the opposite direction, focusing more or less exclusively on reciprocal comparisons while minimizing (at least for the pre-1850 period) the significance of trans-continental connections (including violent ones) and questions of resource endowments and extraction that will figure prominently in later parts of this essay.

But all of us have concluded that the evidence is inconsistent with any assertion that early modern European culture or economic institutions led directly to superior economic performance, much less that they were both necessary and sufficient for the creation of modernity.

Early Modern Economies and the Origins of the Great Divergence

An emerging consensus among European economic historians has moved away from seeing industrialization as a British-centered "Big Bang." Instead, they put industrialization back into its historical context: in long processes of slowly-growing markets, division of labor, many small innovations, and gradual accumulation. The gradual market-driven growth thus highlighted was crucial, but it didn't differentiate Europe from East Asia. Smithian dynamics worked just as well in much of China and Japan, but didn't transform basic possibilities—eventually, highly developed areas everywhere came up against serious resource constraints, in part because commercialization and proto-industrialization accelerated population growth. Britain ultimately needed not only technology and institutions, but also the Americas, coal, and various favorable conjunctures. In Flanders and even Holland, proto-industrialization and productive commercial agriculture led to results more like China's Yangzi Delta or Japan's Kinai region than like England.

Some readers may object to comparing regions within China and Japan to European countries, but China more closely resembles all of Europe than any one European country in its range of environments, living standards and so on. The Yangzi Delta (with about 31.5 million people in 1770, exceeding France plus the Low Countries), the empire's most developed region, can be compared to Britain (or Britain plus the Netherlands) in terms of its prosperity and its position within a larger system. The rice-exporting, cloth-importing Middle Yangzi might be better compared to Poland. Such comparisons illuminate parallels and differences in the structuring of inter-regional relationships within world areas, and relate economic development to larger contexts, rather than searching within each region for its "key to success" or "fatal flaw."

In an influential version of the gradualist story, Jan DeVries has placed the Industrial Revolution within a larger "*industrious* revolution"—a concept which helps resolve a paradox. The grain-buying power of European day wages fell sharply between 1430 and 1550, and took centuries to regain 1430 levels. Yet death inventories from 1550 on show ordinary people slowly gaining more possessions. These trends can be reconciled because people worked more hours per year for money, allowing them to buy both more non-food goods and stable amounts of increasingly expensive bread. Leisure probably decreased—though this is hard to pin down—and people certainly spent less time making goods for their own households. Instead, they specialized more and bought more, including many goods (baked bread, manufactured candles, etc.) which "saved time" on domestic chores.

Chinese trends were similar. The rice-buying power of day wages generally fell in late imperial times, but nutritional standards do not seem to have fallen, or to have been inferior to Europe's. Average Chinese caloric intake in the late 1700s appears to compare well with Europe (and that of the Yangzi Delta with England); China probably led in vitamin intake; and most surprisingly, protein consumption in the Delta and England seems to have been comparable, at least for the vast majority of both societies. Rough nutritional parity is also suggested by Chinese life expectancies, which were comparable to England's (and thus above Continental Europe's) until at least 1750. Moreover, while Chinese birth rates (contrary to mythology) appear to have been no higher than European ones between 1550 and 1850, the rate of population growth was the same or slightly higher, suggesting that Chinese death rates were the same or lower.

There is abundant anecdotal evidence that the consumption of "non-essentials" by ordinary Chinese was rising modestly between about 1500 and 1750, much as it was in Western Europe. Quantitative estimates for various commodities suggest that in most cases China circa 1750 stacked up well against Europe, and the Yangzi Delta fairly well against England. Yangzi Delta labor productivity in the largest sector of all 18th century economies—agriculture—was 90% of England's as late as 1820, leaving both far ahead of almost all of Continental Europe. Total factor productivity was much higher in the Yangzi Delta, because of greatly superior land productivity. In the second largest sector, textiles, the earnings per day of Yangzi Delta producers exceeded those of their English counterparts even in the late 18th century, though the beginnings of mechanization must have caused their productivity to fall behind by then.

The Yangzi Delta may not have stacked up quite as well overall against England as it did sector by sector, because the mix of sectors was different. Lacking much in the way of ores, forest, fossil fuels, or even waterpower (being essentially flat), the Delta had less of its labor force in energy-intensive industry. For example, using one 1704 data set, charcoal was 20 times as costly relative to labor in Canton as it was in London, though real wages were roughly equal. And while the Delta's long-distance trade was very large, it was, as we shall see, leveling off by the late 1700s.

Generally speaking, though, the economic performance of these two regions was surprisingly similar. Europe-China comparisons are more difficult to do than those for England and the Yangzi Delta, because conditions varied much more and statistics are less reliable; but the data we have also suggest fairly close comparability in 1750 and perhaps 1800.

But another feature of East Asian cores was strikingly different from the early modern West (and probably South Asia). From the 16th century on, a growing percentage of rural European workers (whether in agriculture or other occupations) were proletarians—people who owned no means of production and worked for wages. In the most advanced parts of 18th century Europe they became a majority. In China, however (and, for different reasons, also Japan), proletarians were under 10% of the 18th century rural population; almost every household either owned some land or had secure tenancy. On the positive side, this reflected both hard-won customary rights and the state's desire for a peasantry sufficiently independent to be ruled without going through local magnates. More negatively, it reflected very low reproduction rates among those who were proletarianized. Since sex-selective infanticide and neglect skewed male/female ratios, and a few elite males had concubines as well as wives, the poorest men rarely married. (This was perhaps their most intense social grievance; it disappeared for a while after the Revolution, but has reappeared due to sex-selective abortion.)

Given secure tenure, even full-time tenants earned more than twice as much as rural wage laborers. Since urban unskilled wages were very close to rural ones, the poor had little incentive to head for the cities. They were much better off heading for the frontier, where gaining access to land was relatively easy: average incomes were lower, but the chance for a newcomer to reach that average was much better. Consequently, the large non-agricultural labor force in areas like the Lower Yangzi remained embedded in farm households, which produced both agricultural commodities and light manufactures for sale. The resulting economy produced relatively high average incomes, some cushion against market fluctuations, and probably less inequality than in the early modern West, but it needed a continued frontier (both to trade with and to send migrants to), and it produced fewer of the urban agglomeration effects that *may* have been important to early industrial innovation.

Parity did not last. In the 19th century, output and specialization soared in Europe, while in China, per capita non-grain consumption probably declined: 1900 figures for cloth, sugar, and tobacco, for instance, are below even conservative estimates for 1750.

Much of the difference was ecological, but not because "population pressure" was necessarily producing more serious problems within Chinese core areas than in cores of Europe. Dry-farming areas in North China seem to have been maintaining the soil as well as those in England circa 1800; nutrient balances in South China's paddy rice regions (where periodic inundation provided nutrients that supplemented impressive applications of recycled human and animal wastes) would compare very favorably to anything in Europe. Even for wood supply and deforestation there was no clear Western European advantage circa 1750, despite its much sparser population. China used fuel very efficiently, and was actually better off in certain ways than Western Europe, where deforestation, sandstorms, and other signs of environmental stress were all increasing in the 18th century. Still, high fuel prices mattered, since they made people in China unlikely to try substituting heat energy for labor.

One can find some signs of serious problems and of relatively stable conditions in cores at both ends of Eurasia, and the research available leaves many gaps, however, the current state of our understanding no longer supports older, taken-for-granted notions that because they were more densely populated, East Asian cores must have been worse off than European ones in the 18th century. On the whole, the current research seems to suggest rough comparability. What is clear, however, is that in the early 19th century—when both population and per capita consumption were growing as never before in Western Europe—some ecological variables, such as forested area, underwent a surprising stabilization, after declining considerably amidst the much slower growth of the early modern period. In China, by contrast, ecological problems accelerated despite a slowdown in population growth and a probable stagnation or even decline of per capita consumption.

The basic explanation of this ecological divergence appears to be twofold. One is the English transition to fossil fuels. This required new technology, but also luck. Before railways, most of China's coal deposits were far too many land-locked miles away from its core regions to be economical, regardless of any breakthroughs in extraction and use. In England, by contrast, early deforestation and abundant coal outcroppings in places accessible to London caused widespread early use of this less-preferred fuel, but production would have stalled at early 18th century levels without steam engines to pump water from deeper mines. Early steam engines, meanwhile, were so inefficient that for roughly a century their only use was at the pithead, where fuel was virtually free (fuel prices throughout the early modern world were largely driven by transport costs). But once the engines had *some* use, they were worth tinkering with, eventually reaching a point where they revolutionized transport and opened a new world of cheap, energy-intensive production.

Secondly, Western Europe benefited from a surge in imports of various land-intensive products from less developed areas, especially in the Americas. As demand for food, fiber, building materials, and fuel (Malthus' "four necessities") mounted, cores everywhere had to acquire some of these land-intensive products by trading with peripheries that wanted the manufactures, especially textiles, that cores produced.

But that trade tended to run into one of two problems. Where families in the peripheral areas were largely free to allocate their own labor, export booms stimulated population growth through natural increase and/or immigration. Over time, some labor switched into handicrafts, reducing exportable surpluses of raw materials and demand for imported manufactures. The Middle and Upper Yangzi, North China, and other Chinese hinterlands followed this path around 1750-1850, and what had been by far the world's largest long-distance staple trades declined. Moreover, the terms of trade shifted against manufactures: a bolt of medium-quality cloth bought roughly half as much rice in 1850 as in 1750. Core regions felt the pinch: the Yangzi Delta population stagnated while that of China overall was doubling.

In peripheries with less flexible institutions, such as Eastern Europe, these trade-dampening dynamics were weaker. Few people migrated in, people could not switch into handicrafts on any great scale, and since cash crop producers were often coerced, export booms did not necessarily increase their birth or survival rates. But such regions also responded less to external demand for their primary products in the first place. Thus, the Baltic trade had reached a plateau by 1650 at a fraction the size of China's long distance staple trades.

The Americas, however, were different. Smallpox and other disasters depopulated the region, and most of the new labor force were either slaves, purchased from abroad, or indentured whites transported by land-owners in order to generate exports to Europe. Moreover, plantations in particular often became highly specialized; thus slaves, despite their poverty, were a significant market for coarse cloth and other low-end manufactures. Consequently, the circum-Caribbean slave region (from Brazil to what became the U.S. South) was in some important ways the first "modern" periphery, with large bills to pay for imported capital goods (in this case human ones) and a market for some mass consumer goods. Combined with its ecological bounty, this meant that, unlike most Eurasian peripheries, the Americas kept expanding as a source of land-intensive exports.

Thus, contrary to conventional wisdom, Western Europe broke through resource constraints partly because markets in its peripheries *weren't* unencumbered. They were actually freer in East Asia, which led to a more equal dispersion of proto-industry and an ecological cul-de-sac. One reason for China's declining per capita consumption after about 1750 was a shift in population distribution: as the still relatively prosperous Yangzi Delta went from being about 16% of China to being 9% (and 6% by 1950), hinterlands had much more weight in Chinese aggregates. And while living standards in some hinterlands may have kept creeping upwards, others, as we shall see, declined drastically.

Europe in a Chinese Mirror

Once we stop explaining the bottlenecks China hit as due to peculiar pathologies, we can see more clearly the importance of an unexpected relaxing of land constraints—both through coal and through the Americas—in enabling parts of Northwestern Europe to gain population, specialize more in manufacturing, and consume more per capita without raw material prices soaring. Even in 1830—before the great mid-century boom in North American grain, meat, and timber exports, and when its sugar consumption per capita was just 20% of what it would be by 1900—replacing Britain's New World imports with local products would have required about 23 million acres (mostly to substitute for cotton). This exceeds even E.A. Wrigley's estimate of the additional forest acres that would have been needed to replace the coal boom—and either number roughly matches Britain's total arable land plus pastureland. Thus, positive resource shocks, only partly due to technology, allowed England to stretch ecological constraints that might otherwise have slowed its growth, much as the filling up of China's interior hobbled the Yangzi Delta.

In China, ecological problems mounted in the 19th century—not primarily in cores, but in areas like the over-logged Northwest and Southwest, the North China plain, and alongside rivers whose beds rose as highland forest clearance increased erosion. These problems were exacerbated, as we will see, by a decline in transfer payments from richer regions that had been used in large part for environmental management. In short, though European and Chinese cores had much in common, they were hitched to very different peripheries: filling up, turning to handicrafts, hitting ecological constraints, and exporting fewer primary products in China; and vastly expanded, ecologically rich, and outward-oriented in the Americas.

So colonies (and former colonies) mattered a lot—not necessarily because they yielded especially high profits, as dependency models have claimed, but because they were a special *kind* of trading partner—one which allowed European cores to change labor and capital into land-saving imports in a way that expanded trade closer to home couldn't.

East Asia from the Great Divergence to a (Partial) New Convergence

After recovering from mid-19th century shocks, Japan's economy began to grow faster than ever, benefiting both from new technologies (which were adapted to internal conditions) and from new trading partners with different factor endowments. China had a much rougher late 19th and early 20th century. But it is also true that, after suffering huge mid-century disasters—in part because its state was much weaker than Japan's—China's wealthiest regions also resumed economic growth, benefiting from some technological changes and from new trading opportunities that to some extent replaced the primary products, markets for light manufactures, and outlets for emigration once provided by internal hinterlands. Rice from Southeast Asia, for instance, helped to feed much of the Yangzi Delta and rapidly growing Shanghai, replacing lost shipments from the interior; Guangdong and Fujian soon imported rice, too. Timber and other land-intensive products were imported to coastal areas, while old and new light manufactures—cloth, straw mats, cane chairs, cigarettes, and patent medicines—were exported, along with people. It was some of China's hinterlands that had a hundred-year crisis.

Some internal regions, like the Middle Yangzi, gradually recovered to pre-1850 levels after the mid-19th century rebellions and then reached a plateau. Others, such as North China, declined dramatically, with ecological and political problems reinforcing each other. The Chinese state was battered both by rebellion and by foreign incursions. As it began to recover, its priorities shifted to reflect a more dangerous environment. Defending and developing relatively prosperous and now contested coastal regions became a top priority. Conversely, less attention was devoted to an older "reproductive" statecraft: using revenues from rich regions to underwrite flood control, emergency granaries, irrigation, and other efforts to stabilize family farming and Confucian society in poorer, more ecologically fragile areas. For instance, the state sharply reduced its massive subsidies (between 10% and 20% of all government spending from 1820-1850) for flood control and water transport on the Yellow River and Grand Canal (the canal having been superseded by railways and coastal steamships). The savings were largely diverted to paying indemnities for lost wars and attempts at military modernization. Subsidies for deep wells in semi-arid regions disappeared, even though the water table was falling as population grew.

Thus, certain interior regions suffered simultaneously from being pushed into near-autarchy as long-distance internal trade declined, from population growth, and from a loss of state assistance with worsening environmental problems. Floods, droughts and violence all increased dramatically. (That the late 19th century had especially severe El Niños didn't help.) By contrast, new imports and increased government attention helped stabilize at least some ecological challenges closer to the coast, and levels of violence were much lower there.

Thus, this period provided a strong foretaste of a phenomenon much noted in recent decades: an economic decoupling of coastal and interior China, as the coast became more oriented toward external trading partners and once-crucial inter-regional transfer payments declined. Under these circumstances, coastal China—both the parts seized by imperialists (Taiwan, Hong Kong, the treaty ports, and more briefly Manchuria) and the rest—achieved substantial per capita growth in the early 20th century, despite huge problems. Enough of this growth reached ordinary people for some social indicators to improve: for instance, the average height of railway labor recruits from the Lower Yangzi increased at almost Japanese rates from around 1890-1937. Much of this was powered by growth in rural indus-try, which adapted new technologies but built in many other ways on historical precedents. In Jiangsu province (which included Shanghai), almost half of manufac-turing output still occurred in villages on the eve of World War II. However, interior regions experienced little or even negative growth, much greater social unrest, and a shredding of what had been, by pre-modern standards, a relatively effective safety net. Xia Mingfang has estimated that roughly 1.2 million Chinese died in famines between 1644 and 1796, while 38 million died from 1875-1937—almost all of them in the North and Northwest.

It is therefore not surprising that Maoist political economy, while undoubt-edly revolutionary in many ways, in other ways recalled certain tasks and even solutions from the high Qing era. In some sense collectivization made everyone a proletarian, but in another, every rural household was guaranteed access to farm work where, like smallholders or secure tenants, they earned incomes based on their average, not their marginal, product. Subsequent de-collectivization made the comparison to Qing tenures even stronger, though it is now being undermined as farmland as seized for various development projects. (More modest land reforms also preceded industrial booms in Japan, Taiwan, and South Korea.) Massive (if sometimes counterproductive) efforts were made to industrialize the country-side, rather than assuming that higher living standards would have to come from moving people out of the countryside. Migration to cities essentially stopped by 1960. Funds were again directed from wealthier to poorer regions, and (despite the disasters of the Great Leap) emphasis was placed on subsistence security for poor people and fragile regions. The per capita growth rates are unimpressive next to post-1978 achievements, but the social gains were dramatic: literacy soared and life expectancy nearly doubled between 1950 and 1976. So was the creation of infrastructure, including a crucial tripling of China's irrigated area, almost all of it in the North and Northwest.

An enormous amount changed after 1978, but it's also important to notice what did not. Rural industry, which added 130 million jobs before its job creation leveled off (as it became more capital-intensive) in the mid-1990s, was in many ways a more important engine of growth than the more glamorous reorganization of urban economies. Despite rapid urban growth, China remains more rural than other comparably industrial countries (just barely more urban than England in 1840). The diversification of rural economic activities means that by 2000 more than two-thirds of rural income came from non-agricultural activities, about the same level Taiwan reached circa 1980. (In India, by contrast, the figure is about 45%, and in South Korea 20%.) In the more successful parts of the countryside, families with local land-leasing rights also provide much of the industrial work force; indeed, villages often insure that as many native households as possible have some stake in the more lucrative parts of the local economy before any migrants are employed in good jobs. Though this model is now fraying in many ways, it is worth reiterating some of its achievements: enormous poverty reduction and labor-absorption, vastly fewer semi-legal urban slums than in most of the developing world, and so on.

If we look at things regionally, we again see familiar patterns. This rural industrialization is again very concentrated in coastal areas (though it takes in a bit more of the coast than before); as of a few years ago, over half of rural industrial value added came from three provinces. And, as the export boom suggests, those areas are again more oriented towards a wider world than towards the rest of China. China's ratio of foreign trade to GDP now far exceeds the highest levels reached in Japanese history. Both exports and imports play a role here, as coastal China is importing hugely increased amounts of oil, metals, raw cotton, lumber, and so on— just as Japan, Taiwan, and Korea have come to do. Despite those imports, however, coastal China's economy is still far less resource-intensive than that of the interior: for instance, energy use per dollar of GDP in Jiangsu, Zhejiang, and Guangdong is about 40% of what it is in Gansu and Xinjiang.

And there's the rub—or rather, rubs. Being six times the population of Japan, Korea, and Taiwan, China can't ever import the quantities of primary products per capita that the other countries do. Internally, the rapid growth of inland/coastal and urban/rural inequalities is both a problem in itself and a threat to the basic development model. Incomes in rural areas that remain heavily agricultural now lag so far behind those in other areas that guaranteed access to land is no longer enough to keep people in the countryside (the rural population stopped growing in absolute terms in 1996, just about when rural industry stopped adding significant numbers of jobs). Despite still-significant barriers, net rural-urban migration is now approaching 20 million per year. Here China seems to be following Japanese trends, with a 50-year lag; after remaining relatively rural for its level of industrialization until the 1950s, Japan then began two decades of extremely rapid urbanization at the same time that it moved strongly into higher value-added industries. But when Japan began this push, its unemployment rate was 2%, so that even as the cities bulged, everyone found jobs. China's situation is very different, and its success at avoiding massive peri-urban slums will be hard to sustain. And the prospects for the West absorbing a further surge in manufactured imports from Asia are much murkier than in the 1950s.

One result has been the "Go West" initiative: a massive, government-led campaign to jumpstart economic development through mining, hydropower construction, and other capital-intensive, resource-oriented projects in Western China, to generate primary products for the East. Han Chinese migration to these areas (long restricted to avoid provoking ethnic resentment) is now being subsidized to fill skilled jobs. Lakes, mines, and so on—previously off-limits for various reasons— are now being opened, often over local (and sometimes international) opposition. In general, a long-standing paternalism towards minorities here (which, granted, has been slowly weakening for some time) is now being decisively pushed aside. And this initiative also carries huge ecological risks: removing trees at high elevations where re-growth is slow, quick and dirty mining, diversion of water from the Himalayan glaciers and annual snow melt (some of which currently goes to South and Southeast Asia), and so on. Perhaps half the hydroelectric dams built in West China since 1949 are now silted up, and some new ones are expected to provide power for only 20 years.

In one sense, "Go West" is an effort to stitch the country together, increasing interdependence and reducing economic (and perhaps ethnic) differences. In other ways, it may exacerbate differences. The coastal economy is increasingly semi-private—only 20% of industry remains truly state-owned in many coastal provinces—and the new rich are playing an increasing role in providing local services, as elites in rich areas traditionally did. The West, meanwhile, is seeing a revival of state (often military)-led development, with 60-80% of industry state-owned and far fewer high status jobs outside the state sector. Thus, it is not hard to imagine growing regional differences in social and political orientation as well as in living standards. Rather than a projection of the "East Asian" development seen on the coast across more of the Chinese landscape, developments in the interior (especially the far west) seem to have more in common with colonial or "internal colonial" styles of development.

Conclusion

A comparative history of development casts further doubt on the unique advantages of North Atlantic paths to the modern world; it reminds us that more labor-intensive (and less resource-intensive) "East Asian" paths accounted for much of the world's economic growth during both the period before 1800 and the period since 1945, and may sometimes offer a less socially-disruptive transition to modernity. They should be taken as seriously as models drawn from North Atlantic experiences, not pigeonholed as a regionally specific curiosity. But the East Asian path is no panacea, either—when projected onto the gigantic scale represented by China, it eventually runs up against massive social and environmental problems of its own. We still do not know how to have cores without hinterlands. ❑

Sources: For reasons of both length and style, the footnotes have been removed from this paper. Sources (and a more fully developed version of the argument) can be found in a series of publications by Kenneth Pomeranz, including: The Great Divergence: China, Europe and the Making of the Modern World Economy, Princeton University Press, 2000; "Beyond the East-West Binary: Resituating Development Paths in the Eighteenth Century World," Journal of Asian Studies, May, 2002; "Is There an East Asian Development Path? Long-Term Comparisons, Constraints, and Continuities," Journal of the Economic and Social History of the Orient, 2001; "Standards of Living in 18th Century China: Regional Differences, Temporal Trends, and Incomplete Evidence," in Robert Allen, Tommy Bengtsson, and Martin Dribe, eds., Standards of Living and Mortality in Pre-Industrial Times, Oxford University Press, 2005; "Chinese Development in Long-run Perspective," Proceedings of the American Philosophical Society, March, 2008.

Article 7.2

MICROCREDIT AND WOMEN'S POVERTY

Granting this year's Nobel Peace Prize to microcredit guru Muhammad Yunus affirms neoliberalism.

BY SUSAN F. FEINER AND DRUCILLA K. BARKER

November/December 2006

The key to understanding why Grameen Bank founder and CEO Muhammad Yunus won the Nobel Peace Prize lies in the current fascination with individualistic myths of wealth and poverty. Many policy-makers believe that poverty is "simply" a problem of individual behavior. By rejecting the notion that poverty has structural causes, they deny the need for collective responses. In fact, according to this tough-love view, broad-based civic commitments to increase employment or provide income supports only make matters worse: helping the poor is pernicious because such aid undermines the incentive for hard work. This ideology is part and parcel of neoliberalism.

For neoliberals the solution to poverty is getting the poor to work harder, get educated, have fewer children, and act more responsibly. Markets reward those who help themselves, and women, who comprise the vast majority of microcredit borrowers, are no exception. Neoliberals champion the Grameen Bank and similar efforts precisely because microcredit programs do not change the structural conditions of globalization—such as loss of land rights, privatization of essential public services, or cutbacks in health and education spending—that reproduce poverty among women in developing nations.

What exactly is microcredit? Yunus, a Bangladeshi banker and economist, pioneered the idea of setting up a bank to make loans to the "poorest of the poor." The term "microcredit" reflects the very small size of the loans, often less than $100. Recognizing that the lack of collateral was often a barrier to borrowing by the poor, Yunus founded the Grameen Bank in the 1970s to make loans in areas of severe rural poverty where there were often no alternatives to what we would call loan sharks.

His solution to these problems was twofold. First, Grameen Bank would hire agents to travel the countryside on a regular schedule, making loans and collecting loan repayments. Second, only women belonging to Grameen's "loan circles" would be eligible for loans. If one woman in a loan circle did not meet her obligations, the others in the circle would either be ineligible for future loans or be held responsible for repayment of her loan. In this way the collective liability of the group served as collateral.

The Grameen Bank toasts its successes: not only do loan repayment rates approach 95%, the poor, empowered by their investments, are not dependent on "handouts." Microcredit advocates see these programs as a solution to poverty because poor women can generate income by using the borrowed funds to start small-scale enterprises, often home-based handicraft production. But these enterprises are almost all in the informal sector, which is fiercely competitive and typically unregulated, in other words, outside the range of any laws that protect workers or ensure their rights. Not surprisingly, women comprise the majority of workers in the informal economy and are heavily represented at the bottom of its already-low income scale.

Women and men have different experiences with work and entrepreneurship because a gender division of labor in most cultures assigns men to paid work outside the home and women to unpaid labor in the home. Consequently, women's paid work is constrained by domestic responsibilities. They either work part time, or they combine paid and unpaid work by working at home. Microcredit encourages women to work at home doing piecework: sewing garments, weaving rugs, assembling toys and electronic components. Home workers—mostly women and children—often work long hours for very poor pay in hazardous conditions, with no legal protections. As progressive journalist Gina Neff has noted, encouraging the growth of the informal sector sounds like advice from one of Dickens' more objectionable characters.

Why then do national governments and international organizations promote microcredit, thereby encouraging women's work in the informal sector? As an antipoverty program, microcredit fits nicely with the prevailing ideology that defines poverty as an individual problem and that shifts responsibility for addressing it away from government policy-makers and multilateral bank managers onto the backs of poor women.

Microcredit programs do nothing to change the structural conditions that create poverty. But microcredit *has* been a success for the many banks that have adopted it. Of course, lending to the poor has long been a lucrative enterprise. Pawnshops, finance companies, payday loan operations, and loan sharks charge high interest rates precisely because poor people are often desperate for cash and lack access to formal credit networks. According to Sheryl Nance-Nash, a correspondent for Women's eNews, "the interest rates on microfinance vary between 25% to 50%." She notes that these rates "are much lower than informal money lenders, where rates may exceed 10% per month." It is important for the poor to have access to credit on relatively reasonable terms. Still, microcredit lenders are reaping the rewards of extraordinarily high repayment rates on loans that are still at somewhat above-market interest rates.

Anecdotal accounts can easily overstate the concrete gains to borrowers from microcredit. For example, widely cited research by the Canadian International Development Agency (CIDA) reports that "Women in particular face significant barriers to achieving sustained increases in income and improving their status, and require complementary support in other areas, such as training, marketing, literacy, social mobilization, and other financial services (e.g., consumption loans, savings)." The report goes on to conclude that most borrowers realize only very small gains, and that the poorest borrowers benefit the least. CIDA also found little relationship between loan repayment and business success.

However large or small their income gains, poor women are widely believed to find empowerment in access to microcredit loans. According to the World Bank, for instance, microcredit empowers women by giving them more control over household assets and resources, more autonomy and decision-making power, and greater access to participation in public life. This defense of microcredit stands or falls with individual success stories featuring women using their loans to start some sort of small-scale enterprise, perhaps renting a stall in the local market or buying a sewing machine to assemble piece goods. There is no doubt that when they succeed, women and their families are better off than they were before they became micro-debtors.

But the evidence on microcredit and women's empowerment is ambiguous. Access to credit is not the sole determinant of women's power and autonomy. Credit may, for example, increase women's dual burden of market and household labor. It may also increase conflict within the household if men, rather than women, control how loan moneys are used. Moreover, the group pressure over repayment in Grameen's loan circles can just as easily create conflict among women as build solidarity.

Grameen Bank founder Muhammad Yunus won the Nobel Peace Prize because his approach to banking reinforces the neoliberal view that individual behavior is the source of poverty and the neoliberal agenda of restricting state aid to the most vulnerable when and where the need for government assistance is most acute. Progressives working in poor communities around the world disagree. They argue that poverty is structural, so the solutions to poverty must focus not on adjusting the conditions of individuals but on building structures of inclusion. Expanding the state sector to provide the rudiments of a working social infrastructure is, therefore, a far more effective way to help women escape or avoid poverty.

Do the activities of the Grameen Bank and other micro-lenders romanticize individual struggles to escape poverty? Yes. Do these programs help some women "pull themselves up by the bootstraps"? Yes. Will micro-enterprises in the informal sector contribute to ending world poverty? Not a chance. ❑

Sources: Grameen Bank, grameen-info.org; "Informal Economy: Formalizing the Hidden Potential and Raising Standards," ILO Global Employment Forum (Nov. 2001), www-ilo-mirror. cornell.edu/public/english/employment/geforum/informal.htm; Jean L. Pyle, "Sex, Maids, and Export Processing," World Bank, *Engendering Development; Engendering Development Through Gender Equality in Rights, Resources, and Voice* (Oxford University Press, 2001); Naila Kabeer, "Conflicts Over Credit: Re-Evaluating the Empowerment Potential of Loans to Women in Rural Bangladesh," *World Development* 29 (2001); Norman MacIsaac, "The Role of Microcredit in Poverty Reduction and Promoting Gender Equity," South Asia Partnership Canada, Strategic Policy and Planning Division, Asia Branch Canada International Development Agency (June, 1997), www.acdi-cida.gc.ca/index-e.htm.

Article 7.3

REFORMING LAND REFORM

Land reform is back in the international spotlight.

BY RAVI BHANDARI AND ALEX LINGHORN
July/August 2009

Land lies at the heart of many of the world's most compelling contemporary issues: from climate change to armed conflict, from food security to social justice. Since the turn of the millennium, land issues have reclaimed center stage in national and international development debates, which increasingly focus on access to land in promoting economic growth and alleviating poverty.

The distribution of agricultural land in many poor countries is profoundly inequitable, giving rise to social tension, impaired development and extreme poverty. These exploitative imbalances are legacies of colonialism and institutionalized feudalism, posing serious threats to future prosperity and sustainable peace in many poor agrarian societies. Donor-driven development projects focusing on land governance have sought to impose market-led capitalist ideals, further polarizing power and marginalizing the poor. Exacerbating this dire situation are new commercial pressures on land, rapidly transforming it into a commodity to be traded between international banks, multinational companies, governments and speculators. Looming large is the paradigm-shifting presence of globalization, reinforced by international financial institutions seeking to unilaterally impose their macro-economic policies. This toxic blend of national feudalism and international hegemony has placed the world's poor agrarian societies in a perilous predicament. For one sixth of the world's population, nearly a billion farmers, without security of land ownership, the situation is grave. Confronted with this menacing dystopia, it has become increasingly urgent to assess the ways in which land is owned, accessed and regulated.

What is Land Reform?

Land reform is the process of transforming prevailing policies and laws that govern land ownership and access with the aim of instituting a more equal distribution of agricultural land while improving productivity. It can take the form of relatively benign tinkering with land tenure and administration systems or escalate to wholesale redistribution of land from rich to poor. Land reform, also known as agrarian reform, rarely occurs in isolation and is generally accompanied by structural changes to the agricultural sector to assist economic transformation.

The concept of land reform is far from new; since the time of the Roman Empire, nation states have been unable to resist tampering with land ownership and agricultural labor relations. In the last century, no less than 55 countries initiated programs of redistributive land reform, with many more altering their rural land ownership systems. Since the 1950s, powerful international institutions, such as the United Nations and the World Bank, have promoted western forms of private tenure in many developing countries, through the introduction of individualization, titling and registration programs. Their goal was to hasten capitalist transformation by securing land for progressive farmers while hoping that the disenfranchised landless would gain employment in urban industries. Capitalism's litigious obsession with private property rights has proved incongruous in the context of many developing countries which operate customary land ownership systems, where indigenous groups have traditional rights over land they have occupied for centuries.

Despite international interference, the early period of land reform (1950s–1970s) was characterized by nation states seeking to equitably reallocate resources from those who own the land to those who work the land, in a bid to redress historical imbalances and enhance development. These "land to the tiller" programs were particularly prevalent in post-colonial South America, where high levels of landlessness and gross inequity in land holdings exist. Reformation led to state-owned collectivized farming in China, the USSR and Cuba, while locally owned collectives prevailed in Mexico, Honduras and El Salvador. Overall these reforms failed, with a few notable successes clustered in East Asia. In many cases, land became concentrated in the hands of the state and, in feudal countries, real reform failed to materialize from the rhetoric. China's land reform was directly responsible for a famine that killed over 40 million people.

Land reform entered a new phase in the 1980s and 1990s, with widespread decollectivization and a new approach, so-called "market-assisted land reform." This neo-liberal orthodoxy, set forth and funded by the World Bank, aims to redistribute land by facilitating a land market of "willing buyers" and "willing sellers." The World Bank provides the buyers with loans, who are then required to pay full market price and display the clear intention of maximizing productivity. These land markets generously rewarded the rich, who often took the opportunity to offload marginal land, and created an enormous debt burden on the poor. Aided by the World Bank's coercive advocacy, marked-assisted land reform supplanted state-led redistributive land reform as the dominant paradigm.

Since its inception almost 30 years ago, market-led land reform has largely been a failure. In the process of dehumanizing and commoditizing land, it contributed to a rise in landlessness and exacerbated and entrenched the gap between rich and poor. Its fundamental flaws lie in its failure to address existing inequalities or appreciate the gamut of issues associated with land in developing countries—issues such as poverty, conflict, minority and gender discrimination, and environmental degradation. Land, too, is the foundation for enjoying basic human rights. Farmers excluded from land ownership in poor agrarian societies are condemned to a life of extreme poverty and exploitation. In some countries, basic livelihood needs such as access to potable water and firewood, or education and even citizenship, are denied to those without land ownership certificates.

The rise in landlessness and inequality, both corollaries of failed land reform, has fuelled tensions across rural societies and contributed to conflict. In Nepal's case, failed land reform led to a decade-long civil war. In response, landless farmers' organizations have begun to establish themselves into powerful social movements to challenge the status quo and demand their rights to land. Governments and international institutions have finally begun to realize that authentic land reform is a prerequisite to alleviating poverty and achieving sustainable peace and economic prosperity.

All Eyes on Nepal

Nepal is one of the most relevant countries today for contemporary debate on land reform. Nepal made global headlines in 2001 when the crown prince embarked on a murderous rampage through the palace in Kathmandu, slaughtering the king and queen and most of the royal family before killing himself. However, it is the deeper question of land ownership in relation to political and economic power that is actually shaping developments in Nepal, as in so many other poor, agrarian countries around the globe.

This small, mountainous nation, landlocked and sandwiched between the giants of China and India, is home to 30 million people. It is one of the world's poorest countries, with half the population living below the poverty line. The dramatic topography renders 80% of the land uncultivable, yet three-quarters of the population depend on agriculture for their livelihood, one-third of whom are marginal tenants and landless farmers.

Nepal's pattern of land ownership is the corollary of over 200 years of autocratic monarchy, with successive kings treating the land as their personal property, distributing large tracts to military leaders, officials and family members, in lieu of salaries or as gifts. This feudal system deliberately precluded ordinary people from owning land and ensured their continued position as agricultural servants. Non-farmer elites began to accumulate considerable land holdings as a form of security and status, precipitating the now well-established class structure of landlordism: a dismal system whereby those who work the land have little ownership of it.

Landlessness affords no status in communities and disenfranchises millions from their basic human rights. Without a land certificate, people are denied access to many government services such as banking, electricity, telephone service, and potable water. The landless are further victimized by non-government services, preventing them from keeping livestock and prohibiting them from accessing community forestland.

Nepal's land governance was subject to capricious rulers until the first land act was introduced in 1964. In response to a fledgling land rights movement initiated by tenant farmers, the monarchy introduced the act with the aim of "showing a human face." It imposed land ceilings with redistribution of the surplus to needy farmers and pledged to end the ritual of offering vast land grants to royal favorites.

In practice, ceilings were not enforced, little land was redistributed, and landlords, rather than tenants, often benefited. No further significant land reform measures occurred for the next 30 years; the 1964 Land Act remains at the center of Nepal's land reform legislation even today.

The People's Movement of 1990 reintroduced multi-party democracy to the Kingdom of Nepal, bringing new hope. In 1996, amendments to the original land act stipulated that any tenant farmer who had cultivated a piece of land continuously for three or more years would be given the right of tenancy and the right to receive half the land they farmed. As the majority of tenants were unregistered, landlords reacted predictably by evicting them from their land and refusing to grant secure tenancy contracts. In a country as poorly developed as Nepal, where it can take many days to walk to the nearest road, and many more to reach a centralized bureaucracy, these amendments served to formally terminate tenancy rights for over half a million families.

A Community-Led Approach to Land Reform

An innovative model for land reform is rising from the ashes of market-led agendas and centralized state bureaucracies, one loosely termed "community-based land reform." Borrowing from success stories over the past half century and incorporating new insights into sustainable rural development, the model offers a democratized, devolved approach that involves communities in the planning, implementation, and ongoing management of land reform.

In this model, each rural community is authorized to control its own land relations, including redistribution, working within a clear set of parameters laid out by the state. Governments typically fear relinquishing power, but it is precisely through this process of devolution that the majority poor can be included, empowered, and mobilized to ensure the effectiveness and sustainability of the reform. This bottom-up approach is often more cost-effective than top-down methods because of its potential to harness the administrative powers of existing local institutions (in Nepal's case, Village Development Committees). Plus, accurate data on land ownership, tenancy, and other factors such as idle land—an important starting point for any reform program—is more likely to emerge from community-level institutions. Devolved reform offers more room for flexibility across varying ecological zones and social contexts, while locally tested pilot schemes can provide valuable feedback.

Community-led reform is not simply a development buzzword or the latest fad. It has proven success, notably, the elected Land Committees that facilitated Japan's successful reform. Landless populations are pressing for greater inclusion, rightly asserting that they hold the knowledge required to design the most viable model for land reform. Even the World Bank has admitted that "greater community involvement" may be required; the bank now describes market-assisted land reform as only one "option."

The World Bank's mission to proselytize market-assisted land reform had by now reached Nepal. The bank proposed establishing a Land Bank to assist the poor in buying land from the rich. Matching willing buyers with willing sellers is an expensive and difficult process and leaves the door wide open to multi-level corruption. The concept of landless farmers borrowing huge sums of money to purchase land from feudal elites who had not acquired their lands through fair means did little to imbue a sense of justice.

It is clear from experiences in many other countries that international financial institutions (IFIs) such as the World Bank are not interested in pursuing an equitable and sustainable system of land access and ownership, nor are they concerned with enabling landless farmers to lead respectable lives and contribute fully to the socioeconomic and political life of their country. They persistently overlook the long-term benefits of providing secure access to land for the rural poor despite documentary evidence of poverty reduction, increased agricultural productivity, stimulation of the rural economy, and conflict prevention.

Land ceilings also came under attack from the World Bank, which criticized the Philippines, for instance, for implementing "land ownership ceilings [which] restrict the functioning of land markets." Of course, this is the intention of land ceilings. Instead of helping an impoverished farmer to invest in the land, create a livelihood, and improve production, World Bank policies opt to facilitate that farmer in selling it to someone in a better position. In Nepal, so far, the Land Bank has remained on the table, postponed by years of conflict and civil society resistance.

Land reform policies in Nepal have failed to significantly redistribute land, improve agricultural productivity, or realign socioeconomic power imbalances. The main reason for this lies in the conflicts of interest of decision makers. Government leaders are closely tied to landlords, if they are not landlords themselves. This corrupt nexus of power has ensured the continued failure of land

---

Land Grab in Madagascar

In 2008, Daewoo Logistics of South Korea reached a now-infamous deal with the Madagascan government to lease 1.3 million hectares of land (over half the island's cultivable land) on which to grow food for the South Korean domestic market. Madagascar is part of the World Food Program, from which it receives food for the 600,000 people who live at subsistence level. Not a single grain from the Daewoo deal was to remain on the island. Farmers and opposition leaders rose up and took to the streets to demonstrate their disapproval, claiming that the people were losing control of their land, which would also be destroyed by Daewoo's mass deforestation plans. The land minister eventually rejected the deal; nonetheless, it was the last straw for a population increasingly betrayed by its government. The country has now plunged into crisis, with security forces killing over 100 antigovernment protesters and the situation likely to end only by coup or referendum.

reform and the perpetuation of a feudal society. The primary result of imposing land ceilings was concealment of ownership; the primary result of land records reform was authenticating elite ownership; the primary result of tenancy registration was eviction; and the primary result of modernization was abuse of customary rights.

The increasing dispossession of the majority poor and the escalating autocracy of the king led Nepal into a decade of civil war with the opposition Maoists, from 1996 to 2006. Land reform was the rallying cry of the Maoists, who declared themselves the saviors of the poor and enemies of feudalism, colonialism, and foreign imperialism.

Over the next decade, the Maoists came to control over half the country's rural areas and, with public and political opinion turning against the monarchy, the war ended with the signing of the Comprehensive Peace Accord in 2006, paving the way for multi-party elections. The Maoists swept to victory in the 2008 election, confounding the international community but not Nepalese voters. Under intense popular pressure, the king was forced to abdicate and a new Federal Republic of Nepal was declared on May 28, 2008. The People's Movement played a significant role in the Maoist victory and that same civil society is clamoring for the Maoist-led government to deliver on its promises of land reform.

The land rights movement in Nepal has built a significant democratic power base in the form of the National Land Rights Forum, which has over 1.6 million landless members. The organization has developed a major groundswell of momentum to bolster its lobbying and policy advocacy. The movement is united, democratic, people-led, inclusive and peaceful, and should serve as a role model for land rights movements across the world. Nepal's land rights movement pursues a rights-based approach, advocating the intrinsic link between land rights and the fundamental human rights of subsistence, protection, participation and identity. This leverages existing international conventions, laws and constitutions that protect fundamental rights and is an effective way to ensure a framework for land reform which will address the structural causes of poverty. They claim it is the duty of nation states to devise inclusive policies which allow citizens to participate fully in society and not to abandon them to inequitable power structures and a free market system which will ride roughshod over their economic, social and cultural rights.

India also offers examples of successful people-centered movements that are peaceful and community-led. Sustained democratic pressure from India's civil society succeeded in putting land reform on the official agenda. The Janadesh rally in October 2007 witnessed 25,000 people marching 340 kilometers from Madhya Pradesh to Delhi to pressure the government into forming a national land reforms commission, which it duly did.

While it is vital to keep land reform firmly under the political spotlight, it is also essential not to politicize land rights movements. Farmers' organizations in Indonesia became polarized between political parties, each pursuing separate or competing interests, which proved to be a major obstacle to implementing successful land reform. It is critical that land rights movements remain firmly in the hands of the landless farmers, where they are most effective. A sustainable and successful land rights movement needs to be led by those whose future security depends upon its success. The role of civil-society organizations and non-governmental organizations is to support landless farmers in creating a solid institutional base and strong dynamic leadership while facilitating access to government policy-making forums, at local and national levels.

Civil society pressure has led Nepal's Maoist government to embark upon a "revolutionary" program of scientific land reform. Exactly how revolutionary or scientific it will be remains open to conjecture. Following two weeks of mass demonstrations by the land rights movement, the government recently established a Scientific Land Reform Commission to investigate available options and provide concrete recommendations. They have pledged to adopt an inclusive approach closely involving landless people in the process and to end feudal control over land once and for all.

Land Reform in Context

The redistribution of land, either through awarding new land to the landless or granting ownership rights to existing occupants, must not be seen as the final stage in the process but rather the initial stage in creating a viable and sustainable model to ensure livelihood stability and enhanced productivity. In many developing countries there is a trend towards abandoning, selling, or mortgaging awarded lands, often to raise money for medical expenses or because of a lack of credit to finance production. The combined pressures of increasing land prices and a dearth of government-support services has been the main catalyst for selling awarded lands. Without the necessary support systems, deprived farmers will understandably focus on solving their immediate food and economic security problems, reversing the land reform process and undermining the whole basis of a sustainable livelihood model.

In Indonesia, the government places certain obligations upon land reform beneficiaries to ensure a positive outcome: the land must be owner-cultivated and production must increase within two years. Negligent beneficiaries have their land expropriated without compensation. Such conditions are only reasonable if the newly entitled farmers are provided with the support they need, including improved infrastructure and access to markets, accompanied by financial, technical, and social services. Few governments or non-governmental organizations are committed to, or even capable of, providing the necessary support during this critical post-claim period.

The Philippines leads the way in rural support services, having established post-harvest facilities and continuous agricultural and enterprise development which focuses on community capacity building and rural infrastructure and finance. Studies show that when agrarian reform is implemented properly and integrated support services are provided, farmers have higher incomes and invest in their farms more intensively. The examples of Japan, Korea, and Taiwan demonstrate that land reform is not only a social justice measure, but also the foundation for mobilizing agrarian societies towards rural, and, ultimately, urban industrialization.

In the case of Nepal, where broader macroeconomic policies do not support agriculture in general or small-scale producers in particular, land reform alone will not bring substantial income gains to the poor or a reduction in poverty and inequality. Indeed, if the macroeconomic context is adverse to agriculture—if, for example, exchange rate overvaluation and trade policies make agricultural imports too cheap for local growers to compete—then to encourage the poor to seek a living in farming is to lure them into debt and penury. A holistic approach to land reform must therefore be adopted to ensure viable and sustainable benefits.

Nepal is in the process of integrating into regional and global trading platforms that require a series of profound economic policy commitments. As a member of the World Trade Organization (WTO), Nepal has a legal obligation to align its economic policy with global requirements. The landless, near landless, and smallholders face an uncertain future in this era of globalization; Nepal must learn from the experiences of other developing countries that have courted the global players, adopted their policies, and paid the price. Succumbing blindly to globalization's holy trinity of privatization, liberalization, and deregulation is tantamount to self-sacrifice at its altar.

Land reform, and protective measures against unfair trade practices, must be in place before Nepal ventures into any international commitments to open its markets and resource wealth to international speculators. Indeed, the revenues of many transnational companies now far exceed those of the countries in which they operate. Such a concentration of lightly regulated power in international profit-seeking hands is ominous for small producers and even more so for the most marginalized members of agrarian societies. While genuine community-based agricultural investment is to be welcomed, the neocolonial pacts favored by foreign investors pose a serious threat to tenure security and to marginal farmers, many of whom could be pushed out of food production and forced to join the ranks of the rural hungry or city slum dwellers.

In 1995, Indonesia signed the Agreement on Agriculture with the WTO and agreed to open its markets. Liberalization of the domestic market for agricultural commodities spelled calamity for peasant farmers. International free trade agreements are not made with the intention of strengthening poor farmers' land rights. Furthermore, small-scale agricultural production simply cannot compete in a global market controlled by multinational corporations. Developed countries continue to bolster their agricultural export products with significant state subsidies while protecting their domestic market with prohibitive tariffs. Indonesia has since become the largest recipient of food in the world and is experiencing a startling rate of natural resource exploitation; deforestation currently occurs at the equivalent of 300 football fields every hour.

The WTO believes it is better for countries to buy food at the international market with money obtained from exports rather than attempting self-sufficiency; this paves the way for monoculture and contract farming while creating a precarious reliance on imports for basic food commodities. International trade is a natural phenomenon, but a significant degree of autonomy must be maintained; dependence on imports for basic needs such as food is dangerous. Strengthening agricultural self-sufficiency is especially important to developing countries that do not have the resources to sustain expensive food imports long-term.

Monoculture of cash crops in Indonesia has caused landlessness and has made small-scale farmers dependent on expensive agricultural inputs such as high-yield seed varieties, chemical fertilizers, and pesticides, which are often imported. Furthermore, these farming methods compromise ecological integrity and, as has been witnessed in Bangladesh and Indonesia, can lead to large-scale environmental degradation.

The repercussions of IFI interventions in developing countries, namely greater exploitation and inequality, illustrate the danger of imposing a capitalist model upon semi-feudal systems. International trade policies and programs in Indonesia, which were aimed at strengthening the position of agricultural exporters, proved to be overly discriminatory and served to weaken the bargaining position of local farmers. Large corporations were expected to develop farmers' institutions, but instead they exploited them by creating crop-buying monopsonies while forming cartels to raise the prices of their own products.

To accompany market liberalization, IFIs seek to impose the use of modern technology on agrarian societies. If this is not implemented diligently and judiciously, it leads to growth in rural unemployment. In Indonesia, the imposition of modern technology achieved just this, most notably among women, who were evicted from the land and became a pool of cheap labor for multi-national corporations—the same corporations that benefited most from the technology.

The deregulation that IFIs press for must not be carried out too hastily. Without a prior improvement in infrastructure to accompany the dismantling of para-state apparatuses, marginal areas will be alienated. This was seen in sub-Saharan Africa, where only those farmers close to urban centers benefited from the influx of private trade.

Commercialization of Land and the Last Great Global Land Grab

In addition to the globalization of trade, there are new, powerful commercial pressures for landless and marginalized farmers to contend with. Catalyzed by soaring food prices in 2008 and compounded by worldwide financial uncertainty, import-reliant, often oil-rich countries have begun scrambling to secure food sources for their domestic markets, in what has been called "the last great global land grab." Concurrent with this is the rampant growth of subsidized biofuel production to meet ambitious renewable fuel targets in the West, and the inception of carbon trading, which places a commercial value on standing forests and rangelands. Extractive mining and "ecotourism" add to the perilous predicament for vulnerable landless and marginal farmers.

The scramble for land often occurs in countries with a weak legal framework where farmers are not protected by secure land tenure systems. This results in the fertile land of the world's poorest countries becoming privatized and concentrated, creating a direct threat to food sovereignty, local production, and rural livelihoods. The increase in biofuel production is certain to intensify competition for land between indigenous forest users, land-poor farmers, agribusinesses, and financial speculators.

It is clear that potential foreign investment should be carefully analyzed to assess the full impact on the community as compared with the investors' financial interests before any deals are made. Sound investment should be accompanied by skills and knowledge sharing with local communities to establish foundations for long-term cooperation. The exploitation of natural resources for the sole purpose of shareholder gain is unsustainable.

The new REDD (Reduced Emissions from Deforestation and Degradation) scheme, which will offer developing countries financial incentives for preserving biomass stocks in standing forests, is an opportunity for states to define forest tenure and create community-based benefit-sharing mechanisms. Similarly, sustainable tourism can be used to reinforce community governance over biodiversity as a conservation strategy.

Land reform is a pressing issue shared by many developing countries that are shackled by entrenched inequities in land access and ownership. Highly unequal land ownership breeds social tension and political unrest and inhibits economic growth. While each developing country faces its own particular land related issues, some common themes prevail: the lack of political will to formulate and implement effective land reform, entrenched inequitable power structures, exclusive legal systems, poor dissemination of information, and the age-old millstones of corruption and excessive bureaucracy. Across the board, authorities are seen to be rich in rhetoric and poor in deed.

The rising discontent among landless and small-holder farmers has forced open an ideological debate between neo-liberalism, centralized elite domination, and pro-people policy making. The majority rural poor have begun to find their voice, and Nepal's civil war will act as a warning that their land grievances can quickly turn to violence.

Today, the worldwide financial crisis is threatening aid from the West and causing the demand for exports to shrink. Both factors render the billions of dollars of potential investment from multinational corporations and food-hungry, oil-rich nations enormously tempting to impoverished states. Governments must not be lured into exclusive market mechanisms that generate ever greater inequalities and create a profoundly negative effect upon community governance, food sovereignty, and peace building. Effective redistributive land reform, ensuring secure tenancy and ownership systems for marginal farmers, must occur in poor agrarian societies before opening their doors to global trade. The primary responsibility of all governments is to protect the basic human rights of their citizens, paying special attention to the poorest and most vulnerable.

Land reform is beginning to emerge from the vortex of market-led ideology to find itself at the epicenter of topical discourses on poverty alleviation, sustainable rural development, conflict transformation, food security, and fundamental human rights. IFIs continue to push reforms that consolidate and authenticate inequity, but land rights organizations are now enjoying a higher profile with increasing solidarity from a wide variety of state and non-state actors.

It is abundantly clear that the best approaches to land reform are those that integrate security, livelihood, resource management, and community empowerment. Land reform must redistribute land widely enough to preclude any dominant land-owning class and be accompanied by a support structure to sustain productivity. The expansion of rural markets that will follow will generate growth and this will lead to stable peace and national development. All eyes are on Nepal to see if the Maoist government seizes the unique chance to institute such an innovative, rational, and scientific process of land reform. ❑

Acknowledgement: We wish to thank our research assistant, Nabaraj Subedi, for his invaluable help in contributing to this article and the editors of Dollars & Sense for recognizing the importance of the current global debates on land reform and tenure security as a key policy issue for the 21st century.

Sources: Ravi Bhandari, "The Peasant Betrayed: Towards a Human Ecology of Land Reform in Nepal," in Roy Allen (ed.) *Human Ecology Economics: A New Framework for Global Sustainability*; Ravi Bhandari, "The Significance of Social Distance in Sharecropping Efficiency: The Case of Rural Nepal," *Journal of Economic Studies*, September, 2007; Ravi Bhandari, "Searching for a Weapon of Mass Production in Nepal: Can Market-Assisted Land Reform Live Up to its Promise?" *Journal of Developing Societies*, June 2006; Community Self-Reliance Centre Nepal, *Land and Tenurial Security Nepal*, 2008; Elizabeth Fortin, "Reforming Land Rights: The World Bank and the Globalization of Agriculture," *Social and Legal Studies*, 2005; Lorenzo Cotula, *Fuelling Exclusion? The Biofuels Boom and Poor People's Access to Land*, International Institute for Environment and Development, 2008; International Land Coalition, *Land and Vulnerable People in a World of Change*, Global Bioenergy Partnership, 2008; International Land Coalition, *Secure Access to Land for Food Security*, UNDP-OGC, November 24, 2008; Alex Linghorn, "Land Reform: An International Perspective," *Land First*, July 2008; Alex Linghorn, "Commercial Pressures on Land," *Land First*, April 2009; Oxfam International, *Another Inconvenient Truth: How Biofuel Policies are Deepening Poverty and Accelerating Climate Change*, 2008; Rights and Resources Initiative, *Seeing People Through Trees: Scaling Up Efforts to Advance Rights and Address Poverty, Conflict, and Climate Change*, 2008.

Article 7.4

FAMINE MYTHS

Five Misunderstandings Related to the 2011 Hunger Crisis in the Horn of Africa

BY WILLIAM G. MOSELEY
March/April 2012

The 2011 famine in the horn of Africa was one of the worst in recent decades in terms of loss of life and human suffering. While the UN has yet to release an official death toll, the British government estimates that between 50,000 and 100,000 people died, most of them children, between April and September of 2011. While Kenya, Ethiopia, and Djibouti were all badly affected, the famine hit hardest in certain (mainly southern) areas of Somalia. This was the worst humanitarian disaster to strike the country since 1991-1992, with roughly a third of the Somali population displaced for some period of time.

Despite the scholarly and policy community's tremendous advances in understanding famine over the past 40 years, and increasingly sophisticated famine early-warning systems, much of this knowledge and information was seemingly ignored or forgotten in 2011. While the famine had been forecasted nearly nine months in advance, the global community failed to prepare for, and react in a timely manner to, this event. The famine was officially declared in early July of 2011 by the United Nations and recently (February 3, 2012) stated to be officially over. Despite the official end of the famine, 31% of the population (or 2.3 million people) in southern Somalia remains in crisis. Across the region, 9.5 million people continue to need assistance. Millions of Somalis remain in refugee camps in Ethiopia and Kenya.

The famine reached its height in the period from July to September, 2011, with approximately 13 million people at risk of starvation. While this was a regional problem, it was was most acute in southern Somalia because aid to this region was much delayed. Figure 1 provides a picture of food insecurity in the region in the November-December 2011 period (a few months after the peak of the crisis).

The 2011 famine received relatively little attention in the U.S. media and much of the coverage that did occur was biased, ahistorical, or perpetuated long-held misunderstandings about the nature and causes of famine. This article addresses "famine myths"—five key misunderstandings related to the famine in the Horn of Africa.

Myth #1: Drought was the cause of the famine.

While drought certainly contributed to the crisis in the Horn of Africa, there were more fundamental causes at play. Drought is not a new environmental condition for much of Africa, but a recurring one. The Horn of Africa has long experienced erratic rainfall. While climate change may be exacerbating rainfall variability, traditional livelihoods in the region are adapted to deal with situations where rainfall is not dependable.

The dominant livelihood in the Horn of Africa has long been herding, which is well adapted to the semi-arid conditions of the region. Herders traditionally ranged widely across the landscape in search of better pasture, focusing on different areas depending on meteorological conditions.

The approach worked because, unlike fenced in pastures in America, it was incredibly flexible and well adapted to variable rainfall conditions. As farming expanded, including large-scale commercial farms in some instances, the routes of herders became more concentrated, more vulnerable to drought, and more detrimental to the landscape.

Agricultural livelihoods also evolved in problematic ways. In anticipation of poor rainfall years, farming households and communities historically stored surplus crop production in granaries. Sadly this traditional strategy for mitigating the risk of drought was undermined from the colonial period moving forward as

FIGURE 1: FOOD INSECURITY IN THE HORN OF AFRICA REGION, NOVEMBER-DECEMBER 2011.

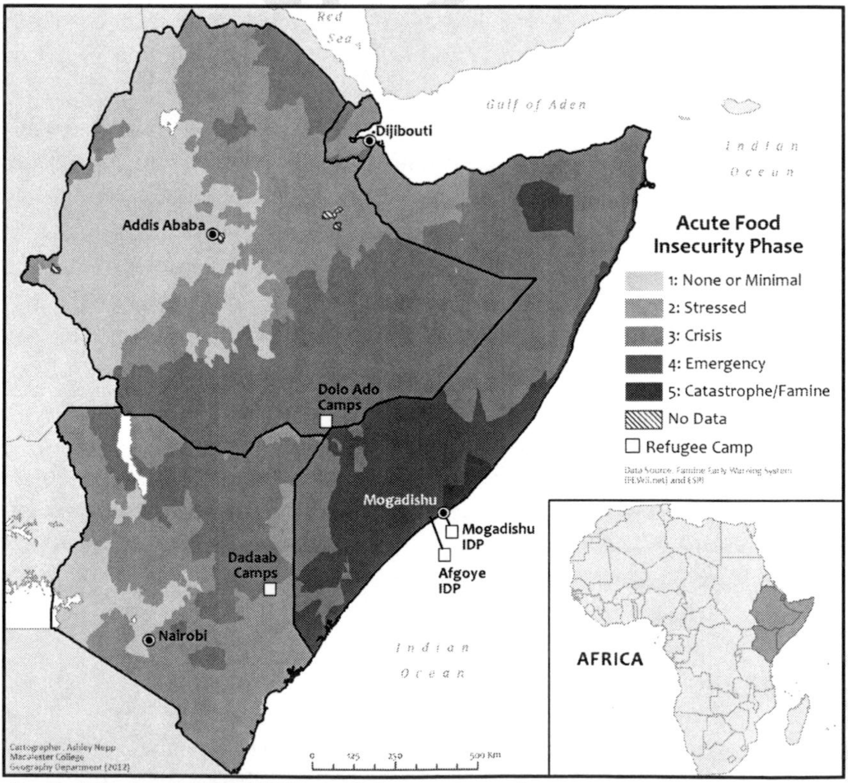

Based on data and assessment by FEWS-Net (a USAID-sponsored program).

Cartography by Ashley Nepp, Macalester College.

households were encouraged (if not coerced by taxation) to grow cash crops for the market and store less excess grain for bad years. This increasing market orientation was also encouraged by development banks, such as the World Bank, International Monetary Fund, and African Development Bank.

The moral of the story is that famine is not a natural consequence of drought (just as death from exposure is not the inherent result of a cold winter), but it is the structure of human society which often determines who is affected and to what degree.

Myth #2: Overpopulation was the cause of the famine.

With nearly 13 million people at risk of starvation last fall in a region whose population doubled in the previous 24 years, one might assume that these two factors were causally related in the Horn of Africa. Ever since the British political economist Thomas Malthus wrote "An Essay on the Principle of Population" in 1798, we have been concerned that human population growth will outstrip available food supply. While the crisis in Somalia, Ethiopia and Kenya appeared to be perfect proof of the Malthusian scenario, we must be careful not to make overly simplistic assumptions.

For starters, the semi-arid zones in the Horn of Africa are relatively lightly populated compared to other regions of the world. For example, the population

---

Land Grabs in Africa

Long term leases of African land for export-oriented food production, or "land grabs," have been on the rise in the past decade. Rather than simply buying food and commodity crops from African farmers, foreign entities increasingly take control of ownership and management of farms on African soil. This trend stems from at least two factors. First, increasingly high global food prices are a problem for many Asian and Middle Eastern countries that depend on food imports. As such, foreign governments and sovereign wealth funds may engage in long-term leases of African land in order to supply their own populations with affordable food. Secondly, high global food prices are also seen as an opportunity for some Western investors who lease African land to produce crops and commodities for profitable global markets.

In the Horn of Africa, Ethiopia (which has historically been one of the world's largest recipients of humanitarian food aid) has made a series of long-term land leases to foreign entities. The World Bank estimates that at least 35 million hectares of land have been leased to 36 different countries, including China, Pakistan, India and Saudi Arabia. Supporters of these leases argue that they provide employment to local people and disseminate modern agricultural approaches. Critics counter that these leases undermine food sovereignty, or people's ability to feed themselves via environmentally sustainable technologies that they control.

density of Somalia is about 13 persons per sq. kilometer, whereas that of the U.S. state of Oklahoma is 21.1. The western half of Oklahoma is also semi-arid, suffered from a serious drought in 2011, and was the poster child for the 1930s Dust Bowl. Furthermore, if we take into account differing levels of consumption, with the average American consuming at least 28 times as much as the average Somali in a normal year, then Oklahoma's population density of 21.1 persons per sq. kilometer equates to that of 591 Somalis.

Despite the fact that Oklahoma's per capita impact on the landscape is over 45 times that of Somalia (when accounting for population density and consumption levels), we don't talk about overpopulation in Oklahoma. This is because, in spite of the drought and the collapse of agriculture, there was no famine in Oklahoma. In contrast, the presence of famine in the Horn of Africa led many to assume that too many people was a key part of the problem.

Why is it that many assume that population growth is the driver of famine? For starters, perhaps we assume that reducing the birthrate, and thereby reducing the number of mouths to feed, is one of the easiest ways to prevent hunger. This is actually a difficult calculation for most families in rural Africa. It's true that many families desire access to modern contraceptives, and filling this unmet need is important. However, for many others, children are crucial sources of farm labor or important wage earners who help sustain the family. Children also act as the old-age social security system for their parents. For these families, having fewer children is not an easy decision. Families in this region will have fewer children when it makes economic sense to do so. As we have seen over time and throughout the world, the average family size shrinks when economies develop and expectations for offspring change.

Second, many tend to focus on the additional resources required to nourish each new person, and often forget the productive capacity of these individuals. Throughout Africa, some of the most productive farmland is in those regions with the highest population densities. In Machakos, Kenya, for example, agricultural production and environmental conservation improved as population densities increased. Furthermore, we have seen agricultural production collapse in some areas where population declined (often due to outmigration) because there was insufficient labor to maintain intensive agricultural production.

Third, we must not forget that much of the region's agricultural production is not consumed locally. From the colonial era moving forward, farmers and herders have been encouraged to become more commercially oriented, producing crops and livestock for the market rather than home consumption. This might have been a reasonable strategy if the prices for exports from the Horn of Africa were high (which they rarely have been) and the cost of food imports low. Also, large land leases (or "land grabs") to foreign governments and corporations in Ethiopia (and to a lesser extent in Kenya and Somalia) have further exacerbated this problem. These farms, designed solely for export production, effectively subsidize the food security of other regions of the world (most notably the Middle East and Asia) at the expense of populations in the Horn of Africa.

Myth #3: Increasing food production through advanced techniques will resolve food insecurity over the long run.

As Sub-Saharan Africa has grappled with high food prices in some regions and famine in others, many experts argue that increasing food production through a program of hybrid seeds and chemical inputs (a so-called "New Green Revolution") is the way to go.

While outsiders benefit from this New Green Revolution strategy (by selling inputs or purchasing surplus crops), it is not clear if the same is true for small farmers and poor households in Sub-Saharan Africa. For most food insecure households on the continent, there are at least two problems with this strategy. First, such an approach to farming is energy intensive because most fertilizers and pesticides are petroleum based. Inducing poor farmers to adopt energy-intensive farming methods is short sighted, if not unethical, if experts know that global energy prices are likely to rise. Second, irrespective of energy prices, the New Green Revolution approach requires farmers to purchase seeds and inputs, which means that it will be inaccessible to the poorest of the poor, i.e., those who are the most likely to suffer from periods of hunger.

If not the New Green Revolution approach, then what? Many forms of bio-intensive agriculture are, in fact, highly productive and much more efficient than those of industrial agriculture. For example, crops grown in intelligent combinations allow one plant to fix nitrogen for another rather than relying solely on increasingly expensive, fossil fuel-based inorganic fertilizers for these plant nutrients. Mixed cropping strategies are also less vulnerable to insect damage and require little to no pesticide use for a reasonable harvest. These techniques have existed for centuries in the African context and could be greatly enhanced by supporting collaboration among local people, African research institutes, and foreign scientists.

Myth #4: U.S. foreign policy in the Horn of Africa was unrelated to the crisis.

Many Americans assume that U.S. foreign policy bears no blame for the food crisis in the Horn and, more specifically, Somalia. This is simply untrue. The weakness of the Somali state was and is related to U.S. policy, which interfered in Somali affairs based on Cold War politics (the case in the 1970s and 80s) or the War on Terror (the case in the 2000s).

During the Cold War, Somalia was a pawn in a U.S.-Soviet chess match in the geopolitically significant Horn of Africa region. In 1974, the U.S. ally Emperor Haile Selassie of Ethiopia was deposed in a revolution. He was eventually replaced by Mengistu Haile Mariam, a socialist. In response, the leader of Ethiopia's bitter rival Somalia, Siad Barre, switched from being pro-Soviet to pro-Western. Somalia was the only country in Africa to switch Cold War allegiances under the same government. The U.S. supported Siad Barre until 1989 (shortly before his demise in

1991). By doing this, the United States played a key role in supporting a long-running dictator and undermined democratic governance.

More recently, the Union of Islamic Courts (UIC) came to power in 2006. The UIC defeated the warlords, restored peace to Mogadishu for the first time in 15 years, and brought most of southern Somalia under its orbit. The United States and its Ethiopian ally claimed that these Islamists were terrorists and a threat to the region. In contrast, the vast majority of Somalis supported the UIC and pleaded with the international community to engage them peacefully. Unfortunately, this peace did not last. The U.S.-supported Ethiopian invasion of Somalia begun in December 2006 and displaced more than a million people and killed close to 15,000 civilians. Those displaced then became a part of last summer and fall's famine victims.

The power vacuum created by the displacement of the more moderate UIC also led to the rise of its more radical military wing, al-Shabaab. Al-Shabaab emerged to engage the Transitional Federal Government (TFG), which was put in place by the international community and composed of the most moderate elements of the UIC (which were more favorable to the United States). The TFG was weak, corrupt, and ineffective, controlling little more than the capital Mogadishu, if that. A low-grade civil war emerged between these two groups in southern Somalia. Indeed, as we repeatedly heard in the media last year, it was al-Shabaab that restricted access to southern Somalia for several months leading up to the crisis and greatly exacerbated the situation in this sub-region. Unfortunately, the history of factors which gave rise to al-Shabaab was never adequately explained to the U.S. public. Until July 2011, the U.S. government forbade American charities from operating in areas controlled by al-Shabaab—which delayed relief efforts in these areas.

Myth #5: An austere response may be best in the long run.

Efforts to raise funds to address the famine in the Horn of Africa were well below those for previous (and recent) humanitarian crises. Why was this? Part of it likely had to do with the economic malaise in the U.S. and Europe. Many Americans suggested that we could not afford to help in this crisis because we had to pay off our own debt. This stinginess may, in part, be related to a general misunderstanding about how much of the U.S. budget goes to foreign assistance. Many Americans assume we spend over 25% of our budget on such assistance when it is actually less than one percent.

Furthermore, contemporary public discourse in America has become more inward-looking and isolationist than in the past. As a result, many Americans have difficulty relating to people beyond their borders. Sadly, it is now much easier to separate ourselves from them, to discount our common humanity, and to essentially suppose that it's okay if they starve. This last point brings us back to Thomas Malthus, who was writing against the poor laws in England in the late 18th century. The poor laws were somewhat analogous to contemporary welfare programs and Malthus argued (rather problematically) that they encouraged the poor to have more children. His essential argument was that starvation is acceptable because it is a natural check to over-population. In other words, support for the poor will only exacerbate the situation. We see this in the way that some conservative commentators reacted to last year's famine.

The reality was that a delayed response to the famine only made the situation worse. Of course, the worst-case scenario is death, but short of death, many households were forced to sell off all of their assets (cattle, farming implements, etc.) in order to survive. This sets up a very difficult recovery scenario because livelihoods are so severely compromised. We know from best practices among famine researchers and relief agencies in that you not only to detect a potential famine early, but to intervene before livelihoods are devastated. This means that households will recover more quickly and be more resilient in the face of future perturbations.

Preventing Famines

While the official famine in the horn of Africa region is over, 9.5 million people continue to need assistance and millions of Somalis remain in refugee camps in Ethiopia and Kenya. While this region of the world will always be drought prone, it needn't be famine prone. The solution lies in rebuilding the Somali state and fostering more robust rural livelihoods in Somalia, western Ethiopia and northern Kenya. The former will likely mean giving the Somali people the space they need to rebuild their own democratic institutions (and not making them needless pawns in the War on Terror). The latter will entail a new approach to agriculture that emphasizes food sovereignty, or locally appropriate food production technologies that are accessible to the poorest of the poor, as well as systems of grain storage at the local level that anticipate bad rainfall years. Finally, the international community should discourage wealthy, yet food-insufficient, countries from preying on poorer countries in Sub Saharan African countries through the practice of land grabs. ❑

Sources: Alex de Waal, *Famine That Kills: Darfur, Sudan*, Oxford University Press, 2005; William G. Moseley, "Why They're Starving: The man-made roots of famine in the Horn of Africa," *The Washington Post*. July 29, 2011; William G. Moseley and B. Ikubolajeh Logan, "Food Security," in B. Wisner, C. Toulmin and R. Chitiga (eds)., *Toward a New Map of Africa*, Earthscan Publications, 2005; Abdi I. Samatar, "Genocidal Politics and the Somali Famine," Aljazeera English, July 30, 2011; Amartya Sen, *Poverty and Famines*, Oxford/Clarendon, 1981; Michael Watts and Hans Bohle, "The space of vulnerability: the causal structure of hunger and famine," *Progress in Human Geography*, 1993.

Article 7.5

MEASURING ECONOMIC DEVELOPMENT
The "Human Development" Approach

BY ALEJANDRO REUSS
April 2012

S ome development economists have proposed abandoning per capita GDP, the dominant single-number measure of economic development, in favor of the "human development" approach—which focuses less on changes in average income and more on widespread access to basic goods.

Advocates of this approach to the measurement of development, notably Nobel Prize-winning economist Amartya Sen, aim to focus attention directly on the *ends* (goals) of economic development. Higher incomes, Sen notes, are *means* people use to get the things that they want. The human development approach shifts the focus away from the means and toward ends like a long life, good health, freedom from hunger, the opportunity to get an education, and the ability to take part in community and civic life. Sen has argued that these basic "capabilities" or "freedoms"—the kinds of things almost everyone wants no matter what their goals in life may be— are the highest development priorities and should, therefore, be the primary focus of our development measures.

If a rising average income guaranteed that everyone, or almost everyone, in a society would be better able to reach these goals, we might as well use average income (GDP per capita) to measure development. Increases in GDP per capita, however, do not always deliver longer life, better health, more education, or other basic capabilities to most people In particular, if these income increases go primarily to those who are already better-off (and already enjoy a long life-expectancy, good health, access to education, and so on), they probably will not have much effect on people's access to basic capabilities.

Sen and others have shown that, in "developing" countries, increased average income by itself is not associated with higher life expectancy or better health. In countries where average income was increasing, but public spending on food security, health care, education, and similar programs did not increase along with it, they have found, the increase in average income did not appear to improve access to basic capabilities. If spending on these "public supports" increased, on the other hand, access to basic capabilities tended to improve, whether average income was increasing or not. Sen emphasizes two main lessons based on these observations: 1) A country cannot count on economic growth alone to improve access to basic capabilities. Increased average income appears to deliver "human development" largely by *increasing the wealth a society has available for public supports*, and not in other ways. 2) A country does not have to prioritize economic growth—*does not have to "wait" until it grows richer*—to make basic capabilities like long life, good health, and a decent education available to all.

The Human Development Index (HDI)

The "human development" approach has led to a series of annual reports from the United Nations Development Programme (UNDP) ranking countries according to a "human development index" (HDI). The HDI includes measures of three things: 1) health, measured by average life expectancy, 2) education, measured by average years of schooling and expected years of schooling, and 3) income, measured by GDP per capita. The three categories are then combined, each counting equally, into a single index. The HDI has become the most influential alternative to GDP per capita as a single-number development measure.

Looking at the HDI rankings, many of the results are not surprising. The HDI top 20 is dominated by very high-income countries, including thirteen Western European countries, four "offshoots" of Great Britain (Australia, Canada, New Zealand, and the United States), and two high-income East Asian countries (Japan and South Korea). Most of the next 20 or so are Western or Eastern European, plus a few small oil-rich states in the Middle East. The next 50 or so include most of Latin America and the Caribbean, much of the Middle East, and a good deal of Eastern Europe (including Russia and several former Soviet republics). The next 50 or so are a mix of Latin American, Middle Eastern, South and Southeast Asian, and African countries. The world's poorest continent, Africa, accounts for almost all of the last 30, including the bottom 24.

INCOME-PER-CAPITA RANKS (2010)

Highest HDI ranks compared to income per capita ranks (difference in parentheses)*	Lowest HDI ranks compared to income per capita ranks (difference in parentheses)
New Zealand (+30)	Equatorial Guinea (-78)
Georgia (+26)	Angola (-47)
Tonga (+23)	Kuwait (-42)
Tajikistan (+22)	Botswana (-38)
Madagascar (+22)	South Africa (-37)
Togo (+22)	Qatar (-36)
Fiji (+22)	Brunei (-30)
Ireland (+20)	Gabon (-29)
Iceland (+20)	United Arab Emirates (-28)
Ukraine (+20)	Turkey (-26)

* The numbers in parentheses represent a country's GDP-per-capita rank minus its HDI rank. Remember that in a ranking system, a "higher" (better) rank is indicated by a lower number. If a country is ranked, say, 50th in GDP per capita and 20th in HDI, its number would be 50 – 20 = +30. The positive number indicates that the country had a "higher" HDI rank than GDP per capita rank. If a country is ranked, say, 10th in GDP per capita and 35th in HDI, its number would be 10 – 35 = -25. The negative number indicates that the country had a "lower" HDI rank than GDP per capita rank.

Source: United Nations Development Programme, Indices, Getting and using data, 2010 Report—Table 1: Human Development Index and its components (hdr.undp.org/en/statistics/data/).

It is not surprising that higher GDP per capita is associated with a higher HDI score. After all, GDP per capita counts for one third of the HDI score itself. The relationship between the two, however, is not perfect. Some countries have a higher HDI than GDP per capita rank. These countries are "over-performing," getting more human development from their incomes, compared to other countries. Meanwhile, some countries have a lower HDI rank than GDP per capita rank. These countries are "under-performing," not getting as much human development from their incomes, compared to other countries. The list of top "over-performing" countries includes three very high-income countries that had still higher HDI ranks (Iceland, Ireland, and New Zealand), three former Soviet republics (Georgia, Tajikistan, and Ukraine), two small South Pacific island nations (Fiji, Togo), and two African countries (Madagascar, Tonga). The list of top "under-performing" countries includes four small oil-rich countries (Brunei, Kuwait, Qatar, and United Arab Emirates) and five African countries (Angola, Botswana, Equatorial Guinea, Gabon, and South Africa).

The UNDP also calculates an inequality-adjusted HDI. Note that, for all the measures included in the HDI, there is inequality within countries. The inequality-adjusted HDI is calculated so that, the greater the inequality for any measure included in the HDI (for health, education, or income), the lower the country's score. Since all countries have some inequality, the inequality-adjusted HDI for any country is always lower than the regular HDI. However, the scores for countries with greater inequality drop more than for those with less inequality. That pushes some countries up in the rankings, when inequality is penalized, and others down. Among the thirteen countries moving up the most, five are former Soviet

TABLE 2: INEQUALITY-ADJUSTED HDI RANKS
COMPARED TO UNADJUSTED HDI RANKS

Highest inequality-adjusted HDI ranks compared to unadjusted HDI ranks (difference in parentheses)	Lowest inequality-adjusted HDI ranks compared to unadjusted HDI ranks (difference in parentheses)
Uzbekistan (+17)	Peru (-26)
Mongolia (+16)	Panama (-20)
Moldova (+16)	Colombia (-18)
Kyrgystan (+15)	South Korea (-18)
Maldives (+14)	Bolivia (-17)
Ukraine (+14)	Belize (-16)
Philippines (+11)	Brazil (-15)
Sri Lanka (+11)	Namibia (-15)
Tanzania, Viet Nam, Indonesia, Jamaica, Belarus (+9)	El Salvador (-14)
	Turkmenistan (-12)

Source: United Nations Development Programme, 2010 Report, Table 3: Inequality-adjusted Human Development Index (hdr.undp.org/en/media/HDR_2010_EN_Table3_reprint.pdf).

republics. Among the ten moving down the most, seven are Latin American countries. The United States narrowly misses the list of those moving down the most, with its rank dropping by nine places when inequality is taken into account.

GDP Per Capita and HDI

The relationship between income per capita and the HDI is shown in the "scatterplot" graph below. (Instead of GDP per capita, the graph uses a closely related measure called Gross National Income (GNI) per capita.) Each point represents a country, with its income per capita represented on the horizontal scale and its HDI score represented on the vertical scale. The further to the right a point is, the higher the country's per capita income. The higher up a point is, the higher the country's HDI score. As we can see, the cloud of points forms a curve, rising up as income per capita increases from a very low level, and then flattening out. This means that a change in GDP per capita from a very low level to a moderate level of around $8000 per year is associated with large gains in human development. Above that, we see, the curve flattens out dramatically. A change in income per capita from this moderate level to a high level of around $25,000 is associated with smaller gains in human development. Further increases in income per capita are associated with little or no gain in human development.

This relationship suggests two major conclusions, both related to greater economic equality.

First, achieving greater equality in incomes between countries, including by redistributing income from high-income countries to low-income countries, could result in increased human development. Over the highest per capita income range,

RELATIONSHIP BETWEEN HDI AND INCOME PER CAPITA (2010)

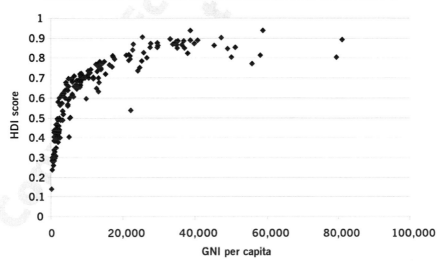

Source: United Nations Development Programme, Indices, 2010 Report - Table 1 Human Development Index and its components (hdr.undp.org/en/statistics/data/).

from about $25,000 on up, increases in income are not associated with higher human development. Decreases in income above this threshold, by the same token, need not mean lower human development. On the other hand, over the lowest income range, below $8000, increases in income are associated with dramatic gains in HDI (largely due to increased public supports). Therefore, the redistribution of incomes from high-income countries to low-income countries could increase human development in the latter a great deal, while not diminishing human development in the former by very much (if at all)—resulting in a net gain in human development.

Second, high-income countries might make greater gains in HDI, as their incomes continued to increase, if a larger share of income went to low-income people or to public supports. Part of the reason that the relationship between per capita income and HDI flattens out at high income levels may be that there are inherent limits to variables like life expectancy (perhaps 90-100 years) or educational attainment (perhaps 20 years). These "saturation" levels, however, have clearly not been reached by all individuals, even in very high-income countries. In the United States, as of 2008, the infant mortality rate for African-Americans was more than double that for whites. The life expectancy at birth for white females was more than three years greater than that of African-American females; for white males, more than five years greater than for African-American males. As of 2010, over 40% of individuals over 25 years old have no education above high school. Over 60% have no degree from a two- or four-year college. It is little wonder that higher income would not bring about greatly increased human development, considering that, over the last 30 years, many public supports have faced sustained attack and most income growth has gone to people already at the top. ❑

Sources: Amartya Sen, Development as Freedom (New York: Oxford University Press, 1999); United Nations Development Programme, Indices, Getting and using data, 2010 Report, Table 1 Human Development Index and its components (hdr.undp.org/en/statistics/data/); United Nations Development Programme, 2010 Report, Table 3: Inequality-adjusted Human Development Index (hdr.undp.org/en/media/HDR_2010_EN_Table3_reprint.pdf); U.S. Census Bureau, The 2012 Statistical Abstract, Births, Deaths, Marriages, & Divorces: Life Expectancy, Table 107. Expectation of Life and Expected Deaths by Race, Sex, and Age: 2008; Educational Attainment, Population 25 Years and Over, U.S. Census Bureau, Selected Social Characteristics in the United States, 2010 American Community Survey, 1-Year Estimates.

Article 7.6

TURNING GAS INTO DEVELOPMENT IN BOLIVIA

BY AARON LUOMA AND GRETCHEN GORDON
November/December 2006

On May 1, 2006, banners reading "Nationalized: Property of the Bolivian people" were hung over filling station entrances and strung across the gates of refineries and gas and oil fields across Bolivia. From the San Alberto field in Bolivia's southern state of Tarija, President Evo Morales stood flanked by his ministers and military before a crowd of television cameras. In a carefully orchestrated public relations event, Morales made the surprise announcement that the military was at that moment securing the country's oil and gas fields.

"This is the solution to the social and economic problems of our country," Morales proclaimed. "Once we have recovered these natural resources, this will generate work; it is the end of the looting of our natural resources by multinational oil companies."

By the time Evo Morales won his unprecedented landslide electoral victory in December 2005, nationalization of Bolivia's oil and gas reserves had become a widespread popular demand. In a national referendum in 2004, 94% of Bolivians had voted to recover state ownership of oil and gas. After then-president Carlos Mesa responded to that vote with only moderate legislative proposals, protests and blockades demanding nationalization rocked the country. Morales and his Movement for Socialism (MAS) party originally supported a more limited reform of the energy sector, but as the protests mounted, MAS joined the call for nationalization. When Mesa resigned, triggering early elections, nationalization became the primary electoral issue.

On paper, the Morales government's oil and gas policy falls far short of what is traditionally meant by nationalization: government expropriation of foreign property to gain total control of an industry. Instead, his administration is taking a softer approach, opening negotiations with private investors to recover a measure of control over the industry and increase government revenues from it.

The May 1 announcement drew strong reactions from both ends of the political spectrum. Gabriel Dabdoub, president of the Santa Cruz Chamber of Commerce and Industry, told the Miami Herald, "We're very concerned about the international repercussions. This might isolate Bolivia from the world." Spanish Prime Minister Jose Luis Rodriguez Zapatero expressed his "most profound concern," warning of "consequences for bilateral relations." At the same time, many on the Bolivian left faulted the policy for not going far enough. The Bolivian Center for Information and Documentation criticized the decree for failing to "recover the oil and gas industry that was privatized in the capitalization process."

A Cochabamba cab driver named Enrique summed up the sentiment of the majority of Bolivians in the middle: "This isn't nationalization; if it were, the multinationals wouldn't be here. But if we kick them out, they'll sue us. So we have to negotiate."

Six months on, Bolivia's government has had mixed results in implementing the decree. Slow progress in negotiations to rebuild the state oil and gas company, political scandals, and logistical problems initially gave Bolivian opposition parties ample opportunity to question the government's intentions and competence. But in October the government reached agreement on new contracts with 10 oil and gas companies, including Petrobras, the Brazilian public-private energy company, and Spanish energy giant Repsol, which together control 74% of Bolivia's gas reserves. The step garnered praise from both foreign and domestic business interests. While the government continues difficult negotiations over remaining issues with foreign energy companies, Bolivians wait to see whether Morales' "nationalization through negotiation" strategy will bring about concrete improvements in their standard of living.

How Did Bolivia Get Here?

At more than 13,000 feet above sea level, the legendary colonial city of Potosi rests at the base of Cerro Rico ("Rich Hill"), once so full of silver it virtually bankrolled the Spanish empire for more than 300 years. Though the glory of Potosi faded as the silver market waned, to this day Bolivian children are taught that a bridge of silver stretching from Potosi to Madrid could have been built from Cerro Rico's bounty. For nearly five centuries, Bolivia has seen its abundant natural resources extracted by outsiders, while the people of Bolivia have remained the poorest in South America.

Today, natural gas is Bolivia's new silver. The country boasts 47.8 trillion cubic feet of certified gas reserves; in South America only Venezuela has more. And proven reserves could rise dramatically since only 15% to 40% of the oil- and gas-rich zone has been explored to date. Until a few years ago, many oil developers regarded natural gas as nothing more than a waste product of the oil extraction process. "The notion that gas might be a moneymaker would have struck most oil executives as absurd," writes Paul Roberts in The End of Oil. With oil becoming increasingly scarce, however, natural gas prices have doubled in the last six years. Gas is now seen as the bridge fuel that will help ease global demand for oil and move industry toward cleaner, non-hydrocarbon energy sources. As analysts continue to debate when oil supplies will peak, the "dash for gas" is already in full swing.

With its price rising and vast reserves to tap, natural gas has become the focus of Bolivia's politics. A keen sense of their own history drives Bolivians' demand that their gas not meet the fate of the silver, rubber, and tin before it—that the people benefit in tangible ways from the wealth beneath their feet. A leader of former state oil workers recounts the words of an Aymara woman from La Paz: "I think that if they take it all now, what will be left for my grandchildren?"

"So for this reason I have to defend it," she explains.

Giving Away the Store

On October 17, 2003, under cover of night, then-President Gonzalo Sánchez de Lozada boarded a jet for Miami after Bolivians took to the streets en masse to demand his resignation. The architect of a radical economic reform in the 1990s, Sánchez de Lozada left behind a devastated economy and a capital in chaos. He also left over 60 people dead and over 400 wounded, casualties of his government's month-long crackdown on mounting protests.

U.S.-educated and known as "El Gringo" for his American accent, Sánchez de Lozada had worked in close collaboration with international lending institutions such as the World Bank and the International Monetary Fund to implement the economic mantra coming out of Washington: a downsized government and unfettered free markets will create a tide that will lift people out of poverty. During his first term in office (1993-1997), Sánchez de Lozada privatized all of Bolivia's most strategic state industries, including telecommunications, electricity, air and rail transportation, and the government's biggest revenue producer, oil and gas.

Sánchez de Lozada claimed his plan, dubbed "capitalization," would ensure that the public would benefit from the privatization of state-owned industries. These would be converted into public-private enterprises, with Bolivians maintaining a 51% interest in the new "capitalized" firms, while foreign investors would receive a 49% share in exchange for putting forth that same value in investment. Bolivia would still have control over the industries but would be able to double their value, spurring job creation and jumpstarting the economy. Almost half a million new jobs would be created in four years, the economy would double in size in ten years, and the dividends from the new capitalized firms would fund an ambitious pension plan for Bolivia's elderly. That was the theory, at least.

Thanks to a mix of backroom deals and grievously unrealistic economic predictions, the reality played out quite differently.

What Sánchez de Lozada's administration actually did was to divide up the assets of the state energy company YPFB (Yacimientos Petroliferos Fiscales Bolivianos) to form three public-private consortiums: two exploration and production firms and one transportation firm. Majority control of these firms—complete with over $11 billion in reserves and infrastructure—was given, free of charge, to foreign corporations such as British Petroleum and Enron in exchange for only a promise of future investment. A new oil and gas law, a condition for an IMF loan, transferred an additional $108 billion of reserves to private control and slashed oil and gas royalties on those reserves by almost two thirds, from 50% to 18%. Then, in 1999, Sánchez de Lozada's successor Hugo Banzer sold off Bolivia's refineries, pipelines, and gas storage facilities at bargain prices, completing the dismantling of YPFB.

In the end, capitalization turned out to be even more destructive than a classic privatization in which the state at least receives compensation for its assets. Under capitalization, Bolivia handed over its most strategic industries and resources, as well as, in the case of YPFB, its most profitable industry. The promised 51/49 split of public versus private control ended up the reverse, leaving Bolivians with no decision-making power over the capitalized firms. The foreign companies that took over Bolivia's oil and gas industry never invested in modernizing its domestic infrastructure or technical capacity, finding it more profitable to export Bolivia's natural gas as a cheap raw material to be processed in Argentina or Brazil. While capitalization brought Bolivia a swath of new foreign investors, the promised trickle-down wealth creation never came. For Bolivians, it was like giving the mechanic the keys to your car, only to see him drive off with it.

Resources and Rents

It may seem contradictory that countries can be "blessed" with valuable natural resources—gold and diamonds, petroleum and natural gas, and so on—and still remain poor. Some economists have argued that natural riches, however, can contribute to stalled economic development.

Industries like mining, oil drilling, and even forestry and fishing are called "extractive" industries. This means they are focused on "extracting" (removing) naturally existing resources. If riches can be easily found, say, by digging a hole in the ground, elites may have little reason to concern themselves with the education or skills of the people as a whole, the improvement of the country's general infrastructure, or other means of general economic development. Instead, they can grow rich and powerful by extracting and selling natural resources—especially if, like gold or oil, these are highly prized and relatively scarce.

The difference between the income that one can get from selling these kinds of goods and what it actually costs to extract them is called a "rent." (Petroleum, for example, may sell for $100 a barrel on the world market. In some parts of the world, however, it can be found relatively easily, and near the surface of the earth, and may cost only $10 a barrel to extract. The rent, then, is $90 per barrel.) In just about every place where there is a concentration of valuable and scarce resources, who will "capture" the rents from the extraction and sale of these resources is a major political issue.

Resource rents may be captured by private individuals or companies, such as those that own oil fields or gold mines. Many a fortune—from Siberia to South Africa to Texas—has come from resource rents. Even when private companies own these resources, workers in the extraction industries may organize to force the companies to "share" some of the rents with them. It may be easier for the owners to pay for labor peace, and keep the wealth flowing out of the ground, than to endure costly work stoppages. For this reason, workers in very lucrative resource-extraction industries have sometimes been comparatively well-paid (for what can be back-breaking and extremely dangerous work).

Resource rents can also be captured by governments. In many countries, valuable natural resources like petroleum are government-owned. (In fact, more than half of all proven

Although average annual gas production rose by 65% between the years prior to (1990-1996) and following (1997-2004) capitalization, government gas revenues increased only 10% due to slashed royalty rates (see figure on page 25). Government revenue from oil and gas, which made up between 38% and 60% of state revenues in the years before capitalization, dropped to under 7% in 2002. Bolivia's finite natural resources were being depleted faster, and the country had little to show for it.

Mark Weisbrot, economist and co-director of the Washington-based Center for Economic and Policy Research (CEPR), views the results of the Washington Consensus experiment in Bolivia this way: "They clearly failed by any objective

---

oil reserves worldwide are controlled by state-owned oil companies.) In some places, state oil companies engage in drilling and extraction. In some, private companies (including large multinationals) may extract and sell the oil, but have to pay "royalties" to the government for the privilege. Elsewhere, private companies may own the oilfields, but the government uses taxes to capture oil rents.

Captured resource rents can be used in many different ways. In some cases, ruling elites may use rents to enrich themselves personally or to build up armies or other forces that solidify their political power (but contribute little to overall economic development or to improving living conditions for the majority). Governments that operate in this way are sometimes known as "rentier states." ("Rentier" (pronounced *ron-tee-AY*) is a French word that means the recipient of income from (economic) rent.) Captured rents, however, may also be used to promote broader economic development (e.g., to build infrastructure or import machinery for new industries). They may be used to provide public services like schooling or education. Governments may even just transfer rents, in cash, to a broad swath of society.

Recent controversies about the control of oil and natural gas in South American countries like Venezuela and Bolivia are largely about government attempts to capture a bigger share of these rents and use them, government leaders say, to improve the lives of ordinary people. One former head of an oil-rich state put the logic of rent capture this way: "We're set up ... where it's collectively [that the people] own the resources. So we share in the wealth when the development of these resources occurs." The government was constitutionally required, this official continued, to "maximize benefits for [the people], not an individual company, not some multinational somewhere, but for [the people]." That was not, however, Venezuela's Hugo Chavez or Bolivia's Evo Morales speaking. The oil-rich state? Alaska. The former official? Sarah Palin.

—*Alejandro Reuss*

Sources: National Petroleum Council, Topic Paper #7: Global Access to Oil and Gas, Working Document of the NPC Global Oil & Gas Study, July 18, 2007; Philip Gourevitch "The State of Sarah Palin: The peculiar political landscape of the Vice-Presidential hopeful," The New Yorker, September 22, 2008.

measure—income per person is less than it was 27 years ago." According to a CEPR report, Bolivia's per capita income has grown by less than 2% in total over the past 25 years, compared to 60% between 1960 and 1980. "In the short run it's the loss of revenue," explains Weisbrot. "Over the longer run it's the loss of control over the resources themselves, which is what you need... as a source of financing for development and as part of a development strategy."

"The majority of government revenues in Bolivia now come from donations and loans," explains Roberto Fernandez, a professor of economics and history at San Simon University in Cochabamba. "We borrow money to pay salaries. What kind of government is this that doesn't even have the autonomy to say, 'I'm going to build a little school'? It has to look for who internationally can give us a loan."

Prohibited by law from running for a second consecutive term in 1997, Sánchez de Lozada regained the presidency in 2002. In October 2003, Bolivians' growing frustration and anger over the dismal state of the economy exploded on the streets, in what later became known as the Gas War. Thousands of primarily indigenous residents of El Alto, the sprawling municipality that surrounds the capital city of La Paz, came out to protest Sánchez de Lozada's plan to export cheap gas to the United States through Bolivia's historic rival, Chile. The protesters erected blockades, strangling La Paz. Sánchez de Lozada declared a national emergency and called out the military.

As a convoy of soldiers carrying cisterns of gas toward La Paz pushed through makeshift blockades of rocks and tires in the streets of El Alto, the city's overcrowded neighborhoods became a battlefield.

"They began to shoot at houses," remembers Nestor Salinas, a resident of El Alto, "shooting at any human being who put themselves in front of the convoy."

"Imagine children just five years old, eight-year-old girls, pregnant women, men, brothers, fathers, teenagers," he continues. "They died to defend our oil and gas."

Within days, Sánchez de Lozada fled Bolivia. As he was landing in Miami, Nestor's 29-year-old brother, David, died from a bullet wound, joining the 59 other civilians killed by government troops.

Morales' Hybrid Energy Policy

Most Bolivians viewed Evo Morales's electoral win last year as a victory for the movement to take back control of the country's natural resources and use them to tackle Bolivia's entrenched poverty. Not an outright nationalization, Morales's oil and gas decree this May set forth a complex series of steps aimed at boosting revenues from gas and regaining some control over the industry. The decree seeks to resurrect the state oil and gas company, YPFB, to assume regulatory functions, direct oil and gas development, and participate in the entire chain of production, from exploration to commercialization.

The decree requires the three public-private energy firms created by Sánchez de Lozada in the mid-1990s, along with the two private firms that bought YPFB's refineries and pipelines at the time, to sell back to the government enough shares (at market prices) to give YPFB majority ownership. To put this in context, these firms hold only 10% of Bolivia's oil and gas reserves. The rest are held exclusively by several foreign companies, including Petrobras and Repsol.

The decree placed a temporary additional tax of 32% on production in the country's two most productive fields, bringing in $32 million a month in new revenues devoted exclusively to rebuilding YPFB. It gave oil and gas companies operating in Bolivia six months to sign new exploration and development contracts.

The decree also reasserted the government's right to establish domestic and export prices. In addition to hiking tax and royalty rates, the Morales administration aims to raise the base prices on which taxes and royalties are calculated. It is currently locked in intense negotiations with Petrobras, arguing that export prices under its existing contracts are far below current market prices. In June, the administration negotiated a 48% increase in the gas price with Argentina, bringing in an additional $110 million a year in revenues—a key achievement of the May 1 decree.

Ultimately, Morales aims to transform Bolivia from an exporter of raw materials into an industrial producer of value-added goods such as electricity, synthetic diesel, fertilizers, and plastics. "The vision is that by 2010 we could see Bolivia as a main exporter of value-added products covering the entire South American market," explains Saul Escalera, a YPFB official. While some critics assert that small countries like Bolivia lack the capital and technology necessary for industrialization, Escalera disagrees. He notes that YPFB has already "received 20 project proposals with a total value of $12 billion from foreign firms that want to invest in Bolivia."

Many of those firms are not the predictable Western players. Gazprom, the Russian state energy giant with more than 25% of the world's gas reserves, has expressed interest in investing more than $2 billion in Bolivia, while inquires have also come from several Asian countries. In May, Venezuela's state oil company, PDVSA, inked a deal to build a gas separation plant to produce fertilizer both for Bolivia's domestic use and for export to Brazil. And an Indian firm, Jindal Steel, has a deal in the works to build a plant that will power the industrialization of Mutún, site of one of the largest iron ore deposits in the world. The $2.3 billion project is projected to generate more than 10,000 new jobs and $200 million a year in government revenue.

According to Hydrocarbons Minister Carlos Villegas, $2 billion of foreign investment has already been committed to expand gas production and export capacity, particularly to Argentina and Brazil. At an International Development Bank conference in Washington, D.C., this July, Villegas declared: "Bolivia has completed its cycle as an exporter of raw materials. The resources are there, but we will give them a new path."

Bolivia's Bumpy Road

The efforts of YPFB to exert control over the oil and gas industry have had mixed results. Shortly after Morales' May 1 announcement, YPFB was involved in a growing corruption scandal and admitted its inability to take over fuel distribution duties as mandated by the nationalization decree. A few weeks later the government declared the nationalization process temporarily suspended due to "a lack of economic resources," creating further unease and confirming critics' concerns that YPFB lacked the capacity, competence, and cash to carry out its new role. In late August the debacle culminated with the resignation of YPFB's president, Jorge Alvarado, who had been accused of signing a diesel contract that violated the decree. It was a major setback for a president who had asserted that YPFB would be "transparent, efficient, and socially controlled."

In August, police and prosecutors searched Repsol's Bolivia offices for the second time in six months in separate smuggling and malfeasance investigations. Repsol expressed outrage, warning that these investigations were jeopardizing the company's continued investment in Bolivia. In this case as in others, the government is pursuing a problematic strategy with foreign energy companies: wielding a strong hand to expose malfeasance and discredit them while simultaneously negotiating for their continued investment in the country.

Despite these obstacles, in late August the government became more assertive in implementing the May decree. After a four-month delay, government threats of expulsion secured the additional $32 million in monthly payments to YPFB due from Repsol, Petrobras, and France's Total, providing the state company with a critical infusion of cash.

In September political problems again flared. A resolution issued by then-hydrocarbons minister Andres Soliz Rada ordered Petrobras to hand over control of exports and domestic sales of gasoline and diesel in its two Bolivian refineries in compliance with the decree. This move backfired, however, after the Brazilian foreign minister said the measure could cause Petrobras to pull out of Bolivia, which led Vice President Garcia Linera to suspend Rada's resolution. Rada responded by tendering his resignation, another setback for the administration. Linera, feeling the political weight of the moment, was resolute in declaring that the nationalization process was "irrevocable" and that the government, while maintaining a posture of "negotiation and tolerance," would be "intransigent" in obligating companies to comply with the decree.

In October, however, the government reached agreement on new exploration and development contracts with 10 major companies operating in Bolivia—a major milestone. Under the new contracts, the foreign companies are to extract Bolivia's oil and gas and hand them over to YPFB, which compensates the companies for production costs, investment, and profit. The tax and royalty rates in the new contracts are variable depending on a company's level of production and whether or not they have recovered past investments. The government claims its take will range between 50% and 80%, although questions remain about how it will be calculated. YPFB president Juan Carlos Ortiz estimates that the new contracts will put annual revenue for 2006 at $1.3 billion; President Morales assured the public that with the increase in exports to Argentina and the new tax rates, annual oil and gas revenue will rise to $4 billion within the next four years.

"Mission accomplished," declared Morales in a press statement at the contract signing. "We are exercising as Bolivians our property rights over natural resources, without expelling anyone and without confiscating. With this measure, within 10 to 15 years, Bolivia will no longer be this little poor country, this beggar country, this country that is always looking to international assistance."

Critics, however, question whether the government got a good deal for the country, pointing out that the contracts don't commit foreign investors to substantial future investments or provide YPFB with the physical resources to participate in all phases of the industry. And tense negotiations continue over control of the five companies which used to make up the state company, prior to capitalization. Petrobras, which owns the two formerly YPFB refineries, has shown reluctance to give up any operational control of these facilities. Considering that Bolivia supplies 50% of Brazil's gas needs and that Petrobras' transactions account for 18% of Bolivia's gross domestic product, both countries have much to lose should a deal not be reached.

Opportunities and Obligations

As Bolivia struggles to work through the pitfalls of implementing Morales' decree, a clear end goal is to achieve a larger shift in power dynamics. Rather than receiving policy prescriptions from Washington or from international institutions and foreign investors, Bolivia aims to draft its own blueprint, joining a growing political shift in the region away from free-market ideology.

YPFB's Escalera describes the difference the nationalization decree has made for the state energy company. "Before, we had big plans—jobs industrialization, value added products—but didn't have the [gas]," he explains. "It was like knocking on the multinationals' door, 'Could you give me a little sugar for my tea?' If they don't want to do it, the deal is off."

"Even if they were willing to give it to me, I'd then have to go talk to Transredes [the public-private pipeline company created under capitalization] to beg for transportation," he explains, "and they would say 'forget it.'"

"Since the May 1st decree," he continues, "everything has changed. We can guarantee everything the investor wants—transportation, volume, price—now it's in my hands."

Many Bolivians hope the government's new resources and new authority will translate into concrete improvements in quality of life for the country's nine million people, including new jobs and increased state resources for education, health care, and infrastructure. But the challenges Bolivia faces in transforming its oil and gas policy cannot be overstated. Whether the nationalization decree can be fully implemented, let alone generate concrete benefits for ordinary Bolivians, depends on multiple factors: not only getting all of the pieces in place to ensure that the anticipated surge in oil and gas revenues actually materializes, but also creating strong and effective governmental and social institutions, mitigating the social and environmental impacts of energy development, and using the new revenues effectively for national development projects.

For Nestor Salinas, a member of the Association of Family Members of those Fallen in Defense of Gas, which is pushing for Sánchez de Lozada to return to Bolivia to stand trial for the killings during the Gas War, the Morales government also carries a moral debt.

"Our name says it clearly: 'Fallen in defense of gas,'" he explains. "This is the importance the country has to place on this issue. The families that lost [loved ones] didn't lose them for nothing, their loss made possible the social, economic, and political change that Bolivia is now living. The government now owes these families justice." ❑

Chapter 8

NATURAL RESOURCES AND THE ENVIRONMENT

Article 8.1

GENETIC ENGINEERING AND THE PRIVATIZATION OF SEEDS

BY ANURADHA MITTAL AND PETER ROSSET
March/April 2001

In 1998, angry farmers burned Monsanto-owned fields in Karnataka, India, starting a nationwide "Cremate Monsanto" campaign. The campaign demanded that biotech corporations like Monsanto, Novartis, and Pioneer leave the country. Farmers particularly targeted Monsanto because its field trials of the "terminator gene"—designed to prevent plants from producing seeds and so to make farmers buy new seed each year—created the danger of "genetic pollution" that would sterilize other crops in the area. That year, Indian citizens chose Quit India Day (August 9), the anniversary of Mahatma Gandhi's demand that British colonial rulers leave the country, to launch a "Monsanto Quit India" campaign. Ten thousand citizens from across the country sent the Quit India message to Monsanto's Indian headquarters, accusing the company of colonizing the food system.

In recent years, farmers across the world have echoed the Indian farmers' resistance to the biotech giants. In Brazil, the Landless Workers' Movement (MST) has set out to stop Monsanto soybeans. The MST has vowed to destroy any genetically engineered crops planted in the state of Rio Grande do Sul, where the state government has banned such crops. Meanwhile, in September 2000, more than 1,000 local farmers joined a "Long March for Biodiversity" across Thailand. "Rice, corn, and other staple crops, food crops, medicinal plants and all other life forms are significant genetic resources that shape our culture and lifestyle," the farmers declared. "We oppose any plan to transform these into genetically modified organisms."

Industrial Agriculture I: The Green Revolution

For thousands of years, small farmers everywhere have grown food for their local communities—planting diverse crops in healthy soil, recycling organic matter, and following nature's rainfall patterns. Good farming relied upon the farmer's accumulated knowledge of the local environment. Until the 1950s, most Third World agriculture was done this way.

The "Green Revolution" of the 1960s gradually replaced this kind of farming with monocultures (single-crop production) heavily dependent on chemical fertilizers, pesticides, and herbicides. The industrialization of agriculture made Third World countries increase exports to First World markets, in order to earn the foreign exchange they needed to pay for agrochemicals and farm machinery manufactured in the global North. Today, as much as 70% of basic grain production in the global South is the product of industrial farming.

The Green Revolution was an attempt by northern countries to export chemical- and machine-intensive U.S.-style agriculture to the Third World. After the Cuban revolution, northern policymakers worried that rampant hunger created the basis for "communist" revolution. Since the First World had no intention of redistributing the world's wealth, its answer was for First World science to "help" the Third World by giving it the means to produce more food. The Green Revolution was to substitute for the "red."

During the peak Green Revolution years, from 1970 to 1990, world food production per capita rose by 11%. Yet the number of people living in hunger (averaging less than the minimum daily caloric intake) continued to rise. In the Third World—excluding China—the hungry population increased by more than 11%, from 536 to 597 million. While hunger declined somewhat relative to total Third World population, the Green Revolution was certainly not the solution for world hunger that its proponents made it out to be.

Not only did the Green Revolution fail to remedy unequal access to food and food-producing resources, it actually contributed to inequality. The costs of improved seeds and fertilizers hit cash-poor small farmers the hardest. Unable to afford the new technology, many farmers lost their land. Over time, the industrialization of agriculture contributed to the replacement of farms with corporations, farmers with machines, mixed crops with monocultures, and local food security with global commerce.

Industrial Agriculture II: The New Biorevolution

The same companies that promoted chemical-based agriculture are now bringing the world genetically engineered food and agriculture. Some of the leading pesticide companies of yesterday have become what today are euphemistically called "life sciences companies"—Aventis, Novartis, Syngenta, Monsanto, Dupont, and others. Through genetic engineering, these companies are now converting seeds into product-delivery systems. The crops produced by Monsanto's Roundup-Ready brand seeds, for example, tolerate only the company's Roundup brand herbicide.

The "life sciences" companies claim that they can solve the environmental problems of agriculture. For example, they promise to create a world free of pesticides by equipping each crop with its own "insecticidal genes." Many distinguished agriculture scientists, corporate bigwigs, and economists are jumping on the "biotechnology" bandwagon. They argue that, in a world where more than 830 million people go to bed hungry, biotechnology provides the only hope of feeding our burgeoning population, especially in the Third World.

In fact, since genetic engineering is based on the same old principles of industrial agriculture—monoculture, technology, and corporate control—it is likely to exacerbate the problems of ecological and social devastation:

- As long as chemical companies dominate the "life sciences" industry, the biotechnology they develop will only reinforce intensive chemical use. Corporations are currently developing plants whose genetic traits can be turned "on" or "off" by applying an external chemical, as well as crops that die if the correct chemical—made by the same company—is not applied.

- The biotechnology industry is releasing hundreds of thousands of genetically engineered organisms into the environment every year. These organisms can reproduce, cross-pollinate, mutate, and migrate. Each release of a genetically engineered organism is a round of ecological Russian roulette. Recently, Aventis' genetically engineered StarLink corn, a variety approved by the U.S. Department of Agriculture only for livestock consumption, entered the food supply by mixing in grain elevators and cross-pollination in the field.

- With the advent of genetic engineering, corporations are using new "intellectual property" rights to stake far-reaching claims of ownership over a vast array of biological resources. By controlling the ownership of seeds, the corporate giants force farmers to pay yearly for seeds they once saved from each harvest to the next planting. By making seed exchanges between farmers illegal, they also limit farmers' capacity to contribute to agricultural biodiversity.

The False Promise of "Golden Rice"

The biotech industry is taking great pains to advertise the humanitarian applications of genetic engineering. "[M]illions of people—many of them children—have lost their sight to vitamin A deficiency," says the Council for Biotechnology Information, an industry-funded public relations group. "But suppose rice consumers could obtain enough vitamin A and iron simply by eating dietary staples that are locally grown?

… Biotechnology is already producing some of these innovations." More than $10 million was spent over ten years to engineer vitamin A rice—hailed as the "Golden Rice"—at the Institute of Plant Sciences of the Swiss Federal Institute of Technology in Zurich. It will take millions more and another decade of research and development to produce vitamin A rice varieties that can actually be grown in farmers' fields.

In reality, the selling of vitamin A rice as a miracle cure for blindness depends on blindness to lower-cost and safer alternatives. Meat, liver, chicken, eggs, milk, butter, carrots, pumpkins, mangoes, spinach and other leafy green vegetables, and many other foods contain vitamin A. Women farmers in Bengal, an eastern Indian state, plant more than 100 varieties of green leafy vegetables. The promotion of monoculture and rising herbicide use, however, are destroying such sources of vitamin A. For example, bathua, a very popular leafy vegetable in northern India, has been pushed to extinction in areas of intensive herbicide use.

The long-run solutions to vitamin A deficiency—and other nutritional problems—are increased biodiversity in agriculture and increased food security for poor people. In the meantime, there are better, safer, and more economical short-run measures than genetically engineered foods. UNICEF, for example, gives high-dose vitamin A capsules to poor children twice a year. The cost? Just two cents per pill.

Intellectual Property Rights and Genetic Engineering

In 1998, Monsanto surprised Saskatchewan farmer Percy Schmeiser by suing him for doing what he has always done and, indeed, what farmers have done for millennia—save seeds for the next planting. Schmeiser is one of hundreds of Canadian and U.S. farmers the company has sued for re-using genetically engineered seeds. Monsanto has patented those seeds, and forbids farmers from saving them.

In recent years, Monsanto has spent over $8.5 billion acquiring seed and biotech companies, and DuPont spent over $9.4 billion to acquire Pioneer Hi-Bred, the world's largest seed company. Seed is the most important link in the food chain. Over 1.4 billion people—primarily poor farmers—depend on farm-saved seed for their livelihoods. While the "gene police" have not yet gone after farmers in the Third World, it is probably only a matter of time.

If corporations like Monsanto have their way, genetic technology—like the so-called "terminator" seeds—will soon render the "gene police" redundant. Far from being designed to increase agricultural production, "terminator" technology is meant to prevent unauthorized production—and increase seed-industry profits. Fortunately, worldwide protests, like the "Monsanto Quit India" campaign, forced the company to put this technology on hold. Unfortunately, Monsanto did not pledge to abandon "terminator" seeds permanently, and other companies continue to develop similar systems.

Future Possible

From the United States to India, small-scale ecological agriculture is proving itself a viable alternative to chemical-intensive and bioengineered agriculture. In the United States, the National Research Council found that "alternative farmers often produce high per acre yields with significant reductions in costs per unit of crop harvested," despite the fact that "many federal policies discourage adoption of alternative practices." The Council concluded that "federal commodity programs must be restructured to help farmers realize the full benefits of the productivity gains possible through alternative practices."

Another study, published in the *American Journal of Alternative Agriculture*, found that ecological farms in India were just as productive and profitable as chemical ones. The author concluded that, if adopted on a national scale, ecological farming would have "no negative impact on food security," and would reduce soil erosion and the depletion of soil fertility while greatly lessening dependence on external inputs.

The country where alternative agriculture has been put to its greatest test, however, is Cuba. Before 1989, Cuba had a model Green Revolution-style agricultural economy (an approach the Soviet Union had promoted as much as the United States). Cuban agriculture featured enormous production units, using vast quantities of imported chemicals and machinery to produce export crops, while the country imported over half its food.

Although the Cuban government's commitment to equity and favorable terms of trade offered by Eastern Europe protected Cubans from undernourishment, the collapse of the East bloc in 1989 exposed the vulnerability of this approach. Cuba plunged into its worst food crisis since the revolution. Consumption of calories and protein dropped by perhaps as much as 30%. Nevertheless, today Cubans are eating almost as well as they did before 1989, with much lower imports of food and agrochemicals. What happened?

Cut off from imports of food and agrochemicals, Cuba turned inward to create a more self-reliant agriculture based on higher crop prices to farmers, smaller production units, urban agriculture, and ecological principles. As a result of the trade embargo, food shortages, and the opening of farmers' markets, farmers began to receive much better prices for their products. Given this incentive to produce, they did so, even without Green Revolution-style inputs. The farmers received a huge boost from the reorientation of government education, research, and assistance toward alternative methods, as well as the rediscovery of traditional farming techniques.

While small farmers and cooperatives increased production, large-scale state farms stagnated. In response, the Cuban government parceled out the state farms to their former employees as smaller-scale production units. Finally, the government mobilized support for a growing urban agriculture movement—small-scale organic farming on vacant lots—which, together with the other changes, transformed Cuban cities and urban diets in just a few years.

Will Biotechnology Feed the World?

The biotech industry pretends concern for hungry people in the Third World, holding up greater food production through genetic engineering as the solution to world hunger. If the Green Revolution has taught us one thing, however, it is that increased food production can—and often does—go hand in hand with more hunger, not less. Hunger in the modern world is not caused by a shortage of food, and cannot be eliminated by producing more. Enough food is already available to provide at least 4.3 pounds of food per person a day worldwide. The root of the hunger problem is not inadequate production but unequal access and distribution. This is why the second Green Revolution promised by the "life sciences" companies is no more likely to end hunger than the first.

The United States is the world's largest producer of surplus food. According to the U.S. Department of Agriculture, however, some 36 million of the country's people (including 14 million children) do not have adequate access to food. That's an increase of six million hungry people since the 1996 welfare reform, with its massive cuts in food stamp programs.

Even the world's "hungry countries" have enough food for all their people right now. In fact, about three quarters of the world's malnourished children live in countries with net food surpluses, much of which are being exported. India, for example, ranks among the top Third World agricultural exporters, and yet more than a third of the world's 830 million hungry people live there. Year after year, Indian governments have managed a sizeable food surplus by depriving the poor of their basic human right to food.

The poorest of the poor in the Third World are landless peasants, many of whom became landless because of policies that favor large, wealthy farmers. The high costs of genetically engineered seeds, "technology-use payments," and other inputs that small farmers will have to use under the new biotech agriculture will tighten the squeeze on already poor farmers, deepening rural poverty. If agriculture can play any role in alleviating hunger, it will only be to the extent that we reverse the existing bias toward wealthier and larger farmers, embrace land reform and sustainable agriculture, reduce inequality, and make small farmers the center of an economically vibrant rural economy. ❑

Article 8.2

IS THE UNITED STATES A POLLUTION HAVEN?

BY FRANK ACKERMAN
March/April 2003

When this article was originally written, the North American Free Trade Agreement (NAFTA) was nearly a decade old, and many of its main effects were already apparent. One of these was the devastating impact of U.S. corn exports on Mexican small-farmer agriculture. As productive as Mexico's small farmers are, they have been not been able to compete with low-priced corn produced on the United States' gigantic, "super-mechanized" farms using the most petroleum- and chemical-intensive methods. Although some numbers and details have changed since this article was written, more recent findings bear out the continuing heavy toll on Mexican farmers. Researcher Timothy A. Wise points to U.S. agricultural subsidies, permitted under NAFTA, as a cause of U.S. producers' export "dumping" (sales a less than cost of production) in Mexico. This has not only cost Mexican farmers about a billion dollars a year (with the largest impact on corn farmers), but also helped turn Mexico into a large importer of corn. Recent spikes in corn prices, due to the promotion of corn-based ethanol as an alternative motor fuel, have inflicted a heavy blow on low-income Mexicans for whom corn is a staple food. Meanwhile, the environmental impacts of chemical-intensive agriculture in the United States remain serious—with agricultural runoff as a top source of water pollution. —Eds.

Sources: Timothy A. Wise, "Agricultural Dumping Under NAFTA," Woodrow Wilson International Center for Scholars, 2010; Timothy A. Wise, "The Cost to Mexico of U.S. Corn Ethanol Expansion," GDAE Working Paper 12-0, May 2012; Environmental Protection Agency (EPA), Water Quality Assessment and Total Maximum Daily Loads Information (epa.gov/waters/ir/).

Free trade, according to its critics, runs the risk of creating pollution havens—countries where lax environmental standards allow dirty industries to expand. Poor countries are the usual suspects; perhaps poverty drives them to desperate strategies, such as specializing in the most polluting industries.

But could the United States be a pollution haven? A look at agriculture under NAFTA, particularly the trade in corn, suggests that at least one polluting industry is thriving in the United States as a result of free trade.

In narrow economic terms, the United States is winning the corn market. U.S. corn exports to Mexico have doubled since 1994, NAFTA's first year, to more than five million tons annually. Cheap U.S. corn is undermining traditional production in Mexico; prices there have dropped 27% in just a few years, and a quarter of the corn consumed in Mexico is now grown in the United States. But in environmental terms, the U.S. victory comes at a great cost.

While the United States may not have more lax environmental *standards* than Mexico, when it comes to corn U.S. agriculture certainly uses more polluting *methods*.

As it is grown in the United States, corn requires significantly more chemicals per acre than wheat or soybeans, the other two leading field crops. Runoff of excess nitrogen fertilizer causes water pollution, and has created a huge "dead zone" in the Gulf of Mexico around the mouth of the Mississippi River. Intensive application of toxic herbicides and insecticides threatens the health of farm workers, farming communities, and consumers. Genetically modified corn, which now accounts for about one-fifth of U.S. production, poses unknown long-term risks to consumers and to ecosystems.

Growing corn in very dry areas, where irrigation is required, causes more environmental problems. The United States also has a higher percentage of irrigated acreage than Mexico. While the traditional Corn Belt enjoys ample rainfall and does not need irrigation, 15% of U.S. corn acreage—almost all of it in Nebraska, Kansas, the Texas panhandle, and eastern Colorado—is now irrigated. These areas draw water from the Ogallala aquifer, a gigantic underground reservoir, much faster than the aquifer naturally refills. If present rates of overuse continue, the Ogallala, which now contains as much fresh water as Lake Huron, will be drained down to unusable levels within a few decades, causing a crisis for the huge areas of the plains states that depend on it for water supplies. Government subsidies, in years past, helped farmers buy the equipment needed to pump water out of the Ogallala, contributing to the impending crisis.

Moreover, the corn borer, a leading insect pest that likes to eat corn plants, flourishes best in dry climates. Thus the "irrigation states," particularly Texas and Colorado, are the hardest hit by corn borers. Corn growers in dry states have the greatest need for insecticides; they also have the greatest motivation to use genetically modified corn, which is designed to repel corn borers.

Sales to Mexico are particularly important to the United States because many countries are refusing to accept genetically modified corn. Europe no longer imports U.S. corn for this reason, and Japan and several East Asian countries may follow suit. Mexico prohibits growing genetically modified corn, but still allows it to be imported; it is one of the largest remaining markets where U.S. exports are not challenged on this issue.

Despite Mexico's ban, genetically modified corn was recently found growing in a remote rural area in the southern state of Oaxaca. As the ancestral home of corn, Mexico possesses a unique and irreplaceable genetic diversity. Although the extent of the problem is still uncertain, the unplanned and uncontrolled spread of artificially engineered plants from the United States could potentially contaminate Mexico's numerous naturally occurring corn varieties.

An even greater threat is the economic impact of cheap U.S. imports on peasant farmers and rural communities. Traditional farming practices, evolved over thousands of years, use combinations of different natural varieties of corn carefully matched to local conditions. Lose these traditions, and we will lose a living reservoir of biodiversity in the country of origin of one of the world's most important food grains.

The United States has won the North American corn market. But the cost looks increasingly unbearable when viewed through the lens of the U.S. environment, or of Mexico's biodiversity. ❏

Article 8.3

CLIMATE ECONOMICS IN FOUR EASY PIECES

Conventional cost-benefit models cannot inform our decisions about how to address the threat of climate change.

FRANK ACKERMAN
November/December 2008

Once upon a time, debates about climate policy were primarily about the science. An inordinate amount of attention was focused on the handful of "climate skeptics" who challenged the scientific understanding of climate change. The influence of the skeptics, however, is rapidly fading; few people were swayed by their arguments, and doubt about the major results of climate science is no longer important in shaping public policy.

As the climate *science* debate is reaching closure, the climate *economics* debate is heating up. The controversial issue now is the fear that overly ambitious climate initiatives could hurt the economy. Mainstream economists emphasizing that fear have, in effect, replaced the climate skeptics as the intellectual enablers of inaction.

For example, William Nordhaus, the U.S. economist best known for his work on climate change, pays lip service to scientists' calls for decisive action. He finds, however, that the "optimal" policy is a very small carbon tax that would reduce greenhouse gas emissions only 25% below "business-as-usual" levels by 2050—that would, in other words, allow emissions to rise well above current levels by mid-century. Richard Tol, a European economist who has written widely on climate change, favors an even smaller carbon tax of just $2 per ton of carbon dioxide. That would amount to all of $0.02 per gallon of gasoline, a microscopic "incentive" for change that consumers would never notice.

There are other voices in the climate economics debate; in particular, the British government's Stern Review offers a different perspective. Economist Nicholas Stern's analysis is much less wrong than the traditional Nordhaus-Tol approach, but even Stern has not challenged the conventional view enough.

What will it take to build a better economics of climate change, one that is consistent with the urgency expressed by the latest climate science? The issues that matter are big, non-technical principles, capable of being expressed in bumper-sticker format. Here are the four bumper stickers for a better climate economics:

- Our grandchildren's lives are important
- We need to buy insurance for the planet
- Climate damages are too valuable to have prices
- Some costs are better than others

1. Our grandchildren's lives are important.

The most widely debated challenge of climate economics is the valuation of the very long run. For ordinary loans and investments, both the costs today and the resulting future benefits typically occur within a single lifetime. In such cases, it makes sense to think in terms of the same person experiencing and comparing the costs and the benefits.

In the case of climate change, the time spans involved are well beyond those encountered in most areas of economics. The most important consequences of today's choices will be felt by generations to come, long after all of us making those choices have passed away. As a result, the costs of reducing emissions today and the benefits in the far future will not be experienced by the same people. The economics of climate change is centrally concerned with our relationship to our descendants whom we will never meet. As a bridge to that unknowable future, consider our grandchildren—the last generation most of us will ever know.

Suppose that you want your grandchildren to receive $100 (in today's dollars, corrected for inflation), 60 years from now. How much would you have to put in a bank account today, to ensure that the $100 will be there 60 years from now? The answer is $55 at 1% interest, or just over $5 at 5%.

In parallel fashion, economists routinely deal with future costs and benefits by "discounting" them, or converting them to "present values"—a process that is simply compound interest in reverse. In the standard jargon, the *present value* of $100, to be received 60 years from now, is $55 at a 1% *discount rate*, or about $5 at a 5% discount rate. As this example shows, a higher discount rate implies a smaller present value.

The central problem of climate economics, in a cost-benefit framework, is deciding how much to spend today on preventing future harms. What should we spend to prevent $100 of climate damages 60 years from now? The standard answer is, no more than the present value of that future loss: $55 at a discount rate of 1%, or $5 at 5%. The higher the discount rate, the less it is "worth" spending today on protecting our grandchildren.

The effect of a change in the discount rate becomes much more pronounced as the time period lengthens. Damages of $1 million occurring 200 years from now have a present value of only about $60 at a 5% discount rate, versus more than $130,000 at a 1% discount rate. The choice of the discount rate is all-important to our stance toward the far future: should we spend as much as $130,000, or as little as $60, to avoid one million dollars of climate damages in the early twenty-third century?

For financial transactions within a single lifetime, it makes sense to use market interest rates as the discount rate. Climate change, however, involves public policy decisions with impacts spanning centuries; there is no market in which public resources are traded from one century to the next. The choice of an intergenerational discount rate is a matter of ethics and policy, not a market-determined result.

Economists commonly identify two separate aspects of long-term discounting, each contributing to the discount rate.

One component of the discount rate is based on the assumption of an upward trend in income and wealth. If future generations will be richer than we are, they will need less help from us, and they will get less benefit from an additional dollar of income than we do. So we can discount benefits that will flow to our wealthier descendants, at a rate based on the expected growth of per capita incomes. Among economists, the income-related motive for discounting may be the least controversial part of the picture.

Setting aside changes in per capita income from one generation to the next, there may still be a reason to discount a sum many years in the future. This component of the discount rate, known as "pure time preference," is the subject of longstanding ethical, philosophical, and economic debate. On the one hand, there are reasons to think that pure time preference is greater than zero: both psychological experiments and common sense suggest that people are impatient, and prefer money now to money later. On the other hand, a pure time preference of zero expresses the equal worth of people of all generations, and the equal importance of reducing climate impacts and other burdens on them (assuming that all generations have equal incomes).

The Stern Review provides an excellent discussion of the debate, explaining Stern's assumption of pure time preference close to zero and an overall discount rate of 1.4%. This discount rate alone is sufficient to explain Stern's support for a substantial program of climate protection: at the higher discount rates used in more traditional analyses, the Stern program would look "inefficient," since the costs would outweigh the present value of the benefits.

2. We need to buy insurance for the planet.

Does climate science predict that things are certain to get worse? Or does it tell us that we are uncertain about what will happen next? Unfortunately, the answer seems to be yes to both questions. For example, the most likely level of sea level rise in this century, according to the latest Intergovernmental Panel on Climate Change reports, is no more than one meter or so—a real threat to low-lying coastal areas and islands that will face increasing storm damages, but survivable, with some adaptation efforts, for most of the world. On the other hand, there is a worst-case risk of an abrupt loss of the Greenland ice sheet, or perhaps of a large portion of the West Antarctic ice sheet. Either one could cause an eventual seven-meter rise in sea level—a catastrophic impact on coastal communities, economic activity, and infrastructure everywhere, and well beyond the range of plausible adaptation efforts in most places.

The evaluation of climate damages thus depends on whether we focus on the most likely outcomes or the credible worst-case risks; the latter, of course, are much larger.

Cost-benefit analysis conventionally rests on average or expected outcomes. But this is not the only way that people make decisions. When faced with uncertain, potentially large risks, people do not normally act on the basis of average outcomes; instead, they typically focus on protection against worst-case scenarios. When you go to the airport, do you leave just enough time for the average traffic delay (so that you would catch your plane, on average, half of the time)? Or do you allow time for some estimate of worst-case traffic jams? Once you get there, of course, you will experience additional delays due to security, which is all about worst cases: your *average* fellow passenger is not a threat to anyone's safety.

The very existence of the insurance industry is evidence of the desire to avoid or control worst-case scenarios. It is impossible for an insurance company to pay out in claims as much as its customers pay in premiums; if it did, there would be no money left to pay the costs of running the company, or the profits received by its owners. People who buy insurance are therefore guaranteed to get back less than they, on average, have paid; they (we) are paying for the security that insurance provides in case the worst should happen. This way of thinking does not apply to every decision: in casino games, people make bets based on averages and probabilities, and no one has any insurance against losing the next round. But life is not a casino, and public policy should not be a gamble.

Should climate policy be based on the most likely outcomes, or on the worst-case risks? Should we be investing in climate protection as if we expect sea level rise of one meter, or as if we are buying insurance to be sure of preventing a seven-meters rise?

In fact, the worst-case climate risks are even more unknown than the individual risks of fire and death that motivate insurance purchases. You do not know whether or not you will have a fire next year or die before the year is over, but you have very good information about the likelihood of these tragic events. So does the insurance industry, which is why they are willing to insure you. In contrast, there is no body of statistical information about the probability of Greenland-sized ice sheets collapsing at various temperatures; it's not an experiment that anyone can perform over and over again.

A recent analysis by Martin Weitzman argues that the probabilities of the worst outcomes are inescapably unknowable—and this deep uncertainty is more important than anything we do know in motivating concern about climate change. There is a technical sense in which the expected value of future climate damages can be infinite because we know so little about the probability of the worst, most damaging possibilities. The practical implication of infinite expected damages is that the most likely outcome is irrelevant; what matters is buying insurance for the planet, i.e., doing our best to understand and prevent the worst-case risks.

3. Climate damages are too valuable to have prices.

To decide whether climate protection is worthwhile, in cost-benefit terms, we would need to know the monetary value of everything important that is being protected.

Even if we could price everything affected by climate change, the prices would conceal a critical form of international inequity. The emissions that cause climate change have come predominantly from rich countries, while the damages will be felt first and worst in some of the world's poorest, tropical countries (although no one will be immune from harm for long). There are, however, no meaningful prices for many of the benefits of health and environmental protection. What is the dollar value of a human life saved? How much is it worth to save an endangered species from extinction, or to preserve a unique location or ecosystem? Economists have made up price tags for such priceless values, but the results do not always pass the laugh test.

Is a human life worth $6.1 million, as estimated by the Clinton administration, based on small differences in the wages paid for more and less risky jobs? Or is it worth $3.7 million, as the (second) Bush administration concluded on the basis of questionnaires about people's willingness to pay for reducing small, hypothetical risks? Are lives of people in rich countries worth much more than those in poor countries, as some economists infamously argued in the IPCC's 1995 report? Can the value of an endangered species be determined by survey research on how much people would pay to protect it? If, as one study found, the U.S. population as a whole would pay $18 billion to protect the existence of humpback whales, would it be acceptable for someone to pay $36 billion for the right to hunt and kill the entire species?

The only sensible response to such nonsensical questions is that there are many crucially important values that do not have meaningful prices. This is not a new idea: as the eighteenth-century philosopher Immanuel Kant put it, some things have a price, or relative worth, while other things have a dignity, or inner worth. No price tag does justice to the dignity of human life or the natural world.

Since some of the most important benefits of climate protection are priceless, any monetary value for total benefits will necessarily be incomplete. The corollary is that preventive action may be justified even in the absence of a complete monetary measure of the benefits of doing so.

Average Risks or Worst-Case Scenarios?

You don't have to look far to find situations in which the sensible policy is to address worst-case outcomes rather than average outcomes. The annual number of residential fires in the United States is about 0.4% of the number of housing units. This means that a fire occurs, on average, about once every 250 years in each home—not even close to once per lifetime. By far the most likely number of fires a homeowner will experience next year, or even in a lifetime, is zero. Why don't these statistics inspire you to cancel your fire insurance? Unless you are extremely wealthy, the loss of your home in a fire would be a devastating financial blow; despite the low probability, you cannot afford to take any chances on it.

What are the chances of the ultimate loss? The probability that you will die next year is under 0.1% if you are in your twenties, under 0.2% in your thirties, under 0.4% in your forties. It is not until age 61 that you have as much as a 1% chance of death within the coming year. Yet most U.S. families with dependent children buy life insurance. Without it, the risk to children of losing their parents' income would be too great—even though the parents are, on average, extraordinarily likely to survive.

4. Some costs are better than others.

The language of cost-benefit analysis embodies a clear normative slant: benefits are good, costs are bad. The goal is always to have larger benefits and smaller costs. In some respects, measurement and monetary valuation are easier for costs than for benefits: implementing pollution control measures typically involves changes in such areas as manufacturing, construction, and fuel use, all of which have well-defined prices. Yet conventional economic theory distorts the interpretation of costs in ways that exaggerate the burdens of environmental protection and hide the positive features of some of the "costs."

For instance, empirical studies of energy use and carbon emissions repeatedly find significant opportunities for emissions reduction at zero or negative net cost—the so-called "no regrets" options.

According to a long-standing tradition in economic theory, however, cost-free energy savings are impossible. The textbook theory of competitive markets assumes that every resource is productively employed in its most valuable use—in other words, that every no-regrets option must already have been taken. As the saying goes, there are no free lunches; there cannot be any $20 bills on the sidewalk because someone would have picked them up already. Any new emissions reduction measures, then, must have positive costs. This leads to greater estimates of climate policy costs than the bottom-up studies that reveal extensive opportunities for costless savings.

In the medium term, we will need to move beyond the no-regrets options; how much will it cost to finish the job of climate protection? Again, there are rival interpretations of the costs based on rival assumptions about the economy. The same economic theory that proclaimed the absence of $20 bills on the sidewalk is responsible for the idea that all costs are bad. Since the free market lets everyone spend their money in whatever way they choose, any new cost must represent a loss: it leaves people with less to spend on whatever purchases they had previously selected to maximize their satisfaction in life. Climate damages are one source of loss, and spending on climate protection is another; both reduce the resources available for the desirable things in life.

But are the two kinds of costs really comparable? Is it really a matter of indifference whether we spend $1 billion on bigger and better levees or lose $1 billion to storm damages? In the real-world economy, money spent on building levees creates jobs and incomes. The construction workers buy groceries, clothing, and so on, indirectly creating other jobs. With more people working, tax revenues increase while unemployment compensation payments decrease.

None of this happens if the levees are not built and the storm damages are allowed to occur. The costs of prevention are good costs, with numerous indirect benefits; the costs of climate damages are bad costs, representing pure physical destruction. One worthwhile goal is to keep total costs as low as possible; another is to have as much as possible of good costs rather than bad costs. Think of it as the cholesterol theory of climate costs.

In the long run, the deep reductions in carbon emissions needed for climate stabilization will require new technologies that have not yet been invented, or at best exist only in small, expensive prototypes. How much will it cost to invent, develop, and implement the low-carbon technologies of the future?

Lacking a rigorous theory of innovation, economists modeling climate change have often assumed that new technologies simply appear, making the economy inexorably more efficient over time. A more realistic view observes that the costs of producing a new product typically decline as industry gains more experience with it, in a pattern called "learning by doing" or the "learning curve" effect. Public investment is often necessary to support the innovation process in its early, expensive stages. Wind power is now relatively cheap and competitive, in suitable locations; this is a direct result of decades of public investment in the United States and Europe, starting when wind turbines were still quite expensive. The costs of climate policy, in the long run, will include doing the same for other promising new technologies, investing public resources in jump-starting a set of slightly different industries than we might have chosen in the absence of climate change. If this is a cost, many communities would be better off with more of it.

A widely publicized, conventional economic analysis recommends inaction on climate change, claiming that the costs currently outweigh the benefits for anything more than the smallest steps toward reducing carbon emissions. Put our "four easy pieces" together, and we have the outline of an economics that complements the science of climate change and endorses active, large-scale climate protection.

How realistic is it to expect that the world will shake off its inertia and act boldly and rapidly enough to make a difference? This may be the last generation that will have a real chance at protecting the earth's climate. Projections from the latest IPCC reports, the Stern Review, and other sources suggest that it is still possible to save the planet—if we start at once. ❑

Sources: Frank Ackerman, *Can We Afford the Future? Economics for a Warming World*, Zed Books, 2008; Frank Ackerman, *Poisoned for Pennies: The Economics of Toxics and Precaution*, Island Press, 2008; Frank Ackerman and Lisa Heinzerling, *Priceless: On Knowing the Price of Everything and the Value of Nothing*, The New Press, 2004; J. Creyts, A. Derkach, S. Nyquist, K. Ostrowski and J. Stephenson, *Reducing U.S. Greenhouse Gas Emissions: How Much at What Cost?*, McKinsey & Co., 2007; P.-A. Enkvist, T. Naucler and J. Rosander, "A Cost Curve for Greenhouse Gas Reduction," *The McKinsey Quarterly*, 2007; Immanuel Kant, *Groundwork for the Metaphysics of Morals*, translated by Thomas K. Abbot, with revisions by Lara Denis, Broadview Press, 2005 [1785]; B. Lomborg, *Cool It: The Skeptical Environmentalist's Guide to Global Warming*, Alfred A. Knopf, 2007; W.D. Nordhaus, *A Question of Balance: Economic Modeling of Global Warming*, Yale University Press, 2008; F.P. Ramsey, "A mathematical theory of saving," *The Economic Journal* 138(152): 543-59, 1928; Nicholas Stern *et al.*, *The Stern Review: The Economics of Climate Change*, HM Treasury, 2006; U.S. Census Bureau, "Statistical Abstract of the United States." 127th edition. 2008; M.L. Weitzman, "On Modeling and Interpreting the Economics of Catastrophic Climate Change," December 5, 2007 version, www.economics.harvard.edu/faculty/weitzman/files/modeling.pdf.

Article 8.4

THE COSTS OF EXTREME WEATHER

Climate inaction is expensive—and inequitable.

BY HEIDI GARRETT-PELTIER

November/December 2011

Two thousand eleven has already been a record-setting year. The number of weather disasters in the United States whose costs exceed $1 billion—ten—is the highest ever. August witnessed one of the ten most expensive catastrophes in U.S. history, Tropical Storm Irene. An initial estimate put the damages from Irene at between $7 billion and $13 billion. In this one storm alone, eight million businesses and homes lost power, roads collapsed, buildings flooded, and dozens of people lost their lives. Meanwhile, Texas is experiencing its hottest year in recorded history: millions of acres in the state have burned, over 1,550 homes have been lost to wildfires as of early September, and tens of thousands of people have had to evacuate their homes. The devastation caused by the storms and droughts has left individuals and businesses wondering how they'll recover, and has left cash-strapped towns wondering how they'll pay for road and infrastructure repairs.

Extreme weather events like these are expected to become more frequent and more intense over the next century. That's just one of the impacts of climate change, which, according to the consensus of scientists and research organizations from around the world, is occurring with both natural and human causes, but mainly from the burning of fossil fuels. According to NASA, since 1950 the number of record high-temperature days has been rising while the number of record low-temperature days has been falling. The number of intense rainfall events has also increased in the past six decades. At the same time, droughts and heat waves have also become more frequent, as warmer conditions in drier areas have led to faster evaporation. This is why in the same month we had wildfires in Texas (resulting from more rapid evaporation and drought) and flooding in the Northeast (since warmer air holds more moisture and results in more intense precipitation).

In response to these dramatic weather changes, the courses of action available to us are *mitigation*, *adaptation*, and *reparation*. *Mitigation* refers to efforts to prevent or reduce climate change, for example, cutting fossil fuel use by increasing energy efficiency and using more renewable energy. *Adaptation* refers to changing our behaviors, technologies, institutions, and infrastructure to cope with the damages that climate change creates—building levees near flood-prone areas or relocating homes further inland, for example. And as the term implies, *reparation* means repairing or rebuilding the roads, bridges, homes, and communities that are damaged by floods, winds, heat, and other weather-related events.

Of these, mitigation is the one strategy whose costs and benefits can both be shared globally. Moving toward a more sustainable economy less reliant on the burning of fossil fuels for its energy would slow the rise in average global temperatures and make extreme weather events less likely. Mitigation will have the greatest impact with a shared worldwide commitment, but even without binding international agreements, countries can take steps to reduce their use of coal, oil, and natural gas.

According to the Intergovernmental Panel on Climate Change, even the most stringent mitigation efforts cannot prevent further impacts of climate change in the next few decades. We will still need to adapt and repair—all the more in the absence of such efforts. But the costs and burdens of adaptation and reparation are spread unevenly across different populations and in many cases the communities most affected by climate change will be those least able to afford to build retaining walls or relocate to new homes. Farmers who can afford to will change their planting and harvesting techniques and schedules, but others will have unusable land and will be unable to sustain themselves. Roads that are washed away will be more quickly rebuilt in richer towns, while poorer towns will take longer to rebuild if they can at all. The divide between rich and poor will only grow.

Given the high cost of damages we've already faced just this year, mitigation may very well be sound economic planning. But it is also the most humane and equitable approach to solving our climate problem. ❑

Sources: NOAA/NESDIS/NCDC, "Billion Dollar U.S. Weather/Climate Disasters 1980-August 2011"; Michael Cooper, "Hurricane Cost Seen as Ranking Among Top Ten," New York Times, August 30, 2011; "Hurricane Irene Damage: Storm Likely Cost $7 Billion to $13 Billion," International Business Times, August 29, 2011; Intergovernmental Panel on Climate Change, Fourth Assessment Report: Climate Change 2007, Working Group II ch. 19; NASA, "Global Climate Change: Vital Signs of the Planet—Evidence"; U.S. EPA, "Climate Change—Health and Environmental Effects, Extreme Events."

Article 8.5

KEEP IT IN THE GROUND

An alternative vision for petroleum emerges in Ecuador. But will Big Oil win the day?

BY ELISSA DENNIS
July/August 2010

In the far eastern reaches of Ecuador, in the Amazon basin rain forest, lies a land of incredible beauty and biological diversity. More than 2,200 varieties of trees reach for the sky, providing a habitat for more species of birds, bats, insects, frogs, and fish than can be found almost anywhere else in the world. Indigenous Waorani people have made the land their home for millennia, including the last two tribes living in voluntary isolation in the country. The land was established as Yasuní National Park in 1979, and recognized as a UNESCO World Biosphere Reserve in 1989.

Underneath this landscape lies a different type of natural resource: petroleum. Since 1972, oil has been Ecuador's primary export, representing 57% of the country's exports in 2008; oil revenues comprised on average 26% of the government's revenue between 2000 and 2007. More than 1.1 billion barrels of heavy crude oil have been extracted from Yasuní, about one quarter of the nation's production to date.

At this economic, environmental, and political intersection lie two distinct visions for Yasuní's, and Ecuador's, next 25 years. Petroecuador, the state-owned oil company, has concluded that 846 million barrels of oil could be extracted from proven reserves at the Ishpingo, Tambococha, and Tiputini (ITT) wells in an approximately 200,000-hectare area covering about 20% of the parkland. Extracting this petroleum, either alone or in partnership with interested oil companies in Brazil, Venezuela, or China, would generate approximately $7 billion, primarily in the first 13 years of extraction and continuing with declining productivity for another 12 years.

The alternative vision is the simple but profound choice to leave the oil in the ground. Environmentalists and indigenous communities have been organizing for years to restrict drilling in Yasuní. But the vision became much more real when President Rafael Correa presented a challenge to the world community at a September 24, 2007 meeting of the United Nations General Assembly: If governments, companies, international organizations, and individuals pledge a total of $350 million per year for 10 years, equal to half of the forgone revenues from ITT, then Ecuador will chip in the other half and keep the oil underground indefinitely, as this nation's contribution to halting global climate change.

The Yasuní-ITT Initiative would preserve the fragile environment, leave the voluntarily isolated tribes in peace, and prevent the emission of an estimated 407 million metric tons of carbon dioxide into the atmosphere. This "big idea from a small country" has even broader implications, as Alberto Acosta, former Energy Minister and one of the architects of the proposal, notes in his new book, *La Maldición de la Abundancia (The Curse of Abundance)*. The Initiative is a "punto de ruptura," he writes, a turning point in environmental history which "questions the logic of extractive (exporter of raw material) development," while introducing the possibility of global *"sumak kawsay,"* the indigenous Kichwa concept of "good living" in harmony with nature.

Sumak kawsay is the underlying tenet of the country's 2008 Constitution, which guarantees rights for indigenous tribes and for "Mother Earth." The Constitution was overwhelmingly supported in a national referendum, but putting the document's principles into action has been a bigger challenge. While Correa draws praise for his progressive social programs, for example in education and health care, the University of Illinois-trained economist is criticized for not yet having wrested control of the nation's economy from a deep-rooted powerful elite bearing different ideas about the meaning of "good living." Within this political and economic discord lies the fate of the Yasuni Initiative.

An Abundance of Oil

Ecuador, like much of Latin America, has long been an exporter of raw materials: cacao in the 19th century, bananas in the 20th century, and now petroleum. Shell discovered the heavy, viscous oil of Ecuador's Amazon basin in 1948. In the 1950s, a series of controversial encounters began between the native Waorani people and U.S. missionaries from the Summer Institute of Linguistics (SIL). With SIL assistance, Waorani were corralled into a 16,000-hectare "protectorate" in the late 1960s, and many went to work for the oil companies who were furiously drilling through much of the tribe's homeland.

The nation dove into the oil boom of the 1970s, investing in infrastructure and building up external debt. When oil prices plummeted in the 1980s while interest rates on that debt ballooned, Ecuador was trapped in the debt crisis that affected much of the region. Thus began what Correa calls "the long night of neoliberalism": IMF-mandated privatizations of utilities and mining sectors, with a concomitant decline of revenues from the nation's natural resources to the Ecuadorian people. By 1986, all of the nation's petroleum revenues were going to pay external debt.

After another decade of IMF-driven privatizations, oil price drops, earthquakes, and other natural disasters, the Ecuadorian economy fell into total collapse, leading to the 2000 dollarization. Since then, more than one million Ecuadorians have left the country, mostly for the United States and Spain, and remittances from 2.5 million Ecuadorians living in the exterior, estimated at $4 billion in 2008, have become the nation's second highest source of income.

Close to 40 years of oil production has failed to improve the living standards of the majority of Ecuadorians. "Petroleum has not helped this country," notes Ana Cecilia Salazar, director of the Department of Social Sciences in the College of Economics of the University of Cuenca. "It has been corrupt. It has not diminished poverty. It has not industrialized this country. It has just made a few people rich."

Currently 38% of the population lives in poverty, with 13% in extreme poverty. The nation's per capita income growth between 1982 and 2007 was only 0.7% per year. And although the unemployment rate of 10% may seem moderate, an estimated 53% of the population is considered "underemployed."

Petroleum extraction has brought significant environmental damage. Each year 198,000 hectares of land in the Amazon are deforested for oil production. A verdict is expected this year in an Ecuadorian court in the 17-year-old class action suit brought by 30,000 victims of Texaco/Chevron's drilling operations in the area northwest of Yasuní between 1964 and 1990. The unprecedented $27 billion lawsuit alleges that thousands of cancers and other health problems were caused by Texaco's use of outdated and dangerous practices, including the dumping of 18 billion gallons of toxic wastewater into local water supplies.

Regardless of its economic or environmental impacts, the oil is running out. With 4.16 billion barrels in proven reserves nationwide, and another half billion "probable" barrels, best-case projections, including the discovery of new reserves, indicate the nation will stop exporting oil within 28 years, and stop producing oil within 35 years.

"At this moment we have an opportunity to rethink the extractive economy that for many years has constrained the economy and politics in the country," says Esperanza Martinez, a biologist, environmental activist, and author of the book *Yasuní: El tortuoso camino de Kioto a Quito (Yasuní: The Tortuous Road from Kyoto to Quito)*. "This proposal intends to change the terms of the North-South relationship in climate change negotiations."

Collecting on Ecological Debt

The Initiative fits into the emerging idea of "climate debt." The North's voracious energy consumption in the past has destroyed natural resources in the South; the South is currently bearing the brunt of global warming effects like floods and drought; and the South needs to adapt expensive new energy technology for the future instead of industrializing with the cheap fossil fuels that built the North. Bolivian president Evo Morales proposed at the Copenhagen climate talks last December that developed nations pay 1% of GDP, totaling $700 billion/year, into a compensation fund that poor nations could use to adapt their energy systems.

"Clearly in the future, it will not be possible to extract all the petroleum in the world because that would create a very serious world problem, so we need to create measures of compensation to pay the ecological debt to the countries," says Malki Sáenz, formerly Coordinator of the Yasuní-ITT Initiative within the Ministry of Foreign Relations. The Initiative "is a way to show the international community that real compensation mechanisms exist for not extracting petroleum."

Indigenous and environmental movements in Latin America and Africa are raising possibilities of leaving oil in the ground elsewhere. But the Yasuní-ITT proposal is the furthest along in detail, government sponsorship, and ongoing negotiations. The Initiative proposes that governments, international institutions, civil associations, companies, and individuals contribute to a fund administered through an international organization such as the United Nations Development Program (UNDP). Contributions could include swaps of Ecuador's external debt, as well as resources generated from emissions auctions in the European Union and carbon emission taxes such as those implemented in Sweden and Slovakia.

Contributors of at least $10,000 would receive a Yasuní Guarantee Certificate (CGY), redeemable only in the event that a future government decides to extract the oil. The total dollar value of the CGYs issued would equal the calculated value of the 407 million metric tons of non-emitted carbon dioxide.

The money would be invested in fixed income shares of renewable energy projects with a guaranteed yield, such as hydroelectric, geothermal, wind, and solar power, thus helping to reduce the country's dependence on fossil fuels. The interest payments generated by these investments would be designated for: 1) conservation projects, preventing deforestation of almost 10 million hectares in 40 protected areas covering 38% of Ecuador's territory; 2) reforestation and natural regeneration projects on another one million hectares of forest land; 3) national energy efficiency improvements; and 4) education, health, employment, and training programs in sustainable activities like ecotourism and agro forestry in the affected areas. The first three activities could prevent an additional 820 million metric tons of carbon dioxide emissions, tripling the Initiative's effectiveness.

Government Waffling

These nationwide conservation efforts, as well as the proposal's mention of "monitoring" throughout Yasuní and possibly shutting down existing oil production, are particularly disconcerting to Ecuadorian and international oil and wood interests. Many speculate that political pressure from these economic powerhouses was behind a major blow to the Initiative this past January, when Correa, in one of his regular Saturday radio broadcasts, suddenly blasted the negotiations as "shameful," and a threat to the nation's "sovereignty" and "dignity." He threatened that if the full package of international commitments is not in place by this June, he would begin extracting oil from ITT.

Correa's comments spurred the resignations of four critical members of the negotiating commission, including Chancellor Fander Falconí, a longtime ally in Correa's PAIS party, and Roque Sevilla, an ecologist, businessman, and ex-Mayor of Quito whom Correa had picked to lead the commission. Ecuador's Ambassador to the UN Francisco Carrion also resigned from the commission, as did World Wildlife Fund president Yolanda Kakabadse.

Correa has been clear from the outset that the government has a Plan B, to extract the oil, and that the non-extraction "first option" is contingent on the mandated monetary commitments. But oddly his outburst came as the negotiating team's efforts were bearing fruit. Sevilla told the press in January of commitments in various stages of approval from Germany, Spain, Belgium, France, and Switzerland, totaling at least $1.5 billion. The team was poised to sign an agreement with UNDP last December in Copenhagen to administer the fund. Correa called off the signing at the last minute, questioning the breadth of the Initiative's conservation efforts and UNDP's proposed six-person administrative body, three appointed by Ecuador, two by contributing nations, and one by UNDP. This joint control structure apparently sparked Correa's tirade about shame and dignity.

Correa's impulsivity and poor word choice have gotten him into trouble before. Acosta, another former key PAIS ally, resigned as president of the Constituent Assembly in June 2008, in the final stages of drafting the nation's new Constitution, when Correa set a vote deadline Acosta felt hindered the democratic process for this major undertaking. The President has had frequent tussles with indigenous and environmental organizations over mining issues, on several occasions crossing the line from staking out an economically pragmatic political position to name-calling of "childish ecologists."

Within a couple of weeks of the blowup, the government had backpedaled, withdrawing the June deadline, appointing a new negotiating team, and reasserting the position that the government's "first option" is to leave the oil in the ground. At the same time, Petroecuador began work on a new pipeline near Yasuní, part of the infrastructure needed for ITT production, pursuant to a 2007 Memorandum of Understanding with several foreign oil companies.

If the People Lead...

Amid the doubts and mixed messages, proponents are fighting to save the Initiative as a cornerstone in the creation of a post-petroleum Ecuador and ultimately a post-petroleum world. In media interviews after his resignation, Sevilla stressed that he would keep working to ensure that the Initiative would not fail. The Constitution provides for a public referendum prior to extracting oil from protected areas like Yasuní, he noted. "If the president doesn't want to assume his responsibility as leader...let's pass the responsibility to the public." In fact, 75% of respondents in a January poll in Quito and Guayaquil, the country's two largest cities, indicated that they would vote to not extract the ITT oil.

Martinez and Sáenz concur that just as the Initiative emerged from widespread organizing efforts, its success will come from the people. "This is the moment to define ourselves and develop an economic model not based on petroleum," Salazar says. "We have other knowledge, we have minerals, water. We need to change our consciousness and end the economic dependence on one resource." ❑

Resources: Live Yasuni, Finding Species, Inc. (liveyasuni.org); "S.O.S. Yasuni" (sosyasuni.org); "Yasuni-ITT: An Initiative to Change History," Government of Ecuador, (yasuni-itt.gov.ec).

Chapter 9

THE POLITICAL ECONOMY
OF WAR AND IMPERIALISM

Article 9.1

IS IT OIL?

BY ARTHUR MacEWAN
May/June 2003

Foreword, October 2012

The long U.S. military engagement in Iraq is over. There were no weapons of mass destruction, so the U.S. government shifted its rationale for the invasion to "regime change" and the establishment of a democratic Iraq. While regime change was accomplished, virtually no one would claim that a meaningful democracy was left in place as U.S. troops departed. Untold numbers of Iraqis died—estimates range from 100,000 upwards to one-million—and over 4,000 U.S. deaths were recorded.

From the perspective of U.S. and other internationally operating major oil companies, however, the U.S. invasion was a success—at least a partial success. ExxonMobil, Shell, BP, Haliburton and others are back in Iraq. Having secured contracts to extract the county's low-cost oil, they are expanding their operations in the country—and expanding their profits from those operations. Iraq's oil production in 2011 stood at 2,798 thousand barrels a day (bpd), surpassing output in all previous years except for the 2,832 bpd in 1989. However, the western firms—the "majors" that have dominated the international oil industry for decades—have not obtained all they had hoped for when the invasion began a decade ago:

The major oil companies have had to share the lucrative Iraqi contacts with newer players in the global industry. Firms from Russia, China, Norway, and elsewhere are getting in on the action. And some U.S. firms—Chevron and ConocoPhillips—have failed to get contacts that they sought.

Substantial opposition to the foreign oil companies has developed in Iraq, including actions by unions and popular demonstrations. This opposition has had an impact in spite of its repression by the Iraqi government.

The Iraqi parliament has never enacted the Iraq Oil Law, a law which would secure the full opening of the country's oil reserves to the major firms and which the U.S. government continues to push.

Iraq events of the decade since this article was originally written have verified the importance of the interests of U.S.-based firms—and especially of the oil companies— in affecting the course of the U.S. government's global policies. At the same time, those events have demonstrated the limits of U.S. power. Neither the government, with all its military might, nor the firms can shape the world's economy exactly as they wish. There are, it turns out, people involved, and they don't always cooperate.

—Arthur MacEwan

Before U.S. forces invaded Iraq, the United Nations inspection team that had been searching the country for weapons of mass destruction was unable to find either such weapons or a capacity to produce them in the near future. As of mid-April, while the U.S. military is apparently wrapping up its invasion, it too has not found the alleged weapons. The U.S. government continues to claim that weapons of mass destruction exist in Iraq but provides scant evidence to substantiate its claim.

While weapons of mass destruction are hard to find in Iraq, there is one thing that is relatively easy to find: oil. Lots of oil. With 112.5 billion barrels of proven reserves, Iraq has greater stores of oil than any country except Saudi Arabia. This combination—lots of oil and no weapons of mass destruction—begs the question: *Is it oil* and not weapons of mass destruction that motivates the U.S. government's aggressive policy towards Iraq?

The U.S. "Need" for Oil?

Much of the discussion of the United States, oil, and Iraq focuses on the U.S. economy's overall dependence on oil. We are a country highly dependent on oil, consuming far more than we produce. We have a small share, about 3%, of the world's total proven oil reserves. By depleting our reserves at a much higher rate than most other countries, the United States accounts for about 10% of world production. But, by importing from the rest of the world, we can consume oil at a still higher rate: U.S. oil consumption is over 25% of the world's total. (See the accompanying figures for these and related data.) Thus, the United States relies on the rest of the world's oil in order to keep its economy running—or at least running in its present oil-dependent form. Moreover, for the United States to operate as it does and maintain current standards of living, we need access to oil at low prices. Otherwise we would have to turn over a large share of U.S. GDP as payment to those who supply us with oil.

Iraq could present the United States with supply problems. With a hostile

ncorrected page proofs.
Economic Affairs Bureau, Inc. CHAPTER 9: THE POLITICAL ECONOMY OF WAR AND IMPERIALISM | 261
o not reproduce or distribute.

YEARS OF RESERVES AT CURRENT ANNUAL PRODUCTION RATES*

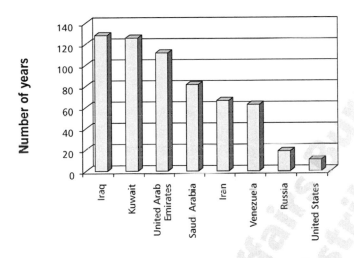

*The number of years it would take to use up existing reserves at current production rate. Past experience, however, suggests that more reserves will be found. In the 1980s, the world's proven reserves expanded by 47%, even as the consumption continued apace. With a more rapid rate of economic growth in the 1990s, and thus with the more rapid rate of oil consumption, the world's reserves rose by almost 5%.

Source: BP Statistical Review of World Energy 2002 <www.bp.com/centres/energy2002>

government in Baghdad, the likelihood that the United States would be subject to some sort of boycott as in the early 1970s is greater than otherwise. Likewise, a government in Baghdad that does not cooperate with Washington could be a catalyst to a reinvigoration of the Organization of Petroleum Exporting Countries (OPEC) and the result could be higher oil prices.

Such threats, however, while real, are not as great as they might first appear. Boycotts are hard to maintain. The sellers of oil need to sell as much as the buyers need to buy; oil exporters depend on the U.S. market, just as U.S. consumers depend on those exporters. (An illustration of this mutual dependence is provided by the continuing oil trade between Iraq and the United States in recent years. During 2001, while the two countries were in a virtual state of war, the United States bought 284 million barrels of oil from Iraq, about 7% of U.S. imports and almost a third of Iraq's exports.) Also, U.S. oil imports come from diverse sources, with less than half from OPEC countries and less than one-quarter from Persian Gulf nations.

Most important, ever since the initial surge of OPEC in the 1970s, the organization has followed a policy of price restraint. While price restraint may in part be a strategy of political cooperation, resulting from the close U.S.-Saudi relationship in particular, it is also a policy adopted because high prices are counter-productive for OPEC itself; high prices lead consumers to switch sources of supply and conserve energy, undercutting the longer term profits for the oil suppliers. Furthermore, a sudden rise in prices can lead to general economic disruption, which is no more desirable for the oil exporters than for the oil importers. To be sure, the United States would prefer to have cooperative governments in oil producing countries, but the specter of another boycott as in the 1970s or somewhat higher prices for oil hardly provides a rationale, let alone a justification, for war.

The Profits Problem

There is, however, also the importance of oil in the profits of large U.S. firms: the oil companies themselves (with ExxonMobil at the head of the list) but also the numerous drilling, shipping, refining, and marketing firms that make up the rest of the oil industry. Perhaps the most famous of this latter group, because former CEO Dick Cheney is now vice president, is the Halliburton Company, which supplies a wide range of equipment and engineering services to the industry. Even while many governments—Saudi Arabia, Kuwait, and Venezuela, for example—have taken ownership of their countries' oil reserves, these companies have been able to maintain their profits because of their decisive roles at each stage in the long sequence from exploration through drilling to refining and marketing. Ultimately, however, as with any resource-based industry, the monopolistic position—and thus the large profits—of the firms that dominate the oil industry depends on their access to the supply of the resource. Their access, in turn, depends on the relations they are able to establish with the governments of oil-producing countries.

From the perspective of the major U.S. oil companies, a hostile Iraqi government presents a clear set of problems. To begin with, there is the obvious: because Iraq has a lot of oil, access to that oil would represent an important profit-making opportunity. What's more, Iraqi oil can be easily extracted and thus produced at very low cost. With all oil selling at the same price on the world market, Iraqi oil thus

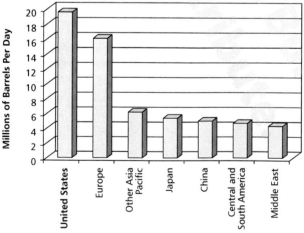

OIL CONSUMPTION 2001

Source: BP Statistical Review of World Energy 2002 (www.bp.com/centres/energy2002

ncorrected page proofs.
Economic Affairs Bureau, Inc. **CHAPTER 9: THE POLITICAL ECONOMY OF WAR AND IMPERIALISM | 263**
ɔ not reproduce or distribute.

presents opportunities for especially large profits per unit of production. According to the *Guardian* newspaper (London), Iraqi oil could cost as little as 97 cents a barrel to produce, compared to the UK's North Sea oil produced at $3 to $4 per barrel. As one oil executive told the *Guardian* last November, "Ninety cents a barrel for oil that sells for $30—that's the kind of business anyone would want to be in. A 97% profit margin—you can live with that." The *Guardian* continues: "The stakes are high. Iraq could be producing 8 million barrels a day within the decade. The math is impressive—8 million times 365 at $30 per barrel or $87.5 billion a year. Any share would be worth fighting for." The question for the oil companies is: what share will they be able to claim and what share will be claimed by the Iraqi government? The split would undoubtedly be more favorable for the oil companies with a compliant U.S.-installed government in Baghdad.

Furthermore, the conflict is not simply one between the private oil companies and the government of Iraq. The U.S.-based firms and their British (and British-Dutch) allies are vying with French, Russian, and Chinese firms for access to Iraqi oil. During recent years, firms from these other nations signed oil exploration and development contracts with the Hussein government in Iraq, and, if there were no "regime change," they would preempt the operations of the U.S. and British firms in that country. If, however, the U.S. government succeeds in replacing the government of Saddam Hussein with its preferred allies in the Iraqi opposition, the outlook will change dramatically. According to Ahmed Chalabi, head of the Iraqi National Congress and a figure in the Iraqi opposition who seems to be currently favored by Washington, "The future democratic government in Iraq will be grateful to the United States for helping the Iraqi people liberate themselves and getting rid of Saddam.... American companies, we expect, will play an important and leading role in the future oil situation." (In recent years, U.S. firms have not been fully frozen out of the oil business in Iraq. For

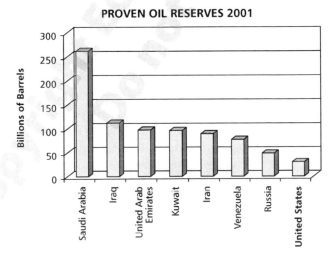

PROVEN OIL RESERVES 2001

Source: BP Statistical Review of World Energy 2002 (www.bp.com/centres/energy2002

example, according to a June 2001 report in the *Washington Post*, while Vice President Cheney was CEO at Halliburton Company during the late 1990s, the firm operated through subsidiaries to sell some $73 million of oil production equipment and spare parts to Iraq.)

The rivalry with French, Russian and Chinese oil companies is in part driven by the direct prize of the profits to be obtained from Iraqi operations. In addition, in order to maintain their dominant positions in the world oil industry, it is important for the U.S. and British-based firms to deprive their rivals of the growth potential that access to Iraq would afford. In any monopolistic industry, leading firms need to deny their potential competitors market position and control of new sources of supply; otherwise, those competitors will be in a better position to challenge the leaders. The British *Guardian* reports that the Hussein government is "believed to have offered the French company TotalFinaElf exclusive rights to the largest of Iraq's oil fields, the Majoon, which would more than double the company's entire output at a single stroke." Such a development would catapult TotalFinaElf from the second ranks into the first ranks of the major oil firms. The basic structure of the world oil industry would not change, but the sharing of power and profits among the leaders would be altered. Thus for ExxonMobil, Chevron, Shell and the other traditional "majors" in the industry, access to Iraq is a defensive as well as an offensive goal. ("Regime change" in Iraq will not necessarily provide the legal basis for cancellation of contracts signed between the Hussein regime and various oil companies. International law would not allow a new regime simply to turn things over to the U.S. oil companies. "Should 'regime change' happen, one thing is guaranteed," according to the *Guardian*, "shortly afterwards there will be the mother of all legal battles.")

Oil companies are big and powerful. The biggest, ExxonMobil, had 2002 profits of $15 billion, more than any other corporation, in the United States or in the world. Chevron-Texaco came in with $3.3 billion in 2002 profits, and Phillips-Tosco garnered $1.7 billion. British Petroleum-Amoco-Arco pulled in $8 billion, while Royal Dutch/Shell Group registered almost $11 billion. Firms of this magnitude have a large role affecting the policies of their governments, and, for that matter, the governments of many other countries.

With the ascendancy of the Bush-Cheney team to the White House in 2000, perhaps the relationship between oil and the government became more personal, but it was not new. Big oil has been important in shaping U.S. foreign policy since the end of the 19th century (to say nothing of its role in shaping other policy realms, particularly environmental regulation). From 1914, when the Marines landed at Mexico's Tampico Bay to protect U.S. oil interests, to the CIA-engineered overthrow of the Mosadegh government in Iran in 1953, to the close relationship with the oppressive Saudi monarchy through the past 70 years, oil and the interests of the oil companies have been central factors in U.S. foreign policy. Iraq today is one more chapter in a long story.

ncorrected page proofs.
Economic Affairs Bureau, Inc. CHAPTER 9: THE POLITICAL ECONOMY OF WAR AND IMPERIALISM | 265
ɔ not reproduce or distribute.

The Larger Issue

Yet in Iraq today, as in many other instances of the U.S. government's international actions, oil is not the whole story. The international policies of the U.S. government are certainly shaped in significant part by the interests of U.S.-based firms, but not only the oil companies. ExxonMobil may have had the largest 2002 profits, but there are many additional large U.S. firms with international interests: Citbank and the other huge financial firms; IBM, Microsoft, and other information technology companies; General Motors and Ford; Merck, Pfizer and the other pharmaceutical corporations; large retailers like MacDonald's and Wal-Mart (and many more) depend on access to foreign markets and foreign sources of supply for large shares of their sales and profits.

The U.S. government (like other governments) has long defined its role in international affairs as protecting the interests of its nationals, and by far the largest interests of U.S. nationals abroad are the interests of these large U.S. companies. The day-to-day activities of U.S. embassies and consular offices around the world are dominated by efforts to further the interests of particular U.S. firms—for example, helping the firms establish local markets, negotiate a country's regulations, or develop relations with local businesses. When the issue is large, such as when governments in low-income countries have attempted to assure the availability of HIV-AIDS drugs in spite of patents held by U.S. firms, Washington steps directly into the fray. On the broadest level, the U.S. government tries to shape the rules and institutions of the world economy in ways that work well for U.S. firms. These rules are summed up under the heading of "free trade," which in practice means free access of U.S. firms to the markets and resources of the rest of the world.

In normal times, Washington uses diplomacy and institutions like the International Monetary Fund, the World Bank, and the World Trade Organization to shape the rules of the world economy. But times are not always "normal." When governments have attempted to remove their economies from the open system and break with the "rules of the game," the U.S. government has responded with overt or covert military interventions. Latin America has had a long history of such interventions, where Guatemala (1954), Cuba (1961), Chile (1973) and Nicaragua (1980s) provide fairly recent examples. The Middle East also provides several illustrations of this approach to foreign affairs, with U.S. interventions in Iran (1953), Lebanon (1958), Libya (1981), and now Iraq. These interventions are generally presented as efforts to preserve freedom and democracy, but, if freedom and democracy were actually the goals of U.S. interventions the record would be very different; both the Saudi monarchy and the Shah of Iran, in an earlier era, would then have been high on the U.S. hit list. (Also, as with maintaining the source of supply of oil, the U.S. government did not intervene in Guatemala in 1954 to maintain our supply of bananas; the profits of the United Fruit Company, however, did provide a powerful causal factor.)

The rhetorical rationale of U.S. foreign policy has seen many alterations and adjustments over the last century: at the end of the 19th century, U.S. officials spoke of the need to spread Christianity; Woodrow Wilson defined the mission as keeping the world safe for democracy; for most of the latter half of the 20th century, the fight against Communism was the paramount rationale; for a fleeting moment during the Carter administration, the protection of human rights entered the government's vocabulary; in recent years we have seen the war against drugs; and now we have the current administration's war against terrorism.

What distinguishes the current administration in Washington is neither its approach toward foreign affairs and U.S. business interests in general nor its policy in the Middle East and oil interests in particular. Even its rhetoric builds on well established traditions, albeit with new twists. What does distinguish the Bush administration is the clarity and aggressiveness with which it has put forth its goal of maintaining U.S. domination internationally. The "Bush Doctrine" that the administration has articulated claims legitimacy for pre-emptive action against those who might threaten U.S. interests, and it is clear from the statement of that doctrine in last September's issuance of *The National Security Strategy of the United States of America* that "U.S. interests" includes economic interests.

The economic story is never the whole story, and oil is never the whole economic story. In the particular application of U.S. power, numerous strategic and political considerations come into play. With the application of the Bush Doctrine in the case of Iraq, the especially heinous character of the Hussein regime is certainly a factor, as is the regime's history of conflict with other nations of the region (at times with U.S. support) and its apparent efforts at developing nuclear, chemical, and biological weapons; certainly the weakness of the Iraqi military also affects the U.S. government's willingness to go to war. Yet, as September's *Security Strategy* document makes clear, the U.S. government is concerned with domination and a major factor driving that goal of domination is economic. In the Middle East, Iraq and elsewhere, oil—or, more precisely, the profit from oil—looms large in the picture. ❏

An earlier version of this article was prepared for the newsletter of the Joiner Center for War and Social Consequences at the University of Massachusetts-Boston. This article was originally prepared largely before the start of the war on Iraq.

ncorrected page proofs.
Economic Affairs Bureau, Inc. **CHAPTER 9: THE POLITICAL ECONOMY OF WAR AND IMPERIALISM | 267**
o not reproduce or distribute.

Article 9.2

THE TRUE COST OF OIL

What are the military costs of securing "our" oil?

BY ANITA DANCS
May/June 2010

When Americans pull up to the pump, the price they pay for a gallon of gas does not begin to reflect the true costs of extracting, transporting, and burning that gallon of fuel.

Most people know that burning fossil fuels contributes to climate change. Every time we drive our cars, we are sending greenhouse gases into the air, which trap radiation and warm the earth's surface. The more the earth warms, the more costly the consequences.

But as bad as the costs of pollution and global warming are, as taxpayers we pay another cost for oil. Each year, our military devotes substantial resources to securing access to and safeguarding the transportation of oil and other energy sources. I estimate that we will pay $90 billion this year to secure oil. If spending on the Iraq War is included, the total rises to $166 billion.

This year, the U.S. government will spend $722 billion on the military, not including military assistance to other countries, space exploration, or veterans' benefits. Defending American access to oil represents a modest share of U.S. militarism.

Calculating the numbers isn't straightforward. Energy security, according to national security documents, is a vital national interest and has been incorporated into military objectives and strategies for more than half a century. But military documents do not attach a dollar figure to each mission, strategy, or objective, so figuring out which military actions relate to oil requires plowing through various documents and devising methodologies.

The U.S. military carves the world up into regions—Europe, Africa, the Pacific, the Middle East, South America and North America—each with its own command structure, called a "unified combatant command." I arrived at my estimate of military spending related to securing oil by tracing U.S. military objectives and strategies through these geographic commands and their respective fleets, divisions, and other units. I only considered conventional spending, excluding spending on nuclear weapons, which is not directly related to securing access to resources.

U.S. Central Command has an "area of responsibility" which stretches from the Arabian Gulf region through Central Asia and was specifically created in 1980 during the Carter administration because of the region's oil reserves. Two-thirds of the world's oil reserves and nearly half of natural gas supplies reside within these twenty countries. Aside from joint training exercises with oil-producing nations, securing oil fields, and a host of other oil-related tasks, the command closely monitors the Strait of Hormuz. Nearly half of all oil transported throughout the world passes through this chokepoint, which has been periodically threatened with disruptions. I estimate about 15% of conventional military spending is directed at supporting the missions and strategies of Central Command, and three-quarters of that spending is related to securing and transporting oil from and through the region, as shown in Table 1.

U.S. Pacific Command ensures transportation of oil, specifically through the Strait of Malacca, one of the two most important strategic oil chokepoints. Fifteen million barrels of oil per day flow from the Middle East and West Africa to Asia. This oil is particularly important to another oil-dependent country—Japan, an important American ally in the region. Pacific Command is the largest of all the commands, covering half of the globe. It is also responsible for the largest number of troops and is an important provider of training and troops to U.S. Central Command. Given information on bases, assigned troops and other indicators, I estimate that about 35% of conventional military spending is required for missions and strategies for this command and about 20% of that amount is needed for securing the transport of energy throughout the region.

U.S. European Command and U.S. Africa Command also have resources devoted to securing access to energy. Initially formed to protect Western Europe against Soviet aggression, European Command is currently postured to project power toward the energy-rich areas of the Caspian Sea, the Caucasus, and the Middle East. Alongside NATO, European Command is increasingly focused on energy security in Europe, especially since the revision of NATO's Strategic Concept in 1999. Finally, the command was also responsible for overseeing the set-up of the newest command, U.S. Africa Command, which was motivated by competition for newly discovered oil reserves. I estimate that around 25% of the military budget is devoted to military strategies relating to Europe and Africa, and of that, about two-

TABLE 1: SECURING ACCESS TO OIL IN FY2010 (IN BILLIONS OF DOLLARS)

Geographic Combatant Command	Percentage of Total Conventional Military Spending	Share of Conventional Military Spending	Percentage Estimated for Securing Oil	Dollar Estimate for Securing Oil
Central Command	15%	$44.7	75%	$33.5
European Command	30%	$89.4	40%	$35.8
Pacific Command	35%	$104.3	20%	$20.9
Northern & Southern Command	20%	$59.6	0%	$0
Subtotal				$90.2
Iraq War				$76.1
Total				**$166.3**

fifths can be attributed to securing oil and energy supplies.

U.S. Northern Command and U.S. Southern Command are responsible for North and South America and the surrounding waters. While Canada, Mexico, and Venezuela rank in the top five countries from which the United States imports oil, I could not find definitive activities connected with either Northern or Southern Command that would justify inclusion in the estimate.

Dividing the military budget according to geographic regions and reviewing activities in those regions leads me to conclude that about $90 billion will be spent this year for securing access to and the transport of oil and other energy supplies.

But that number does not include the vast sums spent on the Iraq War. In spite of the Bush administration's claims that the United States invaded Iraq because of weapons of mass destruction, evidence points to oil. Since World War II and historic meetings between President Roosevelt and the leader of Saudi Arabia, U.S. policy interests have been focused on establishing a stronghold in the region. Prior to the invasion, the Bush administration had already made plans for the oil industry, and currently, the military surrounds and secures the oil fields.

Since 2003, the Iraq War has cost U.S. taxpayers three-quarters of a trillion dollars, as shown in Table 2. Though spending will decline this year, including the Iraq War brings total spending on securing access to oil to $166 billion. Other analysts might point to the strategic importance of Afghanistan in a resource-rich region, but spending on that prolonged war and occupation is not included in this analysis.

Recently, President Obama appeased the oil industry by opening large parts of the East Coast, Gulf waters, and elsewhere to drilling. But this shortsighted policy would only lessen our dependence on foreign oil by a trivial amount. Moreover, if production were increased, oil prices may drop and the average American may choose to drive more. Bring back the Hummer.

Instead, the $166 billion that we are spending right now on the military

TABLE 2: COST OF THE IRAQ WAR	
Fiscal Year	Cost of Iraq War (in billions)
2003 (half)	$53.0
2004	75.9
2005	85.5
2006	101.6
2007	130.8
2008	141.1
2009	94.8
2010 (estimated)	76.1
Total Through 2010	$758.8

Source: Based on Belasco, A. "The cost of Iraq, Afghanistan, and Other Global War on Terror Operations since 9/11" Congressional Research Service, RL 33110, September 28, 2009.

could subsidize and expand public transport, weatherize homes, and fund research on renewable energy. Typically, the federal government invests only $2.3 billion in renewable energy and conservation each year. Even the stimulus bill, which contained an unprecedented amount of spending for renewable energy and conservation, pales in comparison with military spending. Stimulus spending included $18.5 billion for energy efficiency and renewable energy programs, $8 billion in federal loan guarantees for renewable-energy systems, and $17.4 billion for modernization programs such as the "smart" electricity grid, which will reduce electricity consumption. While these healthy federal investments—spent over several years—will encourage a move away from fossil fuels, strategic military operations securing access to those climate-changing resources will continue to dominate our taxpayer dollar.

Put all these numbers in perspective: The price of a barrel of oil consumed in the United States would have to increase by $23.40 to offset military resources expended to secure oil. That translates to an additional 56 cents for a gallon of gas, or three times the federal gas tax that funds road construction.

If $166 billion were spent on other priorities, the Boston public transportation system, the "T," could have its operating expenses covered, with commuters riding for free. And there would still be money left over for another 100 public transport systems across the United States. Or, we could build and install nearly 50,000 wind turbines. Take your pick. ❑

Sources: Energy Information Administration (eia.doe.gov). These estimates are refined and updated from an earlier paper, Anita Dancs with Mary Orisich and Suzanne Smith, "The Military Cost of Securing Energy," National Priorities Project (nationalpriorities.org), October 2008.

Uncorrected page proofs.
Economic Affairs Bureau, Inc. CHAPTER 9: THE POLITICAL ECONOMY OF WAR AND IMPERIALISM | 271
Do not reproduce or distribute.

Article 9.3

"TIED" FOREIGN AID

BY ARTHUR MacEWAN
January/February 2012

Dear Dr. Dollar:

People complaining about the ungrateful world often talk about the "huge" U.S. foreign aid budget. In fact, isn't U.S. foreign aid relatively small compared to other countries? What's worse, I understand that a lot of economic aid comes with strings attached, requiring that goods and services purchased with the aid be purchased from firms in the aid-giving country. This channels much of the money back out of the recipient country. That sounds nuts! What's going on? Katharine Rylaarsdam, Baltimore, MD

The U.S. government does provide a "huge" amount of development aid, far more than any of the other rich countries. In 2009, the United States provided $29.6 billion, in development aid—Japan was number two, at $16.4 billion.

But wait a minute. What appears huge may not be so huge. The graph below shows the amount of foreign development aid provided by ten high-income countries *and* that amount as a share of the countries' gross domestic products (GDP). Yes, the graph shows that the United States gives far more than any of these other countries. But the graph also shows the United States gives a small amount relative to its GDP. In 2009, U.S. foreign development aid was two-tenths of one percent of the country's GDP. Only Italy gave a lesser amount relative to its GDP.

The world's rich countries have long committed to providing 0.7% of GDP to foreign development aid. In 2009, only Norway and Sweden met this goal. The U.S. government did not come close.

Moreover, a large share of U.S. foreign aid is "tied aid"; governments that receive the aid must spend the funds by buying goods and services from U.S. firms. Generally the recipient countries could get more goods and services if they could spend the money without this restriction. So the economic development impact of the aid is less than it appears. Also, whatever the "foreign aid" does for the recipient country, it is a way of channeling money to U.S. firms.

Not only must the recipient country pay more for the goods and services, but the "multiplier impact" is much less. That is, since the money goes to U.S. companies rather than local suppliers, fewer local jobs and salary payments are created; so less is re-spent in the local economy. A 2009 report on aid to Afghanistan by the Peace Dividend Trust notes: "By using Afghan goods and services to carry out development projects in Afghanistan, the international community has the opportunity to spend a development dollar twice. How? Local procurement creates jobs, increases incomes, generates revenue and develops the Afghan marketplace —all of which support economic recovery and stability." Yet most of the aid "for Afghanistan" went to foreign "experts," foreign construction firms, and foreign suppliers of goods.

The U.S. government ties much more of its aid than do most other donor countries. A report by the Organization for Economic Cooperation and Development (OECD) estimated that in the mid-2000s, 54.5% of U.S. aid was tied. Of the 22 donor countries listed in the report (including the United States), the average share of tied aid was only 28.4%. The report notes a "widespread movement to untying [aid], with the exception of the United States."

It is important to recognize that U.S. foreign aid is an instrument of U.S. foreign policy, and is thus highly concentrated in countries where the U.S. government has what it views as "strategic interests." For example, in 2008 almost 16% of U.S. development assistance went to Afghanistan and Iraq, while the top 20 recipient countries received over 50%.

So, yes, the U.S. government provides a "huge" amount of foreign development aid—or not so much. It depends on how you look at things. ❑

Article 9.4

HAITI'S FAULT LINES: MADE IN THE U.S.A.

BY MARIE KENNEDY AND CHRIS TILLY
March/April 2010

The mainstream media got half the story right about Haiti. Reporters observed that Haiti's stark poverty intensified the devastation caused by the recent earthquake. True: hillside shantytowns, widespread concrete construction without rebar reinforcement, a grossly inadequate road network, and a healthcare system mainly designed to cater to the small elite all contributed mightily to death and destruction.

But what caused that poverty? U.S. readers and viewers might be forgiven for concluding that some inexplicable curse has handed Haiti corrupt and unstable governments, unproductive agriculture, and widespread illiteracy. Televangelist Pat Robertson simply took this line of "explanation" to its nutty, racist conclusion when he opined that Haitians were paying for a pact with the devil.

But the devil had little to do with Haiti's underdevelopment. Instead, the fingerprints of more mundane actors—France and later the United States—are all over the crime scene. After the slave rebellion of 1791, France wrought massive destruction in attempting to recapture its former colony, then extracted 150 million francs of reparations, only fully paid off in 1947. France's most poisonous legacy may have been the skin-color hierarchy that sparked fratricidal violence and still divides Haiti.

While France accepted Haiti once the government started paying up, the United States, alarmed by the example of a slave republic, refused to recognize Haiti until 1862. That late-arriving recognition kicked off a continuing series of military and political interventions. The U.S. Marines occupied Haiti outright from 1915 to 1934, modernizing the infrastructure but also revising laws to allow foreign ownership, turning over the country's treasury to a New York bank, saddling Haiti with a $40 million debt to the United States, and reinforcing the status gap between mulattos and blacks. American governments backed the brutal, kleptocratic, two-generation Duvalier dictatorship from 1957-86. When populist priest Jean-Bertrand Aristide was elected president in 1990, the Bush I administration winked at the coup that ousted him a year later. Bill Clinton reversed course, ordering an invasion to restore Aristide, but used that intervention to impose the same free-trade "structural adjustment" Bush had sought. Bush II closed the circle by backing rebels who re-overthrew the re-elected Aristide in 2004. No wonder many Haitians are suspicious of the U.S. troops who poured in after the earthquake.

Though coups and invasions grab headlines, U.S. economic interventions have had equally far-reaching effects. U.S. goals for the last 30 years have been to open Haiti to American products, push Haiti's self-sufficient peasants off the land, and redirect the Haitian economy to plantation-grown luxury crops and export assembly, both underpinned by cheap labor. Though Haiti has yet to boost its export capacity, the first two goals have succeeded, shattering Haiti's former productive capacity. In the early 1980s, the U.S. Agency for International Development exterminated Haiti's hardy Creole pigs in the name of preventing a swine flu epidemic, then helpfully offered U.S. pigs that require expensive U.S.-produced feeds and medicines. Cheap American rice imports crippled the country's breadbasket, the Artibonite, so that Haiti, a rice exporter in the 1980s, now imports massive amounts. Former peasants flooded into Port-au-Prince, doubling the population over the last quarter century, building makeshift housing, and setting the stage for the current catastrophe.

In the wake of the disaster, U.S. aid continues to have two-edged effects. Each aid shipment that flies in U.S. rice and flour instead of buying and distributing local rice or cassava continues to undermine agriculture and deepen dependency. Precious trucks and airstrips are used to marshal U.S. troops against overblown "security threats," crowding out humanitarian assistance. The United States and other international donors show signs of once more using aid to leverage a free-trade agenda. If we seek to end Haiti's curse, the first step is to realize that one of the curse's main sources is…us. ❑

ncorrected page proofs.
Economic Affairs Bureau, Inc. CHAPTER 9: THE POLITICAL ECONOMY OF WAR AND IMPERIALISM | 275
not reproduce or distribute.

Article 9.5

COLONIALISM, "UNDERDEVELOPMENT," AND THE INTERNATIONAL DIVISION OF LABOR

BY ALEJANDRO REUSS
November 2012

The creation of large modern empires, in the last 500 years or so, linked together, for the first time, the economies of different continents into a "world economy." Colonial powers like Spain, Portugal, France, and Britain (also Belgium and the Netherlands) conquered territories and peoples in Africa, Asia, and the Americas, creating far-flung global empires. The horrors of colonialism included plunder, slavery, and genocide on an epic scale. The conquest of the Americas resulted in the greatest "demographic catastrophe" (sudden fall in population) in human history. Many indigenous people were killed by violence or the strains of forced labor, many more by the exotic diseases brought in by European colonists (against which the peoples of the Americas had no natural immunity). Europeans kidnapped and enslaved millions of Africans, many of whom died from the horrors of the "middle passage." Those who survived arrived in the Americas in chains, to be exploited on plantations and in mines.

People often think of colonialism as "ancient history." The United States, of course, began its history as an independent nation with a declaration and war of independence from a colonial power, and has been an independent country for over two centuries. Much of Latin America has been politically independent for nearly as long. Most of the countries of South and Central America gained independence in the 1810s or 1820s. Some countries, especially in the Caribbean, remained colonies much longer (in some cases, to the present day). Unlike in much of the Americas, most of the countries of Africa and Asia have gained independence only in recent decades. The Indian subcontinent was a British colony until the late 1940s, ultimately dividing into three independent countries (India, Pakistan, and Bangladesh) in two subsequent partitions. Much of southeast Asia, likewise, did not gain independence until the 1940s or 1950s. For most current African states, meanwhile, independence dates from the 1950s, 1960s, or 1970s. In South Africa and Zimbabwe (formerly called Rhodesia), a European-descended minority gained independence from a European colonial empire, and continued to rule over a disenfranchised black majority for years afterward. For much of Asia and Africa, then, colonialism is much more recent history than for most of the Americas.

Colonialism and the International Division of Labor

When we speak of the division of labor within a society, we mean that different people specialize in different kinds of work. The international division of labor, in turn, involves different countries producing different kinds of goods. In real life, of course, we rarely see an entire country literally specialize in a single good or category of goods. The economies of different countries, however, can differ dramatically in terms of the relative sizes of different sectors. One country, for example, may be mostly agricultural; another, mostly industrial. Even among agricultural producers, one may produce mostly grains and another mostly fruits and vegetables. Among industrial countries, one may be a major producer of cars or planes, while another may produce clothing.

While the breakdown of total production, among different industries, is often pretty similar for different "developed" (pr "more developed") economies, it is likely to differ quite a bit between "developed" and "developing" ("less developed" or, formerly, "underdeveloped") economies. Sometimes, international trade in goods links together countries that produce similar types of goods. A great deal of world trade goes between different "developed" economies, many of which export the same kinds of goods to each other. However, international trade also links together economies that produce different kinds of goods. It is this second kind of linkage that we have in mind when we talk about the "international division of labor."

Colonialism created patterns in the international division of labor that have proved very difficult to escape. Colonial powers were not, by and large, interested in the development of conquered areas for its own sake. Often, the were interested simply in stripping a colony of all the wealth they could as fast as they could. The original Spanish conquerors of the Americas, for example, were interested first and foremost in gold and silver. First they took all the gold and silver ornaments they could lay their hands on. Then they enslaved the indigenous people and forced them to labor in the mines, shipping vast quantities of gold and silver back to Europe. European empires also began to develop agricultural colonies. Colonies in tropical regions, especially, made it possible to produce goods—like sugar, coffee, and tobacco—which were highly prized and not widely available in Europe. In many places, slaves or other unfree workers (in the Americas, mainly Africans) did the back-breaking plantation work. Sometimes, colonists simply took the lands of local people, leaving them with little choice but to work for meager wages on the plantations.

As some colonial powers began to industrialize, their colonies took on new significance. First, colonies became sources of materials for industry. Britain's textile industry, for example, began with woolen cloth, but gradually shifted toward cotton. Partly, the cotton came from its former colony, the United States, where it was grown primarily on slave plantations in the South. Increasingly, however, it came from colonies like Egypt and India. Second, colonies became "captive" markets for manufactured exports. Colonial powers restricted their colonies' trade with other countries, so one country's colony could not trade with another colonial power. (In effect, the imperial powers were practicing their own form of "protectionism," with barriers to trade surrounding the entire empire.) They sometimes even required that trade *between* their colonies go through the "mother" country, where customs duties (taxes) were collected for the imperial coffers.

Partly, colonial powers got the most out of their colonies by restricting the kinds of goods that could be produced there. They did not want their colonies producing goods that competed with exports from the "mother" country. Before British colonization, for example, India had a large craft industry producing fine textiles. (A "craft" industry involves production by skilled craftspeople, generally without the power machinery typical of modern industrial production.) Textiles, however, were Britain's main export, and the British government wanted the Indian market for its textile manufacturers. Some economic historians argue that colonial restrictions destroyed the Indian textile industry. Others emphasize the cheapness of British-made cloth, made using modern water- or coal-powered machinery. Even if the latter is true, however, India did not have the chance to develop its own machine-powered textile manufacturing industry. If it had been an independent country, it could have imposed tariffs, in order to protect this "infant" industry. But economic policies for India was made in London, and those policies were designed to keep India open to British manufactures. In the end, instead of producing textiles itself, India became a producer of raw material for the British textile industry. This was a pattern that repeated itself across the colonial world, with industrial development stifled and the colonies pushed into "primary goods" production.

Political Independence and Economic "Dependency"

Even after becoming politically independent, many former colonial countries seemed to remain trapped in the colonial-era international division of labor. They had not been able to develop manufacturing industries as colonies, and so they continued to import manufactured goods. To pay for these goods, they continued to export primary products. In many countries, the specialization in a single export good was so extreme that these became known as "monoculture" economies ("mono" = one). In some former colonies, important resources like land and mines remained under the control of foreign companies. In many cases, these were from the former colonial "mother" country. Sometimes, however, a rising new power replaced the old colonial power. After independence from Spain, for example, much of South America became part of Britain's "informal empire." Meanwhile, the United States supplanted Spain and other European colonial countries as the dominant power in Central America and the Caribbean, plus parts of South America.

Critics argued that this situation kept the former colonies poor and "dependent" on the rich industrial countries. (The subordination of the former colonies was so reminiscent of the old patterns of colonialism, that this was often labeled "neo-colonialism" or "imperialism.") The United States' relationship to smaller, poorer, and less powerful countries—especially in its "sphere of influence" of Latin America—exemplified many of the key patterns of post-independence neo-colonialism: Foreign companies extracted vast amounts of wealth, in the form of agricultural goods and minerals, while paying paltry wages to local workers. They employed skilled personnel from their home countries and used imported machinery, so their operations formed economic "enclaves" unconnected to the rest of the country's economy. Finally, they sent the profits back to their home countries, rather than reinvesting them locally, and so did little to spur broader economic development. Critics argued that this system was designed, in the words of Uruguayan author Eduardo Galeano, to bleed wealth out of these countries' "open veins."

Some economists pointed out some major economic disadvantages to specialization in "primary products," which are worth discussing in more detail.

First, economists associated with the United Nations Economic Commission for Latin America (known by its Spanish acronym, CEPAL) observed that the prices of primary products had tended to decline, over time, in relation to the prices of manufactured goods. Economists offered several different explanations for the declining "terms of trade," as this is known. The bottom line, however, was that the lower-income countries had to sell larger and larger amounts of the goods they exported (more tons of sugar, coffee, copper, aluminum, or whatever) to afford the same amounts of the goods they imported (cars, televisions, or whatever). This pattern was one of the reasons for the adoption, in many countries, of "import-substitution" strategies—policies designed to protect and build up local industries to produce the manufactured goods that these countries had imported from the industrialized North.

Second, specialization in primary-product exports exposed low-income countries to wild fluctuations of world-market prices for these goods. Selling a "cash crop" like coffee or sugar in the world market might bring a higher average income, over many years, than growing diverse food crops on the same land. However, the world-market price of a cash crop could be very high one year and very low the next. An especially bad year, or a few bad years in a row, might wipe out any savings farmers or farm workers might have from previous good years, and leave them destitute. Ironically, farmers might go hungry, even if the land was fertile and the weather had been good. For most cash crops, including fiber crops (like cotton) and specialized food crops (like coffee and sugar), the farmers could not survive by eating the harvest if world prices were too low. Why, then, did people in low-income countries not grow basic food crops, like corn (which could be sold or eaten), instead of cash crops for the world market? First, landless farm laborers had no such choice. The landlord or capitalist farmer they worked for chose the crop mix. Second, some individual or family farmers might rent land, work on a share-cropping basis, or depend on credit through the planting and growing seasons. Landlords or lenders might insist that they grow cash crops.

The governments of these countries might have found it difficult to challenge this state of affairs, even had they wanted to. Their economies, after all, were heavily dependent on exports to the dominant country (whose government could cut off access to its markets, should it be provoked). In many cases, however, local political elites have enjoyed close political and economic ties to the multinational companies, and little interest in changing anything. As long as they maintained "order," kept workers from organizing unions or demanding higher wages, and protected the multinational companies' investments, they could be sure to keep the favor of the dominant country's government and the multinational companies. In the cases where opposition movements did arise, calling for changes like the redistribution of land ownership or the nationalization of important resources, the dominant power could intervene militarily, if local elites were not up to the task of putting the rebels down.

Changes in the International Division of Labor

For much of the twentieth century, a key dividing line among capitalist economies was between the "industrial" economies of the United States and Western Europe and the "non-industrial" economies of most of Latin America, Africa, and Asia. The industrial countries were distinguished by their large manufacturing industries, though of course they also had agricultural, mining, and other sectors. The nonindustrial countries, on the other hand, had much smaller manufacturing sectors (relative to the overall size of their economies). The production of "primary products," such as agricultural goods and minerals, therefore, made up a larger proportion of their economies. These two kinds of economies were linked: The high-income industrial economies imported agricultural products and minerals (or "primary products") from the low-income non-industrial economies, and exported manufactured goods (or "secondary products") in return.

In more recent decades, the international division of labor has changed in important ways. Many formerly "non-industrial" economies have developed substantial manufacturing sectors, often by deliberately promoting manufacturing development through government policies like protective trade barriers, low-interest loans, etc. In some cases, what had been "less developed" economies have become major global industrial producers. Since the Second World War, Japan and South Korea are two spectacular examples of countries that developed large and globally competitive manufacturing sectors (in electronics, automobiles, shipbuilding, etc.). In other cases, foreign investment has created a growing "export platform" manufacturing sector. Large corporations have increasingly engaged in "offshoring"—locating production facilities outside the countries where they are headquartered and have their traditional base of operations, and exporting the output back to the "home" market or to other countries. Some low-income countries, then, have gone from importing manufactured goods (which were not produced locally) to producing them for export.

In high-income countries, even as manufacturing employment has declined as a percentage of total employment, other sectors have grown. Over the last few decades, employment in "services" has accounted for an increasing proportion of total employment in high-income countries. When people think of services, they often think of low-wage employment in fast-food restaurants or big-box stores.

Services, however, also include education, health care, finance, and other industries which can involve high-skill—and sometimes highly paid—work. All of these services can be "exported." Some can be done for people physically located in other countries. For example, some educational and health services can be delivered remotely, through global communications. However, they can also be "exported" by having the recipients travel to the place where providers are located (like students from abroad coming to study at U.S. universities or people traveling to the United States for specialized medical care). Economically, this is equivalent to shipping goods to another country for sale, in that in each case the production of goods or services in one country satisfies demand from people who reside (and earn their incomes in) another.

Changing Labels:
"Underdeveloped" or "Developing," "Third World" or "Global South"?

What are now termed "less-developed" or "developing" countries were, until recently, often described as "underdeveloped." The use of this term declined for a couple of reasons:

First, it came to be viewed as having pejorative connotations. That is, it took on very negative unspoken meanings, in particular the view that the people of "underdeveloped" countries were to blame for their own plight. It is now widely viewed as offensive to call a country "underdeveloped."

Second, political movements in many of these countries between the 1960s and 1980s took over and transformed the meaning of the word. Instead of thinking of "underdevelopment" just as a *lack* of "development," they started thinking of it as a *kind* of development, subordinated to the richer, more powerful countries. Their countries, they argued, had not been born "underdeveloped," they had been "underdeveloped" by the colonial powers (or former colonial powers) that dominated the world economy. The shift away from the use of this term was, in part, a way for political and economic elites (both in "developed" and "developing" countries) to silence this argument.

These countries were also once referred to as the "Third World." This usage goes back to the Cold War era, and the division of the globe between the industrial capitalist countries of the West and the increasingly industrial "communist" countries of the East. Countries in neither the "eastern world" nor "western world" were termed the "Third World." The term gained popularity as some governments and many opposition political movements in Latin America, Asia, and Africa came to see their countries and causes as ill-served by aligning closely with either the United States or the Soviet Union.

Today, the term "global South" is sometimes used as an alternative to "developing" or "less developed" countries.

Often, people think the relative decline in manufacturing employment in high-income countries is due only to offshoring—to companies "moving" manufacturing jobs from one country to another. To a great extent, however, the increasing mechanization of production (the substitution of machines for labor) was already driving this process decades before offshoring became a significant factor. Manufacturing *output* in high-income countries, therefore, has declined much less than manufacturing *employment*, since greater mechanization makes it possible to produce more output with the same number of workers. Meanwhile, as assembly-line employment has declined in high-income countries, fields like product engineering and design have accounted for an increasing proportion of the jobs in the manufacturing sector.

The End of "Underdevelopment"?

Advocates of "globalization" have pointed to the growth of export-oriented manufacturing in some less developed countries as a positive sign. "Offshoring," they argue, is finally bringing industrialization to countries that had been caught in a seemingly inescapable cycle of poverty. The countries experiencing the least development, they argue, are those that have remained marginal to the new global economy—especially because government hostility toward foreign investment, official corruption, or political instability have made them unattractive locations for off-shore production. These countries, the globalization advocates argue, need *more* globalization, not less—and therefore should adopt "neoliberal" policies eliminating barriers to international trade and investment

Critics of the current form of globalization, and of the "offshoring" approach to economic development, on the other hand, point to several less-than-shining realities.

First, it is not always true that the least-developed economies have been relatively untouched by the global economy. In many cases, they have suffered under the least beneficial and most destructive forms of global economic integration. Multinational companies, usually with the connivance of local elites, have often seized and extracted valuable resources such as minerals or petroleum, with near-total disregard for the effects on the local population. This process has led to the most extreme patterns of "enclave" development, where the only things developed are the means to get the wealth out of the ground and bound for world markets. Global corporations have captured often enormous "resource rents" from the sale of these riches, with little or no benefit for the masses (though often considerable benefits for ruling elites). Furthermore, the extraction process has often resulted in the ruin of the local environment and of local communities who depend on natural ecosystems (e.g., farmers, fisherfolk, etc.) for their livelihoods.

Second, countries aggressively embracing neoliberal economic policies have not always seen a dramatic increase in manufacturing employment. "Free trade agreements" have typically eliminated both barriers to trade and barriers to international investment. The elimination of trade barriers opened up profitable new markets for multinational companies, while also being an essential ingredient of the offshore-production model. (If a low-income country maintained barriers like tariffs, this would make it more expensive, perhaps unprofitably so, for multinational companies to import materials to an "offshore" production site in that country. Barriers might also result in retaliation by other countries, which would make the re-export of products from the offshore site more expensive as well.) The imports that have flooded in due to the elimination of tariffs and other barriers, however, have battered domestic industries. As a result, many lower-income countries have seen the increase in "offshore" or "export-platform" employment in manufacturing offset by the decimation of domestic manufacturing for the domestic market.

Third, when multinational companies "offshore" manufacturing to lower-income countries, they do not relocate all phases of the manufacturing process. Export-platform production typically involves relatively "low-skill" assembly and finishing work. Meanwhile, functions like engineering, design and styling, marketing, and management largely remain in the company's "home" country. (If you look on the back of an iPhone, for example, you will see that it says, "Designed by Apple in California. Assembled in China.") Some countries, like South Korea, have used foreign investment and low-wage export-oriented manufacturing as a stepping-stone toward the development of domestic industry. These countries, however, did so by heavily regulating such investment, as by imposing "technology transfer" requirements. These regulations ensured that, in exchange for access to the country's workers, multinational companies had to turn over knowledge that could be used to develop domestic industry. Countries whose governments simply throw their doors open to multinational corporations, on the other hand, may remain stuck in the assembly-and-finishing phase—much as "less-developed" countries in an earlier era were stuck as primary-product producers.

In the 1950s and 1960s, radical theorists of economic dependency emphasized that "underdevelopment" was not simply an *absence* of development. Indeed, even in that era, there was visible economic development in so-called underdeveloped countries, as there is today in what are now termed "developing" countries. Rather, they argued that we should think of underdevelopment as a *form* of development—of dependent, subordinated, exploited development. Capitalist development, they argued, produced both development (for countries in the wealthy "core") and underdevelopment (in the poorer "periphery"). While offshore production may bring a certain form of industrial development, and may be changing the international division of labor in some ways, it is also reproducing old patterns of subordination. ❑

Chapter 10

GLOBAL ECONOMIC CRISIS

Article 10.1

PUTTING THE "GLOBAL" IN THE GLOBAL ECONOMIC CRISIS

BY SMRITI RAO
November/December 2009

There is no question that the current economic crisis originated in the developed world, and primarily in the United States. Much of the analysis of the crisis has thus focused on institutional failures within the United States and there is, rightly, tremendous concern here about high rates of domestic unemployment and underemployment. But after three decades of globalization, what happens in the United States does not stay in the United States; the actions of traders in New York City will mean hunger for children in Nairobi. We now know what crisis looks like in the age of globalization and it is not pretty.

This crisis is uniquely a child of the neoliberal global order. For developing countries the key elements of neoliberalism have consisted of trade liberalization and an emphasis on exports; reductions in government social welfare spending; a greater reliance on the market for determining the price of everything from the currency exchange rate to water from the tap; and, last but not least, economy-wide privatization and deregulation. In each case, the aim was also to promote cross-border flows of goods, services, and capital—and, to a far lesser degree, of people.

Despite Thomas Friedman's assertions of a "flat" world, this age of globalization did not in fact eliminate global inequality. Indeed if we exclude China and India, inequality between countries actually increased during this period. The globalization of the last 30 years was predicated upon the extraction by the developed world of the natural resources, cheap labor, and, in particular, capital of the developing world, the latter via financial markets that siphoned the world's savings to pay for U.S. middle-class consumption. What could be more ironic than the billions of dollars in capital flowing every year from developing countries with unfunded domestic needs to developed countries, which then failed to meet even their minimum obligations with respect to foreign aid? Africa, for example, has actually been a net creditor to the United States for some time, suggesting that the underlying dynamic of the world economy today is not that different from the colonialism of past centuries.

These "reverse flows" are partly the result of attempts by developing countries to ward off balance-of-payment crises by holding large foreign exchange reserves. Within the United States, this capital helped sustain massive borrowing by households, corporations, and governments, exacerbating the debt bubble of the last eight years. Meanwhile, the global "race to the bottom" among developing-county exporters ensured that the prices of most manufactured goods and services remained low, taking the threat of inflation off the table and enabling the U.S. Federal Reserve to keep interest rates low and facilitate the housing bubble.

Now that this debt bubble has finally burst, it is no surprise that the crisis has been transmitted back to the global South at record speed.

Measuring the Impact

A country-by-country comparison of the growth in real (i.e., inflation-adjusted) GDP from 2007 to 2008 against the average annual growth of the preceding three years (2005-2007) gives us a picture of the differential impact of the economic crisis—at least in its early stages—on various countries. Consistent data are available for 178 developed and developing countries.

Overall, GDP growth for these 178 countries was down by 1.3 percentage points in 2008 compared to the average for 2005-2007. Of course, the financial crisis only hit in full force in September 2008, so the 2009 data will give us a more complete picture of the impact of the crisis. The International Monetary Fund (IMF) estimates that global GDP will decline in 2009 for the first time since World War II. Currently, the IMF is expecting a 1.4% contraction this year. According to the International Labor Organization, global unemployment increased by 10.7 million in 2008, with a further increase of 19 million expected in 2009 by relatively conservative estimates. As a result, the number of people living in poverty will increase by an estimated 46 million this year according to the World Bank.

The initial impact in 2008 was greatest in Eastern Europe and Central Asia: six of the ten countries with the steepest declines in real GDP growth were from the Eastern Europe/Central Asia region (see Table 1). Joined by Ireland, this is a list of global high-fliers—countries with very high rates of growth (before 2008, that is) that had globalized rapidly and enthusiastically in the last decade and a half. Singapore of course was an early adopter of globalization, touted by the IMF as a model for other small countries, while Seychelles has depended heavily on international tourism. Myanmar would seem to be the exception to this pattern of intensive globalization, given its political isolation. From an economic perspective, however, this was a country whose economic growth depended heavily on the rising prices of its commodity exports (natural gas and gems).

Indeed, if we rank these 178 countries by the share of their GDP represented by exports before the crisis, we find a correlation between dependence on exports and steeper declines in GDP growth. The 50 most export-dependent countries actually saw larger declines in GDP in 2008 than those less dependent on exports (see Table 2). Likewise with certain other key markers of neoliberal globalization.

That globalizers appear to be most affected by the crisis is no accident. It turns out that each of the three primary channels through which the crisis has been transmitted from the United States to other countries is a direct outcome of the policy choices that developing countries were urged and sometimes coerced into making—with assurances that this particular form of globalization was the best way to build a healthy and prosperous economy (see Figure 1 for a summary).

**FIGURE 1: THE CURRENT CRISIS AND IMF POLICIES:
MAKING THE LINKS**

Lowered exports, remittances ("openness")

+

Outflows of portfolio capital ("openness" + no capital controls)

=

Depreciating currencies (floating exchange rates)

=>

Worsening current account balances/debt burdens

X

Falling flows of FDI and development aid

X

"Inflation targeting" and "fiscal restraint"

Transmission Channels of the Crisis

Lowered exports and remittances. The recession in the United States and Europe has hit exports from the developing world hard. Globally, trade in goods and services did rise by 3% in 2008, but that was compared to 10% and 7% in the previous two years. Trade is expected to decline by a sharp 12% in 2009. The United States, the world's most important importer, has seen imports drop by an unprecedented 30% since July 2008. For countries ranging from Pakistan to Cameroon, this has meant lower foreign exchange earnings, slower economic growth, and higher unemployment.

Meanwhile, for many developing countries, the emphasis on export promotion meant the increasing export not of goods and services but of people, who sought work in richer countries and sent part of their earnings back home. Remittance flows from temporary and permanent migrants accounted for 25% of net inflows of private capital to the global South in 2007. These flows are also affected by the crisis, although they have proved more resilient than other sources of private capital.

Migrant workers in construction, in particular, find that they are no longer able to find work and send money back home, and countries in Latin America have seen sharp declines in remittance inflows. However, as Indian economist Jayati Ghosh points out, women migrants working as maids, nurses, and nannies in the West have not been as hard hit by the recession. This has meant that remittance flows to countries with primarily female migrants, such as Sri Lanka and the Philippines, are not as badly affected. The Middle Eastern countries that are important host countries for many Asian migrants have also been relatively shielded from the crisis. As a result, for the developing world as a whole, remittances actually rose in 2008. Because other private capital flows declined sharply post-crisis, remittances accounted for 46% of net private capital inflows to the developing world in 2008.

Outflows of portfolio capital. In the boom years up to 2007, developing countries were encouraged to liberalize their financial sectors. This meant removing regulatory barriers to the inflow (and outflow) of foreign investors and their money. While some foreign investors did buy factories and other actual physical assets in the developing world, a substantial portion of foreign capital came in the form of portfolio capital—short-term investments in stock and real estate markets. Portfolio capital is called "hot money" for a reason: it tends to be incredibly mobile, and its mobility has been enhanced by the systematic dismantling of various government restrictions ("capital controls") that formerly prevented this money from entering or leaving countries at the volume and speed it can today.

Table 1: Steepest Declines in Economic Growth

Top ten countries by decline in 2008 real GDP growth vs. 2005-07 annual average.		
	Country	**Change in 2008 real GDP growth compared to 2005-07 average(in percentage points)**
1	Latvia	−15.56
2	Azerbaijan	−14.44
3	Estonia	−12.26
4	Georgia	−8.42
5	Myanmar	−8.32
6	Ireland	−8.30
7	Seychelles	−7.62
8	Armenia	−6.85
9	Singapore	−6.66
10	Kazakhstan	−6.57

Source: Author's calculations based on data from World Development Indicators online, World Bank, June 2009.

Around the time of the collapse of Bear Stearns in the United States in early 2008, various global financial powerhouses began pulling their money out of developing-country markets. The pace of the pullout only accelerated after the crash that September. One consequence for developing countries was a fall in their stock market indices, which in turn depressed growth. Another was that as foreign investors converted their krona, rupees, or rubles into dollars in order to leave, the value of the local currency got pushed down.

The IMF has long touted the virtues of allowing freely floating exchange rates, where market forces determine the value of each currency. In the aftermath of the financial crisis, this meant a sharp depreciation in the value of many local currencies relative to the dollar. This in turn meant that every gallon of oil priced in dollars would cost that many more, say, rupees. Similarly, any dollar-denominated debt a country held became harder to repay. The dollar cost of imports and debt servicing went up, just as exports and remittances—the ability to earn those dollars—were falling. Predictably, countries with floating (i.e., market-determined) exchange rates were harder hit in 2008 (see Table 3).

Table 2: Exports and Foreign Investment

Change in 2008 real GDP growth compared to 2005-07 average (in percentage points) for countries ranked by:		
	Export share of GDP	**FDI share of GDP**
Average for top 50 countries	−2.25	−1.85
Average for countries ranked 51-100	−1.50	−1.70
Average for the remaining countries	−0.88	−1.07
Total number of countries	167	171

Table 3: Exchange Rate and Fiscal Policy

Average change in 2008 real GDP growth compared to 2005-07 average (in percentage points) for country groupings:			
Exchange Rate Policy		**Fiscal Policy**	
Countries with fixed exchange rate	−1.19	Countries with no inflation targeting	−1.18
Countries with managed float or other mixed policy	−1.19	Countries with inflation targeting	−2.35
Countries with freely floating exchange rate	−2.04		
Total number of countries	178		171

Sources: Author's calculations based on data from World Development Indicators online, World Bank, June 2009 and De Facto Classification of Exchange Rate Regimes and Monetary Policy Frameworks as of April 31, 2008,IMF.

Falling flows of FDI and development aid. Meanwhile, one other source of foreign exchange, foreign investment in actual physical assets such as factories (known as foreign direct investment, or FDI), is stagnant and likely to fall as companies across the world shelve expansion plans. The signs of vulnerability are evident in the fact that countries most dependent upon FDI inflows (as a percentage of GDP) between 2005 and 2007 suffered greater relative GDP declines in 2008 (see Table 2).

Developed countries are also cutting back on foreign aid budgets, citing the cost of domestic stimulus programs and reduced tax revenues. Such cuts particularly affect the poorest countries. With the economic slowdown their governments are losing domestic tax and other revenues, so falling aid flows are likely to hurt even more. The importance of continued aid flows can be seen in the fact that higher levels of aid per capita from 2005 to 2007 were actually associated with more mild drops in GDP growth in 2008 (see Table 2). This may be partly due to the fact that these countries already had low or negative rates of GDP growth so that 2008 declines appear smaller relative to that baseline. Nevertheless, aid flows appear to have protected the most vulnerable countries from even greater economic disaster. In fact the so-called HIPC group (highly indebted poor countries) actually saw an increase of one percentage point in GDP growth rates when compared to the 2005-2007 average.

Both FDI and aid work their way into and out of economies more slowly, so we may have to wait for 2009 data to estimate the full impact of the crisis via this channel.

The simultaneous transmission of the crisis through these three channels has left developing countries reeling. What makes the situation even worse is that unlike developed countries, developing countries are unlikely to be able to afford generous stimulus packages (China is an important exception). Meanwhile, the IMF and its allies, rather than supporting developing-country governments in their quest to stimulate domestic demand and investment, are hindering the process by insisting on the same old policy mix of deficit reductions and interest rate hikes. In an illustration of how ruinous this policy mix can be, countries that had followed IMF advice and adopted "inflation targeting" before the crisis suffered greater relative GDP declines once the crisis hit (see Table 3).

The tragedy of course is that while the remnants of the welfare state still protect citizens of the developed world from the very worst effects of the crisis, developing countries have been urged for two decades to abandon the food and fuel subsidies and public sector provision of essential services that are the only things that come close to resembling a floor for living standards. They were told they didn't need that safety net, that it only got in the way; now, of course, they are free to fall.

For those unwilling to let this tragedy unfold, this is the time to apply pressure on developed-country governments to maintain aid flows. Even more importantly, this is the time to apply pressure on the IMF and the other multilateral development banks, and on their supporters in the halls of power, so that they offer developing countries a genuine chance to survive this crisis and begin to rebuild for the future.

It is worth recalling that the end of the previous "age of globalization," signaled by the Great Depression, led to a renewed role for the public sector the world over and an attempt to achieve growth alongside self-reliance. In the years after World War II, led by Latin America, newly independent developing countries attempted to prioritize building a domestic producer and consumer base. In the long run, perhaps this crisis will result in a similar rethinking of the currently dominant model of development. In the short run, however, the world seems ready to stand by and watch while the poor and vulnerable in developing countries, truly innocent bystanders, suffer. ❑

Sources: Dilip Ratha, Sanket Mohapatra, and Ani Silwal, "Migration and Development Brief 10," Migration and Remittances Team, Development Prospects Group, World Bank, July 13, 2009; Atish R. Ghosh et al. 2009, "Coping with the Crisis: Policy Options for Emerging Market Countries," IMF Staff Position Note, SPN/09/08, April 23, 2009; World Bank, "Swimming Against the Tide: How Developing Countries Are Coping with the Global Crisis," Background Paper prepared by World Bank Staff for the G20 Finance Ministers and Central Bank Governors Meeting, Horsham, United Kingdom on March 13-14, 2009; Jayati Ghosh, "Current Global Financial Crisis: Curse or Blessing in Disguise for Developing Countries?" Presentation prepared for the IWG-GEM Workshop, Levy Economics Institute, New York, June 29-July 10, 2009.

Article 10.2

(ECONOMIC) FREEDOM'S JUST ANOTHER WORD FOR...CRISIS-PRONE

BY JOHN MILLER

September/October 2009

In "Capitalism in Crisis," his May op-ed in the *Wall Street Journal*, U.S. Court of Appeals judge and archconservative legal scholar Richard Posner argued that "a capitalist economy, while immensely dynamic and productive, is not inherently stable." Posner, the long-time cheerleader for deregulation added, quite sensibly, "we may need more regulation of banking to reduce its inherent riskiness."

That may seem like a no-brainer to you and me, right there in the middle of the road with yellow-lines and dead armadillos, as Jim Hightower is fond of saying. But *Journal* readers were having none of it. They wrote in to set Judge Posner straight. "It is not free markets that fail, but government-controlled ones," protested one reader.

And why wouldn't they protest? The *Journal* has repeatedly told readers that "economic freedom" is "the real key to development." And each January for 15 years now the *Journal* tries to elevate that claim to a scientific truth by publishing a summary of the Heritage Foundation Index of Economic Freedom, which they assure readers proves the veracity of the claim.   But the hands of the editors of the *Wall Street Journal* and the researchers from the Heritage Foundation, Washington's foremost right-wing think tank, the Index of Economic Freedom is a barometer of corporate and entrepreneurial freedom from accountability rather than a guide to which countries are giving people more control over their economic lives and over the institutions that govern them.

This January was no different. "The 2009 Index provides strong evidence that the countries that maintain the freest economies do the best job promoting prosperity for all citizens," proclaimed this year's editorial, "Freedom is Still the Winning Formula." But with economies across the globe in recession, the virtues of free markets are a harder sell this year. That is not lost on *Wall Street Journal* editor Paul Gigot, who wrote the foreword to this year's report. Gigot allows that, "ostensibly free-market policymakers in the U.S. lost their monetary policy discipline, and we are now paying a terrible price." Still Gigot maintains that, "the *Index of Economic Freedom* exists to chronicle how steep that price will be and to point the way back to policy wisdom."

What the Heritage report fails to mention is this: while the global economy is in recession, many of the star performers in the Economic Freedom Index are tanking. Fully one half of the ten hardest-hit economies in the world are among the 30 "free" and "mostly free" economies at the top of the Economic Freedom Index rankings of 179 countries.

Here's the damage, according to the IMF. Singapore, the Southeast Asian trading center and perennial number two in the Index, will suffer a 10.0% drop in output this year. Slotting in at number 4, Ireland, the so-called Celtic tiger, has seen its rapid export-led growth give way to an 8.0% drop in output. Number 13 and number 30, the foreign-direct-investment-favored Baltic states, Estonia and Lithuania, will each endure a 10.0% loss of output this year. Finally, the economy of Iceland, the loosely regulated European banking center that sits at number 14 on the Index, will contract 10.6% in 2009.

As a group, the Index's 30 most "free" economies will contract 4.1% in 2009. All of the other groups in the Index ("moderately free," "mostly unfree," and "repressed" economies) will muddle through 2009 with a much smaller loss of output or with moderate growth. The 67 "mostly unfree" countries in the Index will post the fastest growth rate for the year, 2.3%.

So it seems that if the Index of Economic Freedom can be trusted, then Judge Posner was not so far off the mark when he described capitalism as dynamic but "not inherently stable." That wouldn't be so bad, one *Journal* reader pointed out in a letter: "Economic recessions are the cost we pay for our economic freedom and economic prosperity is the benefit. We've had many more years of the latter than the former."

Not to Be Trusted

But the Index of Economic Freedom cannot and should not be trusted. How free or unfree an economy is according to the Index seems to have little do with how quickly it grows. For instance, economist Jeffery Sachs found "no correlation" between a country's ranking in the Index and its per capita growth rates from 1995 to 2003. Also, in this year's report North America is the "freest" of its six regions of the world, but logged the slowest average rate over the last five years, 2.7% per annum. The Asia-Pacific region, which is "less free" than every other region except Sub-Saharan Africa according to the Index, posted the fastest average growth over the last five years, 7.8% per annum. That region includes several of fastest growing of the world's economies, India, China, and Vietnam, which ranked 123, 132, and

ECONOMIC FREEDOM AND ECONOMIC GROWTH IN 2009	
Degree of Economic Freedom	IMF Projected Growth Rate for 2009
"Free" (7 Countries)	-4.54%
"Mostly Free" (23 Counties)	-3.99%
"Moderately Free" (53 Countries)	-0.92%
"Mostly Unfree" (67 Countries)	+2.31%
"Repressed" (69 Counties)	+1.65%
Sources: International Monetary Fund, *World Economic Outlook,: Crisis and Recovery*, April 2009, Tables A1, A2, A3; Terry Miller and Kim R. Holmes, eds., *2009 Index of Economic Freedom*, heritage.org/Index/, Executive Summary.	

145 respectively in the Index and were classified as "mostly unfree." And there are plenty of relatively slow growers among the countries high up in the Index, including Switzerland (which ranks ninth).

The Heritage Foundation folks who edited the Index objected to Sachs' criticisms, pointing out that they claimed "a close relationship" between *changes* in economic freedom, not the *level* of economic freedom, and growth. But even that claim is fraught with problems. Statistically it doesn't hold up. Economic journalist Doug Henwood found that improvements in the index and GDP growth from 1997 to 2003 could explain no more than 10% of GDP growth. In addition, even a tight correlation would not resolve the problem that many of the fastest growing economies are "mostly unfree" according to the Index.

But even more fundamental flaws with the Index render any claim about the relationship between prosperity and economic freedom, as measured by the Heritage Foundation, questionable. Consider just two of the ten components the Economic Freedom Index uses to rank countries: fiscal freedom and government size.

Fiscal freedom (what we might call the "hell-if-I'm-going-to-pay-for-government" index) relies on the top income tax and corporate income tax brackets as two of its three measures of the tax burden. These are decidedly flawed measures even if all that concerned you was the tax burden of the rich and owners of corporations (or the super-rich). Besides ignoring the burden of other taxes, singling out these two top tax rates don't get at effective corporate and income tax rates, or how much of a taxpayer's total income goes to paying these taxes. For example, on paper U.S. corporate tax rates are higher than those in Europe. But nearly one half of U.S. corporate profits go untaxed. The effective rate of taxation on U.S. corporate profits currently stands at 15%, far below the top corporate tax rate of 35%. And relative to GDP, U.S. corporate income taxes are no more than half those of other OECD countries.

Even their third measure of fiscal freedom, government tax revenues relative to GDP, bears little relationship to economic growth. After an exhaustive review, economist Joel Selmrod, former member of the Reagan Treasury Department, concludes that the literature reveals "no consensus" about the relationship between the level of taxation and economic growth.

The Index's treatment of government size, which relies exclusively on the level of government spending relative to GDP, is just as flawed as the fiscal freedom index. First, "richer countries do not tax and spend less" than poorer countries, reports economist Peter Lindhert. Beyond that, this measure does not take into account how the government uses its money. Social spending programs—public education, child-care and parental support, and public health programs—can make people more productive and promote economic growth. That lesson is not lost on Hong Kong and Singapore, number one and number two in the index. They both provide universal access to health care, despite the small size of their governments.

The size-of-government index also misses the mark because it fails to account for industrial policy. This is a serious mistake, because it overestimates the degree to which some of the fastest growing economies of the last few decades, such as Taiwan and South Korea, relied on the market and underestimates the positive role that government played in directing economic development in those countries by guiding investment and protecting infant industries.

This flaw is thrown into sharp relief by the recent report of the World Bank's Commission on Growth and Development. That group studied 13 economies that grew at least 7% a year for at least 25 years since 1950. Three of the Index's "free" and "mostly free" countries made the list (Singapore, Hong Kong, and Japan) but so did three of the index's "mostly unfree" countries (China, Brazil, and Indonesia). While these rapid growers were all export-oriented, their governments "were not free-market purists," according the Commission's report. "They tried a variety of policies to help diversify exports or sustain competitiveness. These included industrial policies to promote new investments."

Still More

Beyond all that, the Index says nothing about political freedom. Consider once again the two city-states, Hong Kong and Singapore, which top their list of free countries. Both are only "partially free" according to Freedom House, which the editors have called "the Michelin Guide to democracy's development." Hong Kong is still without direct elections for it legislatures or its chief executive and a proposed internal security laws threaten press and academic freedom as well as political dissent. In Singapore, freedom of the press and rights to demonstrate are limited, films, TV and the like are censored, and preventive detention is legal.

So it seems that the Index of Economic Freedom in practice tells us little about the cost of abandoning free market policies and offers little proof that government intervention into the economy would either retard economic growth or contract political freedom. In actuality, this rather objective-looking index is a slip-shod measure that would seem to have no other purpose than to sell the neoliberal policies that brought on the current crisis, and to stand in the way of policies that might correct the crisis. ❑

Sources: "Capitalism in Crisis," by Richard A Posner, *Wall Street Journal*, 5/07/09; "Letters: Recessions are the Price We Pay for Economic Freedom," *Wall Street Journal*, 5/19/09/; "Freedom is Still the Winning Formula," by Terry Miller, *Wall Street Journal*, 1/13/09 ; "The Real Key to Development," by Mary Anastasia O'Grady, *Wall Street Journal*, 1/15/08; Terry Miller and Kim R. Holmes, eds., *2009 Index of Economic Freedom*, heritage.org/Index/; Freedom House, "Freedom in the World 2009 Survey," freedomhouse.org; Joel Selmrod and Jon Bakija, *Taxing Ourselves: A Citizen's Guide to the Debate over Taxes*, MIT Press, 2008; International Monetary Fund, *World Economic Outlook,: Crisis and Recovery*, April 2009; Peter H. Lindert, *Growing Public*, Cambridge University Press, 2004; Doug Henwood, "*Laissez-faire* Olympics: An LBO Special Report," leftbusinessobserver.com, March 26, 2005; Jeffrey Sachs, *The End of Poverty: Economic Possibilities for Our Time*, Penguin, 2005.

Article 10.3

THE GIANT POOL OF MONEY

BY ARTHUR MacEWAN
September/October 2009

Dear Dr. Dollar:

On May 9, the public radio program This American Life broadcast an explanation of the housing crisis with the title: "The Giant Pool of Money." With too much money looking for investment opportunities, lots of bad investments were made—including the bad loans to home buyers. But where did this "giant pool of money" come from? Was this really a source of the home mortgage crisis?

—*Gail Radford, Buffalo, N.Y.*

The show was both entertaining and interesting. A good show, but maybe a bit more explanation will be useful.

There was indeed a "giant pool of money" that was an important part of the story of the home mortgage crisis—well, not "money" as we usually think of it, but financial assets, which I'll get to in a moment. And that pool of money is an important link in the larger economic crisis story.

The giant pool of money was the build-up of financial assets—U.S. Treasury bonds, for example, and other assets that pay a fixed income. According to the program, the amount of these assets had grown from roughly $36 trillion in 2000 to $70 trillion in 2008. That's $70 *trillion*, with a T, which is a lot of money, roughly the same as total world output in 2008.

These financial assets built up for a number of reasons. One was the doubling of oil prices (after adjusting for inflation) between 2000 and 2007, largely due to the U.S. invasion of Iraq. This put a lot of money in the hands of governments in oil-producing countries and private individuals connected to the oil industry.

A second factor was the large build up of reserves (i.e., the excess of receipts from exports over payments for imports) by several low-income countries, most notably China. One reason some countries operated in this manner was simply to keep the cost of their currency low in terms of U.S. dollars, thus maintaining demand for their exports. (Using their own currencies to buy dollars, they were increasing both the supply of their currencies and the demand for dollars; this pushed the price of their currencies down and of dollars up.) But another reason was to protect themselves from the sort of problems they had faced in the early 1980s, when world recession cut their export earnings and left them unable to meet their import costs and pay their debts—thus the debt crisis of that era.

This build-up of dollar reserves by governments (actually, central banks) of other countries was also a result of the budgetary deficits of the Bush administration. Spending more than it was taking in as taxes (after the big tax cuts for the wealthy and with the heavy war spending), the Bush administration needed to borrow. Foreign governments, by buying the U.S. securities, were providing the loans.

Still a third factor explaining the giant pool of financial assets was the high level of inequality within the United States and elsewhere in the global economy. Since 1993, half of all income gains in the United States have gone to the highest-income 1% of households. While the very rich spend a good share of their money on mansions, fancy cars, and other luxuries, there was plenty more money for them to put into investments—the stock market but also fixed-income securities (i.e., bonds).

So there is the giant pool of money or, again, of financial assets.

The financial assets became a problem for two connected reasons. First, in the recovery following the 2001 recession, economic growth was very slow; there were thus very limited real investment opportunities. Between 2001 and 2007, private fixed investment (adjusted for inflation) grew by only 11%, whereas in the same number of years following the recession of the early 1990s, investment grew by 59%.

Second, in an effort to stimulate more growth, the Federal Reserve kept interest rates very low. But the low interest rates meant low returns on financial assets— U.S. government bonds in particular, but financial assets in general. So the holders of financial assets went searching for new investment opportunities, which, as the radio program explained, meant pushing money into high-risk mortgages. The rest, as they say, is history.

So the giant pool of money was the link that tied high inequality, the war, and rising financial imbalances in the world economy (caused in large part by the U.S. government's budgetary policies) to the housing crisis and thus to the more general financial crisis.

Again, check out the *This American Life* episode for the details of how this "link" operated. It's quite a story! ❑

Article 10.4

GREECE AND THE EUROZONE CRISIS BY THE NUMBERS

BY GERALD FRIEDMAN

July/August 2012

With its surging debt and sinking economy, Greece has been held up as the poster-child for the need for fiscal discipline and austerity. Instead, it should be seen as a case study in the danger of neoliberal financial integration. Greece's economic problems stem from its joining the eurozone, a single-currency region where monetary policy is managed by a largely independent European Central Bank (ECB). The ECB is based in Frankfurt, Germany, and is committed to maintaining stable prices without regard for levels of unemployment or economic growth. Within the eurozone, Greek industry has been unable to compete with its German competitors. If Greece had retained an independent currency, it could have maintained balanced trade and supported domestic industries and employment by devaluing its currency. Membership in the European Union and the eurozone, though, prevents Greece from adjusting its currency value or otherwise imposing trade restraints, even in the face of a rising tide of German imports which have devastated much of Greek industry. ❑

―――――――――――――

Greece's trade deficits were financed by borrowing, including deposits in Greek banks from Germany and other northern European countries. When the financial crisis began in 2008, however, these countries sought to pull their deposits out of

ANNUAL TRADE BALANCE, PERCENTAGE OF GDP, GERMANY AND GREECE, 1996-2010

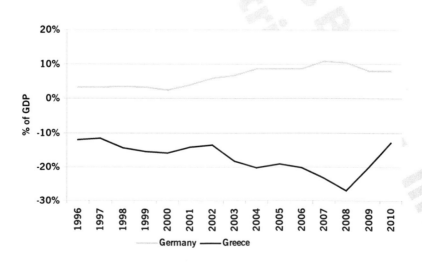

Greek banks and reduce their lending. If Greece had an independent central bank, as it did before joining the euro, that bank would provide liquidity to replace these financial flows and thus guarantee the stability of the Greek banking system. But Greece gave up its own independent monetary authority when it joined the eurozone. Instead, the ECB has used the Greek financial crisis as a tool to drive down Greek wages and living standards.

Binding southern Europe with Germany has allowed Germany to run extraordinary trade surpluses with these other countries. For seven years after 2001, capital flows from Germany balanced German trade surpluses. However, Germany's trade surplus soared with the establishment of the euro in 2002. Most of this surplus was with its eurozone partners, who, without independent currencies, could not adjust to balance their trade.

Greece had a trade deficit even before joining the eurozone, but its deficit soared after it adopted the euro. Germany's surplus and Greece's deficits were balanced with borrowing when Greek banks accepted large deposits from Germans and others.

Throughout the 2000s, the Greek government had a relatively high debt burden but remained stable before the economic crisis. Due to falling tax revenues and increased need for government services during the crisis, Greece experienced a sharp rise in its government deficit. Forcing austerity on Greece to stabilize its financial system has led to soaring unemployment. This has led to falling tax revenues and rising expenditures for unemployment relief, which have actually increased the government deficit.

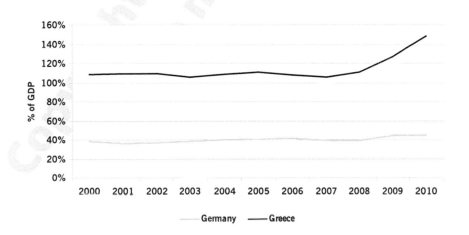

CENTRAL GOVERNMENT DEBT, PERCENTAGE OF GDP, GERMANY AND GREECE, 2000-10

AVERAGE USUAL HOURS WORKED (WEEKLY), EU MEMBERS, 2011

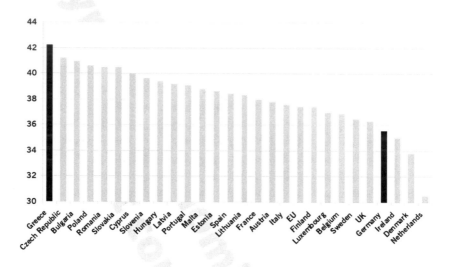

Greece's recent economic troubles come despite the country's work ethic. Relatively poor compared with others in the European Union, Greeks work more hours per week than workers in any other EU member country. By contrast, the relatively affluent Germans work about six hours a week less than the Greeks, and have many more vacation days.

Sources: OECD.stat data base for gross domestic product, government deficits, and unemployment. Eurostat data base for hours worked. International Monetary Fund for trade data.

Article 10.5

WHY THE UNITED STATES IS NOT GREECE

BY JOHN MILLER AND KATHERINE SCIACCHITANO
January/February 2012

For almost two years, we've been hearing a new battle cry in the war against government spending: unless the United States slashes deficits we will become Greece, Europe's poster child for fiscal insolvency and economic crisis. The debt crisis in the eurozone, the 17 European countries that share the euro as their common currency, is held up as proof positive of the perils that await the United States if it continues its supposedly fiscally irresponsible ways.

Take the Heritage Foundation, the Washington-based think tank that specializes in providing red meat for anti-government pro-market arguments. Heritage introduces its 2011 chart on the rising level of government debt (to GDP) with this dire warning: "Countries like Greece and Portugal have suffered or are anticipating financial crises as a result of mounting debt. If the U.S. continues federal deficit spending on its current trajectory, it will face similar economic woes."

Even for those who understand that cutting deficits right now will only weaken a still-fragile recovery, and that weakening the recovery will only increase deficits, getting past the argument that "a eurozone crisis is on its way" is no easy task.

What follows is a self-defense lesson on why the United States is not Greece—or Europe. The U.S. economy is far larger and more productive than Greece. The United States has many more tools in its macro-economic policy box than countries in the eurozone. And while calls for austerity have kept the United States from undertaking government spending and investment large enough to support a robust economic recovery, at least thus far, the United States hasn't undertaken the same self-defeating austerity measures Europe has. If we learn the right lessons from what is happening in the eurozone now, we never will.

Central Banks and Deficit Spending

When economic activity plummeted during 2008 and 2009 in the United States, Europe, and throughout the world, coordinated stimulus spending of nations across the globe prevented the collapse of world output from becoming another Great Depression. Today, deficit spending remains critical as working people continue to struggle through an economic recovery that has done little to create jobs or to lift wages, but much to restore profits.

Governments finance deficit spending by borrowing. Governments sell bonds—promissory notes—to domestic and foreign investors as well as other government agencies, and then use the proceeds to pay for spending in excess of their tax revenues. In the United States, domestic investors, foreign investors, and government agencies hold near equal shares of government bonds issued by the Treasury and receive the interest paid on those bonds.

The Federal Reserve ("the Fed"), the U.S. central bank, can buy U.S. government bonds as well. The Fed can also create money (sometimes metaphorically called "printing money") simply by entering an appropriate credit on its balance sheet and spending it. When the Fed uses this newly created money to purchase bonds directly from the government, it is financing the government deficit. Economists call the Fed's direct purchase of government bonds "monetizing the deficit." By such direct purchases of bonds that finance the deficit, the Fed can fund government spending in an emergency, should it choose to do so. Monetizing the deficit also significantly expands the money supply, which pushes down interest rates, which can also help stimulate the economy.

In the current crisis, the Fed did precisely that. By purchasing government bonds, the Fed financed public-sector spending, and by pushing down interest rates, it encouraged private-sector borrowing. In doing so, the Fed supported a market recovery, but also helped to keep unemployment from rising even higher than it did.

In seeking to lower unemployment, the Fed was exercising what is known as its "dual mandate" under the law to promote both low inflation and low unemployment.

Nevertheless, the Fed's decision to inject more money into the economy has come under heavy fire from those who worry more about inflation than unemployment, and who think that "printing money" is always inflationary. Neither continued low inflation rates nor persistently high unemployment were enough to change the thinking of these inflation-phobes. Back in August, Rick Perry, the Texas governor and candidate for president in the Republican primary, went so far as to insist that if the Fed "prints more money between now and the election" (in November 2012) it would be "almost treasonous."

The central banks of most other countries have much the same abilities as the Fed has to inject money into their economies and to buy government debt. As with the Fed, they may or may not choose to use this power. But the power is unquestionably there.

Europe's Central Bank Is Different

The 17 countries in the eurozone, however, relinquished their ability to print money, expand their money supplies, and lower interest rates when they adopted the euro as their common currency. Only the European Central Bank—known as the ECB—can authorize the "printing of euros," and the ECB maintains control over the money supply of the eurozone.

Unlike the Fed, the ECB does not have a dual mandate to pursue low employment as well as low inflation. The ECB's authority is limited to maintaining low inflation, known as "price stability," which the ECB defines as an inflation rate below 2%.

And the ECB is prohibited from directly buying government bonds. The ECB is authorized to buy government bonds only on the "secondary" bond market, when original purchasers resell them.

The result of these policies is that eurozone countries must sell their bonds on the open market. That leaves them entirely dependent on private bond buyers (i.e., lenders), whether from their own country or other countries, to finance their government deficits. Governments must offer their bonds for sale with rates of returns (or interest rates) that will attract those bonds buyers. Each uptick in the interest rate adds to the debt burden of these countries, and makes deficit spending to stimulate the economy that much more expensive.

Another way a country can stimulate its economy is by increasing exports. Typically, individual countries' currencies (when not fixed to the value of a dominant currency such as the U.S. dollar) lose value, or "depreciate," when an economy falls into a crisis, such as the crisis Greece is in now. As the value of its currency depreciates, a country's exports become cheaper, and that boosts export sales and domestic production and aids recovery. While currency fluctuations can open the door to speculative excesses, the falling value of a country's currency is yet another way to help turn around a flagging economy not available to the eurozone economies. The problem is that all countries in the eurozone have the same currency. So individual countries can't let their currencies depreciate. Nor can they take steps countries outside the eurozone can take to intentionally lower their exchange rates to become more competitive, known as devaluing.

Similarly, central banks outside the eurozone routinely stimulate economies by pushing down key interest rates at which banks lend to each other. This helps lower other interest rates in the economy, such as rates for business and consumer loans, and can lead to the expansion of borrowing and spending. But the ECB targets one interest rate for lending between banks for the whole eurozone. It is not possible to set one interest rate for Germany to fight inflation, and a second, lower, rate in Greece or Italy to stimulate growth.

Without the ability to use separate exchange rates or interest rates to stimulate lagging economies, the crisis-ridden eurozone had but one public policy left to get their economies going again: expansionary fiscal policy. But even that remaining policy option was constrained. The ECB was not about to ease the burden of increased government spending (or the cost of tax cuts) by directly buying government bonds. Eurozone guidelines prohibit budget deficits that exceed 3% of GDP, or national debt in excess of 60% of their GDP. And there is no central fiscal authority with deep pockets to turn to. Contrast this with the United States, where states also share the same currency and the Fed targets one interest rate, but where states can turn to the federal government for assistance in times of economic stress.

In effect, the eurozone countries were left to confront the global downturn and the sovereign debt crisis with one policy hand tied behind their back, and a couple of digits lopped off the other. Market pressure on interest rates made it yet more difficult for eurozone countries to get out of trouble by undertaking countercyclical, or stimulus, spending when economies slowed.

In the few cases where eurozone authorities have provided loans to indebted countries, they have insisted on austerity measures ranging from slashing government spending to public- and private-sector wage cuts as the pre-condition for providing relief. But since cutting government spending in a downturn leads to both a fall in demand and rise in unemployment, this emergency lending is making it even harder for eurozone countries to recover.

No wonder the global downturn hit the most vulnerable eurozone countries so hard, turning their sovereign (or government) debt as toxic as the mortgage-based securities that sparked the initial global downturn. This is what we're seeing played out with the Greek debt crisis.

Greek Austerity

When the 2008-2009 global collapse pushed down GDP and trade, and pushed up budget deficits around the world, Greece already had a large trade deficit and high government debt. Greece had consistently run government deficits greater than 5% of its GDP, and had carried government debt that just about matched its GDP for nearly a decade, both clear violations of eurozone guidelines. Nonetheless, Greek banks, and then banks elsewhere in Europe (including Germany and France), readily lent money to the Greek government, buying their bonds, which regularly yielded a handsome 5% rate of return (the rate of interest on a ten-year government note), and which presumably carried limited risk as the sovereign debt of a developed country unlikely to default.

But as the Greek economy tumbled downward, Greece had to raise its interest rates to above 12% to sell the additional debt it needed to stay afloat. By the summer of 2010, Greece was pushed to the point of default—not being able to pay its lenders.

The European Union and the IMF gave Greece a $140 billion loan so debt payments to the banks could continue. But both the IMF and the European Union insisted on austerity to reduce deficits and ensure repayment. Greece was forced to agree to sharp cuts in government spending, public employment, and wages and benefits of public employees; to tax increases; and to privatization of government assets. The banks that had happily lent Greece money well beyond the allowable eurozone limits escaped without having to write down the value of their loans to the Greek government.

The Greek economy, on the other hand, dropped like a stone. In the year that followed, Greece lost more output than the United States had during the Great Recession. Unemployment rates reached 18.4%, over one-third of young people were unemployed, and more than one-fifth of the population was poverty stricken. The austerity measures did trim the Greek budget deficit. Nonetheless the ratio of public debt to GDP continued to rise as Greek output plummeted.

One year later, Greece was on the brink of default again. The interest rate on Greek government bonds had skyrocketed to above 20% on ten-year government bonds, only adding to Greece's already unsustainable debt burden.

In October 2011 the IMF and the European Union granted an additional $173 billion loan to Greece in return for a new round of austerity measures. More public-sector workers lost their jobs, public pensions were cut further, and the privatization program expanded. The austerity measures were "equivalent to about 14 percent of average Greek take-home income," according to the *Financial Times*, the authoritative British newspaper, or an impact about "double that brought about by austerity measures in the other two eurozone countries subject to international bail-out programmes, Portugal and Ireland."

Also as part of the price for its debt reduction, Greece would have to accept monitoring of its fiscal affairs by the European Union. Greek Prime Minister George Papandreou, forced to cancel a referendum on the second round of austerity cuts, resigned in favor of a "government of national unity" headed by Lucas Papademos, a former banker sure to listen to the markets.

This time, banks and other holders of Greek government bonds seemed not to have escaped unharmed. The value of their bonds were to be written down to 50% of their face value, meaning they could still insist on repayment of half the amount lent, although the market value of those bonds was surely far less than that. In addition, the agreement was "voluntary," and it is yet to be seen if the agreement will be enforced.

As 2011 came to a close with this second round of austerity measures and the near collapse of the Greek economy, the Greek government was paying out a crippling 35% interest rate to attract buyers for their ten-year bonds.

Vortex Europe

European banks are the main buyers of European debt. French and German banks hold large quantities of Greek bonds.

So does the ECB, which began buying Greek bonds and other sovereign debt on the secondary (or resale) market in 2010. It resumed the practice in late 2011 to ease pressures on interest rates. Ordinarily, this bond-buying would also stimulate the economy by increasing the money supply, since the ECB creates the money it uses to buy the bonds. But the ECB also "sterilizes" its bond buying by contracting the money supply in the same amount as its purchases. This eliminates any possibility of inflation, but also negates the stimulus effect.

The bottom line is that because of the extensive holdings of Greek and other government debt within the European banking system, a Greek default would cause substantial losses in the European banking system and destabilize it.

In the last weeks of 2011, the ECB did extend a financial lifeline to banks — exactly what it had refused to give to the Greek government. To help buffer them against sudden losses, the ECB offered the banks $638 billion in three-year loans with the bargain basement interest rate of 1%. The majority of eurozone banks, some 523 of them, took out loans. The ECB's backdoor bailout, as a *Wall Street Journal* editorial called it, was twice the combined size of the two rescue packages for Greece. The banks, unlike governments, would not have to turn to the bond markets for funding if a Greek default occurred. And like banks bailed out in the United States, no requirements were placed on them to continue lending—in Europe's case, to continue lending to governments.

While the ECB move shored up the banks for now, it won't protect them from the large losses that will come with an outright default by Greece or another of the crisis-ridden southern eurozone countries. Such large losses would in turn force countries to bail out banks again, as they did in 2008, to avoid the prospect of cascading banking failures. Because the ECB is prohibited from directly buying European government debt, a new round of bailouts would raise the specter of increasing government deficits, of rising interest rates, and of additional countries defaulting, a sequence that could induce a depression-like downturn.

As a result, private lenders are now insisting on higher interest rates on government bonds not just in Greece, but throughout much of Europe. These interest rate rises began in weaker economies with higher debt levels, including the Italian and Spanish economies, both of which are far larger than the Greek economy. Interest-rate hikes have even spread to France and (very briefly) to Germany, the eurozone's two largest economies. The spikes in rates not only increase the likelihood of default, they put real roadblocks in the way of the spending and investment needed for recovery and long-term growth.

The danger is not only to Europe. The European Union is the largest economy in the world, accounting for nearly 20% of global economic activity. Every region of the world that trades with Europe will be affected by a slowdown there. The eurozone is the largest export market for both the United States and China. The default of any European country would cause losses and instability throughout the global economy. The U.S. financial system would also be sharply affected, for European global banks provide much of the credit for the U.S. economy.

To stem the bleeding, many in Europe and beyond have urged and continue to urge the ECB to step up and find a way to act as most normal central banks would in the situation: inject money into these economies by buying government debt in unlimited quantities. That in turn would lower interest rates, and give countries time to rebuild and restart growth. Germany, the largest and the dominant economy in Europe, continues to block this option on the grounds that printing money is not only inflationary but a "moral hazard" and makes borrowing too easy. At the last European summit, Germany successfully insisted instead on a "fiscal stability union" that will require balanced budgets (before taking interest payments into account). In other words, austerity for workers.

Rejecting Austerity

Austerity won't work for Europe: Europe needs growth, and austerity can't produce growth. Austerity also can't work because the proposed cure—budget cuts—assumes the disease is government spending. But excessive social spending by its government did not cause Greece's debt problems. In 2007, the year before the crisis hit, Greece's social expenditures relative to the size of its economy stood at 21.3% of GDP, lower than the social expenditures in France (28.3% of GDP) and Germany (25.2% of GDP), the two countries most responsible for orchestrating the austerity measures that have slashed social spending in Greece.

Europe didn't have a government debt crisis before the subprime collapse of 2008. It had countries like Germany in the north with large permanent trade surpluses, and countries in the south like Greece with large permanent trade deficits. Fixing these trade deficits and imbalances can't be done by pushing down wages. In fact, repressive wage and labor policies, especially as practiced in Germany, are what lie at the heart of those imbalances that made the weaker southern eurozone countries so vulnerable to the crisis that followed.

Rather, what's needed is government investment and coordination throughout Europe. A public investment program could modernize the infrastructure of the southern eurozone economies and boost the productivity of their workforce by improving workers' health and education.

A recession—or worse—in Europe will slow down growth and raise budget deficits in the United States as well. It will create political pressure for austerity exactly when we need more investment and more stimulus spending.

If this happens, it will be more important than ever to remember that Europe is in the position it is in, first, because it insisted on austerity for Greece and, second, because Europe has a central bank that is prohibited from financing government deficits and whose sole policy mandate is to limit inflation. Without the insistence on austerity, and without having relinquished these basic tools of economic policy—both of which the United States retains—the mess in Europe could never have happened. The United States is not and will never be Greece.

Yet like the crisis in Europe, the crisis in the United States isn't temporary or fleeting. The outcome will determine what kind of jobs and economic security people will have for a long time to come. It will have a huge effect on public-sector unions. And it will affect democracy itself, especially if we stay silent. Austerity in Europe is being imposed from above. There's no reason to let it be imposed here. ❑

Sources: C. Lapavitsas et al., "Breaking Up? A Route Out of the Eurozone Crisis," Research on Money and Finance, RMF Occasional Report, November 2011; Heiner Flassbeck and Friederike Spiecker, "The Euro—A Story of Misunderstanding," Intereconomics, 2011; "The ECB's Backdoor Bailout," Wall Street Journal, December 24, 2011; George Irvin and Alex Izurieta, "Fundamental Flaws in the European Project," Economic & Political Weekly, August 6, 2011; C.P. Chandrasekhar, "The Crisis in Europe," The Frontline, Jul. 30-Aug. 12, 2011; Robert Skidelsky, "The Euro in a Shrinking Zone," Project Syndicate, December 12, 2011; David Enrich, "European Banks Rush to Grasp Lifeline," Wall Street Journal, December 22, 2011; Paul Krugman, "Bernanke's Perry Problem," New York Times, August 25, 2011; Paul Krugman, "Currency Warnings that Europe Ignored," Krugman & Co., November 22, 2011; Andre Leonard, "The Republican plot to turn the U.S. into Greece," Salon.com, July 18, 2011; Sally Giansbury et al., "Greek austerity plans threaten growth," Financial Times, October 17, 2011; James Bullard, "The Fed's Dual Mandate: Lessons of the 1970s," The 2010 Annual Report of the Federal Reserve Bank of St. Louis, April 2011.

Article 10.6

EUROPE AND THE GLOBAL CRISIS

BY JAYATI GHOSH
November/December 2012

Europe is now the epicenter of the global economic crisis. As the world watches each move in that continent with bated breath, whatever happens the current economic structure and trajectory in the region are no longer viable. But any change—whether in the form of a break-up of the eurozone currency union, a revision of its structure towards greater fiscal union, or just a lingering slow-motion death marked by massive social and political upheaval—will have huge implications not only for Europe but for all of global capitalism.

The European Union's (EU) combination of inflexibility, denial, and lethargy bodes ill for the prospects of any immediate resolution. And despite some recent moves by EU economic policymakers that at least recognize the intensifying urgency of the situation, the proposals that are being officially considered are nowhere near meeting the requirements for even a halfway solution.

Dominoes Falling

For a while the talk was all about Greece, and the uncertainty generated by the recent elections. The Greek people at first comprehensively rejected the parties that supported the severe and counterproductive austerity measures being imposed on them by the European Union in return for halting, stingy, and ineffective bailouts. Before the June 17 repeat elections in Greece, other European leaders (including not just German chancellor Angela Merkel but also UK prime minister David Cameron, whose own country is not even a member of the monetary union) openly bullied the Greek electorate, threatening them with the most dire consequences (effectively being thrust out of the eurozone) if they voted for the parties that demanded a revision of the austerity.

As a result of the new elections, the pro-austerity party New Democracy, narrowly defeating the left group Syriza, was able to form a government. Europe's pro-austerity faction, seemingly, got what it wanted. Immediately afterward, however, it became clear that the systemic problems would not go away. While Greece continues to struggle, Spain has become the new front line. Its government was forced to bail out its struggling banks, using a 100 billion Euro credit line from the European Central Bank (ECB). This rapidly proved to be counterproductive, as the move led to a large increase in Spanish government debt, and yet another hammering in the sovereign bond markets. The interest rates on Spanish government bonds spiked. So Spain, whose public debt to GDP ratio (around 55%) is well within European official limits, faces a huge problem of unsustainable debt simply because of higher borrowing costs. There is no doubt that Italy—a huge economy and the second largest exporter in the region (after Germany)—is next on the firing line.

In other words, there is a powerful negative feedback loop between private and public debt in the eurozone. The need for public bailouts of banks that have engaged in risky behavior, for example, has created unsustainable government debt burdens for Ireland and now Spain. This exposes yet another design flaw in the eurozone: a monetary union in which the member states still retain supervisory and regulatory power over national banks, instead of a system in which the common central bank is responsible not just for issuing money but also supervising the banks in the system.

Alternatives to Austerity?

In any case, the view of pro-austerity politicians that popular resistance to austerity measures is responsible for the current crisis is wrong, because the drive for fiscal austerity is completely wrong in the first place. The point sensible economists have been making for a while—that that fiscal tightening is self-defeating because it reduces economic growth, pulls down government revenue, and so makes the deficit-cutting targets even harder to reach—is finally being accepted by many governments.

Greece's national income is already nearly 30% lower than it was four years ago. The country cannot hope to recover (and therefore be in a position to repay debts) with a strategy that is only making output fall further. And Greece is a small but extreme case of the strategy that is being imposed on all of the eurozone's "peripheral" countries that have debt problems. Ireland, which austerity advocates have hailed as a star performer because it has rigorously fulfilled all the draconian austerity measures, is still struggling to grow, as is Portugal. Spain's huge economy is being pushed into a downward spiral as asset deflation (from the collapse of the real-estate bubble) combines with public-spending cuts to throw more people out of their jobs and to make incomes plummet even further. Italy is set to join that group, with massive implications for all of Europe.

On this trajectory, it is only a matter of time before one or more of these countries defaults on at least part of its debt and/or leaves the currency union. Indeed, this is what financial markets and even individual investors are now expecting.

This can only be averted if the union itself becomes more like a real currency union, with a common bond across all countries (no separate "German," "Spanish," or "Greek" bonds), common deposit insurance for all banks within the zone, and fiscal transfers to assist regions in distress. This is what happens, for example, in the United States, where the severe debt problems in states like California and Florida do not result in the sort of crisis that has affected Greece. This is being opposed to the teeth by Germany and some other northern European countries, so the question is who will blink first. At the moment, without significant policy change, it seems that we are headed for the endgame.

No Graceful Exit

The idea that European policy makers are prepared or that financial markets have now "priced in" the possibility of Greek default and exit from the common currency, is laughable—not least because the full implications are impossible to predict. It is foolish to believe that the costs of exit are bad only (or dominantly) for Greece: They are actually likely to be even worse for the eurozone, and for the European Union as a whole, including the non-euro member countries.

There is no formal mechanism—no legal or procedural framework in the European Union treaties—for a member country to leave the eurozone. So what exactly it involves in terms of legal issues and the continued membership of the country in the European Union is also unclear. Even a limited exit of a single relatively small country from the currency union is unlikely to be orderly or manageable. Despite all claims to the contrary, it is impossible for the EU to create an effective "firewall" between Greece and other peripheral economies that are currently under pressure. This is because the exit of any one member creates fundamental uncertainty with respect to other members. Once it is revealed that membership of the eurozone need not be permanent, bond holders will inevitably turn on the countries that are next in line.

All money is essentially about trust, and when this trust is shaken, it has repercussions. Once the genie of possible exit from the currency union is out of the bottle, it cannot simply be shoved back in. So other "weaker" economies will immediately face pressure on their domestic banking systems, as investors both large and small begin to doubt whether their deposits will continue to be denominated in euros in the future. Negative expectations very rapidly become self-fulfilling in such situations, as we know from the classic pattern of a run on a bank. As Mervyn King, governor of the Bank of England, has said, while it may not be rational to start a bank run, it is rational to participate in one. Indeed, it would be individually stupid not to do so, under such conditions.

As it happens, bank runs (or at the very least bank walks or jogs) have already started in Europe. So far they have been rather slow, but such processes can very quickly accelerate and precipitate a crisis. (All financial crises are usually associated with bank runs.) Deposits in Greek banks have fallen by more than one-third since the beginning of the crisis, and around €500million per day was withdrawn in the run-up to the latest election. But banking systems in other countries that do not have such political instability are already experiencing similar slow runs. Deposits held in Spanish and Italian banks have fallen by more than €350 billion since the start of 2012. The "flight to safety" of Europeans has led to increases in German bank deposits of approximately an equivalent amount. But since the banks of northern European countries are also deeply implicated in lending to the peripheral countries, they are not really safe either. (Incidentally, U.S. banks will also be affected.)

If the crisis has not yet exploded, it is because Greek and other banks are being propped up by funds transferred in the form of "emergency liquidity assistance" from the ECB. The terms and amount of such funds are kept secret, but are estimated to be around €500 billion so far, with €100 billion going to Greece alone. This is happening even as the ECB has officially excluded four Greek banks from ordinary borrowing from the ECB because of the ongoing political uncertainty—forcing them to rely on this secret emergency liquidity. Ireland has also been the recipient of fairly prolonged "emergency" assistance of this nature. But such quiet transfers, which have been critical in allowing the monetary system to continue at all, would have to reach stratospheric proportions if the bank runs intensify. Without explicit fiscal transfers (direct aid from the wealthier trade-surplus countries) or immediate creation of eurobonds (shifting the burden from individual countries to the eurozone countries as a group), disorderly defaults are inevitable.

The doomsday scenario was summarised by Martin Wolf of the *Financial Times* (May 17, 2012): "The mechanisms at work would be powerful: runs; the imposition of (illegal) exchange controls; legal uncertainties; asset price collapses; unpredictable shifts in balance sheets; freezing of the financial system; disruption of central banking; collapse in spending and trade; and enormous shifts in the exchange rates of new currencies. Further government bailouts of financial systems would surely be needed, at great cost. Big recessions would also worsen already damaged fiscal positions."

There is no doubt that Europe as a whole has more to lose than Greece from such a disorderly default. Europe is now facing is a banking crisis of potentially enormous proportions. The only way to prevent havoc is to create jointly held eurozone bonds, put in place a common deposit insurance to revive trust in the banking system, and develop a way of dealing with insolvent banks for the entire eurozone. France under new president François Hollande has already declared its support for both the common resolution regime and common bond. But there is continued German opposition, not just from Chancellor Merkel but from both right-wing and left-wing forces within Germany. To a large extent this is because the German public has absorbed the myth that was fed to them by media and policy makers—that they are paying for the extravagant ways of their neighbors through their taxes and savings. This perception ignores the truth that the German economy has been one of the main beneficiaries of the eurozone, which has enabled it to exploit its mercantilist export-driven strategy to the fullest without facing rising real exchange rates that would have reduced its competitive strength.

So a big part of the political obstacles to dealing with the problem is the lack of recognition in surplus-running countries, like Germany, that they have been huge beneficiaries of the monetary union. Far from subsidizing the profligacy of the periphery at their own cost, they have been able to preserve employment through export surpluses and then used these to finance investments (mostly in private non-tradable activities like real estate and some public spending like arms purchases in Greece). Those investments provided their banks high returns for a while, and also further benefited their own industries. In such a context, non-symmetric adjustment that makes only the debtors suffer and pay, is not just unfair—in Europe today it is also simply not possible.

Surplus countries like Germany must make greater, more forceful, and immediate expressions of political solidarity and will if the euro is to survive for long in its current form.

The Rest of the World

It is still not clear how this crisis will finally play out, but the prognosis is not encouraging. While the trigger of this latest round of fierce instability is likely to be Europe, this does not mean that other regions of the capitalist world are in good shape economically. During the Great Recession of 2008–09 and its aftermath, several emerging economies—notably China, but also India, Brazil, Argentina and a number of others—not only experienced less severe downswings but also recovered faster and more strongly, with post-recession GDP growth rates around those of the previous decade. This reinforced belief in the "decoupling" of different capitalist world regions—where the economic fates of some regions are not shared by others. The events of the past year, however, suggest that both internal trends within regions and the closer integration of regions will make it harder to reproduce such differential performance in a coming recession.

The world's largest economy, the United States, is currently perceived to be on a path of recovery. There is much talk of the slight increase in output in the past year, the fall in the unemployment rate, and that fact that some industries are beginning to relocate factories back to the United States. But this is a halting, uncertain and easily reversible recovery. Indeed, a reversal is almost inevitable, because the basic forces underlying the crisis (such as the enormous debt overhang that requires continued deleveraging of the household sector in the face of stagnant wages, rising inequality, and loss of viability of small enterprises) have not been dealt with.

The current rate of U.S. economic growth, 2.2%, is sluggish at best. The unemployment rate has fallen only because more people are leaving the labor force (the "discouraged worker" effect).The number of unemployed remains high, at more than 5 million, and job creation is occurring at low rates that do not resolve the basic unemployment problem. Businesses are cutting back on investment, which will affect future growth. Worse, previous legislation means that, unless a political deal is worked out before the end of 2012, the government will automatically implement sweeping spending cuts and tax increases estimated to reduce consumer spending by at least 4%. Headwinds from Europe will intensify the likely downswing. So, despite very loose monetary policy and the most expansionary fiscal policy of all the large economies (other than Japan), prospects for the U.S. economy are brittle.

In China, the authorities had sought to slow growth because of fears of "overheating," as evidenced by high inflation rates. But the slowdown has been sharper than expected, already leading to calls for renewed state stimulation of the economy. Declining real-estate prices continue to have negative effects for bad loans of the banking sector and for employment in construction, which had been an important part of the increased employment since 2008. However, there are problems in trying to recreate a real-estate and construction boom that had already spiralled out of control. There are growing fears that a further slowdown in exports could result in a "hard landing" for China's economy. The political instability generated by the power struggle within the elite after the fall of former commerce secretary and Communist Party Politburo member Bo Xilai is also likely to have economic implications, though these can still only be guessed at.

In general, given the uncertainties and negative outlook of these major economies, there is no doubt that the world must brace itself for Act II of the ongoing drama—another recession, possibly fiercer than the recent one. The performance of individual countries will depend on the extent to which they are able to insulate themselves by boosting domestic demand in sustainable ways, without further reliance on financial mechanisms that are already too fragile and volatile to last for long. ❑

Earlier versions of this article appeared in Third World Resurgence *(No. 261, May 2012) and* Frontline *magazine (Vol. 29, Issue 11, June 2-15, 2012).*

Article 10.7

RESISTANCE TO AUSTERITY GROWS IN EUROPE

Popular sentiment shifts in Germany's ally-in-austerity, the Netherlands.

BY MARJOLEIN van der VEEN

September/October 2012

The Netherlands made world news when its government collapsed on April 21. The day before it was revealed that an additional 12 billion euro (nearly $15 billion) would be needed in 2013 to meet the rules of the Maastricht Treaty, the treaty that led to the creation of the euro. This was on top of 18 billion euro in cuts (nearly $22.5 billion) over four years that the government had already started implementing. The governing right-wing coalition then collapsed when the right-wing populist PVV party of Geert Wilders refused to support additional austerity.

Resistance to austerity shocked those who saw the Netherlands as Germany's chief ally in pushing European countries to adopt austerity programs. Under the Maastricht Treaty, each country's deficits can be no higher than 3% of GDP, and debt no higher than 60% of GDP. Because the Netherlands' budget deficit was 4.6% of GDP and its debt was 70.2% of GDP, it had to submit a budget to Brussels by April 30 to meet the Maastricht thresholds. Failure to do so would entail a penalty of 1.2 billion euro (nearly $1.5 billion), the possible downgrading of its bonds, and a potential rise in interest rates at which it could borrow.

The collapse of the Dutch government briefly took the spotlight away from Greece and Spain, where the crisis has hit the hardest. By the spring of 2012, the unemployment rate had reached depression levels of 24.4% in Spain and 18.8% in Greece, compared to 5.5% in the Netherlands and 10.8% for the EU as a whole. While Dutch unemployment is not as bad as elsewhere, the economy remains precarious and slipped back into recession during the last half of 2011, mainly because falling housing prices from a bursting housing bubble continue to dampen consumer spending. The Netherlands had one of the largest housing bubbles (depending on which measurement is used) and the highest level of mortgage debt in Europe. The additional proposed cuts were projected to harm the economy further, with real GDP declining by 0.75% in 2012, possibly putting the economy into a "triple-dip" recession. Also of concern is the on-going euro crisis, uncertainties regarding pensions (some of which are tied up in Spanish banks), and the likely damage to exports with a slowing global economy.

Growing frustration with austerity has fueled support for anti-austerity political parties. As in France and Greece, anti-austerity support in the Netherlands is split between the left (the Dutch labor party and Socialist party) and the far-right (the populist party of Geert Wilders). The Socialist Party has made remarkable gains in the polls, doubling its support since the last election, and by late June was leading the governing pro-business VVD party in the polls. If the Socialist Party wins the September elections or enters a coalition government, it will be a historic first for the party. Following the victory of the

Socialists in France, the party could help chart a new course for Europe and challenge the austerity policies forced upon Greece and other European countries in crisis.

The Menu of Cuts

The initial cuts of 18 billion euro (about $22.5 billion, about 3% of GDP) over four years were deep and wide-ranging. Public transportation would have been cut by 40%. Cuts to programs that employ disabled workers would have scrapped 70,000 out of 100,000 jobs. In education, 300 million euro (about $370 million) would have been cut from programs for special-needs kids, resulting in 5,000 teachers and coaches losing their jobs. University students would be penalized with fines of 3,000 euro (about $3,700) per year for taking longer to finish their studies. In the health sector, the budget for professional interpreters would have been cut, and co-payments would have been introduced. Arts programs faced a 25% cut, and taxes on tickets to many cultural events would have risen from 6% to 19%. Foreign development assistance would have been cut almost 25%. In addition, the pension age would have been raised to 66 in 2019, and a value-added tax (VAT—a type of sales tax) raised from 6% to 7% (and from 19% to 21% for luxury goods).

Dutch workers actively resisted with strikes and public protests. On March 7, teachers held the largest one-day strike since 1982, with 50,000 teachers filling a stadium in Amsterdam. A one-day strike of workers with disabilities brought 15,000 people to The Hague on March 22. On April 25, about 600 health care workers protested wage cuts, the deterioration of quality in health care, and the "flexibilization" of labor contracts (making it easier to hire and fire workers). Transportation workers and students also had days of protests. While there was no general strike, as in Spain or Greece, protests have nonetheless succeeded in slowing down the cuts. The new budget accord brokered after the government collapse pared back and even eliminated some cuts (e.g. for special needs education, development assistance, and public transportation).

After the government collapse on April 21, VVD leaders scrambled to broker an agreement with the opposition, such as the Green-Left party, in order to close the additional budget hole. On April 26, a new budget accord was produced that relies on a two-year freeze on public sector wages, and an increase in the VAT by 2%. Also, the

---

Three Ways to Reduce the Deficit/GDP Ratio

There are three ways a government can reduce its deficit/GDP (or debt/GDP) ratio: (1) Cutting government spending; (2) Raising taxes; or (3) Boosting GDP

GDP may be boosted through government spending, in such a way that GDP grows more than the deficit and brings the deficit/GDP ratio down. Austerity policies usually focus only on the first way—cutting government spending. Typically, these spending cuts end up hurting poor and working classes most. Elites tend to studiously ignore other ways of reducing the deficit/GDP ratio (such as raising taxes on the wealthy and corporations). Even though the causes of the crisis lay mostly with the banks, the burden of the crisis is shifted onto the shoulders of working people.

increase in the retirement age would be phased in as early as 2013. The package contained other measures, such as scrapping a mortgage deduction for new homebuyers, elimination of rental subsidies, cuts in travel subsidies, some "sin" and luxury taxes, a doubling of the bank tax, a tax on high incomes, and a series of new environmental taxes and subsidies. While these spending cuts and tax increases are more progressive and bear a little more heavily on higher income households, they will still have a contractionary effect on the economy, and could drive the Dutch economy back into recession.

Why did Dutch government deficit exceed the Maastricht thresholds and lead to this belt tightening? First, the crisis of 2008-09 caused tax revenues to fall and government expenditures on unemployment insurance to rise. Then there was the bank bailout, to the tune of 30 billion euro (about $37 billion), with another 200 billion euro (around $250 billion) in loan guarantees. The government also implemented expansionary fiscal policies, all of which led to rising deficits.

In some cases deficits and debt may be problematic (especially the rising cost of borrowing, as in Greece, Spain, and Italy), but only after the recession is over and full employment is restored should governments turn to reducing deficits and debt.

"Expansionary Austerity"?

The standard view in economics is that trying to reduce a deficit during a recession leads to a slowdown of the economy, thereby worsening the recession. But in 2009, Harvard economists Alberto Alesina and Silvia Ardagna proposed that austerity could actually be expansionary by raising confidence and expectations of lower taxes, spurring private investment and encouraging consumers to spend. Examples were taken from obscure cases (e.g. Denmark in 1982-86) and then used to inform austerity programs in Europe and elsewhere.

Another reason for thinking austerity could be expansionary is that it would help boost net exports. The eurozone countries cannot devalue their currency to make exports competitive—unless they break from the euro, a prospect with costs attached. An alternative is "internal devaluation," which reduces wages and prices. Austerity would help achieve "internal devaluation," as cutbacks in government spending and resulting layoffs and wage freezes would contribute to driving down real wages overall. Lower labor costs then reduce the price of exports, enabling exports to become competitive and expand the economy.

The Role of the European Central Bank (ECB)

Running deficits to stimulate growth may bear the risk of raising interest rates. When European countries gave up their national monetary policy tools to join the eurozone, they gave up the ability for their central banks to accommodate expansionary fiscal policies with monetary policy. One solution lies with the European Central Bank (ECB), which could step in by buying government bonds (even if only in the secondary market). Last December, the ECB started injecting money into private banks to allow them to buy government bonds, though it has still resisted directly buying government bonds in a major way, insisting on using the ESM to solve the crisis. The ECB also should include lowering unemployment in its mandate, which is currently focused solely on keeping inflation low.

There are several problems with these "expansionary austerity" theories. First, expectations of higher taxes have not significantly discouraged business investment; in many countries taxes have already been lowered over several decades of neoliberalism. More significant in discouraging business investment was insufficient aggregate demand due to the economic collapse. Falling household wealth and income have dampened consumer spending, and with so much excess capacity (empty factories, office buildings, and unused equipment), firms are reluctant to expand investment and build up even more productive capacity. The low interest rates provided by central banks were not enough of an incentive to invest. Nor were consumers likely driven to spend by expectations of lower taxes. Rather, the austerity cutbacks led to *lower* consumer confidence and spending, as households became worried about their jobs and incomes and about the value of their houses and pensions.

The policy of "internal devaluation" was also wrong-headed. If the crisis was contained to only one country, then promoting export competitiveness through devaluation might work. However, when the crisis is global, all countries can't simultaneously export themselves out of it. The squeeze on real wages and incomes only exacerbates problems of insufficient aggregate demand. Plus, it can initiate a competitive race to the bottom, as each country and trading partner tries to devalue to maintain its competitive position for its exports.

Austerity Was Contractionary

So how did the theory of "expansionary austerity" hold up? By 2011 and 2012, after two years of austerity in Europe, country after country experienced slowdowns or recessions and rising unemployment. Not only did GDP growth decline, the austerity policies did little to reduce debt as tax revenues fell with slumping economies. The failures of the austerity policies imposed on European countries were finally recognized by the S&P ratings agency in January 2012, when it downgraded the debt of nine European countries, including France, Spain, Italy and Portugal, although not the Netherlands. As Paul Krugman noted in a blog post, an S&P FAQ stated:

> We also believe that the agreement [the latest euro rescue plan] is predicated on only a partial recognition of the source of the crisis: that the current financial turmoil stems primarily from fiscal profligacy at the periphery of the eurozone. In our view, however, the financial problems facing the eurozone are as much a consequence of rising external imbalances and divergences in competitiveness between the EMU's core and the so-called "periphery". *As such, we believe that a reform process based on a pillar of fiscal austerity alone risks becoming self-defeating, as domestic demand falls in line with consumers' rising concerns about job security and disposable incomes, eroding national tax revenues.*

Not only did austerity policies decrease GDP and tax revenues, and thereby increase government deficits and debt, they also had a terrible effect on workers, who were thrown into unemployment and slipped into poverty. Even those fortunate to keep their jobs were often worked more intensely, as employers expected the same amount of work from smaller numbers of people, and as fear of layoffs compelled workers to comply. The public at large also faced negative consequences from austerity. Cutbacks in employment and services often meant an inferior quality of service provided (whether in public transportation, health care, education, etc.), which in some cases could even jeopardize the safety of consumers or the public (e.g. more train accidents, medical mishaps, faulty economic theories, etc.).

Other Agendas

If austerity policies have been shown to fail, why are they still being implemented by policymakers? Undoubtedly there are other agendas at stake. The economic crisis is being used to push through "structural reforms," at a time when workers and their political parties are thought to be weak. (Ironically, the greatest need for structural reforms remains in financial markets, not labor markets.) In Greece, the bailouts have included vast privatization of state assets. The cuts to public education, healthcare, and transport will merely open these sectors to private corporations producing on a for-profit basis. At a time when existing markets are becoming saturated and private investors find it more difficult to find new investment opportunities, investors are eyeing these public services as new profit opportunities.

In the Netherlands, business interests are eager to weaken unions and push through labor-market flexibility and an increase in the retirement age. With unions in a state of disarray, they are imposing wage freezes and reductions aimed at boosting profits. Business also seeks to institutionalize austerity measures with the new fiscal pact signed in March, the European Stabilization Mechanism (ESM).

Alternatives to Austerity

There are several alternatives to austerity. First, as long as unemployment remains high, the focus should be on reviving the economy. Growth could lower the debt/GDP ratio if growth in GDP is larger than additional debt. Growth promotion should ideally be done

---

The European Stabilization Mechanism (ESM)

The ESM is a 500 billion euro permanent bailout fund established in March 2012. It places rules on borrowing countries' structural deficits (that part of the deficit that is not the result of cyclical downturns), imposing a maximum structural deficit of 0.5% of GDP (unless a country has a debt to GDP ratio of less than 60%, in which case it is allowed a maximum structural deficit of 1%). Failure to meet these thresholds results in fines or other penalties. At the June EU summit, European governments agreed to use the ESM to directly bail out banks in Spain and Italy, and exempted these countries from complying with the austerity requirements imposed on other countries such as Greece. In what amounts to a victory for the banks, the ESM funds for Spain's banks would not have seniority over private claims, meaning that shareholders would be paid back before taxpayers.

in a way that is environmentally sustainable and does not add to CO_2 emissions. A green "New Deal" program could create jobs through public investment in renewable energy, energy efficiency and conservation, public transportation, and other investments that are geared toward reducing poverty and future climate change emissions.

Second, deficits can be reduced through tax increases, rather than spending cuts. Since raising taxes will slow down the economy, attempts to balance budgets should wait until economies have fully recovered and full employment restored. Then, taxes should be levied on those institutions responsible for the crisis in the first place (i.e. the banks). Workers and ordinary people should not have to pay for the crisis they did not cause. Tellingly, the total package of Dutch austerity cuts now amounts to 30 billion euro (about $37 billion), which is precisely the amount of the Dutch bailout of the banks! Taxes could be raised on financial speculation, capital gains, dividends, profits of financial institutions, and executive compensation packages. Loopholes could be eliminated and taxes raised on foreign corporations with head offices in the Netherlands, which has become a tax haven for foreign corporations taking advantage of an effective tax rate of 5%.

Lessons and Implications for the Future

Deficit cutting is misguided during periods of high unemployment, and likely to worsen the economy while providing only a weak remedy to budget deficits. What has happened in Europe is an important lesson for the U.S., which is engaging in austerity at the state level as states try to balance their budgets. The U.S. federal government should also heed the lessons from Europe, as it too is facing possible fiscal contraction when various tax cuts and spending programs expire on Dec. 31, 2012.

The Dutch case is important as an indicator of the changing mood in Europe. Will voters elect an anti-austerity government in September? Will the Socialist party achieve a victory and help in reshaping policy in the European Union in a direction more favorable to workers and the unemployed, as they did in France? Or will the current governing parties hold onto power and continue to push austerity, as they did in Greece? Will Dutch voters be presented with fear-mongering and divide-and-rule politics that seek to split the working class vote, aided by right-wing populism? Dutch voters are in for heated debates as temperatures rise and election campaigning gears up over the summer months. ❑

Sources: "Short-term Forecasts June 2012," June 14, 2012 (cpb.nl); "Details miljardenakkoord op een rij," April 26, 2012 (rtl.nl); Paul Krugman, "Bleeding Britain," *New York Times* blog, November 30, 2011; Paul Krugman, "Fiscal Fantasies," *New York Times* blog, June 18, 2010; Paul Krugman, "S&P on Europe," *New York Times* blog, January 14, 2012.

CONTRIBUTORS

Frank Ackerman, a founder of *Dollars & Sense*, is a senior economist at Synapse Energy Economics in Cambridge, Mass. His extensive publications on economics and the environment are available at frankackerman.com.

David Bacon is a journalist and photographer covering labor, immigration, and the impact of the global economy on workers.

Tom Barry is a senior policy analyst and director of the TransBorder Project at the Center for International Policy in Washington, D.C.

Dean Baker is an economist and co-director of the Center for Economic and Policy Research (www.cepr.net) in Washington, D.C.

Drucilla K. Barker is professor of economics and women's studies at Hollins University. She is co-author of *Liberating Economics: Feminist Perspectives on Families, Work, and Globalization.*

Ravi Bhandari (co-editor of this volume) is the Chevron Endowed Chair of Economics and International Political Economy at Saint Mary's College of California, visiting professor at Tribhuvan University and Kathmandu University's School of Management (KUSOM).

Sarah Blaskey is a student at the University of Wisconsin-Madison and a member of the Student Labor Action Coalition.

Roger Bybee is the former editor of the union weekly *Racine Labor* and is now a consultant and freelance writer whose work has appeared in *Z* Magazine, *The Progressive, Extra!, The Progressive Populist, In These Times,* and other national publications and websites.

Anita Dancs is an assistant professor of economics at Western New England College and a staff economist for the Center for Popular Economics.

Elisa Dennis is a consultant to nonprofit affordable housing developers with Community Economics, Inc., in Oakland, Calif.

Susan F. Feiner is professor of economics and women's studies at the University of Southern Maine. She is co-author of *Liberating Economics: Feminist Perspectives on Families, Work, and Globalization.*

Anne Fischel teaches media and community studies at the Evergreen State College in Olympia, Wash.

Ellen Frank teaches economics at the University of Massachusetts-Boston and is a *Dollars & Sense* collective member. She is the author of *The Raw Deal: How Myths and Misinformation about Deficits, Inflation, and Wealth Impoverish America.*

Gerald Friedman is a professor of economics at the Univeristy of Massachusetts-Amherst.

Heidi Garrett-Peltier is an associate research professor at the Political Economy Research Institute at the University of Massachusetts, Amherst.

Phil Gasper teaches at Madison College and writes a column for *International Socialist Review.*

Jayati Ghosh is a professor of economics at the Centre for Economic Study and Planning at Jawaharlal Nehru University.

Gretchen Gordon is a research associate with the Cochabamba-based Democracy Center and a contributor to the book *Dignity and Defiance: Stories from Bolivia's Challenge to Globalization.*

Mara Kardas-Nelson is a freelance writer currently based in Cape Town, South Africa. She has written on health, the environment, and human rights for the *Globe & Mail* and the *Mail & Guardian.*

Marie Kennedy is professor emerita of Community Planning at the University of Massachusetts-Boston and visiting professor in Urban Planning at UCLA. She is a member of the board of directors of Grassroots International.

Gawain Kripke is a senior policy advisor at Oxfam America.

Alex Linghorn has worked closely with the land rights movement in Nepal. He is currently a postgraduate at the School of Oriental and African Studies (SOAS), University of London.

Aaron Luoma is a research associate with the Cochabamba-based Democracy Center and a contributor to the book *Dignity and Defiance: Stories from Bolivia's Challenge to Globalization.*

Arthur MacEwan, a founder of *Dollars & Sense*, is professor emeritus of economics at the University of Massachusetts-Boston and is a *D&S* Associate.

John Miller is a member of the *Dollars & Sense* collective and teaches economics at Wheaton College.

Anuradha Mittal, founder and director of the Oakland Institute in Oakland, Calif. She is an internationally renowned expert on trade, development, human rights, and agriculture issues.

William G. Moseley is a professor of geography at Macalester College in Saint Paul, Minn.

Lin Nelson teaches environmental and community studies at the Evergreen State College in Olympia, Wash.

Immanuel Ness is a professor of political science at Brooklyn College-City University of New York. He is author of *Immigrants, Unions, and the New U.S. Labor Market* and editor of *WorkingUSA: The Journal of Labor and Society.*

James Petras is an advisor and teacher for the Rural Landless Workers Movement in Brazil and an activist-scholar working with socio-political movements in Latin America, Europe, and Asia.

John Perkins is the author of *Confessions of an Economic Hit Man.*

Robert Pollin teaches economics and is co-director of the Political Economy Research Institute at the University of Massachusetts-Amherst. He is also a *Dollars & Sense* Associate.

Kenneth Pomeranz is a professor of history at the University of California at Irvine and author of *The Great Divergence: China, Europe, and the Making of the Modern World Economy.*

Smriti Rao teaches economics at Assumption College in Worcester, Mass., and is a member of the *Dollars & Sense* collective.

Dan Read is a London-based freelance journalist specializing in human rights and current affairs.

Alejandro Reuss is a co-editor of *Dollars & Sense* and an instructor at the Labor Relations and Research Center, UMass-Amherst.

Patricia M. Rodriguez is an assistant professor of politics at Ithaca College.

Peter Rosset is is a researcher at the Centro de Estudios para el Cambio en el Campo Mexicano (Center of Studies for Rural Change in Mexico), and co-coordinator of the Land Research Action Network. He is based in Oaxaca, Mexico.

Katherine Sciacchitano is a former labor lawyer and organizer. She teaches at the National Labor College in Silver Spring, Maryland, and as a freelance labor educator.

Chris Sturr is co-editor of *Dollars & Sense*.

Bob Sutcliffe is an economist at the University of the Basque Country in Bilbao, Spain, and the author of *100 Ways to See an Unequal World*.

Chris Tilly is director of the Institute for Research on Labor and Employment and professor of urban planning at UCLA and a *Dollars & Sense* Associate.

Marie Trigona is an independent journalist based in Buenos Aires. She is also a member of Grupo Alavío, a direct action and video collective.

Ramaa Vadsudevan is an assistant professor of economics at Colorado State University.

Marjolein van der Veen is an economist who has taught economics in Massachusetts, the Seattle area, and the Netherlands.

Mark Weisbrot is an economist and co-director of the Center for Economic and Policy Research (www.cepr.net) in Washington, D.C.

CPSIA information can be obtained at www.ICGtesting.com
Printed in the USA
BVOW011241181112

305795BV00004B/2/P